A SOUL'S DELIGHT

YOUR
STEP - BY - STEP
HIGHER SELF INTEGRATION
JOURNEY

JoyBeth

TRAFFORD PUBLISHING

W9-BON-324

KNOW YOUR SOUL . . .

2ⁿᵈ Edition
Cover Artwork, Logos, and Illustrations: JohnEB
Author Photo: William Brehm

National Library of Canada Cataloguing in Publication Data

JoyBeth.
  A soul's delight

ISBN 1-55212-599-8

  1. Spiritual life. I. Title.
BL624.J69 2001   291.4   C2001-910013-2

TRAFFORD

This book was published *on-demand* in cooperation with Trafford Publishing.
On-demand publishing is a unique process and service of making a book available for retail sale to the public taking advantage of on-demand manufacturing and Internet marketing.
On-demand publishing includes promotions, retail sales, manufacturing, order fulfilment, accounting and collecting royalties on behalf of the author.

Suite 6E, 2333 Government St., Victoria, B.C. V8T 4P4, CANADA
Phone   250-383-6864   Toll-free   1-888-232-4444 (Canada & US)
Fax   250-383-6804   E-mail   sales@trafford.com
Web site   www.trafford.com   TRAFFORD PUBLISHING IS A DIVISION OF TRAFFORD HOLDINGS LTD.
Trafford Catalogue #01-0001   www.trafford.com/robots/01-0001.html

10   9   8   7   6   5   4   3

TABLE OF CONTENTS

WHO'S WHO

YOU are an unique being.   The information, activities, and techniques contained within this book, *A Soul's Delight*, may or may not fit or work well for you.   It is your response-ability to choose what you want to include or exclude in your own life.   The author and publisher are not in any way responsible for your own individual choices . . .

****

REV. DR. JOYBETH is a well-traveled Soul currently providing *Soul Attunement through The Higher Self Integration Process* consultations, workshops, retrievals, trainings, writings and more. She has a special understanding of what it is to be human through having manifested many of life's intriguing and fascinating adventures. Her personal stories are available through **her companion book, BEYOND BELIEF INTO KNOWING: My Soul's Journey.**

JoyBeth has a Bachelors Degree in Social Work and Rehabilitation, Sociology and Psychology, a Masters Degree in Clinical Social Work, and a Doctor of Ministry in Spirituality. Over 30 years of working as a community organizer, educator, psychotherapist/counselor, workshop leader, and creator of new programs has added to her understanding of the current human condition that masks our Souls. She also serves as an Interfaith Minister. Her third book is *The WE That Is ME: A Creation Spirituality Guidebook For You.*

"Dr. Joy" is also a Healing Arts Practitioner, sharing and teaching a whole array of body-mind-spirit understandings and techniques. Having developed knowledge and skills that enable her to communicate in the metaphysical dimensions of spirit and Soul, she functions as a mystical psychic and spiritual healer/educator dedicated to *Soul Evolution.*

Correspondence can be addressed to **JoyBeth**
PO BOX 19, E. Orland, Me. 04431   WWW.SOULINTEGRATORS.COM   SoulDelite@aol.com
Her books can be ordered through all bookstores & 1-888-232-4444 or www.Trafford.com

****
****

A BIG HUG ...

This book is dedicated to *YOU!*

I GRATEFULLY THANK AND ACKNOWLEDGE all those who have played a special role in the manifesting of   *A Soul's Delight*   and its companion autobiography   *Beyond Belief Into Knowing,* especially those humans having a conscious spiritual experience who have been a part of both my personal and professional Soulfull journey. I am so blessed to have developed my Soul Powers of intimate human, nature, Soul, and spirit connection and communication. As a result, I have many wonder-filled relationships that support me in playing my part in spreading SOULWORK: HUMANITY'S NEXT STEP.   I give special kudos to the folks at Trafford Publishing …

****

WHAT AM I GETTING INTO?
OR *THE INTRODUCTION*

"THERE IS MORE TO LIFE THAN THIS ... "

How many times have you heard this rumble deep inside your Being? How many times has this thought kept you going, pushing past pain and barriers, into a new phase of life? How many times -when external forces have said, "That's all there is"- have your insides cried out for something more?

Some of us have a personal history or herstory of feeling "different": of not really belonging in the traditional systems of schooling, religion, relationshipping, and work. While we may have tried to fit in and feel, act, and think "normal," in certain moments and times a deeper part of ourselves would jump out and proclaim "I AM!" This "I AM" would make waves and force issues. It would think, feel, and act in ways that others would raise an eyebrow to, call us names, and exit right out of our lives.

My *I AM, SOUL, HIGHER or TRUE SELF* never would stay buried or even quiet for very long. Just when I would have this "being like others" stuff down, out of my mouth and behaviors would pop some sort of contradicting thought, feeling, and truth that would expose me for what I really am: *an evolving Soul who just can't quit.* For many years, I had no conscious idea as to where these different thoughts, feelings, and behaviors came from. I tried my best as a child to hide from what I now know were psychic and spiritual abilities. But at age twenty, my Soul would no longer take NO for an answer. It was then that I claimed my "strangeness," beginning an extensive and continual search to understand the fullness of myself and the whole of life.

Twenty-five years ago simply claiming that eating a semi-vegetarian, natural foods diet was a healthy choice proved risky. The putdowns and rejections were plentiful. Yet today, it is a well-known fact. Yes, today there is so much more available in literature and workshops throughout the world covering physical and mental health and fitness. The Body-Mind Connection actually makes the news and the mainstream ads these days. However, it is still relatively risky to tell everyone I meet that I talk with spirits, healed my dog's abscess with my hands, and can know who they are and what they have been through by reading their energy body. These skills and much more have become a natural part of my daily, very human life. They represent a few of the natural abilities every single one of us Souls in human form have waiting to be developed, if we choose so.

I've discovered that all the existential questions, such as "Who Am I? Is there a God? Have I existed before?" and then some, *can* be answered and, more importantly, can be directly experienced. The knowledge behind those answers can then be utilized in our daily lives. In fact, in order to be whole or "holy healthy," tools and skills that integrate that cosmic knowledge *have* to be utilized and expanded as we grow along. The Human Potential Movement has encouraged us as humans to recognize that we have all the potential in the world to be totally healthy, which includes incredibly creative and awesomely prosperous. Yet, we humans have also shown each other that we can be incredibly destructive and awesomely unhappy. The point is that we do indeed have a personal, interpersonal, and planetary choice!

Personally, it has taken me years and years (as well as quite a few life times) of external research, inward searching, and reworking of my thoughts, feelings, and behaviors to truly believe and know that every one of us has a real quality of life choice and to understand what that choice is all about. Believing that we have the choice of living life joyfully in its fullest - with loving respect towards Earth, all of its creatures and other inner and outer worlds - is in itself quite a feat. It requires us to move beyond what most of us are taught by "mass consciousness" about life.

We have to change most aspects of how we think, feel, and behave acquiring mind, body, and spirit skills that science is still confused about and that, in the past, have been relegated to those few and rare geniuses. After my personal search and witnessing the search of many others, I can honestly and forthrightly say: "Genius, recognize yourself!" Yes, I am writing about *YOU* . . .

Through Science we've learned that most of us are using only 1/10 - 1/4 of our potential brainpower. Throughout the centuries, Mystics of many religions and belief systems have demonstrated unlimited powers of mind and spirit. Christianity's Jesus The Christ proclaims "all this and more." Throughout human history are reminders that there are higher abilities and skills that are ours for the development.

Yet, there are also reminders of powers gone awry, of widespread misinformation and confusion about the development of "Higher Abilities," and a lack of motivation to live in wholeness. This is based on disbelief, mistrust, and a lack of general knowledge in all we need to know in order to be able to choose to live in true health, love, and prosperity. Many systems of wellness are being taught that are based on real limited definitions of health. As a result the statistics for illness and dis-ease, for mental and emotional difficulties, including addictions, and for social and planetary dysfunction and destruction continue to rise.

It is time for us all to quit hiding under the guise "Is it scientifically proven?" Does our planet, our world and you have the time to wait until that magical and illusive "proof of the pudding" is documented in enough ways and enough decades to get through all of our defenses and mistrusts? If we humans are going to break through our barriers of ignorance and arrogance, then each one of us needs to access The Mystic, The Healer, The Artist, *and* The Prophet inside ourselves in order to become part of the proof.

There is an incredible amount of knowledge and techniques to learn that will, can, and do enable us to attain wholeness. This wholeness includes all the happiness, health, and prosperity that accompanies a way of life that is connected with our True Self, our *Soul expressing through our Higher Self,* as the God/Goddess Life Force Energy. So many of us are awakening to the awareness that there is indeed a healthier way to be on this planet we inhabit currently. Presently, there are available numerous workshops, retreats, conferences, books, audio and video tapes, computer programs, web sites, therapists, teachers, and guides designed to enable us in discovering and developing our potentials.

While this is exciting, it also gets confusing with many of us feeling lost as to what direction to attune to, what to follow, what to believe, and what to incorporate into our own lives. This confusion is a result of the patterns of self-denial and the disconnection we have been taught between the physical, mental, spiritual and Soulfull aspects of our Being. Most of us are out of touch with ourselves and our natural abilities to tune in and receive the HIGHER GUIDANCE and information that is available and designed for our own unique selves. We are not consciously aware of THE STAGES OF EVOLUTIONARY SOUL DEVELOPMENT we all can intentionally move through. Therefore, we cannot appropriately assess our current, or this lifetime's, SOUL PURPOSE AND TASKS.

Many are very wary of techniques and tools of self-transformation that have been labeled "New Age." Ancient history through to our present shows us that there is nothing new about EVOLVING SOULS and the basic methods available to understand and consciously connect with the omnipresent Whole Creative Life Force, named by many as "GOD."

A Soul's Delight, is an integral **HIGHER SELF INTEGRATION PROCESS AND PROGRAM** designed to help open us up to *realigning with our Soul's Knowledge and Skills. Integrating our Higher Self* enables us to more consciously use our physical, mental, and spiritual energies to live joyfully prosperous, *Soulful* lives while journeying here on Earth. The information and tools provided focus on educating and understanding *what life in its totality* is all about. They speak to how each one of us can become "holy healthy" by reuniting and realigning with The God/Goddess Love and Light.

This book is designed to move an individual (you) through their (your) blocks and limitations into consciously choosing and working to become the really creative and loving being you actually are. *A Soul's Delight* teaches us how to uncover our Soul, understand its development, and re-form a body, personality, mind, and spirit that is more appropriate to our own individuated *SoulSelf*. It defines a *Psychology of the Soul,* along with *The Journey Of The Soul,* teaching practical skills of *Higher Self Integration* that are aligned with the current available energies on Earth and other dimensions.

The Higher Self Integration Process is intense, requiring an UNENDING COMMITMENT to becoming a most loving, creative, and holy healthy being. Not all of us are at the SOUL CONSCIOUSNESS and personality developmental levels that are necessary in order to be able to make this commitment and stick with all the work, time, and energy it takes.

Being in denial of who we really are as a Soul often exhibits itself through active substance and process addictions, major chronic and life threatening dis-eases, and violently angry and hostile attitudes and behaviors. If you are experiencing any of these behaviors and circumstances, you may need to seek professional help in those specific areas before you will be clear enough to actively work through the information and tools put together in this book.

To be ready to really focus on *Higher Self Integration* means that you need to have learned some basic personal processing skills, healthy physical and nutritional skills, and the beginning mental skills that one can obtain through meditation or learning to really concentrate and focus the mind. While this program encourages you to go at your own pace, to take special care of yourself as you explore, and to design your own program based on what you are currently experiencing in life, it still is and will be an intense journey of which you need to monitor yourself closely. Although this program emphasizes becoming your own guide through your own Higher Sense Perceptions and Abilities that you are or will be developing, do not hesitate to seek or continue with other human and spirit teachers, guides, activities and tools if you feel so moved.

The information gathered together in this book draws from many systems, teachers, and dimensions. However, there are so many different types of activities available to use in learning necessary *Higher Self Integration* skills that it is not possible to contain them all in this book. Therefore, the **process** of *Higher Self Integration* is emphasized, leaving room for whatever other tools and activities you are drawn to which can enable you to transform your beliefs and behaviors in the most appropriate way that works best with your own unique development.

This book/program was designed and written to work with you energetically on many levels. You will find that the reading and working of the information and activities, in order to achieve real TRANSFORMATION AND INTEGRATION, will be enhanced by approaching it in these ways:

◆ Plan on **lots of time** over an extended period of time in order to work this program. This may take many years, if not your entire lifetime, depending on where you start and how far in your *Soul Development* you choose to go in this present life. Long-term changes take long-term commitment. None of the processes, skills, stages, and levels covered in this book are overnighters. Some will take days to understand and incorporate into your daily life; others may take weeks, months, years and sometimes decades.

◆ Don't skip around, at first, even if you are familiar or have worked with the concepts you are currently reading. Read and study the entire book before you design your own program. Get and stay **relax**ed. Take walking and stretching **break**s. Don't overload yourself, but read and **work at a pace that enables the highest comprehension.** Read and **reread.** Then be prepared to revise your own program as your abilities develop and expand.

◆ Work the activities and go back and **do them again** and again. In order to attain the skill level necessary for *Higher Self Integration*, you will need to become proficient and advanced with all the skills and processes covered in this book. This occurs with **"practice, practice, practice!"** The **capitalized words** in every chapter form a quick review and type of index when used as a skimming and loading your biocomputer technique. Studying **the indexed glossary** can be helpful in making the language of the Soul so comprehensible that *SoulSpeak* becomes a natural part of your daily thinking and verbalizing habits.

◆ If you jam up with emotions such as anger or confusion over something you are reading or trying to do, **use emotional clearing methods** in order to move past the energy that is stopping you. Then, try again later. This may mean hours, weeks, months, or even years later. It may also mean backing up and continuing to work with some previous concepts and activities.

Remember, that if you have chosen or choose to "go for" *Higher Self Integration*, you are or will be on the grandest of all adventures possible for us humans. As you focus on your *Soul Development*, life as you know it will never be the same again, and that is a guarantee! The Holoverse is a magnificent place in which to consciously explore. So put on your thinking, doing, and being hats and join us on

THE JOURNEY OF A LIFETIME and beyond...

CHAPTER ONE
THE ALL OF LIFE

THE FURTHER YOU REACH, THE HIGHER YOU CLIMB . . .

GETTING STARTED

"There's more to life than this!" Indeed, there *is* much more to life than being born, living some years on Earth "struggling through the best I can," and then dying. *And* there is a lot more to living on Earth than feeding, clothing, and housing ourselves and others.

So many of us emerge from childhood with a limited and distorted understanding of what life is all about and how we are to live it. Many of the beliefs and skills we were taught in order to live our lives were not based on a true understanding of the potential and truth of each and every one of us, but on survival-based fears which produce unhealthy and very limited ways of living our life. As a result, as a species and as individuals, we humans appear to be a fairly unhappy and life-destructive lot. And, if we buy into the mainstream media images we are presented, we appear to be perpetuating this unhappy destructiveness year after year.

However, at the same time, there also appears to be a spreading opportunity for an "AWAKENING OF CONSCIOUSNESS" occurring in present day humans. There is quite a bit of knowledge being amassed and available to all of us as we open our perceptions and develop the skills and abilities necessary in assimilating and integrating "the wholeness of life." Information and understandings about how our physical, mental, and spiritual bodies function as a whole unit, in conjunction with our Soul and the Creative Life Force Energy (God/Goddess), are being researched, channeled, and made available to anyone who so desires to know and understand. Today, the processes that lead to wholeness, enlightenment, and *Soul Attunement* or *Higher Self Integration*, are available for us all to study, practice, and integrate.

We don't have to withdraw from modern life completely in order to attain love and joy that knows no bounds. To the contrary, daily life experiences are some of our Soul's most poignant teachers and laboratories. However, these processes do require an ongoing commitment and a reworking of belief and lifestyle systems that take much dedicated work, time, and energy over an extended period of time.

You are invited to journey through the words and activities, information and perceptions collected and created in *A Soul's Delight*. You are also encouraged to work with all the suggested activities, taking your time, going at a pace that works best for your own transformational process. Once you are familiar with the concepts and skills that are involved in the *Higher Self Integration Process*, you will be guided in forming your own *Higher Self Integration Program* that will change and expand as you do.

ACTIVITY: <u>THE READINESS FACTOR</u>

For most activities covered in this book, it is helpful to first put yourself into A STATE OF OPEN RELAXATION, where your body and mind are relaxed, clear of distractions, and focused on the task at hand. Here are a few suggestions on how to obtain that readiness state:

1. If your body is stiff and tense, stretch gently for a few minutes.
2. Use BREATHING/RELAXATION EXERCISES that relax your body and focus your mind:

A. While breathing deeply, pay attention to your breath as it moves in/out of your body.

B. While inhaling tense up your feet, releasing them slowly on exhaling. Cover every part of your body in this way adding each progressive body part with the next inhalation.

C. As you continue breathing deep and slow, keep repeating silently to yourself "Relax - or - I am relaxed, open, and alert" as you slowly exhale.

3. Become aware of any thoughts that keep distracting you from your task at hand. LABEL THOSE THOUGHTS NONJUDGMENTALLY with an appropriate word, such as "planning, anger, fear, remembering." Then LET THE THOUGHTS GO by returning your focus to your breath.

4. While breathing slowly and deeply, explain the assigned task/activity to yourself making sure that you are with the program, understanding what you are to do. Recheck for any tightness or emotional reaction to the assignment. IF YOU HAVE HAD A NEGATIVE EMOTIONAL REACTION, SEE IF YOU CAN WORK IT THROUGH AND RELEASE IT: Fear, anger, and confusion jam our flow and creative juices.

5. Take a deep, long, slow breath and begin.

ACTIVITY: <u>JOURNALING</u>

An ongoing activity that is beneficial and necessary in the *Higher Self Integration Process* is called JOURNALING. You will use writing about your own thoughts and experiences as a creative, therapeutic processing tool.   You will also use journaling in a variety of ways, but the basic principles - of honesty and uncensorship, as well as following the flow of your thoughts and feelings until they naturally ebb - need to be upheld whenever you use journaling as a tool in your *Higher Self Integration Program*.

Get a thick notebook with lots of empty pages and title it "My HSI Journey."   Keep it in a safe, private place. Form an understanding with the members of your home that they will respect your privacy and right to have a notebook that is not to be looked at by any other human being, unless you give them specific permission.

Title a section of your NOTEBOOK, "My Journal."   In your journal section you want to allow whatever comes up for you to be released in words without concern about how others would react. Whatever you write in this journal section needs to be kept so that you can use your writings in different ways, reasons, and times throughout your journey.   You are on a journey of self-transformation that will elicit all kinds of feelings, thoughts, awareness', and learning that you will need to become aware of, process, and review through the help of your journal.

In your journal, you are not to be concerned about misspelled words and run on sentences nor how "good" your writing is.   You are to WRITE FREELY whatever your thoughts and feelings are saying to you in the moment you are writing, being as honest as you know how to be. Practice NONJUDGMENTALNESS with what comes out of you, allowing yourself to express in writing the intensity of what you are feeling until the flow stops naturally on its own.

For your first journaling activity, after you have reached an OPEN STATE OF RELAXATION, allow yourself to free-flow write expressing your present thoughts and feelings about: 1. *The Higher Self Integration Process* and what you anticipate or imagine will need to change in the way you think, feel, and behave if you are to be joy-filled, prosperous, and living up to your highest potential, and 2. Your concerns and hopes about how these physical, mental, and spiritual changes could affect your relationships with others, and your present home/work/planetary life.

> **TRUE ANSWERS STAND THE TEST OF TIME,**
> **PROVING THAT THEY WORK FOR THE BEST OF ALL CONCERNED . . .**

LIFE'S QUESTIONS

We humans tend to be curious creatures. We spend vast amounts of our time, energy, and monetary resources scientifically investigating everything and anything. Therefore, it seems strange that the basic, essential, and existential questions of life often have us stumped and in worldwide major conflicts trying to defend systems of beliefs that often don't make any real logical, let alone intuitive, sense at all.

Most of us have been taught that there are many questions about life that just can't be answered. Questions that are extremely significant in our everyday life often remain unanswered. These are essential questions that affect the quality of our lives, such as: Why and how does one person get cancer and the next doesn't? - to - How can each child raised in the same family turn out so different? - to - What happens when we die? - to - Why am I here now? For lots of us, many of the answers we have been presented in the past from some sort of authority figure just haven't made much sense or worked for us.

In the *Higher Self Integration Process* it is very important to learn to be aware of your questions, to dare to ask, and to remain open to receiving the answers. In seeking real knowledge or truth, it is also important that one's answers can stand the test of time, demonstrating and proving that they make sense and work FOR THE BEST OF ALL CONCERNED. Everything is interconnected in this world, as are the questions and the answers that fit and ring true.

All of the true answers will fit into a life system that makes sense and fits into COMPASSIONATE INTELLIGENCE. Life *is* very understandable when you are aware of all of its parts. Think of life as a jigsaw puzzle that works as a cohesive whole when all the pieces are available and fitted into their appropriate part of that whole.

ACTIVITY: <u>YOUR LIFE'S QUESTIONS</u>

Open up your HSI Notebook and label a few pages as "My Life's Questions."

1. Get into a relaxed and open state of consciousness.

2. Allow yourself to "brainstorm" all of the questions you have about life, recording each question in your notebook. BRAINSTORMING is a thinking tool that enables your mind to explore any area you are focused upon UNCENSORED. Do not judge, analyze, or delete any question your mind centers on, but record every question about life that your thoughts uncover. You are not looking for the answers to the questions in this activity, only for the questions.

3. When it seems as if your mind has slowed down and has no more Life Questions, recognize that this means only that you have ridden one wave of your mind's thoughts. Prepare yourself to RIDE ANOTHER WAVE of questions by breathing slowly and deeply for a couple of minutes. Then see if any more questions come into your awareness.

4. You can use a question that you already uncovered as a focal point, allowing other questions to be flushed out by the focus of another question. You can also use these titles to focus upon, encouraging your mind to keep riding those thought waves: Questions about God, about spirituality, about death, about other dimensions and existences, about your personal life including your work, health, relationships, resources, skills and abilities, and personality issues.

5. As you read and work through this book, other questions will be stimulated. Keep on recording your Life's Questions as they come up.

A Soul's Delight: Your Step–by–Step Higher Self Integration Journey is based on a whole and comprehensive system of the answers to Life's Questions. These truths have been handed down throughout the history of this planet and beyond. They are currently being channeled, tested, and integrated by many Truth Seekers throughout this planet and other dimensions. Many of these truths, however, are not easy to accept or to apply in our lives when we have been programmed to think and act in ways that are not in synch with the true understandings of how life really works.

Part of being human involves the process and intelligence of free will and the ability to choose what we want to believe and how we run our lives. The rest of this book is devoted to the voicing of the truth about what life is really about, detailing processes and tools that can enable you to prove the truth of life to yourself when you have filled in the missing pieces and learned certain skills.

It is of utmost importance to your growth and development that you prove to yourself the knowledge that is being shared through this book. Many of the concepts you will be reading about are hard for many of us to accept and believe at first. What most of us have or have not been taught about life by our families, educational systems, religions, or what is called MASS CONSCIOUSNESS, will more than likely be challenged by the concepts, beliefs, practices, skills, and systems taught in this book.

It takes time and actively working with these concepts before you will prove to yourself their validity and be able to "GET IT!" Getting it means that you wholly understand a concept so that it has made complete connections within your thinking programs (the light bulbs in your mind are flashing), thus enabling you to integrate it behaviorally and emotionally in your daily life. You will have to intimately experience the concepts yourself before they can provide you a belief and lifestyle system that actually does explain The All Of Life in a way that makes both logical or rational and intuitive or metaphysical sense. It is by fully integrating into your daily world The Truth Of Life that you will be able to achieve real joy, prosperity, and enlightenment.

ACTIVITY: <u>REACTIONS</u>

As you read this book and the recommended readings, as well as work the activities, be consciously aware of the reactions you have to the material being presented. For example, stop your flow of reading to check in and label what's going on for you, as in "I'm finding this interesting" or "I'm bored" or "Now I'm really confused." The more intense your reaction (either positive or negative) the more emotional energy will run through you requiring you to release, understand, and work through the reaction which has surfaced.

One constructive EMOTIONAL RELEASING METHOD for dealing with intellectual processes that have jammed or blown apart because of emotional reactions involves journaling. UNCENSORED, let your emotional reaction be expressed through WRITING freely in your journal. Ride the wave of your reaction until it starts ebbing through your writing. Then ask yourself what was it that you connected to (in positive reactions) or felt threatened by (in negative reactions). Freely explore this focus until it begins to naturally wane. If you are once again relaxed, open, and flowing, resume reading.

Another releasing method for emotional reactions is to MOVE THAT JAMMED ENERGY THROUGH PHYSICAL MOVEMENT AND SOUND. Freeform dancing, running, jumping up and down and other aerobic movements that allow you to heat up and breathe more deeply help. Add to that movement any sounds from your mouth that are not words, but which connect to what you are feeling: be it screaming, laughing, hissing, growling, and the like. Marching around the room banging on pots and pans or drumming can help move the energy and change your mental and emotional state. Once you feel the energetic shift of needing-to-release to time-to-move on, see if you are clearer about why you emotionally reacted and what you need to do in order to continue on with the activity.

> **BY FULLY INTEGRATING INTO OUR DAILY WORLD "THE TRUTH OF LIFE"**
> **WE ARE ABLE TO ACHIEVE REAL JOY, PROSPERITY, AND ENLIGHTENMENT...**

WHERE DO WE COME FROM?

Let's start with the question and answer from which all other questions about life evolve: **"Is there a God?"** Yes! Absolutely. Practically. Realistically. It's the Truth!

We are not talking about a silent, male-human look alike that randomly dishes out the traumas and dis-eases "for your own good." There is a Higher Intelligence, a fundamental creative power or energy in the HOLOVERSE (every physical universe as well as every spiritual dimension at every level) which is the source and substance of all existence. We humans have named this omnipresent energy source God, Goddess, Higher Power, The Light, Eternal Love, Yahweh, The Great Spirit, The Holy Spirit, Infinite Intelligence, The Christ Consciousness and more.

All these various names do speak to the essence of this All Pervading, Intelligent Energy Source. It is Light. It is Love. It is Power. It is All Energy including both feminine and masculine, the Yin and the Yang. It is Higher Consciousness. It is Divine Order and Universal Law. And it is indeed in everything and everywhere all the time and for all time. Thus, this Highest Creative Intelligence is within you and me. We are inherently connected with (or come from) The Higher Source, yet we appear to have somehow broken that connection. Or have we?

In reality, we are not separated from Our Original Source, God, in anyway except through the illusion of form and misbeliefs. We have tricked ourselves into believing that we are separated from God. This has been done through cutting off our ways and means of being directly and consciously aware of the ever-flowing communication between we humans and Our Creator's Love and Intelligence that is inside us, as well as all around us.

A most exciting and challenging bit of knowledge is that we can develop the consciousness and abilities it takes to directly and intimately communicate and consciously work and reunite with God or Goddess, The Great Spirit! You and I are Souls with a spirit body temporarily encased in a particular human body while here on Earth. Our SOUL is the Life Force Individualized. As is the Life Force or God, our Soul is immortal and infinitely intelligent. MIND is our activator and connector to that Infinite Intelligence.

We are Souls, individuated and animated life force energy conglomerates which are connected through intelligence or mind. Each of our Souls has a SPIRIT BODY that is made of light and energy. This spirit body allows us to interact in the worlds of spirit or on spiritual planes of different dimensions. When we as Souls choose to enter THE EARTH PLANE, we can remain in spirit form or we can take on a material form in order to work in the Earth's particular world of physical form and matter. We become HUMAN when our SOULSPIRIT enters into another human womyn's egg-sperm-fetus cell interaction. As our body is slowly being prepared in a womyn's womb, we are still knowing SOUL CONSCIOUSNESS and everything is being recorded in our Soul's mind.

The functioning of a human body on The Earth Plane depends on the bodily organ, our BRAIN. Our brains take a while to develop enough to work with different parts of our mind's (Soul's) knowledge, forming what seems to be a lag time in which our Soul's consciousness does not appear to be evident in our human consciousness. That, along with: (1.) the restrictive and limiting modeling or programming most of us receive as a child, (2.) the particular type of karma and learning we have come back into the Earth Plane to work on, and (3.) the energy vibrations of the planets, our names, and living circumstances, usually puts us into a consciousness developmental level in which we struggle with being human.

We get caught up in working with our five senses, usually to the extent that they are being modeled around us. Blocking out our MULTI AND META-SENSORY POTENTIALS AND ABILITIES, we are often unable to tune back into our Soul Consciousness and our inner knowledge, thus learning to depend on external forces to show us how to live an Earthly life. Through the cycles of time, a mass consciousness has developed which does not incorporate the knowledge, wisdom, and truth of the Soul. MASS CONSCIOUSNESS is the prevailing human view of life usually based on misbeliefs and disbeliefs that have been handed down from centuries of restricted human programming. To break the cycle of operating under mass consciousness, we must find a way to return to SOUL CONSCIOUSNESS. That's what living as a human on Earth is really about.

The Earth Plane is one of our many "SOUL SCHOOLS" with a particular emphasis on materialization and relationship. Its energy is denser than other planes or dimensions, thus enabling us to interact with energy as matter and form in a unique way. Our Soul's choose to use the energies of the Earth over and over again, for as the Earth evolves and interacts with mass consciousness other opportunities to learn in different ways are presented. It is particularly equipped as a classroom in which to learn THE POWER SKILLS OF COMMUNICATION, PERCEPTION, TRANSFORMATION, MANIFESTATION, AND COCREATION.

How many lifetimes or incarnations we/you have chosen and will choose to have as a human on The Earth Plane depends on several factors. These are: how developed a Soul you are, what types of karma you have chosen to create, which *SOUL CONSCIOUSNESS LEVELS* you achieve, and your level of conscious awareness and commitment to knowing "The Whole of Life." We continue to experience being human on Earth at different times during our Soul time/space continuum until we have moved to the deeper levels of conscious Soul/God connection that are experienced on other spiritual planes and dimensions.

Although our Souls exist in the spiritual planes of existence inbetween our Earthly schooling and incarnations, we remain in a type of holding pattern until we have used our human experiences to move us through the stages or levels of *Earthly Soul Consciousness* that allows us to "graduate" from our Human/Earth school. At that point we have the SOUL CHOICE to become a SPIRIT GUIDE for others who are in human form on the Earth Plane and to move through quite a variety of spiritual dimensions as consciously reconnected Souls.

IN REALITY, WE ARE NOT SEPARATED FROM OUR ORIGINAL SOURCE, GOD, IN ANYWAY EXCEPT THROUGH THE ILLUSION OF FORM AND MISBELIEFS...

ACTIVITY: <u>DEFINING GOD</u>

Throughout your life you have been receiving "programming" about all things and concepts that humans deal with. These programmings have greatly influenced your thinking, feeling, and behaving patterns. In order to clear and rework our mind thoughts so that we are able to perceive "Higher Truths," we have to become consciously aware of what is already programmed in our brains, so that we can clear or erase the tapes that no longer fit our development. There are techniques and activities that can help us become aware of what has been programmed into our brains and where that programming came from. This activity begins to teach mind clearing and awareness processes through focusing on the concept and reality of "God."

1. Get into an open relaxed state of consciousness.

2. FREE ASSOCIATION is a mental technique that can aid us in becoming aware of what's in our minds and in opening up our thinking processes in more creative directions.

A. In this first Free Association Exercise, say to yourself silently the word "God," recording in your HSI notebook the very first word that your mind then says or associates with the word God. Take that new word and record the next word that comes up for you. Keep repeating this step until you want to stop. each new word a few more times. Example: God -father-son-me-sad-distance-gone.

(continued on page 16)

B. In this second Free Association Exercise, using God as your base word, you will record your one word association but this time will go back to the base word and start again. Example: God - Truth, God - Light, God - invisible, God -dictator, etc. Continue on until your mind ceases with anymore associations.

C. Look over your word association lists, looking for patterns and insights into your thoughts about God. Was this hard or did your word associations flow out furiously? Are there contradictions and confusions that show up? Are you surprised by anything? Are you having an emotional reaction to anything? What are you seeing about your own concept of God? Where do you think your various associations come from: The Bible, a religion, your parents, a program on TV, etc.? Keep on thinking about what has come out of your head.

3. Now, use BRAINSTORMING together with the phrase, "God is . . ." as your focus. Remember that in Free Association and Brainstorming there are no right or wrong answers. There is just whatever comes up in your own mind.

A. Record whatever words, phrases, or paragraphs of thoughts that come out of the focus "God is . . ." Follow your train of thought until it runs out.

B. Then, take a little break, deep breathe, and start again. Let everything you've ever heard about or thought about God come back into your awareness through brainstorming. Let all your questions, experiences, expectations, and hopes concerning God come pouring out.

C. Now, brainstorm *the possibilities* of God. No censoring or judging, no limiting or refusing. Go past what others taught you.

THE SOUL INDIVIDUATION PROCESS can be thought of as similar to the connection and bond between a human and its genetic birth mother. A human came from its mother and appears to be a separate being. However, the mother's energy and essence remains within the human through genetic coding, and brain synchronizations or patterning that took place while in the womb. Even if the human psychologically and physically denies the existence of its birth mother, they are still linked energetically, often showing up in various behaviors that are similar to one another.

A Soul comes from God, only appearing to be separated from God while in Spirit and human form. God's energy is our energy. In essence, we are still of God. As our individuation process began, we became Souls with mind/intelligence, forming Light Bodies or Spirits in order to work in SPIRITUAL or ASTRAL DIMENSIONS (see Index Glossary) that require energetic form. When we chose to start experiencing physical form on The Earth Plane, our Souls with mind and spirit bodies entered a womb, helping to form our dense human body. Our brains run our physical form, while our mind and spirit, or energetic body, work with the brain to help produce what we need while on Earth. When we die or pass on, our Soul through mind and spirit moves back into the spiritual realms and dimensions, while our physical form dematerializes.

While on Earth, we Souls now in human form have to construct PERSONALITIES in order to interact with one another and other materialistic matter. These patterns of thinking, feeling, and behaving are influenced by our previous SOUL JOURNEYS on the Earth, our genetic and biological programming, our Earthly surroundings or environment, planetary influences, and the personality modeling we receive from those who surround and teach us their ways of adapting to Earth Living. While the development of personality is essential in order to navigate through the complex living patterns that have developed over time on this planet, humans have generally gotten caught up in their personalities or EGOS. One of the greatest myths that have developed in the human race is from the "I am my personality" misbelief. It entraps us in a cycle of earthly lives in which we devote most of our life force energy to battling our various "selves" or still empowered personality parts. It masks and covers up our Souls and causes us to forget "from where we came."

ACTIVITY: <u>BEGINNING TO DECIPHER PERSONALITY</u>

The *Higher Self Integration Process* is one that requires you to get to "KNOW THYSELF" more intimately than you thought was possible. SELF-AWARENESS is one of the major keys to real CONSCIOUS LIVING. This activity helps you to start seeing more clearly how you developed the particular characteristics that you previously thought defined who you are. If you can decipher or figure out and connect from where in the past you learned your different behaviors, it is then easier to choose to unlearn or change thinking, feeling, and behaving patterns that are no longer appropriate for your unique Being in the here and now.

1. Get in an open and relaxed state. TALK TO OR ASK YOURSELF to help you to figure out how and where you learned to behave as you do. This helps your mind to focus by giving it a direction and task. Then, scan your memory in order to remember if you have been told, "You remind me of your ____." (mother/father/brother/best friend, etc.), "You sound just like_____." or anything similar. Several techniques useful in SCANNING MEMORY are: A. Keeping your mind focused on the task at hand and paying attention to what pops up. B. Selecting and thinking about a certain time period of your life while focusing on the current task. C. Selecting a particular person in your life that influenced you greatly, recalling specifics about their behavior, and then scanning your memory for similar behaviors coming from yourself.

2. Breathe slowly and deeply as you help to awaken your memory banks with this VISUALIZATION (see Index Glossary): With your eyes closed, imagine or visualize a big movie type screen on the back of your eyelids, inside your head. Your brain is the projector and can play for you anything that you have stored away in your memory banks. On your MENTAL SCREEN, let your brain/mind complex show you a scene where you are behaving a certain way. This could be a past scene of you interacting with someone, shopping, cooking, parenting or any type of activity. As you watch yourself, try to connect if you have seen anyone else act in your same manner. Are you stirring the pot the same way your mother did? How did you form your opinion or belief about what you are doing, thinking, or feeling? Does your parenting style remind you of your father's? Have you heard someone else say those particular words in the same tone you used? Allow yourself to see on your mental screen the image of yourself and the other who behaves or sounds similar.

3. Once you have recalled from where your behavior originated, be aware of your own reaction to the connections you have made. Are you comfortable or uncomfortable with your behavior? Do you choose to keep it or would you prefer to think, speak, or act differently? Keep using MEMORY WORK, VISUALIZATION, and CONNECTIVE ANALYZATION to become aware of how and where you picked up your smallest to most intense types of behaviors, reactions, beliefs, and verbalizations.

WE ARE SPIRITUAL BEINGS HAVING A HUMAN EXPERIENCE ...

WHO ARE WE?

We are light beings, Souls with spirit or energetic form, temporarily encased in a human body here on Earth. We are not humans striving to have a spiritual experience. WE ARE SPIRITUAL BEINGS HAVING A HUMAN EXPERIENCE. On Earth we enter into and take on a material or Earthly body thus becoming part of the Human Race. In order to function on the Earth as Humans, we develop a personality, a set way of thinking, feeling and behaving, which allows us to assess and respond to what we perceive is happening around us in our material and human environment.

Usually this personality that is created is quite a hodgepodge of characteristics we acquire due to our genetic, environmental, planetary, and karmic influences. However, our personality or everyday consciousness is only one aspect of our being. In the process of adapting to our earthly environments, we loose touch with our direct and very real connection with God - Universal Mind/Divine Light - as a living entity. Our Soul Consciousness becomes covered up by our Earth-bound awareness. We are no longer in touch with our *Soul's Knowledge and Wisdom*.

The personalities most of us form are not based on HIGHER SPIRITUAL ENERGIES AND CONSCIOUSNESS, but on lower human mass consciousness ways of thinking, feeling, and behaving. We form our "LOWER SELF PERSONALITY" which is human and earth based, very limited compared to our potentials. In order to reawaken to our SOUL'S KNOWLEDGE, we have to very consciously create personalities (ways of thinking, feeling and behaving) that enable us to integrate our Soul's energies and knowledge into our everyday consciousness. We have to form or uncover our "*HIGHER SELF*" based on the unlimited potential of our multisensory capacities, our Soul/Spirit connection and reality. The process of becoming our *Higher Self* is called *Higher Self Integration* or "*SOUL ATTUNEMENT.*"

ACTIVITY: <u>WHO AM I?</u>

Get in an open and relaxed state. Sit in front of a mirror and while looking at your reflection ask yourself, "Who Am I?" Take note of your reply to yourself. Repeat the question, "Who Am I?" Take note. Repeat this question over and over and over again. Do this for at least 15 minutes. Do it at other times, building up to 30 minutes and more.

This is a lot harder and trickier than it looks on paper, so be aware of yourself if you start having different types of reactions, such as: frustration, sadness, boredom, and confusion. This seemingly simple activity is an ancient one used throughout human history to enable an individual to start removing the mask of human or lower personality. Keep on going with it, watching where it leads you, releasing your various reactions, and then always going back to the all encompassing question: WHO AM I? WHO AM I? WHO AM I? WHO AM I? WHO AM I?

Our Soul, which communicates through our "*Higher Self*", is directly connected to Higher Intelligence or God. It is by contacting and integrating our Soul on The Earth Plane through becoming our *Higher Self* that we connect or tap into the deep storehouse of Holoversal or Divine Knowledge and Wisdom. Taping into this Divine Light, we become channels of love.

Our Soul talks to our personality through INTUITION and a wide range of HIGHER SENSE PERCEPTIONS OR METAPHYSICAL ABILITIES. As we consciously transform into our *Higher Selves*, our lower self gradually lets go and we begin to be guided, taught, and encouraged by an Inner Wisdom that is true unconditional love and oneness. As we connect with our *Higher Selves* and experience HIGHER ENERGY STATES, our bodies and minds expand and transform. Our thinking and feelings change. How we live our lives evolve with LIFESTYLE CHANGES playing an important part. We gain more awareness of the path of HUMANITY'S EVOLUTION and our part in it. We discover our *Soul's Life Work,* gaining the tools to carry it out. We work on SOUL RETRIEVAL.

Our growth allows us to trust more, keep our heart open, and reach new levels of sharing and intimacy. We learn to trust our ability to sense energy. We hear inner guidance clearly. We are able to harmonize with the energies of all kinds of people and able to transmute negative energy. We gain an ability to sense, see, and hear the subtle vibrations of other dimensions. Our higher abilities of clairvoyance, clairaudience, clairsentience and other psychic/metaphysical/higher sensory abilities become enhanced as tools to further our growth.

Through integrating our *Higher Self*'s abilities and knowledge daily in our lives, we develop self-confidence, self-love, clarity of mind and other important QUALITIES OF THE SOUL. We are able to create rapid positive changes in our physical bodies and gain greater skills in healing ourselves and helping others to learn how to heal themselves. Our human journey becomes more joyfully transformative. We learn to: reach deep levels of concentration, focus, awareness, visualization, and perception. . . develop our higher senses. . . control our thoughts and feelings. . . continually "Soul Review" replacing all personality weaknesses. . . search for the good in all things abstaining from criticism and judgment. . . live in en-joy-ment with patience and tranquility as we work in Divine Order. . . work with The Universal Spiritual Laws making them a practical reality in our everyday lives. . . become one with the Higher Truths. . .

Our Soul housed within our Spirit or Etheric body helps to form THE HUMAN ENERGY FIELD which is the manifestation of Universal Energy that is intimately involved with human life. Our Human Energy Field, or our Aura, can be described as a luminous body that surrounds and interpenetrates the physical body emitting its own characteristic radiation. Our AURA is divided into seven major layers that interpenetrate and surround each other. These seven layers are also connected to seven major CHAKRAS, which are swirling energy vortexes that extend out from our bodies through our aura.

A spinal flow functions as our main vertical power current. In addition, we also have smaller chakras or energy points located throughout our etheric body correlating to points throughout our physical body. In actuality, we are, each and every one of us, pulsating masses of energy. In essence, ENERGY MANAGEMENT is what it's all about. As Richard Gelber, MD, knows and writes in his book, Vibrational Medicine: "We, as human organisms, are a series of interacting multi-dimensional subtle energy systems. If these energy systems become imbalanced there will be resulting pathological symptoms which manifest on the physical/emotional/mental/spiritual planes . . ."

What has happened and happens with us is that we get stuck. We literally get blocked. Throughout our Soul's journey and development, we create "ENERGY BLOCKS" that jam us up and keep us from growing and integrating our Higher Selves. Unless we become consciously aware of, release, and heal these blocks, we remain stuck with jammed energy circuits. To be truly whole, to have all parts of our lives running at maximum potential, and to run the Divine Life Force through our beings at 100%, we have to release our energy blocks.

As Shakti Gawain writes in Creative Visualization: "A 'block' is a place where energy is constricted, not moving, not flowing. Usually blocks are caused initially by repressed emotions of fear, guilt, and/or resentment (anger) which cause a person to tighten up and close down spiritually, emotionally, mentally, and physically. . ." Some of our unreleased/unhealed past life, childhood, and present emotions, physical traumas, habits, thoughts (false beliefs, attitudes, etc), and crises or traumatic oriented experiences have remained within our personal energy field. These ENERGETIC DISTURBANCES eventually cause mental, physical, and life style problems, weaknesses and susceptibilities, illnesses, and dis-eases. These blocks manifest on every level: physically, mentally, and spiritually (etherically). They also manifest in our lifestyle patterns such as: what and whom we attract in our lives and relationships, our financial and material resources, and what we give of ourselves.

Originally, the energy gets stuck, plugged up, blocked, or blown apart etherically and then begins to manifest mentally, physically, and in our lifestyle. Pain of any kind is an indication that there is something out of balance within your system/life. Any discomfort anywhere in your body/life is a direct message about how you are out of alignment with your *Soul/Higher Self*. "BLOCK BUSTING" is an essential part of managing our Being's energy and of being able to *Integrate Our Higher Self or Soul* into our daily lives.

As Sanaya Roman channels in her book, Spiritual Growth: "Your Higher Self is the very essence of who you are and holds accumulated knowledge from all your lifetimes. It heals and evolves you as you bring its high, fine vibration into your body and all your energy systems. Spiritual Growth comes from increasing contact with your *Higher Self*, in becoming and being your Higher Self, allowing it to become the director of every part of your life . . ."

ACTIVITY: __DISCOVERING BLOCKS__

     1. Label a section of your HSI Notebook, "My Block Indicators." Divide some pages into these categories: 1. Physical Aches and Pains, Illnesses and Diseases, Limitations and Restrictions, 2. Lifestyle Difficulties and Discomforts, 3. Mental and Behavioral Imbalances and Troubles, and 4. Past Life, Childhood, and Present Life Traumas.

     2. Get in an open and relaxed state of consciousness. Spending time on each category, use the skills you have been learning of FREE ASSOCIATION, BRAINSTORMING, MEMORY SCANNING, and VISUALIZATION to become aware of those things in all the areas of your life that indicate the presence of energy blocks. These are ongoing lists that you will add to as you work with *The Higher Self Integration Process* and your life continues on.

**AS WE CONSCIOUSLY TRANSFORM INTO OUR HIGHER SELVES,
OUR LOWER SELF GRADUALLY LETS GO AND WE BEGIN TO BE GUIDED
BY AN INNER WISDOM THAT IS TRUE UNCONDITIONAL LOVE AND ONENESS...**

WHERE ARE WE GOING?

Have you ever dared to envision what your life would be like if you were consistently physically fit, **mentally alert and advanced, emotionally peaceful, spiritually attuned, and Soulfully connected?** What if you really could create a life where you had financial independence and freedom, whole health, true place success, joyfilled relationships, peace of mind, and lived a happy and nurturing lifestyle in a safe and beautiful environment? Do you dream of the human world on our Earth becoming an advanced civilization with love and respect for all life as its foundation?

     It is time to put your whole heart and Soul into uncovering those wishes and dreams and making them a reality. Life does not have to be primarily about suffering or pain and struggle. That is a choice, one most of us don't even know we have if we have listened to mass consciousness. SOUL CONSCIOUSNESS teaches us something very, very different.

     As Souls in human bodies, we can move past the lower-human-self misbeliefs about life and start living a life in tune with HIGHER CONSCIOUSNESS based on THE UNIVERSAL LAWS. Bruce McArthur in *Your Life - Why It Is The Way It is And What You Can Do About It : Understanding The Universal Laws* defines, "Universal Laws as unbreakable, unchangeable PRINCIPLES OF LIFE that operate inevitably, in all phases of our life and existence, for all human beings and all things, everywhere, all the time." Once we become aware of these life sustaining and fulfilling principles, we can start working hand-in-hand with them instead of unknowingly beat our heads against brick walls.

     Imagine if we fully understood and integrated THE UNIVERSAL LAW OF CAUSE AND EFFECT - FOR EVERY EFFECT THERE IS A CAUSE - in every area of our lives. Wouldn't we be a lot more cognizant of our choices and their possible outcomes? Wouldn't our defenses, based on blame and denial, be so invalid that taking full responsibility in our lives would take on a meaning infused with "for the best of all concerned"?

Take THE UNIVERSAL LAW OF MANIFESTATION which centers around the power of the mind with "AS YOU BELIEVE, SO IT BECOMES FOR YOU."   Just imagine the changes you and your life will go through when you have fully understood and integrated that it is your thoughts and the energies or emotions you choose to run that create your life's situations and circumstances. Whoa! No more "Poor Pitiful Me - It's Not My Fault" song and dance routines. They just won't stand up to TRUTH once it's been uncovered.

These represent just a couple of the many PRINCIPLES OF LIFE that, once known and fully integrated in our daily lives, can revolutionize the activities of Humans on The Planet Earth. And in the meantime, what if we/you work diligently to discover and transform our/your individual blocks to living a "HOLY HEALTHY LIFE"? Just imagine yourself not only physically well but also living up to the potentials housed within your Being!

What do you think your life would be like if you knew how to manifest every material and financial resource you needed? How would your life change if you were in daily communication with Higher Beings who helped you to know the best-for-all-concerned way to do everything? If you knew how to get balanced when you got imbalanced or to heal when you became ill, don't you think you'd also learn how to stay balanced and whole?

Wouldn't what you produced or the goals you set up be on a whole different scale if you were cocreating with The Infinite Love and Intelligence as your direct partner? And what about being able to read your loved one's energy to find the repressed links concerning what's causing them such low self-esteem or to manifest cancer? Or avoiding a car accident because you accessed information that told you that it would be safer if you chose another route?

We can all learn using ALTERED STATES OF CONSCIOUSNESS to access memories and feelings that are causing us blockage, discomfort, and pain. We can all learn various ways of SELF AND OTHER HEALING through mental/psychic/spiritual work that tunes us into limitless information and creativity through communication with HIGHER DEVELOPED SOULSPIRITS.   There are skills and abilities, called HIGHER SENSE PERCEPTIONS (ESP), that every one of us are capable of developing.   These can change the very flavor of our daily life.

All these skills and abilities, experiences and situations, are ours for the taking. We each have within us what it takes to develop manifesting, cocreating, transforming, healing, energy reading, and higher communication skills. It's up to us, each and everyone, to consciously and purposely decide where we are going. The problem has been that it is hard to make a conscious choice when we don't know all of our options.

As you adventure through your *Higher Self Integration Process*, actively reworking your personality and skills to reflect your Soul and Divine Spark as your *Higher Self*, your perceptions, ideas and thinking possibilities will take you in directions your lower-self couldn't even imagine! And they are directions based on JOY, COMPASSION, and LOVE.

**WE CAN MOVE PAST THE LOWER-HUMAN-SELF
MISBELIEFS ABOUT LIFE AND LIVE A LIFE ENTUNED WITH HIGHER
CONSCIOUSNESS BASED ON THE UNIVERSAL LAWS OR PRINCIPLES OF LIFE. . .**

ACTIVITY: <u>HIGHER VISIONING</u>

Once you are in an open and relaxed state, focus on your breath, putting whatever distracting thoughts that pop up into the mouth of the bird of your choice you see on your mental screen. Every time you have a distracting thought give it to your bird and watch as it flies off, carrying that thought away.   Keep BREATHING SLOWLY and deeply using this visualization to help clear your mind.

(continued on page 22)

In your mind's eye or on your mental screen, VISUALIZE yourself lying on a warm, sunny beach. Feel yourself being warmed by the sun, allowing yourself to relax even more. Feel your muscles melt as the heat penetrates deep within you.

Slowly float up toward the clouds, feeling lighter and lighter, relaxing more and more. As you float higher and higher, you FEEL LIGHTER AND CLEARER. As you float upwards you feel a LOVING ENERGY move into your energy field, helping you to feel safe and receptive. You float into a lovely mountain range formed by clouds and sit on the highest peak. As you look around, you see a BEING OF LIGHT, representing your *Higher Self Energy* moving towards you. Welcome it with open arms and feel the unconditional love and acceptance as it is absorbed into your energy field.

ASK your *Higher Self* to present to you through imagery, words, and feelings an understanding of what you will look like, feel like, and be doing as your *Higher Self* functioning at 100%. Ask your *Higher Self* to present images of the ideal life for you once you have integrated your *Soul's Self* into your life. Ask and explore details including home environment, relationships, work, finances, recreation, creative forms of expression, and your physical, emotional, mental, spiritual health and practices.

OBSERVE what you are receiving without judgment or analyzation. If you tighten up and feel any emotions or disbelief, take a mental note of what is going on for you so that you can work with it after this activity is over. If your conscious mind begins to place negativity and limitations on your images, RECENTER YOURSELF. Ask it gently to let go of any preconceived limitations. Then allow the VISIONS to continue to SURFACE.

When you have received all that you are ready to receive, THANK your *Higher Self* for the images and knowledge. Float down to the beach, relaxing a few more minutes in the sun. Then slowly and gently come back to your present environment.

Don't be concerned if you felt like you were making things up more than perceiving or receiving from a different channel than your everyday lower-self consciousness. In time as your abilities open up, the quality of your HIGHER SELF VISIONING will change significantly. This is an activity you will return to time and time again throughout the passing of time. It can serve as a CHECK IN as to your progress every few weeks, or months, or years, depending on the timing you choose for your transformation and development.

Where we are going is largely dependent upon our awareness, understanding, and intentional connecting and working with and through the different *Levels and Stages of Earth-based Soul Consciousness.* There are very real and practical levels and stages we all must go through before we are ready to move out of human incarnation, having learned and integrated into our beings all that Earth living has to offer. Even though each one of us as individuated Souls in human form go through these stages in our own ways, taking our own time (be it ten or a hundred lifetimes), there are certain understandings, experiences, and tools that are most helpful in moving through these LEVELS OF SOUL CONSCIOUSNESS EXPERIENCED ON EARTH.

The more we understand how the SOUL EVOLVES, the better we can direct our CONSCIOUS, SUBCONSCIOUS, and SUPERCONSCIOUS INTENTIONS to happily dance along with natural evolution, instead of rebelliously warring against it. At a certain point in our Soul Development as a human, we have to make an UNWAVERING COMMITMENT TO SOUL MASTERY before we are able to make further progress on our *"Journey home to God."* We have to align the energies of our personality to the energies of our Soul and The Divine Love Light. We have to develop and enact characteristics that are in tune with our Soul's energy, such as being balanced, compassionate, patient, inspirational, vibrant, and harmonic, as well as many other Soul attributes.

**WE HAVE TO MAKE AN UNWAVERING COMMITMENT
TO SOUL MASTERY IN ORDER TO JOURNEY HOME TO GOD...**

ACTIVITY: <u>TUNING INTO RESOURCES</u>

Attunement to Soul or *Higher Self Integration* has everything to do with learning to TURN INWARD FOR GUIDANCE.   It is all about developing the abilities to be aware of and perceive guidance from higher more developed sources than the general human race. However, our Souls and other advanced Souls only in spirit form (angels/spirit guides and teachers) use what's available on this planet in the form of written and taped materials, workshops, human teachers, situations, circumstances, and nature to help us out in our growth/transformation.

In every chapter, additional resources and recommendations will be included that could prove helpful in understanding each chapter's focus.   However, the most important link between yourself and choosing those resources that can work best for your own unique self in each given moment, are your abilities to:

A. ASK for what you are seeking.
B. Remain OPEN to receiving what you are seeking (often coming in forms that you never would have guessed fit or were possible).
C. Learn to receive, using DISCERNMENT instead of interpretation and critical judgmentalness.
D. Give THANKS for what you have received and experienced.

When a resource - be it an article, book, movie, a sentence a stranger is speaking, or a workshop- fits for you, you will know it. You will have a reaction to it (either positive or negative or both) because your Being will be stimulated or hooked into its energy. It will feed you in some way.

Once you have obtained an open and relaxed state of being, allow yourself to feel which resources you know of that would be the most appropriate ones for you presently. Feel what your gut has to say and if it bites, let it feed.

In the hours, days, months, and years to come, be on the look out for "coincidences" or more accurately, SYNCRONICITIES (see Glossary). Watch for the book that falls on your head, or the person you "just happened to meet" who has been studying what you are interested in. Keep your mind, heart, eyes, ears, and all your senses open and alert to taking advantage of all your LEARNING OPPORTUNITIES that are being manifested every day of this life.

Three books useful in understanding the concepts covered in this chapter are:
1. Gary Zukav, <u>The Seat Of The Soul</u>, Fireside/Simon & Schuster, 1990.
2. John Randolph Price, <u>The Superbeings</u>, Fawcett Crest, N.Y. 1981.
3. Sanaya Roman, <u>Spiritual Growth:Being Your Higher Self</u>, H.J. Kramer, 1989.

CHAPTER TWO

THE SOUL'S SELF

**IT IS THROUGH THE PROCESS OF SEARCHING FOR OUR SOUL THAT
WE ARE ABLE TO MOVE FROM HUMAN INTO SOUL CONSCIOUSNESS . . .**

SOUL SEARCHING

Twenty-five years ago I used to think that "The Soul" was an elusive concept designed to help us to fill in the blank when there were no physical explanations to many of life's mysterious happenings. Since then, I've learned that Soul is much more present, permanent, powerful, and penetrating than the human body. It not only can be defined, but it can be felt, seen, touched, heard, and intuited. It's just that you and I have to open up the specific abilities that enable us to be aware of, know, attune and integrate Soul in our daily lives.

We've got to develop the characteristics, or thinking, feeling, and behaving patterns, that encourage Soul to make itself known in the material or Earthly environment. As Souls, we have within our beings the highest and most powerful Divine Energy/life force that needs comparable means of expression. Through our human conditioning, we stifle, block, and inhibit our Soul, developing a personality, or means of life expression, that is oriented toward human or mass consciousness. This LOWER SELF PERSONALITY has to be transformed into a *HIGHER SELF PERSONALITY* if we want to let the wholeness and fullness of our Souls shine forth.

As pure Souls, we have no limits, no boundaries that our Soul's energy cannot penetrate and transform. It is our perception and belief of being a limited human with strict material boundaries that has covered up our Soul's energy, requiring SOUL RETRIEVAL. It is through the process of searching for our Soul that we are able to move from human or mass consciousness back into Divinely Connected Soul Consciousness. As we do so, we uncover our real abilities and POWERS or THE ABILITY TO MAKE THINGS HAPPEN.

As Souls in human bodies, we can develop the powers of COMMUNICATION, SELF-EXPRESSION, PERCEPTION, ENERGY READING, TRANSFORMATION, HEALING, MANIFESTATION, DEMONSTRATION, COCREATION, and CAUSATION. Through developing these powers on a Soul level, we can know everything about life past, present, and future. We can gracefully change what is no longer valid for living attuned as a spiritual being through human form, experiencing full PROSPERITY. Our natural skills of clairaudience, clairvoyance, and clairsentience, which include channeling or spirit communication and mediumship, and auric vision, mental telepathy, psychokinesis, out of body travel, psychometry, materialization, spiritual and hands on healing, and others, develop and become a daily reality.

Most human beings have had experiences in which they realized that they knew what they did through INTUITION, which is THE ACT OR FACULTY OF KNOWING WITHOUT THE USE OF RATIONAL PROCESSES. Many of us have known things ahead of time, seen scenes inside our mind that actually took place at a later date, made a decision based only on a gut reaction that turned out to be right on, and saw or heard dead loved ones speak. Some of us have used the ability to help relieve illness symptoms and discover another person's life traumas through physical touch. At this moment, someone is probably breaking another's record for mental or physical achievement. There are a few documented cases of people levitating or flying, of developing stigmatas (physical replications of the wounds caused by the nails that pierced Jesus The Christ's hands and feet), of bringing others back to life, and of consciously choosing to leave their physical body permanently (conscious dying), among other abilities that some people still want to believe are impossible.

Our Soul's abilities and energies are capable of moving out beyond the illusional limitations and belief systems of mass consciousness and our lower selves or ego personalities. This not only includes developing and using abilities of mind, body, and spirit that go way beyond what has traditionally been labeled normal or ordinary, but also includes the abilities and skills that enable one to live one's life in full Prosperity.

PROSPERITY CONSCIOUSNESS is the study and practice of the spiritual laws of wholeness. It includes being and having financial independence and freedom (to have all the financial and material resources you need in order to be free to give, express, and cocreate as your *Higher Self or Soul*), whole health, true place success, joyful relationships, peace of mind, and a whole and spirit filled lifestyle and environment. In other words, Prosperity is being fully integrated into and as your *Higher Self*, because true Prosperity is the result of DELIBERATE HIGHER THOUGHT AND ACTION. True Prosperity is having all the time, energy, financial, material, spirit, human, and nature resources to do and be my/your/our Soul highest, wholest, and happiest each and every moment. And this requires SOUL POWER!

Each and every one of us has the SOUL POTENTIAL for developing and integrating all the SOUL POWERS AND ABILITIES mentioned in the last few pages. All the EXTRA SENSORY or HIGHER SENSE PERCEPTIONS we have read or heard about are ours for the recognizing and developing. They are our very NATURAL ABILITIES, which over human history have been covered up and given a bad rap due to fear involving the perceived misuse or possible misuse of POWER. Because of Soul, it is a natural and normal part of life to use these powers and abilities. To keep denying and pretending that we do not have these METAPHYSICAL ABILITIES and cannot develop these skills is a very false and destructive way to live life. It only creates stuckness, frustration, illness/dis-ease, and destruction.

Because of the previous Soul adventures we have all had in other physical and multidimensional incarnations, all of us have bits and pieces of these Soul powers and abilities already developed. The SOUL MEMORIES of the specifics are held in the recesses of our SOUL MIND. Therefore, it always seems like certain powers, abilities, skills, and tools are more easily developed for each of us than are others.

TRUE PROSPERITY MEANS HAVING ALL THE TIME, ENERGY, FINANCIAL, MATERIAL, SPIRIT, HUMAN, AND NATURE RESOURCES TO DO AND BE OUR HIGHEST AND WHOLEST EACH AND EVERY MOMENT . . .

ACTIVITY: <u>WHAT COMES NATURALLY</u>

In consciously developing your *Higher Self*, or Soul abilities, it helps to start with those areas, abilities, and skills you seem to have retained or are already using a little bit of.   AWARENESS is one of the most necessary ingredients or skills to develop in your life in order to function from Soul. Knowing your inner and outer self and environments can only become a reality through the development of CONSCIOUS COGNIZANCE, the sure recognition and thorough knowledge of something sensed, felt, or perceived. This activity uses the Development of Awareness in the quest of discovering what comes naturally.

(continued on page 26)

1. After you have gotten into your open and relaxed state, take a long and deep look at each one of these Soul Power Categories, recalling if you have directly experienced any of their skills, abilities, and happenings: A. CONNECTING through COMMUNICATION/SELF EXPRESSION: Transmission - the exchange of thoughts, feelings and actions - connection - listening to and sending out messages human to human/animal/plant/spirit - to know, express, and share one's self . . .

B. KNOWING through PERCEPTION/READING ENERGY: To become aware of and achieve understanding in one's mind - to detect or observe through the senses - to know something through the reading of its energetic vibrations . . .

C. CHANGING through TRANSFORMATION/HEALING: To change the nature, function, or condition of - set right or amend - to become whole and sound . . .

D. ATTRACTING through MANIFESTATION/DEMONSTRATION: To show, demonstrate, prove and reveal - to teach, describe, or illustrate by experiment or practical application . . .

E. CREATING through COCREATION/CAUSATION: To cause to exist, bring into being, originate in physical form through connecting with one's *Higher Self* - the process of effect, result, or consequence . . .

2. In your journal under the title "What Comes Naturally," list the categories A-E, writing in detail the different things you have experienced in each of these power areas. After you have written about all you can remember, put a circle around these words every time you have used them or their equivalent:
A. HEARD - A VOICE INSIDE MY HEAD OR CHANNELED - IT CAME THROUGH ME
        BUT I KNEW IT WASN'T ME,
B. INTUITED, FELT OR SENSED,
C. HEAT, TINGLES, AND ENERGY EXPERIENCED,
D. SAW, VISUALIZED, IMAGINED, OR PERCEIVED,
E. KNEW THINGS I COULDN'T HAVE KNOWN, DID THINGS I DIDN'T KNOW I
        COULD, EXPANDED KNOWLEDGE AND ABILITIES.

3. Looking over what you have written and circled, FIND THE PATTERNS in your behavior that stand out. Notice your own reaction to what you are becoming aware of. Acknowledge which areas/powers/abilities you seem to naturally gravitate towards. STUDY the various powers and abilities so that your knowledge and understanding deepens.

4. Get into an even deeper state of relaxation and PROGRAM into your mind the intention and request to be on the alert or to be consciously aware of any of the previously mentioned happenings occurring in your daily life. This can be done in a variety of ways, including using DIRECT AND DELIBERATE WORD REPETITION, VISUALIZING what you wish to occur, ASKING for internal help with your request, and scheduling a time at the end of each day to RECORD any related events or REALIZATIONS. Watch for your increased daily awareness of what is happening in and around you.

Our true Soul's abilities and powers need to shine forth through the clarity and wisdom of *Higher Consciousness*. Lower-self personality characteristics run distorted and negative energy currents that inhibit Soul's real and full light to shine into and over the denseness of The Earth Plane. However, there are a lot of personality characteristics, abilities, skills, and energies that run the energy currents compatible with Divine Love's Light. It is these *Higher Self* personality characteristics that Developing Souls need to understand and integrate as their ways of being, thinking, feeling, and doing in the everydayness of life on Earth.

When one is running TRUE SOUL ENERGY, the personality one uses to express that Soul energy will often be labeled ECCENTRIC because one is departing or deviating from the conventional or established norm, model, or rule. In today's world, mass consciousness has established negative and destructive personality characteristics and lifestyles as the norm. The process of *Higher Self Integration* usually necessitates changing and transforming one's personality characteristics and lifestyle habits from a conglomerate of modeled behavior taken from our childhood familial and societal environments into thinking, feeling, and behaving patterns as perceived through our more *Higher and Divine Inner Guidance and Knowledge.*

Impatience has to be transformed into patience, rigidity into flexibility, and critical judgmentalness into detached discernment. One has to DEVELOP ADVANCED LEVELS of awareness, focus, concentration, creativity, organization, problem solving, decision-making, goal attaining, whole thinking skills, mindfulness, meditation, trance, and inner/spirit communication. And these abilities have to become so natural that their essence permeates every part of one's life.

If you keep your car and house in a mess, then it's pretty much a guarantee that your emotional and thinking processes will be too. It's hard to hear Soul through tons of clutter. It's hard to find who you really are if you are covered under a thick pile of garbage.

The lighter energies of joy, enthusiasm, appreciation and thankfulness, wonder and playfulness, and loving connection are what keep our Souls (including our spirit and physical bodies) vitally vibrant. Knowing, living, and being compassion, forgiveness, and love are absolutely essential to wholeness and channeling our Soul's Self. Inside each and every one of us is a manifestor, transformer, connector, communicator, co-creator, manager, problem solver, healer, discerner and seer of reality, visionary, and teacher just waiting to be recognized and facilitated into being.

ACTIVITY: <u>TO BE ALL I CAN BE!</u>

1. Reread the first four pages of Chapter Two, focusing on all the Soul powers, abilities, skills, and characteristics mentioned. Be aware of any emotional reactions and questioning you experience in your own mind and body. Listen in particular for DOUBTS AND FEARS.

2. Get into a relaxed, open state and then list in your HSI Notebook all the Soul powers, abilities, skills, characteristics, and energies you can think of. Over time, keep adding to this list. Don't forget about using Brainstorming and Visualizing.

3. One at a time, take each thing listed and allow yourself to think about, investigate, and research the SOUL MEANING of each. Whether it is the POWER OF MANIFESTATION, THE ABILITY TO KNOW, THE SKILL OF ASTUTE INTELLIGENCE, THE CHARACTERISTIC OF INSPIRATIONAL or THE ENERGY OF GRACE, there are higher meanings and realities to all of them that you will need to access, become aware of, work with, and integrate into your daily life. Being helpful means and looks like one thing when coming from a lower consciousness patterned on control issues and sympathy, and a whole other thing when based on Divine Consciousness patterned on unconditional love and compassion. Be aware that you will be working on this activity for a long time to come.

4. As you learn the real and higher meaning of Soul powers, abilities, skills, energies, traits and characteristics start dealing with how they fit in your own life. As you do so you will be naturally UNCOVERING many of the FEARS, DOUBTS, CONFUSIONS, FRUSTRATIONS, AND LIMITATIONS you have accumulated in working with yourself and your life from a lower or mass consciousness standpoint. Make sure you write out all the BOOGA-BEARS you uncover so that you can easily work on them in the future. What are the things deep inside you and within your present life style that seem to be keeping you from living and being YOUR SOUL'S POTENTIAL or BEING ALL YOU CAN BE? Keep on EXCAVATING!

EARTH IS A LEARNING ENVIRONMENT FOR DEVELOPING SOULCONSCIOUSNESS PROVIDING US OPPORTUNITIES TO MOVE FORWARD IN OUR KNOWLEDGE AND RECOGNITION OF OUR HIGHER SELVES AND GOD . . .

SOUL CONSCIOUSNESS

To what extent and level we bring out each of our Soul characteristics and abilities has everything to do with which levels of *Evolutionary Soul Consciousness* **we are actively working in and on.** Remember that Earth is a learning environment for developing SOUL CONSCIOUSNESS, providing us opportunities to move forward in our knowledge and recognition of our *Divine or Higher Selves*, including our oneness with God/Goddess/The All Of Life. As such, there are very real and practical stages that we all must go through, before we are ready to move out of human incarnation having learned all that human Earth living has to offer.

This journey takes lifetimes. In every one of our lifetimes, we move through a series of distinct stages or levels of *Soul Consciousness*. Each of us, as individuated Souls in human form, go through these stages or levels in our own way taking our own time. All of these stages are necessary and valid. Whichever ones we are currently working in are neither good nor bad, right nor wrong. It is simply just WHERE WE ARE AT. There are, however, certain tools, understandings, and experiences that are most helpful in moving through each of these stages of Soul Consciousness. And we do have a choice in how smooth or rough the going gets.

For the purposes of communication and application, these stages are named level one through level seven, paralleling the seven major chakras or energy centers of our spirit bodies. Starting in level one, each Soul stays working in that level until we have the motivation, knowledge, and skills to move into the next level. Many of us will move from one level into another, stopping at a certain stage/level while in a particular lifetime. It is common, though, to be working within two consecutive levels simultaneously.

When we are born again, we will start back at level one. But we will have the Soul and human knowledge and skills available within our memory banks and spirit essence to move quicker through the repeated stages into new, more advanced stages of Soul Consciousness, if we so choose. Those who have worked through all seven stages or levels of Soul Consciousness possible on Earth do not continue taking Earthly human forms. Instead, we permanently move on into OTHER DIMENSIONAL STATES OF BEING.

◆ *LEVEL ONE*

Each time we are born as a human, we start in LEVEL ONE SOUL CONSCIOUSNESS. How fast we can work through the lessons necessary to gain the knowledge and motivation to move into level two depends on many factors. These factors include the personality we start forming which is based on a variety of energies coming from genetic, environmental, planetary, and karmic influences. KARMIC INFLUENCES include finished and unfinished business from our previous Soul journeys and the general mass consciousness we are and have been a part of. We are each involved in making human history that is intertwined within our body/mind/spirit.

As Souls, we choose the circumstances of our births based on the lessons we need to learn and the reasons we are becoming human once again. Our first years on this planet are dedicated to becoming aware of our immediate environments and learning survival skills. These include developing our thinking and communicating abilities and will power. Many of us get caught up in the issues of survival and security, staying there all our lives. Others of us keep on pushing ahead to learn more than just survival and fitting in with the status quo or mass consciousness.

One of the central reasons we are each here on this planet is to work on the issue of POWER. We have to become conscious of how to use those powers and the total response-ability that comes with the POWER OF CHOICE. In level one, we are primarily going along with our society's program. Carolyn Myss, in *Anatomy of the Spirit,* calls it our "Tribal Culture." Some folks will choose to envelop themselves with the darker or negative side of that culture, while others will gravitate towards what's more balanced while staying within that culture's boundaries.

In Level One Soul Consciousness, we do not have a working comprehensive awareness of our true identity. We remain within the confines of the personality we form during our first years on Earth. In this level, we see ourselves as our personality, and will even fight with our life at stake for what we have decided are our rights. Many of us will cling to tightly confined roles, rules, and behaviors. In doing so, we can experience limitation, illness, loneliness, frustration, isolating judgmentalness, and other problems or unhappiness in many areas of our lives.

Within level one, we find a range of people behaviors. These behaviors can run the gamut of outwardly destructive actions, feelings, and thoughts all the way to the outwardly positive who are, by society's standards, good citizens. Whether one is a convicted murderer or a "regular guy" doing his or her family/work thing, the linking factor is that the person is operating without a real understanding, nor integrated actions, of what it means to be a Soul or spirited being.

We can operate as a dedicated humanitarian or service worker in level one, but the real reason for our actions is self-serving, confined to a limited knowledge of what life is really about. We can also be religious confessing to believe in God without integrating God's knowledge and wisdom in our everyday lives. Our motivations are often based on anger, ridicule, and needing to rescue others, protect ourselves and our loved ones, or prove our worth to others. Our real Soul abilities, which shine forth in the light of joy and prosperity, are not yet integrated in our lives.

We can develop a strong self-image as a human being, occasionally overcoming handicaps and achieving a degree of success by determination and will power, while operating under Level One Soul Consciousness. However, we are operating under a faulty and hole-ridden belief system. This can cause us to crumble if life does not turn out to be what we fantasize or dream that it ought or should be. It also causes us to block out in-depth relationships due to self-absorption. We operate as if we are The Center of the Universe and that all others (outside of ourselves and sometimes our immediate family) are not.

In level one awareness we can, on occasion and on what appears to be a random basis, tap into Higher or Extra Sensory Perceptions so that we know that they exist. But in level one, we don't even consider that they are natural abilities that can be developed and used to increase the quality of life here on Earth. We are not aware of the importance of consciously reconnecting, as *Awakened Souls*, to Divine Light and Love. If we explore ESP and the like, it is more oriented toward the negative/dark side of the occult trying to desperately learn to control others in order to feel some relief from overwhelming fears, pain, and insecurities.

Level one includes learning to relate to our self, although many of us get caught up in a pretend self that perpetuates a narrow and limited self-involvement. In this day and age, the result is quite visible by addictive behaviors, limited abilities, and daily problems. Level oner's, who stay there for a while, see life as limited and a struggle. We get hooked into feeling fleeting moments of happiness based on "the good things" that happen to us on the outside.

We rely on the false highs that come from feeding addictions: be it through food, drugs, adrenaline, money, violence and control struggles, sex, material objects, relationships, work, battling time, or the myriad of addictive thought and emotional processes. These include using crises and catastrophic thinking, living on the edge, busyness and distractions, and feeding off of others energy in order to keep feeling needed, worthy, and alive. To move ahead within level one, a person has to learn enough EMOTIONAL CONTROL along with a sense of CONSCIENCE in order to not hatefully and purposefully harm others.

When a Soul is ready to adventure into level two, it is because of a growing awareness that there is more to life than just trying to survive and do one's family/work thing. Sometimes, it's because we are experiencing so much pain and struggle that we feel forced to look around and see what else there is: Can't I do better than this? Other times, it's because we are attracting people and circumstances in our lives who are "on to something good" and we feel a growing desire to have it too.   Or perhaps, it is because we are having experiences that can't be explained, although we know they are real: curiosity gets fired up and becomes stronger than the fear of the unknown.

The old shallow and circular thinking patterns, that keep us in one mode-of-operandi, begin to be tested and to not make as much sense anymore.   Whether we are aware of it or not, our Soul is beginning to stretch.   The conscious intellectual exploration of what life is really about begins.   In order to consciously begin working in level two, a Soul on Earth must experience a crack in its established shell of mass consciousness, allowing a bit of **"There is more to life than this . . ."** light to begin opening one up to greater life possibilities.   A HUNGER FOR MORE starts growling in our bellies.

We have learned MASS CONSCIOUSNESS SURVIVAL SKILLS, but we still experience dissatisfaction. Whatever we have and are experiencing just isn't enough.   We don't feel that we have enough POWER AND CONTROL over our own lives.   We often don't know what it is that we want, but we're starting to get a SNEAKING SUSPICION that it's out there somewhere.   In order to move into level two, a Soul has to find the COURAGE to step outside of the defined norm and begin SEARCHING AND RESEARCHING.

WHETHER WE ARE AWARE OF IT OR NOT, OUR SOUL IS BEGINNING TO STRETCH . . .

ACTIVITY: <u>LOOK BEFORE YOU LEAP</u>

Part of becoming your *Higher Self* is learning high level OBSERVATION SKILLS. You become an avid observer of life in all its forms and realms through making a conscious daily effort to notice and watch attentively whatever is happening all around and in you. In order to be a keen observer, one has to learn how to not let one's own thinking and feeling processes interfere, distort, or fictionalize what one is observing.

PEOPLE WATCHING is so full of life's information and lessons. Since there are many folks all over this planet who are "level ones" purposefully observing them will give you plenty to notice and think about. It will also help develop those investigating skills that a person has to have in order to work in level two. Observation skills enable us to look before we leap which often proves very helpful as we start to explore life and all its possibilities on a wider scale.

BARRIERS to becoming keen observers are past-based expectations, prejudices and critical judgmentalness, deeply held fears, previously programmed negative attitudes, and emotional attachments towards what one is observing. All these keep us separated from what we are observing in ways that also inhibit us learning the ESSENCE and SYMBOLISM of what we have experienced. A keen observer sees the energy behind the action and the life lesson or real meaning behind what is occurring. One misses these things if one operates from a closed mind.

Study the previous information about level ones and let connections between what you have studied and what you are observing hold CONVERSATIONS WITHIN YOUR HEAD. Learn to RECOGNIZE whenever you plug into your OLD EXPECTATIONS, BIASES, PREJUDICES, JUDGMENTS, FEARS, NEGATIVE ATTITUDES, and EMOTIONAL ATTACHMENTS. Remember that these will all take concerted effort to release and transform, so don't get on your own case. Just recognize your own created barriers and start working on LETTING THEM GO. Keep going back to your observations. When you learn to QUIT REACTING, watch for THE GIFTS WHICH LIE BEHIND YOUR FEARS.

◆ *LEVEL TWO*

During level two, one intellectually searches for more complete answers to the questions about life that she or he cannot any longer ignore. We talk with others in more depth than previously, searching for and finding new READING MATERIALS, and ATTENDING CLASSES, WORKSHOPS, AND SEMINARS. We attempt to consciously learn more about what it means to be human and how best we can travel through life. Our understanding faculties are beginning to develop individually, but are still boxed in by the PERSONALITY LIMITATIONS we are carrying with us.

While our minds are beginning to open, experiencing an interest and enthusiasm in studying new ideas, we keep running old habitual emotions of disappointment, frustration, and boredom. These emotions are how we learned to handle our fear of change and our distrust of anything different. They distort whatever we are discovering. We are fascinated by what we are finding out. Yet, we do not have the beliefs, knowledge, motivation, and discipline to integrate what we are learning in a whole way throughout our daily lives.

This is the stage of THE DABBLER: trying a little bit of this and that. Ideas and techniques of self actualization, mental powers, the mind/body connection, meditation, astrology, channeling, expanding one's creativity, improving one's body, and the like become interesting to us. We often move from one idea, teacher, or practice to another until we land on something that seems to work for us, at least for a while.

Meanwhile, all the ideas we are encountering do begin slowly changing parts of how we have thought, felt, and acted in the past. We reach out more intimately than we could before, discovering more about how we relate to others. We become more aware of our emotions and the need to learn to handle our lives differently. As this happens, many seek guidance through psychological THERAPEUTIC PROCESSES and/or religious counsel.

Many of us can get stuck in level two through getting addicted to the INTELLECTUAL STIMULATION. We can get caught in someone else's (or a certain sect/cult's) need to control our thoughts and feelings. We can also shut off our exploration due to fear of the changes we begin realizing are required if we are to move ahead.

There is a strong tendency in Level Two Soul Consciousness to NARROW OUR EXPLORATIONS due to feeling overwhelmed by the complexity of what we are learning. We have trouble trying to judge truth from fiction. This can keep us fragmented and confused, though we might want to believe that we are really close "to getting it." We can get quite attached to what we are learning and head very enthusiastically into some painful DEAD ENDS.

During level two, we have many opportunities to develop STUDYING, LISTENING, and NONHURTFUL EXPERIMENTING AND EXPLORING skills. But many people stay in this level due to FEAR OF CHANGE and LACK OF SELF-DISCIPLINE to see one completely through the change processes. Many greatly underestimate what it really takes to be whole, shying away from the deeper psychospiritual and Soul issues. Many times level two's get stuck on NUTRITION/PHYSICAL FITNESS as the be all and end all. We have advanced into the "You are what you eat" mode, yet continue to leave out the truth of "You are what you think and feel." We're still greatly limited, although we can fool ourselves that we are not. In level two, we're a long way from clearly recognizing and integrating into our lives real response-ability for everything we are a part of. In order to move into level three, we have to start CONNECTing the new CONCEPTS being studied directly TO our PERSONAL selves and LIVES. Techniques have to be tried and practiced, weeded through, and delved into deeper.

**WE HAVE ADVANCED INTO THE "YOU ARE WHAT YOU EAT" MODE,
YET LEAVE OUT THE TRUTH OF YOU ARE WHAT YOU THINK AND FEEL . . .**

ACTIVITY: <u>THE WHOLE PICTURE</u>

Level Two is all about opening up and stretching toward life's possibilities, only we aren't anywhere close to seeing and integrating the whole picture. It is important and helpful to do whatever you can do to **LOAD YOUR MIND-COMPUTER** to see, hear, and touch what is out there in the multidimensional life you are a part of.

1. After you have moved into an open and relaxed state, list through Brainstorming every area you can think of in life.   Example: family, clothes, hobbies, home, religion, etc.

2. Divide these larger categories into smaller ones.   Examples:
House - building, water, furnishings, appliances, electronics, electricity, etc.
Psychic Abilities – Clairaudience, telepathy, finding empty parking places, knowing who is calling, etc. Keep going over your two lists adding anything else that comes to mind in the time to come.

3. For every life arena/awareness you have named:
A. Think about how you handle or work with it now,
B. What are your other choices in dealing with it,
C. What's keeping you from changing   and
D. Where, how, what are your resources in learning and implementing those NEW WAYS into your life. Set up some pages in your HSI notebook in this manner, adding to it as new awarenesses, ideas, barriers, and resources come your way.

Example:

AWARENESS	CHOICES		BLOCKS	RESOURCES
General/Specific	A. Current	B. Other Possibilities	C. Barriers	D. How, When & Where
1. My Body's physical workout -	walk	swimming	scared of water	YMCA, fear release
		Hatha Yoga	don't know how	Yoga classes
		<u>(with lots more detail)</u>		

◆ *LEVEL THREE*

At the beginning of level three, we are still working from a basic intellectual approach with little spiritual or superconsciousness. The more one begins to APPLY what one has read and heard about life theories and greater mental abilities, the more CHANGES in thinking, feeling, and behaving occur. These personal changes begin to SHIFT our relationships, work, and financial resources into NEW PHASES. We now recognize that many of the old ways we were taught to believe are no longer valid. We can't turn back completely, no matter how hard we try. Even a little backpedaling becomes dangerous, creating painful dis-eases, broken relationships, financial disasters, and other such TILT indicators.

The ROLLER-COASTER RIDE of level three has begun. We know too much to turn back, but not enough to know where we're going, let alone how to get there. As we practice specific MENTAL SKILLS, our higher abilities open up more systematically. As this happens, we cling to what we're able to accomplish, often soothing the chaos our lives seem to have plunged into with an old technique: FALSE EGO.

We start convincing ourselves about how much we know and how skilled we are, shouting and demanding for others to follow us. We can become righteous in our own way: deceptively critical and judgmental towards everyone and every system that does not comply to our new ways of thinking. Many folks can get very stuck at this level for a long time.

Our emotions that we run become more intense so that we have the opportunity to feel the amount of anger, resentment, and frustration we have been living under for years, even though we had not been fully aware of it. Our denial defenses have broken down and we're directly staring at a self, our lower self, that we're often ashamed of or confused by. But the old system of guilt and blame no longer works for us. Therefore, we feel pretty OUT-OF-CONTROL of our lives.

While we are making some INTERESTING CONNECTIONS and demonstrating some unusual skills, we haven't advanced enough to put it all together in a true holistic system. Many parts of us are still clinging to the old negatively conditioned thoughts, feelings, and behaviors. We become aware of conflicts within our lives between our old and new ways. As a result, we become conscious of THE WAR WITHIN OURSELVES. All of our "booga bears" start showing their faces. Our fears and addictions not only keep jumping out at us, but continually trip us up. Through these INNER BATTLES, we start to realize that our Souls/spirits have to be heard and, thus, our truth or SPIRITUAL FACULTIES begin to emerge.

As we start combining HEALTHIER AND WISER physical, mental, and spiritual theories and TECHNIQUES in our daily lives, we attract more opportunities to demonstrate higher abilities and truths. Yet our enthusiasm and optimism often gets ahead of our understandings and abilities, resulting in errors of judgment that can baffle us into a "How can this possibly happen?" state of mind. We have to keep on going BACK TO THE DRAWING BOARD again and again. Level three often feels like the most difficult because we seem to keep banging ourselves over the head. There are many dark alley's full of ego traps that we have to move beyond.

MEDITATION, MENTAL DEVELOPMENT TOOLS AND SKILLS SUCH AS VISUALIZATION, AFFIRMATION, PRAYER, NUTRITION, AND FITNESS TECHNIQUES INCLUDING MASSAGE AND ACCUPRESSURE are all necessary. BELIEF REPROGRAMMING is a must. Learning FORGIVENESS of self and others moves us more into the arena for attaining real SELF ESTEEM and LOVE. PSYCHOSPIRITUAL SUPPORT from other beings tends to keep us on track, providing a mirror effect that helps us to recognize our own ego trips. Approaching our problems and dis-eases HOLISTICLY is the only way that we're now able to move on and really heal.

Through this roller coaster ride of our life, we can emerge with a new and deeper sense of WILL and SELF-DISCIPLINE that is totally necessary for the next level. Many of the false beliefs we learned about life have been broken down and we are going through a very necessary PURIFICATION PROCESS. We are now able to know more of what taking responsibility for our own energy really means as we stand in the doorway to *Higher Consciousness . . .*

AS WE START TO REALIZE THAT OUR SOULS/SPIRITS HAVE TO BE HEARD, OUR TRUTH OR SPIRITUAL FACULTIES BEGIN TO EMERGE . . .

ACTIVITY: <u>THE THINGS THAT GO BUMP IN THE NIGHT</u>

Behind all stuckness, limitation, frustration, anger, and depression is FEAR. Behind all failure, disappointment, pain, illness, and trauma is fear. Fear is at the root of all our destructive patterning and programming. It is absolutely essential to recognize and rework your "Pandora's Box," which holds all your deepest to pettiest of fears. You'll be working on fear for a long time to come because there are tons of them that have taken hold in the human body, psyche, and life.

1. Once you are in your Open and Relaxed State, start Brainstorming YOUR FEARS, listing them in your HSI Notebook. Write down every fear you can think of. Believe me that you have more tucked away inside of you than you can possibly imagine at this time.

(continued on page 34)

2. Use specific Life Areas to help stimulate those hidden fears to the surface.
Example:
      What are your fears regarding people: your individual family members, strangers, the opposite sex, a certain ethnic group of people, etc.?

3. Pay attention to your DREAMS, your fear REACTIONS to movies and TV programs as well as to what others share about their lives, and to the FEARFUL THOUGHTS that flit in and out of your mind every day. Use EMOTIONAL INTELLIGENCE to be aware of every time a feeling/emotion/energy spurt of fear moves throughout your being, no matter how light or intense it's being run. Look at different sights, smells, touches, tastes, sounds, and patterns of behavior that seem to stimulate the sensation of fear in your being.

4. See if there are some MAJOR CATEGORIES your fears fit under such as the FEAR OF REJECTION, the FEAR OF VIOLATION, the FEAR OF DISASTER, etc. Look for your particular FEAR PATTERNS your Fear List will show. Are you more fearful of your own self, of others, or of the unknown? What are your different fears based on: a past trauma, the modeling and programming you received from a parent, your own vivid imagination, etc.? Keep asking yourself EXPLORATORY QUESTIONS concerning your fears.

5. Pick out a few of your fears and brainstorm a few SAFE WAYS to begin WALKING THROUGH YOUR FEARS. You will need to learn the ways that work best for you to overcome your various fears through AWARENESS, RELEASE, REPROGRAMMING, DESENSITIZATION, and CREATING SAFE, REALITY-BASED, AND JOYFUL WAYS of feeling, thinking, and behaving. Begin CONTEMPLATING DIVINE SAFETY.

♦ *LEVEL FOUR*

At the beginning of level four, we start to notice that our positive thoughts, feelings, actions, and results are beginning to outweigh the negative. Our consciousness starts being directed towards positive, joyful understandings and experiences at least 51% of the time. While we will continue our EMOTIONAL CLEANSING for quite some time, the most painful stages have begun to lift. We also start viewing the pain we do feel in a more OPTIMISTIC and POSITIVE light. We are starting to truly see that the Earth is our classroom. We begin making much more WHOLE and CONSCIOUS DECISIONS about how and what we choose to learn and focus on.

Our outer lives begin to STABILIZE once again, as we more HOLISTICLY HANDLE the changes naturally coming our way. Our resistances begin to melt away. We experience more harmony and resources and less pain and dis-ease. As our higher thoughts and abilities continue to progress, we recognize them as the natural result of an uplifted consciousness. *We shift from exploring higher consciousness, because we seek to eliminate pain, to exploring because it feels so wonderful.* This is an extremely important shift!

Our hearts are truly opening. We work willingly with the FORGIVENESS PROCESS. During this level, we often experience very deep sadness and hurt, but are able to process it through without sinking into the old style of depression. We shift our focus from the old angers we have felt about others, to the ANGER and dislike we have FELT about and TOWARDS OURSELVES. As our DEEPER MEMORIES of ourselves AS SPIRITED SOULS become conscious, our UNDERSTANDINGS ABOUT WHO WE ARE AND WHY WE ARE HERE begin to broaden in leaps and bounds.

Whereas we often seemed to have raged war with parts of our lives in level three, we now experience our real "DARK NIGHT OF THE SOUL" as we can no longer hide nor avoid the darkest parts of ourselves. We also now have the tools we need in order to enter into our most outrageous craziness, without frying our bodies and minds. As we strip away more of our superficialities, we start feeling more and more CONNECTEDNESS with THE HIGHER SOURCE and THE HIERARCHY OF SPIRITUAL BEINGS who are here to help us. Sometime along the way, we find that our struggles have become joyful and our deep loneliness has opened us up to an unlimited Holoverse.

We now recognize that we are STANDING IN THE DOORWAY of a whole new life/world. We can clearly see and feel the old mass consciousness world we are beginning to emerge from. We are being more drawn into what was previously an unknown, yet strangely familiar WORLD OF SPIRIT AND LIGHT. We now absolutely know there is "a God" and that we are spiritual beings in a temporary human form. We begin LOOSING OUR FEAR OF DEATH at the same time our LONGING TO "GO BACK HOME TO GOD" increases. Yet, we still need all the help and protection we can get in order to take the next step, which is the *total commitment to Higher Self Integration and Soul Mastery.*

In order to Soul progress any further, an UNWAVERING VOW/COMMITMENT to becoming one with God through INTEGRATING OUR HIGHER SELF must be made on the deepest Soul level. We have to be willing to let go of all attachment to living as our lower self and to developing fully our *Higher Self.* No other goal, commitment, or focus is as important as this one. Nothing and no one can ever again have precedent over our commitment to SOUL MASTERY and INTEGRATING GOD'S UNIVERSAL TRUTHS OR PRINCIPLES into our daily personality and affairs.

When a being is ready to make this commitment, the process occurs gradually, although we are fully and constantly aware that it is going on. There is a UNITATION WITH ALL LIFE that begins to seep into every cell of one's body. Our awarenesses open even further into THE INTRICATE WONDERS AND JOYS OF EARTH LIVING, INTERDEMENSIONAL COMMUNICATION, AND DIVINE LOVE. This is a deeply personal time, when we are being rebirthed into a new understanding of the power within us. This power will now continue to develop at a rate that is balanced and healthy in all aspects.

As our MENTAL ABILITIES EXPAND even more, we keep developing our abilities of AWARENESS, CONCENTRATION, FOCUS, MEDITATION, TRANCE WORK, WHOLE THINKING PATTERNS, AND CONTEMPLATION. HUMANITY RAGE and SEPARATION SADNESS are two of the SOUL PROCESSES that are necessary to become aware of and work through. An individual's SOUL REVIEW takes place gradually, with PAST LIFE RECALL and ENERGETIC TRANSFORMATION two skills that are developed and used often. SPIRIT GUIDANCE, ANGELIC COMMUNICATION, and DIRECT SOUL ATTUNEMENT start to occur more. A JOYFILLED LIGHTNESS TICKLES OUR LAUGHTER BUTTON and our joy starts getting spread around through our everyday beingness. We have developed the higher understandings about life and now need to feel them within our core. Knowing is sufficient for now as we experience more love and laughter in our lives, which helps to prepare us for the next level of Soul Consciousness: *active demonstration of Divine Truth and Power.*

NOTHING AND NO ONE CAN EVER AGAIN HAVE PRECEDENT OVER OUR COMMITMENT TO SOUL MASTERY AND INTEGRATING GOD'S UNIVERSAL TRUTHS OR PRINCIPLES INTO OUR DAILY PERSONALITY AND AFFAIRS . . .

ACTIVITY: <u>I'VE GOT THE JOY, JOY, JOY</u>

We start to become "spiritually of age" when we are able to make that most important switch of being growth oriented because of the pure joy in reconnecting and integrating our *Soul/Higher Self* instead of to escape or get rid of pain. In order to make this SWITCH IN MOTIVATION AND INTENTION, we must be able to see, touch, taste, smell, intuit, perceive, visualize, believe in, think about and feel deep, inner JOY.

1. After entering an open and relaxed state, ask yourself to bring to the forefront of your mind all the things that already elicit high pleasure/happiness/joy for you in your daily life. Let your pen just flow over a page or two in your HSI notebook. Remember to use KEY WORDS and MEMORIES to help you ride your various joy-waves. Add to this list as time passes on.

2. Become aware of anything that seems to block your natural ability to feel joy: fears, aches and pains, doubts, critical judgments, negative programming, rigidity, angers, frustrations, other people's behaviors, irritations, etc. Take a good look at these, and over time, really DELVE INTO EACH one of these BARRIERs or BLOCKs to running this higher energy current called JOY. Utilize all the skills and tools you are learning about to lift yourself above your specific barriers to feeling happiness and joy. Learn to TALK YOURSELF INTO JOY, instead of pain.

3. Freeing oneself to really running joy and feeling joyful in everything you do and everything that is a part of your life, usually takes quite some time. In the meantime, make sure you intentionally and purposefully DO at least a few things EVERYDAY that bring JOY into focus for you. Intentionally increase that fresh, childlike wonder that is sometimes buried beneath society's heavy view of what being an adult means. Your goal is to make your life JOY-FULL AND WONDER-FULL.

♦ *LEVEL FIVE*

We have now begun the true and conscious journey to *Higher Self Mastery*. Consciously REDESIGNING and RECONSTRUCTING ONE'S PERSONALITY to be able to be and communicate *Higher Truths and Consciousness* becomes a priority. As we go through this meticulous process, higher possibilities of human life become a natural part of our daily thinking and feeling processes. The deep recognition and reality that we are a COCREATOR with the Higher Power/God/Goddess, continues to change our beliefs about who we are, why we are here, and what Earth Living is really all about.

Our creativity begins to open up in many different ways. We begin to understand that we have the power and abilities to live a fully prosperous and wholly healthy life, and we begin to USE these POWERS ACCORDINGLY. We find our life being DIRECTLY SHAPED BY OUR THOUGHTS, FEELINGS, AND ACTIONS. HIGHER VISIONS and dreams fill our waking and sleeping hours. We discover that we do have the LONG TERM MOTIVATION AND WILL to make these higher possibilities a very real and daily reality. BRINGING OUR PERSONAL LIFE UP TO OUR HIGHEST VISIONS is the main focus of this level.

We integrate TRUE COMPASSION, HIGHER WISDOM, and DIVINE CONNECTEDNESS into every moment. The drive to discover and understand why we are here this lifetime, leads us to recognizing our LIFE TASKS, LESSONS, PURPOSE, and particular ABILITIES and SERVICES that we have evolved into enough to offer others. We strive to ever deepen the connection with our angels/spirit guides and continue to EXPLORE with an open heart the INNER AND OUTER WORLDS that are forever all around us.

As we continue to evolve and transform, we are guided to the work, relationships, environments, material/financial human/spirit resources that we are best able to serve and be served by. We are still most concerned about BRINGING ALL PARTS OF OUR LIFE UP TO THE STANDARD OF LIVING THAT BEST SERVES OUR *Higher Self*. This includes having all the financial and material resources we need in order to achieve our higher purposes.

Our BODIES become more and more BALANCED AND HEALTHY. We are BALANCED EMOTIONALLY and our ADVANCED MENTAL and SPIRITUAL ABILITIES are guided by our loving selves united in COSMIC CONSCIOUSNESS, not by our lower self ego needs. Our relationships are also transformed and we are freed from negative relationship attachments, addictions, and bigotry. The relationships we choose become loving and caring relationships, based on the HIGHER CONSCIOUSNESS RECOGNITION OF THE DIVINE WITHIN US ALL. We are now oriented towards SPIRITUAL PARTNERSHIPS.

While the main focus of level five may appear outwardly to be a very self-involved one, it is a time of INTENSE CONNECTION to every aspect of life there is. As we form and integrate our *Higher Selves* into our Earthly lives, all peoples and energies around us benefit from our transformation. The peace, love, and wisdom we radiate moves way beyond us, affecting everything we come into contact with. We become well aware of this fact, recognizing that there is no separation of energies between ourselves and others. As we develop our conscious abilities to create and handle energy, we constantly work with "THE BEST FOR ALL CONCERNED" from a Soul point of view.

It is during level five that our powers of COMMUNICATION & SELF-EXPRESSION, PERCEPTION & READING ENERGY, TRANSFORMATION & HEALING, MANIFESTATION & DEMONSTRATION, and COCREATION & CAUSATION really start coming into their own. Our abilities to CONSCIOUSLY MANIFEST AND PURPOSEFULLY MANAGE ALL THE RESOURCES we need improve rapidly. We are able to RECOGNIZE AND UTILIZE EVERY LIFE LESSON that is a part of our daily lives. We have developed the skills to very swiftly RECOGNIZE OUR OWN BARRIERS and BLOCKS as they crop up and to TRANSFORM their NEGATIVE STUCK ENERGY into forward propelling insights and actions.

One has to have CLEARED OUT MANY RESTRICTING ENERGY/KARMIC BLOCKS and have DEVELOPED many of the HIGHER ABILITIES available as embodied Souls within The Earth Plane to be working and living in level five, and to advance into levels six and seven. Therefore, although the work is more complex and advanced, the learning process will go much SMOOTHER. The COCREATIVE PROCESS becomes as natural and normal as eating and sleeping, thus enabling Earth-oriented Souls to joyfully complete our Earth lessons in ways that facilitate Soulfull balance and harmony and provide a much needed service to and for Earth and all of its inhabitants of every kind.

> **THE RECOGNITION AND REALITY THAT WE ARE A COCREATOR WITH GOD**
> **CONTINUES TO CHANGE OUR BELIEFS ABOUT WHO WE ARE,**
> **WHY WE ARE HERE, AND WHAT EARTH LIVING IS ALL ABOUT . . .**

ACTIVITY: <u>SHOW AND TELL</u>

To consciously attract to you everything you need to fully express your *Higher Self*, you have to be able to ENVISION YOUR HIGHEST GOOD. You also have to make these visions into reality through the power of your mind, emotions, and actions. This activity helps to increase your ability to really see and touch something that hasn't yet manifested, so that your intentions help to increase your ability to attract and manifest energy.

(continued on page 38)

Allow images of your Higher Good to come into your mind's eye through light trance work (your open, relaxed state). Look up in your HSI notebook the ideas and images you received by doing the Higher Visioning Activity in Chapter One. Using paper of different sizes and a combination of cut out pictures and drawings with paint, crayons or whatever, CREATE COLLAGES of your visions of your *Higher Self* and the life you will live as your *Higher Self*. Don't be shy about using small natural objects such as shells and feathers. Give yourself permission to really create images that stir and motivate you. Place these collages around your living and workspaces so that you can use them to help you FOCUS, THINK, AND MEDITATE on your *Higher Self Visions*.

▪ *LEVEL SIX*

It is now obvious that we are moving our life into a more integrated stage, that includes WHOLENESS IN BODY, MIND, AND SPIRIT. As we continue to advance, we are able to more quickly and efficiently fulfill the earthly needs we have. This frees us up further in order to start devoting more ENERGY AND TIME INTO THE ADVANCEMENT OF HIGHER KNOWLEDGE AND ABILITIES.

As our mental and spiritual abilities continue to develop, we often go through different steps of the utilization and sharing of these skills and abilities in order to get to know them intimately, enabling us to see where they ultimately fit in the world. Therefore, different people on different levels at different times are attracted to us for guidance, giving us the opportunities to demonstrate what we have and are learning. As we grow, we continue to attract people who are advancing themselves. In level six, we will spend much time and energy DEVELOPING OUR SKILLS AND UNDERSTANDING WHERE WE FIT INTO THE LARGER COSMIC PICTURE.

Eventually, we will find our own unique way to share what we have learned. Finding A WAY TO COMMUNICATE THE ANCIENT TRUTH TEACHINGS in a mode that works for the present Earth environment and consciousness levels is a task that we will spend much effort on in level six. The services we have provided until this time, have been necessary for our growth and the growth of others. They matched our developmental levels at the time. However, as our *Higher Selves* are fully integrated in our Earthly lives, we are able to develop NEW WAYS OF THINKING AND TEACHING BASED ON THE EXTENSION OF DIVINE WISDOM AND KNOWLEDGE. We focus our creativity and love on absorbing these concepts and on FORMING THE ADVANCED MESSAGES we are here to bring to Earth.

We are now committed to SERVICE ON A MUCH DEEPER AND BROADER SCALE. We are in the public eye, DELIVERING THE MESSAGES that have been DESIGNED TO HELP ADVANCE HUMAN EVOLUTION. Moving our higher visions for humanity into the greater world requires a tremendous amount of CLARITY. This cannot be done effectively unless we have been and remain fully dedicated to the *Integration of Our Higher Self*.

This very OUTWARD PUBLIC TIME is just another testing point, unless we are FULLY GROUNDED IN GOD'S LOVE AND LIGHT, knowing that we are A COSMIC MESSENGER. Any unfinished business concerning our own self-created blocks will be shown in the light of public service and will need to be immediately transformed. Any steps we have bypassed or hurried through now become symptomatic demanding to be reworked and finished. Any remaining ego trips we've held onto will show themselves as we land directly in the ego traps that are set up by mass consciousness through the student-teacher roles. Even so, our powers and abilities as demonstrators and guides are heightened. We have been works of art in progress and through the process have become MASTER TEACHERS.

FINDING A WAY TO COMMUNICATE THE ANCIENT TRUTH TEACHINGS
IN A MODE THAT WORKS FOR THE PRESENT EARTH ENVIRONMENT AND
CONSCIOUSNESS LEVELS IS A TASK WE WILL SPEND MUCH EFFORT ON . . .

ACTIVITY: <u>WHAT AM I TEACHING YOU?</u>

Each and every person's energy and essence you come into contact with functions as a teacher for you and, in turn, you function as a teacher for them. In CONSCIOUS LIVING, it is important to be aware of what you are modeling, demonstrating and teaching in each moment of your life. You are responsible for what you teach. And YOU TEACH HOW YOU LIVE.

1. Once in an open and relaxed state, look back on your day and your contacts with others. REVIEW THE SCENES in your head with the question "What did I teach them?" as your focus. What did you model or demonstrate? Was it complaining, blaming, or lying? How about balanced giving, peace of mind, or effective decision-making? Etcetera. Be honest. This is about what you actually did, not what you wished you had done or been.

2. Think about and decide what you would like to be presently teaching others you come in contact with. Figure out what is keeping you from doing so and form A LONG RANGE PLAN and process that enables you to move through any barriers to teaching consciously. As time moves on, update and continue to use this activity.

3. What do you imagine you will teach if you choose to become a MASTER TEACHER OF LIFE?

▪ *LEVEL SEVEN*

There comes a point or a time that THE HIGHER MESSAGES we have helped to spread on the planet have formed a momentum of their own. We have helped to give birth to a new fountain of energy, which is then drunk up by others who are thirsty and readily in need. When the work we have helped to cocreate has formed a life of its own, we no longer need to be its chief dispenser nor protector. There will come a time that we will, once again, move on.

Level Seven of Earthly Soul Consciousness, that we can learn while living as humans on the Planet Earth if we so choose, provides us the opportunity to SERVE IN MORE UNIVERSAL OR HOLOVERSAL WAYS. While still living in a physical body, we devote our energy to the EVOLUTION OF ALL SOULS by WORKING IN MORE DIMENSIONAL/ SPIRITUAL WORLDS. We separate ourselves from the human masses becoming even more available to work within the spiritual realms.

We have achieved complete *Higher Self Integration* and are constantly, consciously, and directly connected to God/Goddess/The Source. We are able to achieve total oneness with all creation. We are peace and love. We are now MASTERS OF LIFE.

Our HIGHER SENSE PERCEPTIONS, including the skills of clairvoyance, clairaudience, clairsentience, time travel, telepathy, healing, materialization, and spirit projection have BECOME a very natural part and WAY OF LIFE. We have mastered living on Earth. Therefore, we can FREELY MOVE IN AND OUT OF THE EARTH PLANE WHILE MAINTAINING OUR PHYSICAL EXISTENCE.

If we have achieved Level Seven Soul Consciousness, we have LEARNED ALL THE LESSONS Earth Living has to teach and do not need to keep incarnating in a physical body on Earth. Since we are consciously aware that we will no longer choose to be a human on The Earth Plane again, we joyfully do, experience, and FINISH UP ANY REMAINING EARTHLY AND HUMAN THINGS THAT WE ENJOY. We work on completing our earth lessons and our Soul-chosen reasons for our present Earth Life. When we no longer need our Earthly body, we can CONSCIOUSLY CHOOSE when TO separate our spirit body from our body of Earth matter ("DIE"). Our Souls now remain in the spiritual worlds, although we may choose to become a spirit guide for The Earth Plane.

WE ARE NOW MASTERS OF LIFE . . .

ACTIVITY: __MY LAST HUMAN LIFE__

Just suppose that this is your last human life and there are no limits on what you could do, who you could influence, and where you could go. Now, get into a relaxed and open state and let your imagination, and your higher and often hidden dreams, wishes, and hopes take you through the rest of this present life unlimited. Who, what, where, how, why?????

If you don't like what's popping out of you, give yourself a break in energy, lift yourself up through inspiring readings, music and/or movement, and try again. Watch how this changes as you learn more over time.

HIGHER OR TRUE SELF INTEGRATION CAN ONLY BE ACHIEVED THROUGH USING COMBINATIONS OF INTEGRAL PRACTICES DESIGNED TO FIT THE LEVELS OF SOUL CONSCIOUSNESS EACH HUMAN BEING IS OPERATING AT . . .

SOUL ACTIVATION

It takes a long time and continuous effort to uncover and integrate Soul into our daily Earthly life. Mounds of unhealthy, destructive beliefs and thinking patterns, emotions and habits, and ways of behaving and communicating have to be EXCAVATED AND RELEASED. New, healthier SOULFUL PATTERNS have to be programmed and established as normal and natural ways of being. This PERSONAL PROCESS WORK seems to take the most time and energy from us mass consciousness influenced humans. The layers of the onion are thick, gooey, and plentiful. We have to keep peeling back layer after layer, month after month, and year after year.

Soul Activation/Attunement requires what is called Integral Practices in order to be able to incorporate all its components, layers, levels, and stages into daily living routines and patterns. In his book, *The Future of the Body: Explorations Into the Further Evolution of Human Nature*, Michael Murphy defines INTEGRAL PRACTICE as "a discipline to cultivate the physical, vital, affective, cognitive, volitional, and transpersonal dimensions of human functioning in an integrated way." Integral Practices include studies, activities, techniques, tools, skills, and experiences that connect the physical, mental, emotional, spiritual, and Soulful elements and aspects of being.

Higher Self Integration can only be achieved through using combinations of Integral Practices designed to fit the levels of Soul Consciousness each human being is operating at or moving into. Our own Soul knows best how we need to do this, but until we can quiet down our lower selves and the din of mass consciousness programming or conditioning in order to be advanced enough TO HEAR and KNOW SOUL, we have to use some formulas that have worked for other fledgling SOUL SEEKERS.

ACTIVITY: <u>**OPENING TO RECEIVE**</u>

In order to be able to COCREATE A QUALITY LIFE, one has to believe and know that it is there for the manifesting and that they are able and worthy of living a quality life. Many of us, due to unhealthy self-images and thinking/feeling patterns, have shut off our ABILITY TO IMAGINE, VISUALIZE, AND PERCIEVE a Prosperously Soulfilled Life. By doing so, we limit our ability to receive all the precious and enjoyable gifts of life.

After entering your relaxed open state, ask yourself and then write down in your HSI Notebook any reasons why you should not have everything you need in order to live a quality life as your *Higher Self*. As you take a long look at these barriers, PROMISE YOURSELF you will free yourself, in time, from the thoughts, feelings, and lifestyle habits that are holding you back.

Now, enable yourself to enter an even deeper relaxed state recalling all the wonderful things you have already received in your life. Let these loved, happy, and taken-cared-for feelings flow freely in your being. While staying with these feelings, MENTALLY INVITE even more wondrous things to come to you.

Whenever you start hearing or feeling a blockage in the form of fearful, doubtful, or unworthy thoughts, make up a few AFFIRMATIONS that are appropriate for you. An affirmation is a strong, positive statement that something is already a reality. Two examples are: "I am receiving all the wondrous gifts of life." and "I am worthy of living a quality life." Affirmations are an OPENING AND REPROGRAMMING TOOL. Repeat your affirmations aloud and silently over and over focusing on bringing back those good feelings of worthiness, prosperity, and possibility.

Once you are back in the flow "of all good things" open up to new prosperous thoughts, more harmonious emotions, physical energy, and abundance in every area of your life. Visualize CREATING THE MENTAL, EMOTIONAL, AND PHYSICAL SPACE for these wonderful things to be in your life. Imagine yourself standing in the sunlight and with every ray that hits your being, you are filled with more and more vital life force energy and every thing else you need to be "HOLY HAPPY AND HEALTHY." Take these good energies with you as you continue your daily routines.

ACTIVITY: <u>**RUN WITH IT**</u>

As you are READING, LISTENING, and OBSERVING in your effort to grow and learn, start taking various concepts and ideas, and instead of quickly and forgetfully letting them in and moving on to the next, take them and run with them. As you read, mark the sentences that warrant more time and head space in order to deeply comprehend. After deep breathing and relaxing more, go back to those ideas and let your thinking cap take a plunge into their intricacies. No more blasting past. Work with what you have just read, heard, or seen. LET IT SINK IN AND FORM ANEW. See if you can directly APPLY what you just took in TO YOUR DAILY LIFE. Try to look at or think about it in a WHOLE WAY that is IN RELATION TO EVERYTHING ELSE it touches upon.

As your abilities to understand and apply whole concepts to your everyday life improves, go back and read, listen to, and observe the same books, tapes, and teachers again. You'll become aware of things on a whole new level than you were able to before. Then after some more time has elapsed and changes have occurred in your life, GO BACK AND DO IT AGAIN. TRUTHS have many energetic levels they work with us on, requiring a deep and repeated delving into in order to comprehend and apply their multilayered and intricate realities.

Gary Zukav's, *The Seat Of The Soul*, mentioned in Chapter One is a good one to run with. Be sure to check each author's Bibliography for more directions as you utilize BIBLIOTHERAPY to learn and grow. Here are a few more possibilities appropriate to this Chapter's focus: Michael Murphy and his *The Future of the Body*, Jean Houston's *The Possible Human*, *Your Psychic Powers and How to Develop Them* by Hereward Carrington, & Al G. Manning, <u>*Helping Yourself With E.S.P.*</u>

CHAPTER THREE

KNOW THYSELF

> "KNOW THE TRUTH AND THE TRUTH WILL SET YOU FREE" . . .

YOUR LEARNING PROCESS

To **KNOW one's SOUL is to be involved with the WHOLE OF LIFE.** And one has to know, work with, and HONOR all elements of one's being (physical, mental, spiritual and Soul) in order to recognize and be whole/SOUL.

Denial of aspects of our being, of life, and the resulting energy fragmentation that gets expressed through disease and dysfunctional life systems, appears to be an all-pervading epidemic in our Human World. In order to consciously change aspects of our being that have proven separating and destructive, we've got to be aware that they exist, understand the reason they have been a part of our life up until this time, and purposefully develop aspects of being which are connecting, vitalizing, and SOULFUL.

The problem lies in the reality that we aren't motivated to KNOW THYSELF and do all the intricate and intimate work that truly knowing one's self entails if we feel that CHANGE is a dirty word. Acquiring knowledge or LEARNING goes hand in hand with TO CHANGE and its synonym, TO TRANSFORM.

Since the root of why we deny and divide lies in fears of being overwhelmed and out of control, LEARNING in order to achieve TRANSFORMATION OF BEING is an essential part of the *Higher Self Integration Process*. It is through acquiring knowledge about something that helps one to not feel overwhelmed and out of control. Why is it so scary for so many of us to even think about a spirit world being all around us, just waiting to communicate with us? Isn't it because we don't know about, let alone understand how to work with such a world? Aren't we so scared, because of IGNORANCE or NOT KNOWING, of "LOOSING IT or GOING CRAZY" or in other words: to be out-of-control?

In many of us creative humans, ignorance invites our imaginations to go wild, especially when fueled by fear and superstition. The attainment of knowledge can stop a fear-fueled tailspin cold. Working with A POSITIVE LEARNING PROCESS can keep us on track, enjoying all the various road stops along the way. However, many of us seem to be negatively influenced and scarred by our learning processes.

In *Higher Self Integration*, where honesty and openly learning about oneself is absolutely essential, we can automatically sabotage our work on ourselves because of faulty, ineffective, and destructive learning habits. In learning to work with *Life's Multidimensional Realities*, including *The Whole Person,* as a *Master of Life/Higher Self/Attuned Soul*, there is a tremendous amount to discover, get to know, and integrate. It is virtually impossible if one has only learned faulty learning mechanisms and processes, such as: rigid shallow thinking patterns, scattered mind syndrome, teacher rebellion, and what-if-I-make-a-mistake-panic.

Relearning faulty learning processes, patterns, and habits takes some effort. However, the pay off in being able to learn and transform so much faster and effectively is well worth the time. Being aware of and improving your learning processes is a very practical as well as necessary place to venture from as you consciously and intentionally explore yourself, fully applying the ancient and modern wisdom of "KNOW THYSELF" and the Universal Law of "KNOW THE TRUTH AND THE TRUTH WILL SET YOU FREE."

ACTIVITY: <u>LEARNING MISS-TAKES</u>

1. Using the tools of LIGHT TRANCE (your open, relaxed state), BRAINSTORMING, FREE ASSOCIATION, MEMORY SCANNING, IMAGE PERCEPTION, VISUALIZATION, FOCUSED QUESTIONING, and THOUGHT RECOGNITION (recording on paper any thoughts and feelings you hear within your own head), bring into your awareness anything you have experienced, or been programmed concerning your ability to learn and change. In your mind, go back to where you grew up and went to school, reviewing the thoughts, feelings, beliefs, successes and failures, awards and punishments, praise and putdowns you received in the name of learning and education. Remember that the people (young and old) you lived with before your official schooling were your first teachers in helping to establish your learning patterns.

2. After you bring back into your conscious awareness the experiences concerning your learning process, use your EMOTIONAL RELEASING TOOLS to let go of any hanging on of negative feelings such as: anger, confusion, frustration, shame, or UNFINISHED BUSINESS. Concerning some of your past incidences, actively engaging in THE FORGIVENESS PROCESS may prove necessary.

3. Once you have ATTAINED AWARENESS and then PROCESSED AND RELEASED EMOTIONALLY, you are better equipped with clarity and insight to FIGURE OUT THE MESSAGES YOU RECEIVED about learning, change, and growth. These messages or programs influence your ability to learn. You have to become conscious of them so you can have the choice of changing their influence on your life. The following are examples of Negative Learning Programs that are destructive and distractive to *Higher Self Integration*:

"Old dogs can't learn new tricks"... Expecting to be instantly rewarded... Learning is not any fun and boring to boot... "No pain no gain"... I can't, I'm not good/smart/creative/worthy enough... Someone else can do it better or do it for me... It's not any good unless I have others approval... Dancing around the cause by treating the symptoms... You don't learn by doing but by thinking/reading... Being addicted to The Regurgitation Process, going through the same verbalizations and feelings, or doing whatever, over and over without really releasing and experiencing new moves... Having preset expectations and judgments so that, if it doesn't turn out the way you had planned, you label it wrong and yourself a failure... No one has anything new to teach me... Assuming you already learned all you can learn... Expecting "to get it" the first time and when you don't, you give up or blame yourself or someone/thing else... Believing you understand it all when you have really just begun... Your average focus and concentration rate is only 6 to 15 seconds at a time... and lots more...

ACTIVITY: <u>TO BE THE GENIUS I AM</u>

Once you have become aware of your traumatic past learning experiences, released their residue emotions/energy, and become aware of the exact programming tapes you have been living with, you have to develop a vision of what you want to be and how to get there. You are actively changing your learning foundation, being aware of the fact that a house needs a foundation. If you get rid of the faulty one, you still have to construct a new one or at least make repairs that fit the remodeling on your house. In whatever personal reconstruction project you work on yourself, always remember that you have to replace the negative or ill-fitting energy you have let go of with new, more positive fitting energy. You don't want your "house" to come crashing down.

In the LEARNING PROCESS AND SKILLS department, you need to have these understandings and skills as part of your Learning Foundation:
I CAN, I can, I can . . . It is mine to learn, have, be, and do . . . Learning is fun and joyful . . . Learning is an ongoing, stimulating, and exciting process . . . I am fully capable of learning and doing this . . . I am calm, relaxed, and open while learning new things . . . AWARENESS, FOCUS, and ONE-MINDED CONCENTRATION . . . WHOLE THINKING SKILLS, including both logical and intuitive, situational and relational, right and left brain connections . . . Able to learn or be taught through others, experiences, and circumstances . . . KNOWING SYMBOLIC MEANINGS . . . Trust based on DISCERNMENT . . . POSITIVE MOTIVATION AND FOLLOW THROUGH (long term if necessary) . . . Being patient with the necessity of REPETITION . . . LEARNING BY DOING/EXPERIENCING . . .

Develop a PLAN OF ACTION concerning how you will learn or enhance each one of the above listed skills and understandings. ACTION PLANS need to be practical and realistic to your circumstances, safe yet stimulating and challenging, and based on principles of Holism (body, mind, spirit and Soul). Be sure to use the skills covered thus far such as: brainstorming, visualization, and affirmations, in order to formulate and incorporate your learning goals into your everyday life. You will be exposed to many more helpful skills and activities within *A Soul's Delight*. Other helpful information and activities oriented towards Learning Processes can be found in:
<u>Superlearning</u> by Sheila and Nancy Ostrander and Lynn Schroeder, Delta Books, 1979.
<u>The High Preformance Mind</u> by Anna Wise, Jeremy P. Tarcher/Putnam, 1997.

> **IN PERSONAL RECONSTRUCTION, ALWAYS REMEMBER
> THAT YOU HAVE TO REPLACE THE NEGATIVE OR
> ILL FITTING ENERGY YOU LET GO OF WITH MORE POSITIVE HEALTHY ENERGY . . .**

YOUR LIFE'S REVIEW

In order to KNOW THYSELF, we have to be able to assess our life, where we've been, where we are presently, and where we are going. Since generally we aren't trained how to do PERSONAL, LIFE, or SOUL ASSESSMENTS, the following activity serves as a guide. Ira Progoff's, *At a Journal Workshop* and *The Practice of Process Meditation*, are two other books that prove helpful to this process.

ACTIVITY: *DEVELOPMENT ASSESSMENT GUIDE*

Please take a lot of time to work with this personal assessment, once you get into your open and relaxed state. It may require several different sessions in order to work through the whole guide. By using your HSI Notebook to record your answers, you can take all the space you need to be as honest and thorough as you can be. It may prove helpful to rework this assessment guide biannually, for it also acts as a way to chart your progress.

SCALE RATING:

1	2	3	4	5
Not feeling good about this at all.	Starting to feel a little better.	Comfortable but need to move forward.	Good for now.	Functioning at my best.

1. A. List the major pains/difficulties/crises you have been through thus far in this lifetime (including addictions, dis-eases, relationship problems, etc.). Go into some detail. Deeply listen to what flows out of your writing:

   B. List your "feel good about" accomplishments thus far in this lifetime. Again, go into detail and listen to yourself through your writing:

2. A. Describe your present life in detail:

   B. Overall, what is your scale rating concerning your life? _____

3. Describe any and all Past Lives you are aware of in as much detail as you can. Make sure that you record your feelings about what you have learned concerning your Soul's journey thus far:

4. What are your conscious ideas about where your present life is going?

5. If you have accessed your *"Higher Self Vision,"* describe it in as much detail as you can. Include anything you have become aware of concerning *Your Life's Purpose, Lessons, Tasks, Goals, Missions,* and *Your Particular Abilities* which you have discovered thus far:

6. A. Scale rate how you feel about your physical body: _____

   B. List all physical pains/limitations/symptoms you currently experience:

   C. Detail your posture, weight, strength, movement, flexibility, & vitality:

7. A. Describe your dietary habits, also listing any drugs, herbs, & nutritional supplements (include sugar, caffeine, alcohol, nicotine, etc.). Be sure to include any related behavior disorders such as Bulimia and Compulsive Overeating:

   B. Scale rate your satisfaction concerning your dietary habits: _____

8. A. Describe any emotional discomforts/imbalances you experience (such as irritability, lack of self-confidence, victimization, fears, loneliness, depression, confusion, etc.):

   B. Scale rate your satisfaction related to your emotional stability/clarity: _____

9. A. Describe any behavior patterns you don't feel good about (such as nail biting, sleeping problems, communication difficulties, sexual confusion, etc.):

   B. Scale rate your satisfaction related to your behavior patterns: _____

10. A. Describe any mental/intellectual processes within your brain/mind complex you don't feel good about or are ready to change (such as negative thinking, judging/blaming, memory retention and recall, thought control, etc.):

   B. Scale rate your satisfaction related to your mental/intellectual processes: _____

11. A. Describe any spiritual processes you are confused or concerned about (such as your connection with God, the death and dying transition, prayer, meditation, spiritual support, etc.):

 B. Scale rate your satisfaction related to your spiritual processes: _____

12.   List the physical/emotional/mental/spiritual activities, practices & systems you are engaged in (such as yoga, meditation, swimming, psychotherapy, spirit channeling, etc.):

13. List the teachings, books, teachers, workshops that have helped you the most thus far:

14. A. What do you do to relax?

 B. What do you do to play?

 C. What do you do to freely create?

 D. What do you do to nurture yourself, others, the Earth?

15. List your enjoyments (in-joy-moments)

16. Describe aspects of your lifestyle you feel good about and those you don't:

	Feel good	Don't feel good
A. Life's work-		
B. Finances-		
C. Home Environment-		
D. Earth's Environment-		
E. Living Partnerships-		
F. Family Relationships-		
G. Social Relationships-		
H. Recreation-		
I. Spiritual/Religious Beliefs & Connections-		
J. Creative Activities-		
K. Time management-		

17. Describe other aspects of your personality you are aware of, such as various subpersonalities you run and from whom or where you picked up your different thinking, feeling, and behaving characteristics:

18.   Studying the Seven Levels Of Evolutionary Soul Consciousness available here on Earth, determine which level or levels you are currently working in:_____ _____

19. Scale Rate- 1. not at all,   2. once in a while,   3. often/getting there,   4. fully integrated in life

DO YOU/ARE YOU:

*eat consciously _____
*regularly detox physical body _____
*aware of your breathing _____
*meditate _____
*use affirmations_____
*practice concentration_____
*use focusing _____
*Soul dance_____
*do Tai chi _____
*enter into The Silence _____
*use rituals _____
*use observation _____
*cleanse your chakras _____
*cleanse your aura _____
*use Divine Love Light Energy_____
*receive Higher Self guidance_____
*be the Healer you are and heal_____
*neutralize all incoming energy_____
*multitrack _____
*consciously release negative energies/blocks/emotions_____
*live prosperously _____
*give clearly to others_____
*work with The Universal Laws_____
*use your intuition_____
*freely laugh_____
*be the Artist you are and create_____
*see & understand auras_____
*able to forgive_____
*being in the moment/mindfullness_____
*aware of subpersonalities_____
*spiritually contemplate _____
*use massage and accupressure _____
*attune with nature _____
*use Flow States_____
*compassionate _____
*in decision making use "the best of all concerned" _____
*lucid dream _____
*perform inspirational/charismatic speaking & writing _____
*aware of the different levels of Soul Consciousness_____
*consciously developing many of your Soul Powers _____
*use long distance viewing
*out of body travel _____
*sense Earth Traumas _____
*relationship healthily & happily_____
*know your Soul Core Issues _____
*communicate with your Guardian Angel _____
*worked through your dark night of the Soul _____
*know your Soul's Life Purpose _____
*journal _____

*stretch your body _____
*exercise your body _____
*practice breathing exercises _____
*visualize_____
*pray_____
*still your mind thoughts _____
*enter into silence_____
*body prayer _____
* do Qi Gong _____
*be the Mystic you are and connect_____
*use art as meditation/spiritual practice _____
*work directly with God/Goddess_____
*work with spirit guides_____
*clearly hear your "Soul's Voice"_____
*integrate daily your Higher Self _____
*use a grounding cord_____
*nurture yourself_____
*rework limiting beliefs_____
*do your Personal Process Work _____
*use Astrology_____
*use self healing skills_____
*work with your past lives_____
*clearing childhood traumas_____
*work with your dreams_____
*wonderfully creative_____
*be the Prophet you are and compassionately celebrate_____
*flow with life_____
*perceive visions & spontaneous info_____
*work with healing energy_____
* dowse _____
*use witness consciousness _____
*developing your 5 powers _____
*consciously work with Kundalini_____
*enter into Cocreative States_____
*communicate with elementals _____
*use mental telepathy _____
*prophesize _____
*superperform _____
*find missing objects _____
*visit the Akashic Records _____
*work with Divine Order _____
*read Soul's Journeys _____
*manifest all the resources you need __
*have freed your inner child _____
*shape and time shift _____
*practice thankfulness _____
*aware of what you teach _____
*use blessing _____

YOUR ENERGETIC REALITIES

We Souls, with our minds, are housed within our spirit or etheric "bodies" first and always before **and after we take on human incarnations that add physical bodies and brains to the mix.** Therefore, we have to understand and know our etheric selves in order to truly "Know Thyself." Those of us who have developed our AURIC VISION can verify that human discomfort and dis-ease always show up in our etheric bodies before it manifests as symptoms of imbalance and pain in our physical bodies. We're all pulsating masses of energy and ENERGY MANAGEMENT is what it's all about for each and every one of us.

We exist within energy fields and have a variety of energetic forms that we feed ourselves with. THE HUMAN ENERGY FIELD is the manifestation of universal energy that is intimately involved with human life. Commonly called THE AURA, it can be described as a luminous body that surrounds and interpenetrates the physical body emitting its own characteristic and individualistic radiation. Our aura is divided into seven layers or bodies that interpenetrate and surround each other in successive layers. Each layer moves at a higher rate of vibration and interacts as a whole system with what we call our Chakras.

To the trained eye and hand, our auras are full of vibrating colors and heat sensations. Krilian Photography can capture human auras on film. Human babies attention is often captured by someone who has brilliant dancing colors within their aura. Often the baby isn't staring at us per say, but at our energy fields. All the colors, forms, and vibrations within our energy field indicate what types of thoughts, feelings, behaviors, circumstances, and health (or the lack of) we are manifesting currently. This includes things from our past that we have not let go of or healed.

There is a vertical flow of energy that pulsates up and down our energy field in our human spinal column and through our arms and legs. This spinal flow is our main vertical power current running through our physical bodies. It helps to bring in both the UNIVERSAL AND HOLOVERSAL ENERGIES we need to have in order to maintain our physical bodies on Earth.

CHAKRAS are energy centers that penetrate our physical bodies through our etheric double or spirit body. They are swirling cone-shaped vortexes with their tips pointed into the main vertical power current. Their open ends extend to the edge of each layer of the field they are located in. Each chakra corresponds to or is associated with the different layers in our aura's. There are seven major chakras and four smaller ones (in the hands and feet) which are essential that we get to know and consciously attend to. These major chakras are specialized energy transformers that take in subtle energy and distribute it to the major glands, nerve centers, and organs of the physical body.

We can train our eyes to see chakras and auras and our hands to feel the energy of the aura and its seven body layers, energy channels, and chakras. However, it is through training our minds to directly work with our own energy centers and fields that enable us to become wholly healthy and fully integrated as our *Higher Selves*. We have to get into the daily habit of CONSCIOUSLY WORKING WITH OUR ENERGETIC COMPONENTS, taking care or nurturing our spirit body just like we do our physical body. We have to consciously and willfully DAILY CLEANSE, FEED, EXERCISE, USE, AND REST OUR ETHERIC DOUBLE in order to enable it to utilize the energies we run when integrated as our *Higher Selves*.

The more we get to know our aura and chakras the more we see the interconnectedness of all of life's various components. There is a lot to learn about our human and spirit energy fields. It is imperative that you study the chakras, learning the skills necessary to developing vitally healthy energy centers and using this information/skills in your daily life. Below is a summary of the significance of our chakras upon our lives. This information has been collected from at least 15 different books by various authors who have studied the chakras (all of which are listed in this book's Bibliography), as well as channeled and applied knowledge and experiences by this author.

WE HAVE TO GET INTO THE DAILY HABIT OF CONSCIOUSLY
WORKING WITH OUR ENERGETIC COMPONENTS, TAKING CARE OF
OR NURTURING OUR SPIRIT BODY JUST LIKE WE DO OUR PHYSICAL BODY . . .

ACTIVITY: <u>INGRAINED BRAIN</u>

You need to get the Chakra System's information firmly planted in your mind. In order to do so you must STUDY, research, and study some more! PRACTICE, experiment, and practice some more! To "ingrain something on your brain" you must STUDY RELAXED AND EXPERIENCE FOCUSED. REPETITION helps to train the synapses. MAKING IT REAL etches it in permanently. TAKING A CONCEPT, APPLYING IT DIRECTLY to you and your life, and then MAKING NEW CONNECTIONS with it makes it a part of your own creation.

These two books can function as "block busters" helping us to move past both our ignorance and suspicion of what we don't already know. Take your time with these two books. QUESTION. DISCOVER. LET YOUR MIND STRETCH . . . Barbara Ann Brennan, *Hands of Light: A Guide to Healing Through the Human Energy Field*, Bantam Books, 1988 & Caroline Myss, *Anatomy of The Spirit:The Seven Stages of Power and Healing*, Harmony Books, 1996.

◆ *1ST OR ROOT CHAKRA*

HOW SECURE & SAFE WE FEEL IN THE MATERIAL WORLD. . . ALL IS ONE GROUNDING, SECURITY / FEAR, WORRY, FIXATED ON SURVIVAL

Location: Base of spine - legs, bones, feet, rectum.

Nature: Life force, heat, strength, will, ambition, to warm. Survival related to the basic processes of absorption, assimilation, excretion, and reproduction. Groundedness, connection to the Earth, survival instincts, physical body support. Need for logic, order, structure, law. Houses the Kundalini energies that are the primal energies of creation, manifestation, and the building of Higher Consciousness.

Correspondences: <u>Color</u>-red denoting heat, the life force, physical existence, strength, energy & vitality, <u>aura body</u>-etheric double, <u>musical tone</u>-C, <u>chant</u>-OOH, <u>skill</u>-survival, <u>physical sense</u>-smell, <u>temperature</u>-hot, <u>element/direction</u>-earth/north, <u>vibration rate</u>- lowest. Access to mineral intelligence, stars & planets.

Function: Grounding, releasing excess energy, a part of reproduction, blends earth & cosmic energies, contains programming necessary to keep your body alive/your personality intact/your soul attached to your body, the ability to adapt and make changes, a will center with the will to live manifesting in physical energy, issues dealing with food/shelter/safety/taking care of self, learning about loyalty, honor, and Divine Justice.

Healthy/Balanced Functioning: Have to address one's personal/familial/societal issues keeping the positive influences and discarding the negative ones, positive & safe family group identity and bonding, comfortable with one's place in society, being committed to one's reality, able to stand up for self, to be connected to Planet Earth and the natural world, the ability to adapt & to let go, to have healthy children, to satisfy and provide for one's physical needs/life's necessities, physical balance/health, to know how to take care of one's self, feeling safe and secure, to be responsible for oneself, good body image, stability, vital energy, alertness, good circulation.

Blocked/Imbalanced: Unresolved family and physical survival issues (including incest/abuse/neglect), problems concerning one's house/family/sexual identity/race, fears of physical survival & abandonment, loss of physical order, freaking out, alienated, unable to produce healthy children, pre-occupied with survival, paranoid, unable to take care of one's self and provide for life's necessities, not able to stand up for one's self, poor body image, anxiety, unsupported by others, feeling homeless, holding onto the past/old outdated thoughts & program tapes, limited awareness and lack of understanding results in immersion in the material plane, fearing/doubting/distrusting the environment, negative & limiting psychological programming from one's early years. Too much Root Chakra Energy results in ungroundedness/fear/panic/nervousness/ unnecessary survival struggle.   Too little results in lethargy/depletion/feeling cold/resistant to change.

Examples of Root Chakra Imbalances: Various mental illnesses generated out of family dysfunctions including multiple personalities/obsessive-compulsive disorder/depression, drug/alcohol & other addictions, victimized by society, aging problems, anorectal bleeding, rectal tumors/cancer, diarrhea, constipation, Alzheimer's, foot problems, planter warts, sprains, hemorrhoids, leg and knee problems, varicose veins, survival oriented money and material resource difficulties.

ACTIVITY: <u>**YOUR GROUNDING CORD**</u>

Emotions are energy patterns that we are picking up from others or are creating and running ourselves. This activity can be used on a DAILY BASIS as often as needed throughout the day as you become more aware of feeling various emotions that you really would rather not keep so alive and volatile. Remember that the more you practice this MENTAL/ENERGETIC CONNECTION, the realer it becomes. After awhile, you will actually see and feel the change in your being. Once you have established this activity within your system, it will only take a few moments of focused relaxation and awareness to bring it into your consciousness as needed.

Close your eyes and become aware of your breathing. Breathe deeply and evenly until you are relaxed keeping your focus upon your breathing, letting all distracting thoughts leave as soon as they enter. Place your attention in your pelvic cradle at the base of your spine. With every breath you take, visualize that you are drawing into your pelvic cradle long threads of golden energy. Make these threads of energy into a long cord that is attached to the base of your spine, going all the way into the center of the earth.

This is your GROUNDING CORD. It helps to stabilize you and is used to drain out unwanted energies from your being. When you are feeling uncomfortable emotions/energies, visualize them moving down to the base of your spine and out your grounding cord. They have been released. You no longer own them.

♦   *2ND OR BELLY CHAKRA*

**HOW WE RELATE TO OTHER PEOPLE . . . HONOR ONE ANOTHER
SEXUALITY, EMOTIONS / DISAPPOINTMENT, FRUSTRATION, BOREDOM**

Location: Below naval at the center of the abdomen - pelvis, vagina, cervix, uterus, ovaries, gonads/penis, prostate, large intestines, appendix, lumbar vertebrae, hip, Genitourinary System.

Nature: Emotions, sexuality/sensuality, tastes/appetites/desires, seeks to create, the power of choice in relation to others, duality (male-female, yin-yang, day-night), Law of Cause and Effect.

Correspondences: <u>Color</u>-orange, <u>aura body</u>-emotional/astral, <u>musical tone</u>-D, <u>chant</u>-OH, <u>skill-</u> clairsentience, <u>physical sense</u>-taste, <u>temperature</u>-warm, <u>element/direction</u>-water/west. Wisdom of the plant kingdom & the devic life that accompanies it.

Functions: To experience all levels of feeling (emotions, sensations, tactile, sexual), picking up the vibes (feelings) of another, socializing, relationshipping, body communication, balance of male & female energy in the body, procreation, creativity given to the world, sexuality, ability to recover from loss, personal and professional decision-making ability & talent, ability to protect oneself, fight or flight instinct, personal ethics/values/morals, to learn what motivates us to make the choices we make.

Healthy/Balanced Functioning: To feel the full spectrum of your emotions clearly & at your will, to be able to distinguish your emotions from the emotions of others, empathy, validation of another, reaching out & embracing life, a positive and realistic personal identity, relationships/partnerships based on mutual respect & support, physical intimacy, physical openness, balance, healthy risk taking, complementarity (drawing on the other side for completion), life becomes a creative communion, desire to create with music, art, words, science and medicine.

Imbalance/Blocked: Fear of loosing control and being controlled by others, betrayal, hysterical, acting out the emotions of others, controlled by sex, using sex to manipulate another, using money/blame/guilt to control the dynamics of our relationships, using blame or guilt to control ourselves or to be controlled by another, controlled by flattery, using flattery to manipulate another, sympathy (becoming the emotions or problems of another), no boundaries, forming relationships that handicap growth.

Examples of Belly Chakra Imbalances: Hardening of the arteries, hernia, sexual dysfunction, AIDS, venereal diseases, PMS/menstrual problems/menopausal difficulties, ob/gyn problems, pelvic problems, colitis, low back pain, sciatica, bladder/urinary problems, penile/testicle/prostate problems, sexual obsessions/addictions.

ACTIVITY: <u>CHAKRA CLEANSING</u>

After you have gotten into your open and relaxed state, reconnect yourself with your grounding cord. Concentrate on mentally visualizing CLEANSING and grounding EARTH ENERGIES coming into your being through your left and right feet chakras. Allow this energy to flow strongly up your legs, into your pelvis or Root Chakra, WASHING OUT all unwanted energies down your grounding cord. Visualize this Earth Energy in whatever brilliant and vitally alive looking color that feels like it's vibrating especially to meet your needs.

COLORS VIBRATE at different rates providing different types of energies. Once you see your color need in your minds eye, continue bringing this energy up through your feet chakras, up your legs and spinal column, WASHING OUT EACH OF YOUR SEVEN CHAKRAS. Once you have completed washing out all unnecessary and negative energy from your Crown Chakra down your grounding cord, bring the cleansing earth energies up through your feet and out your Crown Chakra, directing it to WASH OVER YOUR AURA. Let these energies slide down your aura and out your grounding cord.

This is only one example of many energetic cleansing methods. Play around with this one, making it your own. You might choose to try using the whole spectrum of rainbow colors coordinating them with the MATCHING CHAKRA VIBRATION (red-Root Chakra, Orange-Belly Chakra, yellow-Solar Plexus Chakra, etc.) Since our aura's have seven corresponding levels, the rainbow colors as a whole can brighten up and clear out our aura once we have really developed the mental abilities to make this type of cleansing real.

♦ *3RD OR SOLAR PLEXUS CHAKRA*

HOW WE RELATE TO OURSELF OR PERSONAL POWER . . . HONOR ONESELF

SELF-ESTEEM, CONFIDENCE, RESPECT / ANGER, RESENTMENT, LIMITATION

Location: Just below the sternum - upper abdomen, small intestine, adrenal glands, neural center, pancreas, stomach, liver, gall bladder, spleen, kidney, middle spine/back/lumbar vertebrae, General Digestive System.

Nature: Personal power in relation to self and one's external relationships, place of personality & ego equilibrium, body distribution point for psychic energies, digestion and purification, intellect, balance, nourishment, stimulation.

Correspondences: Color-yellow, gland-adrenals or pancreas, aura body-lower mental, musical tone-E, chant-AW, skill-balance/astral travel, physical sense-sight, temperature-warm, element/direction-fire/south. Window into animal kingdom/our animal nature and the power & nobility inherent in the higher orders of physical life.

Functions: Power center, energizes body by distributing vital life force energies to every part of the body, transmutes psychic energies into physical energies, balance of emotion & intellect, to face our strengths/weaknesses/fears/secrets, center of astral travel and astral influences, receptivity to spirit guides and psychic development, personal power issues of discipline/commitment/will.

Healthy/Balanced Functioning: Taking responsibility for one's energy, setting limits for one's self, being in control of one's energy, self-starter, self-motivator, balance of giving & receiving, out of body experience, to travel to the past or the future, to be in the present time, mental & emotional peace and self-confidence, good use of nourishment and prana, good self-esteem/respect/discipline, the ability to generate action, ability to handle a crises, generosity, determination, a strong sense of responsibility, endurance/stamina.

Imbalanced/Blocked: Fear of rejection/criticism/looking foolish, failing to meet one's responsibilities, insecurity concerning one's physical appearance, having no energy/drained/ fatigued, inability to say no, cannot finish projects, unorganized, needing outside motivation from others, victim consciousness, low self worth/image, overeating, undereating, ego tripping, controlled by fear (unable to move), being dogmatic, domination, intimidation, inability to trust others, anger, abuse of others, cowardly & submissive, fear of assuming responsibility or making decisions for self, being stuck in the past or in the future.

Examples of Solar Plexus Chakra Imbalances: Nervousness, closure of psychic abilities, disharmony, disruption of digestion, gastric or duodenal ulcers, eating disorders such as Anorexia & Bulimia, psychic disturbances, mental instability, stomach cramps, nausea, adrenal problems, arthritis, allergies, appendicitis, overweight & underweight, middle back problems, colitis, intestinal problems, gall stones, gas pains, indigestion, liver problems, hepatitis, Parkinson, stomach ulcers, pancreatitis/diabetes, motion sickness.

ACTIVITY: <u>**ALL YOU NEED IS LOVE**</u>

This is an example of working to OPEN UP AND STRENGTHEN A SPECIFIC CHAKRA.

Once you have gotten into your relaxed and open state, focus your attention on your Heart Chakra. Lay your right hand on your heart area and try to pick up whether it feels cold, medium, or hot to you. Visualize and sense your right HAND putting HEALING and opening energy directly into your Heart Chakra.
(continued on page 54)

As you do so, allow any EMOTION that is SURFACING to enter your awareness. If you need to, allow your being to cry, or sigh, or giggle: whatever it needs to do. Do not analyze what you are feeling. Simply allow yourself to FEEL IT. Once the emotion has subsided, MIND-WHISPER sweet nothings to your heart/yourself, such as: "I love you" and "You are a wonderful being with a right to be happy" or whatever is positively appropriate for yourself. You want to provide UPLIFTING and STRENGTHENING energies and programs for and to yourself.

Next, visualize your Heart Chakra FILLING UP AND GLOWING with a new spring-like color green. As you do so allow yourself to SOFTEN and feel the glow that love provides us with. Let this new green provide you with a breath of fresh air, gently blowing out any Heavy Heart Energy you might have been harboring. Allow yourself to feel refreshed, revitalized, and a little more lovelike.

◆ *4TH OR HEART CHAKRA*

UNCONDITIONAL LOVE . . . LOVE IS DIVINE POWER
SELF AND OTHER LOVE / HURT, AT WAR, HOSTILITY

Location: At the center of the chest near the heart - thymus, blood, vagus nerve, ribs, breasts, lungs, circulatory System, diaphragm, esophagus, heart & cardiovascular system, shoulders, arms, hands.

Nature: The higher love nature (in expressing love toward self & others), compassion/caring, emotional perceptions, healing, higher intelligence, the meeting place of the lower/upper chakras.

Correspondences: Color-green/rose, Ductless gland-Thymus, aura body-Higher mind, musical tone-F, chant-AH, skill-love/compassion/joy, physical sense-touch, temperature-cool, element/direction-air/east. Intended domain and the linking bridge between the outer manifestation of the created material universe (3 lower chakras) & inner nature (the top 3 chakras).

Functions: Affinity (to be at one with/to become one with), life expectancy, self-concept, keeps body alive by drawing the soul (affinity) to the body, learning the power of love.

Healthy/Balanced Functioning: To be at one with one's self (all dimensions at one with the others), to be at one with another, to be at one with a group of others, to be at one with an idea, to be at one with the planet, to be at one with God/Goddesss, loving & accepting one's self, loving & accepting others, at peace with one's self, compassion, kindness, trust, generosity, to reach out & connect with others, to have what one wants & needs, prosperous, inspiring, dedication, hope, joy, ability to heal oneself and others, to act out of love and compassion, to know that the most powerful energy is love.

Imbalanced/Blocked: Fears of loneliness/commitment/emotional weakness and betrayal/inability to protect oneself emotionally. To be at war with one's self, to be at odds with another, self-absorption, selfishness, inability to receive love or give love to self or others, to experience hurt & pain about one's self, controlled by love addictions, suicidal, acting nice/loving when one really does not feel it, a sense of emptiness/isolation/deprivation, inferiority feelings, Depression, grief, loneliness, critical, judgmental, jealousy, bitterness, revengeful, issues with forgiveness, hatred.

Examples of Heart Chakra Imbalances: Aches, allergies, breast problems, breast cancer, upper back pain, rounded shoulders & shoulder pain, skin problems, blood problems including anemia, cancer, leukemia, blood pressure problems, strokes, immune response diseases such as Lupus, Rheumatoid Arthritis, lung cancer, bronchial pneumonia, emphysema, growths, Hodgkin's Disease, flue, lymph problems, Mononucleosis, spinal curvature, stroke, thymus problems, cholesterol problems, heart problems such as congestive heart failure/myocardial infarction/mitral valve prolapse.

ACTIVITY: <u>MY DAILY TUNE IN</u>

Part of KNOWING THYSELF means being aware of what energies you are running in the present moment. USING THE CHAKRA SYSTEM as part of your RECOGNITION PROCESS helps one to not only focus on physical happenings but also functions as a mental/emotional/ psychological/spiritual gage. You are ready to do the following DAILY TUNE IN once you have LOADED YOUR MIND-COMPUTER with The Chakra Information.

Lying down in your open and relaxed state, focus your attention one at a time on each of your chakras starting with the Belly Chakra up to your Crown Chakra.

1. MENTALLY SCAN the area of each chakra for energetic sensations, tension, comfort, discomfort, and pain. Make a mental note of what you pick up on, writing it down at an appropriate time in your HSI Notebook under Daily Tune In.

2. While focusing on each chakra, allow yourself to feel any emotions that are still hanging inside of you. Become aware of any of the Chakra Issues and Lessons you are currently engaging. The healing/transforming process will go much smoother if you are aware of where you are at: what is in-balance and out-of-balance, what lessons you are working on, and what issues have you up-in-arms. You can often modify your daily schedule in order to better meet your own needs if you are aware of what is happening inside you.

◆   *5TH OR THROAT CHAKRA*

WILL POWER . . .   SURRENDER PERSONAL WILL TO DIVINE WILL
SELF EXPRESSION, COMMUNICATION/ INABILITY TO EXPRESS SELF

Location: Throat - mouth, teeth & gums, thyroid & parathyroid, vocal chords, trachea (bronchial & vocal apparatus), esophagus, hypothalamus, cervical vertebrae, Respiratory System.

Nature: Communication, mastery of the will (discipline), speech, expression, hearing, creativity, artistry, spirituality, independence, inner trust.

Correspondences: <u>Color</u>-light blue, <u>ductless gland</u>-thyroid and parathyroid, <u>aura body</u>-lower spiritual, <u>musical tone</u>-G, <u>chant</u>-EH, <u>skill</u>-clairaudience, <u>physical sense</u>-hearing, <u>temperature</u>-cool, <u>element/direction</u>- ether/center. Access to the angelic kingdom/seat of telepathic dialogue.

Functions: To communicate with another, to express oneself, learn the power of choice, to hear energy, sense of self within one's society or profession, receptivity to higher vibrational influences, clairaudience/to hear out-of-body spirits, telepathy, where your spirit or soul communicates with your body or personality.

Healthy/Balanced Functioning: To express one's self verbally, meaningful listening & speaking with others, to tone or sing, to dance, to write, to follow one's dreams, to hear astral music, clear telepathy (giving & receiving thoughts), communication with parts of one's self (inner voice & spirit guides), faith, knowledge, controlling and having positive thoughts and attitudes, making positive choices, loyal sincerity, self-confidence in abilities. Having learned that actions motivated by personal will that has trusted in The Divine create the best effects.

Imbalanced/Blocked: Fears regarding our own choices and of others owning our will, confusion of all the voices within (other's thoughts, inner voice, spirits), tuning others out (choosing to ignore by not hearing them), not able to express one's self, issues with personal expression, not following one's dreams, self-thrashing (putting one's self down).

Examples of Throat Chakra Imbalances: Sore throats & laryngitis, bronchitis, bruxism, Meniere's, sagging lines, snoring, tonsillitis, accidents, ear/hearing problems, jaw/mouth/teeth/gum problems, nose problems, neck problems, speech difficulties such as stuttering, thyroid problems, cancer of the larynx, scoliosis, swollen glands.

ACTIVITY: <u>**HEALING CONNECTIONS**</u>

Our chakras function as an interconnected whole: when one is out of balance, the others will be too. However, many of us have certain chakras that cry out for more of our healing attention than others because of our need to learn its particular lessons in the moment. Each chakra's lessons and issues also have their particular levels and stages. It's all A LAYERING SYSTEM leading us into the core and depth of life.

Once you have brought to your awareness what chakra balances/imbalances and lessons/ issues you are currently running, there are a variety of healing and learning methods to apply. Taking the information about the chakras and your Daily Tune In charts, list each of your chakra's imbalances (blocked)/balances (healthy functioning) and the issues/lessons you are learning or will need to learn. As you learn more about healing/transformational skills and tools, devise a HEALING PLAN for each of your chakra's. Look at each chakra's correspondences in order to apply the appropriate colors, sounds, etc. as you utilize various healing techniques such as TONING and COLOR VISUALIZATION ENERGY WORK. You will continue to update this plan as you learn more and evolve.

♦ *6TH OR BROW CHAKRA*

PERSONAL VISION . . . SEEK ONLY THE TRUTH
PERCEIVING, IMAGING / ILLUSIONAL NEGATIVE THINKING

Location: The center of the forehead (third-spiritual eye) - pituitary gland, eyes, ears, lower brain, autonomic nervous system.

Nature: Mind, intuition, inner vision, truth, knowledge, primarily spiritual, introspection, perception, imagination, visualization, psychic healing, clairvoyance, seeing auras, ideals and idealism. The brow center helps to direct the higher spiritual forces into the third eye. The process of subtle energy assimilation through the brow chakra assists the individual in intuitive decision-making and in seeing beyond the physical level (clairvoyance).

Correspondences: <u>Color</u>-indigo, <u>ductless gland</u>-pituitary, <u>aura body</u>-middle spiritual, <u>musical tone</u>-A, <u>chant</u>-IH, <u>skill</u>-clairvoyance, <u>physical sense</u>-all senses, <u>temperature</u>-electric, <u>element/direction</u>-planet/below. Domain of archangels.

Functions: To perceive & project reality, to see & manage energy, intellectual abilities and skills.

Healthy/Balanced Functioning: To see & appreciate beauty, to have vision, to use intuitive skills/insight/ wisdom, to know knowledge, to see into the past & probable-possible futures, to see all energy formations & patterns, to see mental image pictures, creative visualization, telepathic links, psychic healing, to be intelligent, positive imagination, clairvoyance-to clearly see spirits without physical bodies, to see auras & chakras, "I AM" awareness, beingness rather than doingness, entuned to the will of God/Goddess, opening & clarity of mind, developed impersonal mind, acting on internal guidance, using our mental and reasoning abilities and our psychological skills in evaluating our beliefs and attitudes, ability to learn from experience, emotional intelligence.

Imbalance/Blocked: Unwillingness to look within and excavate one's fears, fear of the truth, clouded reason, fear of one's shadow side (dark, lower, or negative energy), to be confused, not be able to think in logical sequences, inadequacy, closed to ideas, paranoia, refusal to learn from life experience, illusional, to be blind to beauty, over-rationalizing or over-intellectualizing problems, to see monsters & other lower energy levels.

Examples of Brow Chakra Imbalances: Headaches, loss of balance, brain problems including strokes & tumors, amnesia, eye problems, thinking disorders, major endocrine imbalances, learning disabilities, seizures, neurological disturbances, blindness, deafness, full spinal dificulties.

ACTIVITY: <u>GOD'S GLOW</u>

After you have entered your relaxed and open state, use a MIND SWEEPER to clear out any more random thoughts. Visualize a THOUGHT CLEANSING PROCESS such as seeing yourself taking a broom and sweeping away any thought concerns and distractions. Or seeing a giant vacuum cleaner gently sucking all your hyper thoughts bagging them until later, when you can sort them in order to throw out the ones you don't want.

Next, visualize the sun's healing and warming rays enter into your aura and body through the top of your head. As the sun's warmth fills you from head to foot, you relax and open even more. Once you are very calm, relaxed, and centered, concentrate on bringing and visualizing GOD'S DIVINE LOVE WHITE LIGHT ENERGY into your being through your Crown Chakra. Gradually fill your whole self with this most vibrant, healing, and transforming of all energies. Allow yourself to really feel what it's like to BATHE IN THE GLOW OF DIVINE LIGHT. Experience the melt down of tension and the joyous uplifting experience of unconditional love.

♦ *7TH OR CROWN CHAKRA*

SEEING THE LARGER PURPOSE IN LIFE . . . LIVE IN THE PRESENT MOMENT
FAITH, COSMIC CONSCIOUSNESS / SPIRITUAL CRISES, MENTAL DISORDERS

Location: At the crown (top) of the head - Pineal Gland, Central Nervous System, Skeletal and Muscular Systems.

Nature: Attunement toward inner searching for the meaning of life and oneness with all that is, spiritual seeking, related to one's attitudes/faith/values/ethics, courage, humanitarianism, transcendence, connection with God/Goddess, knowingness or pure intuition, bringing in Cosmic energy here, the spiritual quest.

Correspondences: <u>Color</u>-violet & then white, <u>ductless gland</u>-pineal, <u>aura body</u>-higher spiritual, <u>musical tone</u>-B, <u>chant</u>-EEE, <u>skill</u>-pure knowing/spiritism, <u>temperature</u>-electric, <u>element/direction</u>-universe/above. Key to our Divine Nature-the indwelling spirit/Soul.

Functions: To know energy, to bring in cosmic energy, to connect one to the Cosmos, to release excess energy and toxins, integration of Higher Personality with life & spiritual aspects of humankind, meditation, trance work & spiritism, spirituality, prana and grace, to have all physical/psychological & emotional illusions removed from one's life.

Healthy Functioning: To know without using reason, to have faith, connection with All Intelligence, acquiring attitudes/values/ethics & courage, trance mediumship (when the soul of a particular body leaves their body & allows another soul/spirit to use their body to communicate to the physical world), going beyond self to a merging with God, total oneness with all creation, higher levels of cosmic energy, Cosmic Consciousness, total integration and peace, prayer, running energy that generates Divine Devotion, inspirational and prophetic thoughts, transcendent ideas and mystical connections, ability to see the larger pattern and truth, humanitarianism, trust of life, meditation, symbolic sight.

Imbalanced/Blocked: Fears relating to spiritual issues such as spiritual abandonment, loss of connection and identity with life and people around us, staying stuck in The Battle of the Selves and in The Dark Night Of The Soul, getting lost in one's past lives, having no faith, inability to trust life, uncontrolled trance mediumship, being controlled by spirits, self-absorbed, inability to see the larger pattern of life and of one's particular life.

Examples of Crown Chakra Imbalances: Skull problems, mental disorders, unable to handle spiritual energy, stress diseases, cerebral dysfunctions, bone cancer & bone problems, Multiple Sclerosis, genetic disorders, paralysis, Lou Gehrigs Disease, comas, insanity, epilepsy, senility, spiritual crisis, mystical depression, chronic exhaustion that is not linked to a physical disorder, extreme sensitivities to light/sound/and other environmental factors, energetic disorders.

ILLUSTRATION #1 : THE HUMAN AURA AND CHAKRAS

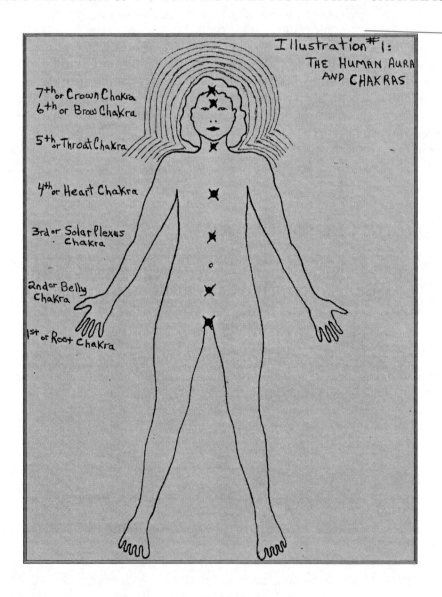

CHAPTER FOUR

TO BE HOLY HEALTHY

> THE HIGHER SELF INTEGRATION PROCESS IS A
> TRANSFORMATIVE, HEALING JOURNEY INTO WHOLENESS OR REAL HEALTH . . .

THE POSSIBILITIES

Health is not just the absence of any signs of medically diagnosable physical, psychological, or lifestyle symptoms, illnesses, and dis-eases. HEALTH IS THE ZEST FOR LIVING, the ability to wake up eager to begin the day. It includes NATURAL WELL BEING without chronic reliance on stimulants such as caffeine, nicotine, alcohol, and adrenaline highs or medicinal painkillers and other drugs. It is vitality and feeling fully alive, a loving and harmonious home life, a sense of meaning and purpose that provides a profound experience of inner satisfaction, and a positive state of well-being and internal harmony.

Enjoying real health means being trim, physically fit, and free from major and minor complaints (from cancer to allergies to headaches to indigestion). It is being clearheaded, able to concentrate, and radiant with clear skin, glossy hair, and sparkling eyes. It means that we are active and creative, able to relax easily, free from worry/anxiety, and optimistic. Satisfied with work and the direction of our life, able to communicate assertively, and being balanced in the use of our sexual/life force energy is included in the definition of whole health. Being healthy means living free from destructive health habits such as smoking, ingesting unhealthy amounts of sugar and fats, undersleeping, and placing oneself in physically/verbally violent situations.

Past research, indicated by Dr. Harold H. Bloomfield and Robert B. Kory in their book *The Holistic Way To Health & Happiness*, shows that when a person has proven to be real healthy they also radiate these characteristics: spontaneity and expressiveness, clear perception of reality and clarity of thought, and acceptance of self, others, and nature. A sense of self-sufficiency, integrity, frequency of joyful peak experiences, interpersonal competence, and a nonauthoritarian democratic personality are also characteristics of the healthy person. More characteristics include active creativity, an integrated use of concrete and abstract thinking, and the ability to express love and affection.

But that's not all! REAL HEALTH IS BEING BALANCED AND WHOLE IN THE PHYSICAL, MENTAL, SPIRITUAL PARTS OF OUR BEING SO THAT WE LIVE UP TO AND IN OUR SOUL POTENTIAL. These potentials include a real and practical direct connection with God and the hierarchy of spiritual beings developmentally past the need to take human form. Also included is developing our Higher Sense Perceptions that so enable us to take better, safer, more creative care of ourselves, one another, and our dear planet Earth. Knowing why we are here, what we need to learn currently, and what best we can give while being a part of the human and earthly community is a potential that provides the greatest peace and well-being feelings, which in turn influence and produce whole health.

Whole Health means exactly that: the sum of all its parts. We humans can not live and act separate from our bodies, minds, spirits, and Souls without becoming dis-eased, ill, out of balance, problemed, and at least a wee bit whacko. In trying to fool ourselves into believing that we can achieve real health through ignoring parts of ourselves and our lives, we become fragmented and imbalanced, thereby manifesting painful physical, mental, and lifestyle symptoms.

REAL HEALING IS A JOURNEY WITHIN ONESELF TO REUNITE BODY, MIND, SPIRIT, AND SOUL. It is the recognition that wholeness comes when our physical, mental, emotional, spiritual, and Soul senses are in balanced relationship. It is becoming a conscious co-creator, connected through our spirit and Soul with the Divine Life Force. True and real WHOLE HEALTH AND HEALING go hand in hand with *Higher Self Integration*.

> **REAL HEALING IS A JOURNEY WITHIN ONESELF**
> **TO REUNITE BODY, MIND, SPIRIT, AND SOUL . . .**

ACTIVITY: <u>HOW HEALTHY CAN I BECOME?</u>

Many of us receive a very limited, false, and unhealthy picture of what healthy/happy living is all about from the world around us. To consciously go about actively creating true health, we have to EXPAND OUR VISION as to what living in real health actually means.

1. After you have achieved your relaxed and open state of consciousness, FOCUS ON the CONCEPT of physical health allowing IMAGES, FEELINGS, and WORDS to come forth that will help you define what physical health and wholeness means to you. Then EXPLORE IN GREAT DETAIL what it would feel, look, and be like to live in full and vital physical human health (from the hair on top of our heads down through to our toenails and everything inbetween). Next, try to VISUALIZE what YOU personally will look, act, and feel like when you have achieved whole physical health.
Really sit with this, allowing it to sink in. BE AWARE OF any DOUBTS or MISGUIDED IMPOSSIBILITIES your thoughts and feelings conjure up, dismissing them in order to return to your physically healthy images. Renew this activity once in awhile, noting how your health concepts expand as you do. Remember, aging is natural; degeneration is not.

2. For some, it seems even harder to picture in minute details what mental, spiritual, and Soul health looks like. However, give these all a try, one at a time. As you advance through your *Higher Self Integration* program, your knowledge and clarity about what whole health is will increase, eventually enabling you to get images, words, and feelings which PUT ALL THE PUZZLE PIECES of complete physical, mental, spiritual, and Soul health TOGETHER.

Health and healing also have everything to do with TO PROSPER and PROSPERITY CONSCIOUSNESS. To Prosper means to flourish, succeed, thrive. Prosperity's root means "WELL-BEING AND WHOLENESS." *Higher Self Integration*, whole health, and prosperity are synonymous with one another. We are all prosperous to the degree that we are experiencing peace, health, and plenty in our world/lives. And the *Higher Self Integration* process moves us along into the Soul Consciousness Levels where our Soul powers and skills enable us to PERCEIVE, EXPRESS, TRANSFORM, COCREATE, and MANIFEST all we need in order to be prosperous: "Holy Healthy."

The *Higher Self Integration* process is a SELF-HEALING journey. Self-healing means SELF-TRANSFORMATION. Self-healing of physical, psychological, intellectual, spiritual, social, and environmental dis-ease or discomfort includes INTENSE SELF EXPLORATION, CHANGING DESTRUCTIVE EVERYDAY THINKING, FEELING, AND LIVING HABITS to helpful and healthfilled ones, RELEASING PAST TRAUMAS and psychodynamics, and REBALANCING the way you run your ENERGY. This includes clearing, charging, and RESTRUCTURING YOUR ENERGY FIELD: WORKING knowingly and intentionally WITH YOUR CHAKRAS. It is FULLY LOVING and NURTURING YOUR body/mind/spirit/SOUL.

Self-Healing has everything to do with PAYING ATTENTION TO YOUR INNER SELF, learning who you really are as a Soul. It is taking FULL SELF-RESPONSIBILITY for all of your life, bringing the power of your life back home to you. It is becoming EMPOWERED as your *Higher Self,* consciously attracting everything you need in order to become Holy Healthy.

DISCOMFORT anywhere in our bodies and lives IS a DIRECT MESSAGE to us about how we are out of healthy alignment. Our symptoms are messages from our being letting us know that something or things in our lives and the systems that govern our bodies are out of balance and in need of healing. HEALING occurs THROUGH UNDERSTANDING the cause of our imbalances, releasing and REWORKING what has thrown us out of balance, and then BRINGING those thoughts, feelings, behaviors, energies, situations, experiences, skills and abilities into our lives that help to keep us in balance or healthy.

When we are in dis-comfort or dis-ease, we have the choice as to patch ourselves up (the Bandaid Approach) by just treating the symptoms or we can truly heal ourselves. If we try to eliminate the symptoms through just surgery, drugs and/or nutrients and herbs without dealing with the underlying causes, these imbalances or impairments to healing and full health will continue. Ill symptoms will continue to resurface again and again as either the same dis-ease or as another illness or dis-ease which is similar in its systemic patterning. We can also choose to use conventional allopathic and/or complementary holistic treatment methods to help ease our symptoms, so that we will have the time and energy to use the self healing techniques necessary in creating health that lasts.

Science is starting to catch up with the knowledge some humans have always known: that our bodies, minds, and spirits are one. Our bodies reflect what is happening in our minds and spirits. IN ORDER TO ACHIEVE REAL HEALTH, WE HAVE TO BE FULLY INTEGRATED AND BALANCED PHYSICALLY, MENTALLY, AND SPIRITUALLY AS SOULS. It is very important to understand how this works when working with the *Higher Self Integration* process. Fortunately, there is more and more information becoming available for all of us if we will just take the time to educate ourselves.

SELF-HEALING IS TAKING FULL SELF-RESPONSIBILITY FOR ALL OF YOUR LIFE, BRINGING THE POWER OF YOUR LIFE BACK HOME TO YOU . . .

It is crucial for wholeness that we each UNDERSTAND HOW OUR BODIES FUNCTION and what particular state our own UNIQUE BIOCHEMISTRY is in. As Joseph Pizzorno, a Naturopathic Doctor, points out in his book *Total Wellness*, we each have a unique "biochemical individuality" that is influenced by our thoughts and feelings, beliefs and reactions, foods we eat, the environments in which we live, our lifestyle, and our genetic susceptibilities. All of our major body functions are regulated by our nervous system and our hormonal or endocrine system through our brain. Imbalances in any of our hormones or biochemical components can cause widespread dysfunction.

PSYCHONEUROIMMUNOLOGY is the study of the interaction between the mind, body, and immune system in health and illness. Medical researchers have now proven a chemical link between our thoughts/emotions (energies) and our bodily systems: NEUROPEPTIDES. Neuropeptides are biochemical messengers or chemicals that are directly triggered by emotions and that hook up to receptors in our cells located throughout our bodies. In other words, our direct thoughts, beliefs, attitudes, moods, feelings and emotions have a significant and direct impact on which chemical messengers are sent and in how they are received. OUR THOUGHTS and EMOTIONS DIRECTLY INFLUENCE OUR BIOCHEMICAL BALANCE causing dis-ease or health.

These neurotransmitters translate our every fleeting to obsessive thought, reaction, and emotion, conscious or unconscious, into physiological changes. The cells that manufacture and receive emotional chemistry in the brain are present throughout the body.   Dr. Candace Pert, the neurobiologist who provided proof that thoughts are converted into matter through neuropeptides, has shown that our emotions are stored in every cell of our body and that mind is located in every bodily cell. She calls neuropeptides our "biochemical correlates of emotion."   As is stated in *Total Wellness,* "These peptides constitute a psychosomatic communication network in which the mind is literally spread throughout the body."

Our thoughts, emotions, and brain communicate directly with our immune, nervous, and endocrine systems and with our organs of our bodies as a whole, interwoven, and interconnected organism. "The mind can no longer be thought of as being confined to the brain or to the intellect; it exists in every cell of our bodies," emphasizes Dr. Christiane Northrup in *Women's Bodies, Women's Wisdom.* Soul, mind, and etheric (also named life force, prana, chi, orgon, etc.) energy together resides within every cell of the human body.

Our human energy field surrounds and carries with us the emotional energy created by both our positive and negative inner (thought) and outer (recorded directly through emotion and thought) experiences.   As Dr. Carolyn Myss in *Anatomy of the Spirit* points out, "In this way your biography - that is, the experiences that make up your life - becomes your biology." In other words, you are what you think and feel. Dr. Myss, as a Medical Intuitive, proclaims what others are also coming to understand, that EMOTIONAL AND SPIRITUAL STRESSES OR DIS-EASES ARE THE ROOT CAUSES OF ALL PHYSICAL ILLNESSES.

Not only that, but certain emotional and spiritual crises correspond quite specifically to problems in certain parts of the body. Louise L. Hay, in her best seller, *You Can Heal Your Life,* has a helpful list that correlates various dis-eases and illnesses with the psychological/emotional thinking patterns that help to create the specific imbalance. For instance, urinary infections are correlated to being "pissed off" and blaming others for not getting one's own needs met. You'll find a pattern of feeling unloved and victimized, along with anger, criticism, and resentment, in people who have manifested arthritis.

Taking it one step further, these negative thought/feeling/behaving patterns and their corresponding dis-eases can be classified under the various chakras.   Plant into your mind the realization and truth that YOU ARE AFFECTING THE HEALTH OF YOUR BODY (AND THE STATE OF YOUR AFFAIRS) BY CHOOSING THE FEELINGS OR EMOTIONS THAT OCCUPY AND INFLUENCE IT. Think of it this way: Ill health is an illness of vibration, of misdirected energy. Biochemical imbalance is a consequence of that misdirected and blocked energy/life force.

To jump even deeper into the truth about why our lives are the way they are, we have to acknowledge that we create - through our thoughts, emotions, beliefs, attitudes, moods, actions (including what we choose to ingest for nutrients) and reactions - health and ill health. WE EACH CREATE/ATTRACT TO/MANIFEST OUR LIFE ACCORDING TO OUR SPECIFIC THOUGHTS, FEELINGS, AND BEHAVIORS. Our mind, with its thoughts, attitudes, emotions, and activities it runs, is creating our present and future life.

We are 100% responsible for our pains as well as for our joys, our struggles as well as our successes, our functional as well as our dysfunctional relationships, and all that lies inbetween. Nothing happens randomly. God is not rolling dice saying, "He gets a divorce, she gets cancer, and they get a burned out home." We create everything in our lives through the power of our minds, and we're not talking about just a limited this-life-mind.

Our minds hold within them all that we've been as Souls. Our thoughts run from programming set up this lifetime, which is based on our needs as a Being that has unfinished business holding on from other existences. TRUE HEALING, REAL TRANSFORMATION, REQUIRES LEARNING SOUL CONSCIOUSNESS, BECOMING AWARE OF HOW AND WHY WE THINK, FEEL, AND BEHAVE AS WE DO. Then, we can go for whole health by transforming the power of our mind.

**AS SOULS,
WE ARE 100% RESPONSIBLE FOR WHAT'S HAPPENING IN OUR LIVES . . .**

ACTIVITY: <u>THE TRUTH ABOUT MY BLOCKS</u>

Energy blocks within our etheric body caused by repressed negative emotions, beliefs, and traumas, are the precursors to bodily pain, limitation, illness, and dis-ease. In order to move past and heal our body symptoms, we have to TRACK DOWN THE ENERGETIC BLOCK or blocks that caused the imbalance.

1. Once in your state of open relaxation, decide to FOCUS on one physical difficulty, imbalance, limitation, or illness you are currently experiencing. This can be anything from restricted movement in your groin area, eyes that ache/blur/tire easily, or vaginitis and herpes to growing warts, heart problems, and Rheumatoid Arthritis. For now, just pick one, close your eyes, breathe slowly and deeply, silently asking yourself to show you the TRUE MEANING of your discomfort. Behind every discomfort is a CAUSE AND A LESSON: what you need to know, learn, change, and integrate into your life that will correct your imbalance.

2. RESEARCH the physical or medical information concerning your focus, the complementary or holistic information related, the emotional/psychological connections, and the metaphysical realities involved. This includes understanding which chakras are imbalanced, enabling yourself to discover and understand your own personal issues involved.

3. Be open to RECEIVING IMAGES AND THOUGHTS within your mind that are connected to your focus. In the time period coming up, be aware of any connected dreams, memories, coincidences, synchronicities, and related information coming your way. Once you UNDERSTAND THE UNDERLYING EMOTIONAL ISSUES involved, do memory and emotional releasing or PERSONAL PROCESS WORK in order to connect your originating cause or causes and the events to the thinking/feeling/behavioral and situational patterns that have continued to feed this imbalance.

4. Keep working on it allowing NEW CONNECTIONS to surface. Write it all down and come back to it later. Keep practicing this process over time, using other focuses as you peel back the layers and masks which cover and hide your Soul and your natural health.

THE PROBLEMS

While we dare to imagine what our lives will be like when we are truly HOLY HEALTHY or *Higher Self Integrated*, the truth of the matter is that there just aren't that many of us Souls in human form who are whole. The vast majority of us are Level One, Two, Three-ers, with the lesser amounts of Level Four, Five, Six, and Seven-ers spread out across the planet far and wide. While these more Conscious Souls are involved in trying to move mountains of mass consciousness in order for Truth to be visible, they are not necessarily a known everyday household entity. WE NEED MORE WHOLE HEALTH MODELING AND EDUCATION!

As the human species, we're obviously out of balance enough to have manifested lots of dis-eases, addictions, and discomforting lifestyles and relationships. For the majority, Soul Vision and Truth appears to be covered over and distorted by pain, negative emotions, confusion, fatigue, and false beliefs about life. If Soul Attunement and Whole Health is natural and what we are all about, why don't more of us appear to be INTEGRATED AND WHOLE? And for those of us that are already working towards the goal of Whole Health and Soul Attunement, why does it seem to take so much time and effort in the quest for balance?

After all, it is easy to tell when we are out of balance, if we'll listen. OUR BODIES LET US KNOW by aches and pains, illnesses and dis-eases. OUR MINDS LET US KNOW through fuzzy and forgetful thinking processes and negative thoughts and emotions. Feeling separated and disconnected, drained and devitalized are SIGNS FROM OUR SPIRIT/SOUL. Relationship, home, work, and environment indicators such as conflicts with others, addictive lifestyle patterns, and lack of financial and material resources show us that "all is not well." Many of us who have been diagnosed with dis-eases, such as cancer, or who have been through lifestyle and relationship difficulties, such as divorce, realize afterwards that there were physical, mental, and emotional signs that warned us of imbalance and pending problems.

So, how is it so easy to get off balance? Why do we often choose to ignore the obvious? How did we get so unaware of who we really are? What do we need in order to be in balance or Holy Healthy and fully integrated as Souls?

One of the central reasons so many of us appear as unhealthy and unaware Souls is that WE DON'T KNOW HOW! Most of us were not taught what real health and *Soul Attunement* is nor how to achieve it. We were not given the opportunity to practice, learn, and integrate the knowledge, skills, and tools of whole health in our daily lives. There are not that many clear whole health and *Higher Self Integrated* role models in our lives and in the world which media brings to us. Not only were we "left in the dark" about whole health, we were often shown how to live by doing the opposite of what is necessary to achieve health. IGNORANCE, or not knowing, and FAULTY LIVING PATTERNS really keep us limited and spinning.

Most of us grew up fragmented in our knowledge of how best to take care of our bodies, minds, spirits, or Souls. Most of our familial, educational, medical, and religious systems do not recognize our wholeness. Consequently, many of our innate abilities and skills for *Higher Self Integration* that are necessary in achieving whole health, such as high levels of awareness and concentration, whole thinking and problem solving, intuition, reading energy, and tuning in for Higher Guidance, were not developed.

Instead, most of us were taught inadequate and often mistaken ways to think and live. WE'RE UNTRAINED IN THE REAL LIFE SKILLS OF MIND, BODY, SPIRIT, AND SOUL. We're taught to ignore what we observe and feel, learning a deep internal dishonesty and cover up of who we really are as Souls. We get off balance easily because we are taught to live imbalanced. We often ignore the obvious because we don't know what the obvious means. We don't know about so many things because we've been taught that they don't exist, even though they do.

Our Soul Vision is covered over with tons of MIS-BELIEFS AND DIS-BELIEFS we've been taught about health and living. For those of us that feel that our current life is going reasonably well despite a few problems here and there, it is hard to go for full health and prosperity due to all the "Just put up with it" and "Don't rock the boat" status quo types of attitudes. Many of us have learned well how to "Just make do!" in a world that teaches us that we are innocent victims to painful and crippling body ailments, torturous death, dysfunctional relationships, warring world conditions, and to supposedly limited economic and resource supplies.

We could all probably live and settle into an OK life, buying into that line of perception, if we just keep on "pulling ourselves up by the bootstraps." But if that doesn't work, and the pain or dysfunction worsens, then we can "take a pill and get instantly cured of our ills," right? Wrong! Isn't it true what we were taught, that "The Doctor knows best" and all we have to do in order to feel better is to "Do as I say."? Wrong again! In order to move through these BELIEF TRAPS, we've got to know and understand what Whole Health is really about. WE'VE GOT TO GET WHOLLY EDUCATED!

WE'RE UNTRAINED IN THE REAL LIFE SKILLS OF MIND+BODY+SPIRIT = SOUL . . .

ACTIVITY: **AN APPLE A DAY**

The most powerful hindrances to achieving Whole Health/*Higher SelfIntegration* are the very destructive and unhealthy misbeliefs and disbeliefs about health. MISBELIEFS are wrong or faulty mental acceptances or convictions in the truth or actuality of something. DISBELIEFS are the refusals or reluctances to mentally accepting that something is true and real.

Accept the fact that you have a lot more of these than you yet recognize. Many of them operate seductively from your SUBCONSCIOUS (see Index Glossary), having a power over you and your life that can move beyond destructive into insidious. In order to disempower these faulty thoughtforms and belief systems, you have to first acknowledge their existence consciously.

1. After you have achieved your open and relaxed state, use free associative and brainstorming techniques to start recognizing and listing separately your MISBELIEFS and your DISBELIEFS regarding health and healing. Keep your eyes and ears open during your daily life to recognize all the crazy misbeliefs and disbeliefs constantly coming your way in the form of your own thoughts, others conversations, radio and TV advertisements and programs, etc. You'll have to keep on educating yourself with new information regarding Whole Health and Healing as a way to enable you to recognize the old, outdated, and untrue pseudo-facts and nuances which have been, both subtly and not so subtly, planted in your mind/brain complex.

These are just a few more of the many implanted crazy and sickness-causing thoughtforms: "An apple a day keeps the doctor away." "I cannot heal myself. I'm just too sick." "It doesn't matter what I eat." "My spiritual beliefs have nothing to do with the health of my body." "Praying doesn't do any good at all: it's not real." etc., etc., etc. KEEP ON DIGGING!

2. After you have uncovered those thought forms that have led you astray from whole health and your natural abilities to heal, then you need to CONSCIOUSLY OBSERVE how they influence and often control your life, feelings, and behaviors. Next comes your very conscious and INTENTIONAL CHOICE as to whether you want these misbeliefs and disbeliefs to be active in your life. If you choose "No way," then consciously PROGRAM into your mind the TRUTHS, purposefully and consistently allowing and making them play an important role in how you behave and function within your life. Choose one or two and follow them all the way through the process. Help yourself to BE CREATIVE with each step. Don't freak out. It's really important to HAVE FUN with this.

As a result of having learned some untruths about health/healing and many false beliefs and perceptions as programmed by our limited life experiences, many of us form very unhealthy personality habits, characteristics, and patterning. It seems that most of us learn very destructive lifestyle and thinking habits and patterns that end up making personality issues a major stuckness, miserability, and often life-threatening factor in our lives. These crazy ways of thinking, feeling, and behaving also make up the reasons why "people don't heal." They are the very FACTORS THAT HAVE TO BE CHANGED in order for healing and health to be real instead of an illusional fantasy. Transformation of these factors are a requirement for *Higher Self Integration.*

In this highly addictive and codependent society we are all apart of, we are taught to be dependent on a medical authority to tell us how to get better. We're hung up on instant gratification, wanting someone else to "make it better now." We want rational, easy explanations with even easier "cures."

We fear death, even though it is a very natural transition to being back in the spirit world continuing on with our Soul's Journey in another dimension. The "reward-punishment" belief system we're taught sets us up even further to resisting and struggling with life. We've learned to feed energetically on the negative fear-based emotions and behaviors of anger, blame, jealousy, critical judgmentalness, self-absorption, producing more/bigger/better, and competitive motivation which is hung up on the win-loose concept.

Many of us are quite attached to what Carolyn Myss calls, "Woundology," which includes relating to others and our lives through and with our pain. "Misery loves company" is an old saying that many are trying to prove true. We get stuck in the misbelief that "I am my personality" falsely believing that we're incapable of changing our ways of thinking and behaving. For the majority, the word CHANGE evokes images of being thrown out of our present family, relationship, work, and housing situations: "left alone without a clue." Somehow the truth that life is naturally about change has alluded us and to see change as inherent and even joyful and fun is blasphemy to those addicted to pain and suffering.

As a result, we can dishonestly vow that we're ready to change, when we aren't at all because of the fear that's shaking our very Soul. That fear is the fear of rejection, of abandonment, of isolation from what has been feeding us, even if it was poison. Our fear of change plants deep-seated self-destructive and self-sabotaging patterns "in concrete" in our body/mind/spirit complex.

We, in turn, skirt, trick, and runaway from the amount of work it takes to clear ourselves of these most limiting and destructive beliefs and patterns of behavior. Many choose to remain living off of destructive ways of behaving, feeling, and thinking because they tire of all the reprogramming and repatterning it takes to manifest wholeness and *Soul Attunement or Higher Self Integration.* The old destructive ways are familiar; "It's what I know, even if it kills me."

In order to "GO FOR" Whole Health/Soul Attunement, one has to STAY WITH ONE'S COMMITMENT through the many stages that sometimes feel more painful and a lot more confusing than sticking with the old ways of doing things. However, to be able to stick with such an all-encompassing commitment, the WILLINGNESS/READINESS FACTORS HAVE TO COME FROM KNOWLEDGE AND JOY, not from the need to escape pain and misery.

For the long term commitment and consistency needed in real self-transformation, one has to be willing to WORK TOWARDS THE RESOLUTION OF THE KARMIC LESSONS or energy patterns of the relationship and personal patterning that are getting in the way of knowing and being one's Soul. Of equal importance is the need to have or be DEVELOPING more POSITIVE and ENERGIZING PLACES TO PUT THE ENERGY that was being used to create pain and dysfunction.

This means that we have to let go and transform our negative stuckness into positive movement. We have to LET GO OF THE PAST. We have to MOVE PAST running the negative emotions, thoughts, and behaviors centered on ANGER, RESENTMENT, and BLAME. We have to be WILLING TO FORGIVE - our circumstances, life, God/Goddess, others, and ourselves - anything we have blamed for what we think are injustices (acts or conditions that cause us to suffer hardship or loss undeservedly).

In order to get over what we perceive are injustices, we have to be willing to accept the SoulTruth that we, each and everyone of us, create or ARE RESPONSIBLE for everything that has manifested in our lives. And that's where a lot of people choke, protest, rebel, and scream in anger. "Give up my victimhood and all I get from fighting with my life? You've got to be kidding?" No, The Great Cosmic I/We is not.

What we all have to realize is that EACH AND EVERYONE OF US IS CREATING OUR EXPERIENCE OF REALITY FROM A SOUL LEVEL. The Truth or Universal Principle/Law that our human external reality reflects our internal one - or as Edgar Cayce channeled "SPIRIT IS THE LIFE, MIND IS THE BUILDER, PHYSICAL IS THE RESULT" - encompasses our SUPERCONSCIOUS or Soul Knowledge. Our Soul Knowledge includes the lessons and energy or karma we are working on as a Soul, not just as a limited-to-this-lifetime programmed personality. Our Soul is not judging these lessons as right or wrong, fair or unfair. They are just ways and methods we have chosen to learn from.

As Souls, we choose circumstances, relationships, and experiences that contribute to our consciousness's growth and development. These SOUL CHOICES, made on both super and sub-conscious levels, include rebirthing and dying processes. If, as this lifetime personalities, we do not understand or are uncomfortable with what we are manifesting and creating, we can CHOOSE TO BECOME CONSCIOUSLY AWARE OF our LESSONS and

CONSCIOUSLY CHOOSE HEALTHIER AND MORE POSITIVE WAYS TO LEARN them. We can also always consciously choose how we react to anything, what attitude we display. ATTITUDE ADJUSTMENT SKILLS are just as important in our lives as is reading, writing, and arithmetic.

Higher Self Integration is about CLAIMING OUR POWER TO CHANGE AND CREATE, TRANSFORM AND MANIFEST, HEAL AND GROW. It is not about wallowing in self or other blame, or running guilt and self-recrimination. It is not about being disempowered. It is about making decisions and choices based on what we know in each moment, and adding to what we know if we want different results for and in the future. It is about INCREASING OUR ABILITY TO RESPOND (response-ability) appropriately, not only in the interest of our present personality, but for the best for all concerned and for/as Soul. We have to cultivate the ability to APPRECIATE THE REALITY WE'VE CREATED and the problems in it as gifts and blessings that can help us grow and evolve.

One's knowledge and response-ability levels have to match. Knowledge without responsibility and integration is a game of pretense, and one that keeps us stuck and dead-ended. It's full of blaming, betraying, scapegoating, and hostage-holding. Knowledge without response-ability is living a lie. Knowledge with response-ability is WISDOM.

As Shakti Gawain, both in her book, *The Path Of Transformation*, and an article from ARE's Venture Inward March/April 1994, *Don't Blame Yourself*, puts it: "Yes, I am a powerful, creative being, learning about what it's like to be in physical form, learning how to create. Now that I see and appreciate what I've created, how can I learn from my reality - refine and improve it?" We have to FORGIVE, to let go of judging what is happening in our lives as right/wrong or good/bad, so we can SEE THE TRUTH, LESSON, GIFT and BLESSING of each moment as a Soul. Then we are emotionally free and clear to APPLY WHAT WE'VE LEARNED in order to heal and prosper.

> **IN ORDER TO GO FOR WHOLE HEALTH/SOUL ATTUNEMENT,**
> **THE WILLINGNESS/READINESS FACTOR HAS TO COME FROM KNOWLEDGE**
> **AND JOY, NOT THE NEED TO ESCAPE PAIN AND MISERY . . .**

ACTIVITY: THE WHOLE TRUTH AND NOTHING BUT THE TRUTH

It is impossible to operate with real response-ability if we're thinking and perceiving a situation in narrow, egocentric, and limited terms. And running negative emotions muddles up the situation even further. Real RESPONSE-ABILITY requires WHOLE THINKING SKILLS and EMOTIONAL CLARITY. It involves looking at each and every situation THROUGH THE EYES OF SOUL, not through conditioned automatic Lower Self Response Patterns.

1. After you have achieved an open and relaxed state, review your current life circumstances looking for a seemingly complex situation that will soon be demanding a response, or a decision, about what you are going to do. Pick one that you consider important, with possible significant outcomes, which is stimulating a negative reaction from you in the form of fear, anger, frustration, grief, etc. For this first practice run, pick a physical health-related issue. As you continue to work with this particular response-ability learning activity in the time to come, pick situations from every area of your life. (continued on page 68)

If you were going to respond based on your emotional reaction, what would it be? This is your automatic not-stopping-to-think-of-the-consequences reaction mode. Mentally roleplay that response. MENTAL ROLEPLAYING is imagining how a situation, scene, or interaction will turn out by acting out the various roles of you, others, and the circumstances and systems involved in certain ways inside your mind. Pay attention to your feelings as you mentally roleplay.

2. Next, release the negative emotion you are feeling about the real situation. Let out your anger, etc. through journal writing, nonhurtful physical release, crying, talking it out with an objective or nonattached friend, and/or various other types of PERSONAL PROCESS WORK.

3. Only after you have released the emotion, begin thinking about it using these steps:

A. Recognize your ATTACHMENT to the situation - What are you scared of? What FEARS are being triggered? What are you imagining you might have to loose or give up? What's the "WORST CASE SCENARIO" which is torturing you by teasing you and lying back in the shadows of your thoughts?

B. Find any linkages between this current situation and similar situations in your past. LET GO OF THE PAST, allowing this current situation to be just what it is. Don't mix it up with unfinished business that has nothing to do with the here and now. Be aware of the NEXT LEVEL OF FEARS stemming from past experiences, lack of confidence, and low self esteem.

C. Make sure you know any FACTS that are involved. Research and educate yourself about the various elements concerning your situation. Look at the individual parts of the whole picture and then look at the situation as a whole.

D. Figure out the situation's LESSONS AND GIFTS. This cannot be done easily if the above steps have not been completed. This requires being able to look beyond your old beliefs about life and your old ways of feeling and thinking. Your work with the previous steps helps to open your eyes to new light, different ways of seeing your life, and to the truth of the situation. Get into a deeper relaxed and open state of consciousness, asking for internal guidance concerning the truth of the situation. If others are involved, try to see the whole truth about their involvement and the whole truth about your involvement. Think beyond personality. THINK SOUL. THINK KARMIC INVOLVEMENT. THINK LIFE LESSONS.

E. PRAY FOR GUIDANCE. Work with DIVINE ORDER. Open yourself through MEDITATION, PRAYER, and CONTEMPLATION to HIGHER TRUTH AND WISDOM. LET GO AND LET GOD. LISTEN to the still small voice within. And listen some more. Let INFINITE INTELLIGENCE, your specific guides, and your Soul's wisdom fill in any gaps that the rational, logical human mind cannot comprehend on its own.

F. With what you now know after gaining emotional clarity and looking at the situation as a whole, once again Mental Role Play, but this time your scene is based on "the whole truth and nothing but the truth." Note the differences in how you feel and think.

SELF HEALING SKILLS HAVE US DELVE DEEP WITHIN OURSELVES BECAUSE THEREIN LIES THE CRUX OF WHAT'S GOING ON IN OUR OUTER LIFE...

THE PRACTICALITIES

It takes COMMITTED AND MULTI-FACETED DEEP INNER WORK to discover and integrate into our daily lives the physical, mental, emotional, spiritual, social, familial, work/service, and environmental changes necessary for each one of us to be happily holy healthy or *Higher Self Integrated*. The more we are out of balance and not experiencing wholeness, happiness, and *Soul Attunement*, the more work we have to do in order to heal/transform our lives. Most of us are dis-eased and discomforted because we are out of touch as to who we really are and what is really healthiest for us. Self-healing skills have us delve deep within ourselves because therein lies the crux of what's going on in our outer life.

Learning and integrating self-healing techniques and skills requires ongoing time, energy, and personal resources. If you lack ORGANIZATIONAL SKILLS, you better learn them because you'll have to use them in your own life in order to get the most from your energy and time allotments. If you lack COMMITMENT and SELF-DISCIPLINE, you better learn these because true wholeness cannot be achieved without them. The mental-based self healing tools of visualization and affirmation can not take hold and change our biochemical and physical structures and processes, nor our conditioned and programmed cognitive patterns, if we do not know how to use INTENTIONALITY and to DEEPLY CONCENTRATE. Emotional distractions and scattered thinking patterns can render mental healing techniques useless.

Which healing techniques are appropriate for us as individuals has everything to do with personal SOUL EVOLUTION, the level of Soul Consciousness one is in. A Level One usually sticks to the "fix up my symptoms quick, Doc" system, while a Level Three usually finds traditional allopathic drug, cut, and fry methods harmful. What is important is to START WHERE YOU ARE and expand your goals and techniques as you prove to yourself that your self-healing program designed for uniquely you is working. Don't try to pretend to be more advanced in your self-healing abilities than you are for "You can't fool Mother Nature."

Reach out and utilize the support you need from others in order to be able to HEAL YOURSELF. Allopathic Medicine can often help with diagnostics, pain relief, and with buying more time in which to keep plugging away on your holistic healing goals and plan. Figure out what you can do yourself and who needs to be a part of YOUR PARTICULAR HEALING TEAM. Each part of your life you have been able to change/transform will help you in bringing the others into a balanced match.

BLENDING BACK INTO BALANCE means to DISCOVER, MIX, UNITE, AND INTEGRATE THOSE ELEMENTS OF LIVING THAT WILL CREATE AND MAINTAIN A HARMONIOUS AND STABLE STATE. While each of our journeys into wholeness and balance need to be designed for our individually unique selves, there are general guidelines and signposts that can help guide our way. These simple sounding, yet very loaded questions can get us started in sorting through life's mazes: 1.What is out of balance in my life? 2. How did I get that way? 3.What do I need to know and do in order to heal? ATTEND/CONNECT/EXPRESS...

The first step to finding what is out of balance in our lives is to realize that we have a right to live in balance. We also have to recognize that if we have gotten out of balance somehow, then it stands to reason, if we correct the causes of the imbalances that we can get back into balance or wellness. Feeling trapped, hopeless, or fearful of changes often keeps us in a state of denial. DENIAL blocks our abilities to be aware of our signals or symptoms that try to alert us that we're out of balance. Denial, blaming, and projecting just keeps the focus off ourselves, keeping us stuck and in pain. Many times it's not until after we change a destructive behavior, relationship, or job that we really realize just how much it had caused dis-ease.

Keeping track of one's imbalances requires turning inward and learning the skills of listening and watching our own life. It involves becoming a "WITNESS" to one's personality. We've got to learn to nonjudgmentally, and without setting unreal expectations of "how things should be," see our own body, hear our own thoughts, feel our own emotions, connect with our own spirit, and channel our own Souls.

Remember that if you have had a breakdown physically, then you have also had a breakdown emotionally, mentally, and spiritually in some form or fashion. To be oriented towards the cause, you have to go beyond diagnoses and symptom control, into EXPLORING the EMOTIONS (energies) you have been running, the THOUGHTS (including misbeliefs and disbeliefs) that have occupied your mind, and the separation from your spiritbody and Soul that is always behind every breakdown, imbalance, or disease.

Causes of imbalances are directly tied into how we live our lives on a daily basis. Many of our breakdowns occur because we are not in balance in what we eat, how we think and feel, the pace we keep, the creativity we express, and the love we share. One can eat reasonably healthy, take regular relaxing vacations, and enjoy a positive significant-other relationship. But, if the body is not exercised as it needs to be, the job is unfulfilling and stressful, and one is disconnected from the Earth and Spirit, then a breakdown is inevitable.

The causes of our imbalances are found in the exploration of who we are and how we run our lives. Our physical bodies are many systems within a greater whole that are all interconnected within its physicality, let alone with our mind, spirit, and Soul. In *Total Wellness*, Joseph Pizzorno's research reveals seven underlying, health-sustaining systems of our physical body that must be treated these ways in order to enhance healing and ensure well-being or health: "We must STRENGTHEN THE IMMUNE SYSTEM, DECREASE TOXICITY, NORMALIZE INFLAMMATORY FUNCTION, OPTIMIZE METABOLIC FUNCTION, BALANCE THE REGULATORY SYSTEM, ENHANCE REGENERATION, and LIVE IN HARMONY WITH THE LIFEFORCE."

**REMEMBER THAT IF YOU HAVE HAD A BREAKDOWN PHYSICALLY,
THEN YOU HAVE ALSO HAD A BREAKDOWN EMOTIONALLY, MENTALLY,
AND SPIRITUALLY IN SOME FORM OR FASHION . . .**

ACTIVITY: TEAMWORK OR YELL FOR HELP

As you move through the various Levels Of Soul Consciousness, you will develop your abilities to tune inward into more-knowing energies than "the ordinary human." However, and in the meantime, there are some humans and organizations whom have combined research and experience that can be quite helpful in putting together your own unique healing plan/program.

EDUCATE YOURSELF about the physical body and how it functions (do the same for your mind and spirit, too). EXPLORE YOUR CHOICES for treatments and therapies, both allopathic and complementary (formerly known as alternative). EXPERIMENT and PRACTICE tools, techniques, activities, and abilities you can do yourself. ELICIT the SUPPORT and knowledge of others who are on a wavelength that works for you.

For a list of books, magazines, and organizations that have proven helpful for others in their whole healing journey, look in A Soul's Delight's Bibliography/Resources Section, as well as the recommended book's various bibliography/reference sections. These reading resources can further your knowledge of the concept's covered in this chapter:

The Holistic Way To Health & Happiness, by H. Bloomfield & R. Kory, Fireside, 1980

Book of Stress Survival, by A. Kirsta, Fireside, 1986

Dr.'s Deepak Chopra's and Andrew Weil's books . . . (see Bibliography)

Total Wellness: Improve Your Health By Understanding The Body's Health Systems, by J. Pizzorno, Prima Publishing, 1996.

Light Emerging: The Journey of Personal Healing, by B. Brennan, Bantam Books, 1993.

Women's Bodies, Women's Wisdom: Creating Physical and Emotional Health & Healing, by C. Northrup, Bantam Books, 1994

Vibrational Medicine: New Choices for Healing Ourselves, by R. Gerber, Bear & Co., 1988 (1996 update)

There are some core similarities to real healing that stand true for each and everyone of us. The more we are out of balance, the more we will need to be organized and self-disciplined in whatever healing techniques fit best for where we are currently. Healing takes ongoing commitments of motivation, focus, time, energy, and resources. Learning to recognize and work through our ego resistances is absolutely necessary, incorporating instead "the two P's": PATIENCE AND PERSEVERANCE. Being able to recognize and celebrate our accomplished steps towards the ultimate goal of lasting balance and whole health is essential in keeping our motivation going through the uncertainty and change that is an integral part of the movement into balance.

Physical movement/exercise, special care with our diets and nutrition, positive and life-giving thought patterns, beliefs, and emotions, as well as staying in touch with Spirit through meditation and prayer are core components of a balanced-living life program. As important is a loving connection with nature and finding a way to serve fellow beings with life-affirming intentions. We need to consciously choose clothing and a home environment that help us to release our creative self-expression. Personal challenge, intimacy, and pleasure along with real friends and lots of love enable us to be balanced in our giving and receiving.

The particular blend of knowledge, resources, techniques, and skills needed in order to find and stay in balance can come to each and everyone of us in many different ways if clear intent and openness to being whole and *Higher Self Integrated* is acknowledged and continually expressed. There is a wealth of Life Force/God Given Energy for us all to use: there for the sincere and honest asking.

"ALL THIS AND MORE, IN FAITH, WE CAN DO . . ."

ACTIVITY: <u>HUMAN HEAL THYSELF!</u>

Self-healing ability is a built-in reality for us humans. Our physical bodies are oriented towards health and healing on a moment-to-moment basis. It's natural for us. What we have to do is to GET OUT OF OUR OWN WAY. We've got to give our bodies the nutrition, movement, rest, relaxation, respect, and nurturing they require. We've got to use our brain/mind abilities for growth and healing, not negativity, stagnation, and destruction. We've got to RUN THE ENERGIES, emotions, and expressions that energize our Souls, not burn us out. We've got to CREATE SITUATIONS in which we can share our joy and love, not waddle in our insecurities.

There are many self-healing skills, techniques, and tools that we can all learn to use and integrate into our daily lives. These are some of the general categories:

body movement/exercise	journaling	meditation
bodywork (massage, etc.)	visualization/imagery	prayer
nutrition (herbs, minerals, etc.)	affirmations	forgiveness
relaxation exercises	emotional release work	energetic cleansing
breathing exercises	belief reprogramming	laying on of hands
body talk	reworking fear-based thoughts/behaviors	spirit guidance
working with pain	present/past life memory work	using White Light
sound/toning/music	trance work/hypnosis	integrating Higher Self
colorwork	sub-personality work	joy and unconditional love
using crystals and gemstones	mind control & expansion	Divine Love & Light
aromatherapy & flower essences	whole thinking skills	Soul nurturing

(continued on page 72)

There is a lot to do and incorporate into our daily lives when we are oriented towards self-healing, whole health, and *Higher Self Integration*. It helps to DESIGN SEQUENCES or routines that include the various physical, mental, and spiritual healing and developing activities you are currently working with, in ways that allow them to flow and feed right into one another.

Below is a Self-Healing Sequence that incorporates the basic sequence principles of:

* <u>OPENING UP</u> through STRETCHING, RELAXING, and BREATHING

* <u>HEALING</u> through FOCUSING, CLEANSING, and REWORKING

* <u>WRAPPING UP</u> through AFFIRMING, PROTECTING, and APPRECIATING

Try this SELF-HEALING SEQUENCE. Over time, let it change as you do, using different activities you are drawn to, designing and using your own Self-Healing Sequences. Remember that the deeper your concentration, one-minded focus, and self-healing confidence and beliefs are, the deeper and realer the effects will be. A few suggestions for activity substitutions are in parenthesis at the end or beginning of the activity explanations.

*** OPENING UP ***

STRETCHING- While standing, rotate forward/backwards/circling each of your hands, feet, knees, hip joints, shoulders, elbows, arms, and neck for a minute each. Keeping your head straight ahead, swing your arms back and forth from side to side rotating your spine. Now, shake your entire body for a few minutes letting any tenseness be shaken loose . . . (Sun Salutes, 10 minutes of floor stretching exercises, Tai Chi, etc.)

RELAXING- Concentrate on watching your breath. Continue breathing, saying silently to yourself "love" on the inhale breathing in love, and "fear" on the outbreath breathing out all your fears. From your toes to your skull top be aware of each body part, saying silently to each, "Relax," feeling all tensions drain out . (various visualizations concentrating on relaxation, self-massage and pressure point work, progressive body holding and release, etc.)

BREATHING- Slowly breathe deeply for a few breaths. Then breathe in to a silent count of four, hold for four, breathe out for four, hold empty for four. Breathe this way for three to five minutes . . . (vary counts, left/right nostril breathing, exhale through O-shaped mouth, etc.)

*** HEALING ***

FOCUSING- Mentally scan your body from the top of your head to the bottom of your feet registering any pain and tightness you feel. Become consciously aware of your pains/discomforts. Focus in on a part of your body that seems to need more pressing attention, release, and healing. Breathing deeply, breathe into that body part relaxing into the discomfort. Allow the discomfort to make itself known to you as intensely as it needs to. Within yourself, ask that body part what it needs . . . (mentally dialogue and roleplay with your body part, mentally review your his/herstory with a particular body part or body system, visualize your Being expressing its needs through various images which provide you a particular focus, etc.)

CLEANSING- Imagine yourself lying on a warm, peaceful beach. Hear the waves gently lapping at the shore and relax deeper. Feel the warm sunrays penetrate into your body, especially in the area that you need special healing. Visualize the sunrays as sparkling Life Force energy penetrating your discomfort, clearing away all painful negativity. Continue focusing on this imagery, cleansing away all negativity and pain . . . (Grounding Cord activities, chakra and auric cleansing activities, color cleansing visualizations, etc.)

(continued on page 73)

REWORKING- While deep breathing and being aware of your focus, rub your hands together visualizing healing energy forming and generating from them. Keeping your mind clear of distracting thoughts, put your right hand on your area of focus, letting the healing energy move into the place that needs healing . . . (use toning and soundwork, become aware of the emotional issues involved using emotional releasing abilities, seek spirit and/or Soul guidance, etc.)

*** WRAP UP ***

AFFIRMING- (Affirm out loud, make up specific affirmations for your direct focus, write out your affirmations, etc.)   Affirm mentally to yourself:

> I make up my mind that it is time to be healed. With such a mindset,
> I set into motion a process that affects every part of my body, mind, spirit, Soul.
> Opening my mind to the idea of healing, I let Divine Life work in and through me
> and others so that healing is real. I am being healed now! Whatever I need, the
> spirit of life is within me to heal and restore me. Divine Life pulsates throughout
> my body. Healing is a natural process that is constantly taking place within me . . .

PROTECTING- Remaining relaxed, visualize your crown chakra opening and Divine White Light streaming into your Crown Chakra, throughout all your chakras and spine, into your legs and arms, and throughout your aura, cleansing and healing. Keep running this healing and protecting light as long as you can remain focused . . . (Pray for protection and guidance, Divine White Light environment surrounding visualization, Divine Safety affirmations, etc.)

APPRECIATING- Breathing deep and evenly, see yourself as you are in this moment in your mind's eye, projected as if on an invisible mental movie screen. What do you see? Then, visualize yourself fully healthy in every way, being in-joy. Really get into this image. Now put both images side by side connecting them with a silver cord. Let the joy and lightness of the healed image fill your other unhealed self. Watch the two images merge in joy and health. Thank the joyful healthy you for being seen and felt . . . (Thank your pain for its teachings, send your pain or Being love in the form of thoughts/colors/ images, plan some special nurturing for yourself, etc.)

CHAPTER FIVE
BEAUTIFUL BEING

> IT IS OF THE UTMOST IMPORTANCE TO UNDERSTAND AND WORK VERY
> CONSCIOUSLY WITH OUR HUMAN BODIES FROM A POSITION, ATTITUDE, AND
> INTENTION OF LOVE AND ACCEPTANCE, RESPECT AND RESPONSE-ABILITY. . .

WHAT IT IS . . .

In the journey and development of Soul Consciousness, being human provides our Soul opportunities to experience an Earthly World absolutely teeming over with stimuli and sensation, choices and creations. Our human body provides us the vehicle in which to interact in and with such a world of materiality. While we are on Earth, our human body houses our Soul. The more entuned with our Soul's needs and energies we allow our bodies to be, the more we are able to express Soul here on Earth. In *The Higher Self Integration Process*, it is of the utmost importance for us to work very consciously with our human bodies from a position, attitude, and intention of love and acceptance, respect and responsibility (response-ability).

As Souls, we exist within our spirit/etheric bodies through our minds. Mind cannot be separated from our Soul's spirit. One cannot exist without the other because they are one, beyond separation. Our Souls exist in spiritual dimensions through our mindspirit. But if we, as Souls, are to experience Earthly life in all its material density, we must assume human bodies with which to interact with Earthly matter. Our Souls exist through mindspirit without a human body, but a human body cannot exist without a Soul's mindspirit. When a Soul's mindspirit leaves its human body (through what's called death), the physical body ceases to exist.

The human body never comes into being without the influx and connection to mindspirit, Soul. It is truly misleading to talk about and care for a body separate from mindspirit. The mass consciousness, scientific, and orthodox medical focus on the human body as a machine separate from mindspirit has no place and reality in *Higher Self Integration or Soul Consciousness*. Indeed, a Soul in human form who is wanting to move from Level Three Soul Consciousness into the higher levels cannot do so until they DAILY RECOGNIZE AND WORK WITH THEIR BODYMINDSPIRIT AS THE INTERCONNECTED WHOLE IT IS.

In general, our society has come up with a superficial definition of a beautiful body which is dependent upon all the body's parts being proportioned a certain way. This false focus eats away at self esteem, orienting many folks towards misleading distractions, such as: calorie and fat counting obsessions, fitness addictions and its rebellious counterpart "Couch Potatoes Unlimited," designer infatuation, and the urge to falsify reality through implants, nips and tucks, etc.

In actuality, BEAUTY IS RADIATED. It is made up of energy, not mass. In-proportion body parts are just in-proportion body parts, unless there's a glow from within. And that shine from within is Soul, not a specific tooth whitener. The more we are entuned with our Soul's energy, the easier it is to treat our beings in the ways they require in order to run the types of energies necessary in being beautifully healthy and whole.

Lower personality ways of thinking, feeling, and behaving are what get us out of balance, blocking out our Soul's Divine LoveLight Energy, and causing dysfunction, premature aging symptoms, and dis-ease. There have been times in my life when my physical body looked and acted 15 years older than it was. At those times, my personality's way of running my life had caused so much stress that my body was symptomatically dis-eased.

And there are also times when folks mistake me for being 20 years younger than I am, exclaiming that I am one of the most beautiful people they have ever seen. During these times, I am very centered or entuned with my Soul's energy. I run positive, loving thoughts and feelings and am truly enjoying my life. I literally glow from within and that glow outshines any bodily imperfections that are just a part of me. With Soul shining forth, my angular jaw line, scars, damaged teeth, slumped shoulders, etc. are overshadowed. Soul brings forth the Beautiful Being that is in all of us. It allows our bodymindspirit to RUN THE AMOUNT OF DIVINE LIFE FORCE THAT ENLIVENS OUR BEING, not sicken and deaden it.

Many of the thoughts, feelings, behavior patterns, attitudes and belief systems we have been taught about our physical bodies, or more accurately our bodymindspirit physicality, set us up for imbalance, illness, dis-ease, destruction, and obsessive activities. Just look at the differences between two people the same age, one who stays stuck in anger, hostility, and negativity and one who joyfully flows with life. Anger hardens the face, causes deep lip-pursing wrinkles, stiffens and pains the body, and dis-eases the heart. It is not a pretty picture.

As one develops consciousness, THE INTENTION behind all of one's actions and behaviors carries more weight in outcome and in learning one's current lesson in order to move to the next. In Level Two Soul Consciousness, one can do a regular fitness workout coming from the orientation of not wanting to be fat and not be way off track for that level of consciousness. But one cannot move out of Level Three if still stuck in thinking and feeling patterns of "I'm not good enough, pretty enough, thin enough," etc.

In terms of Soul Consciousness, being stuck in a fat and calorie counting contest is still buying into the mass consciousness's false belief systems of body beautiful, the very ones that have instilled compulsive overeating, bulimia, and other eating disorders as a way of life in our society. When one is entuned with one's Soul, when one is *Higher Self Integrated*, one naturally eats, sleeps, moves, cleanses, rests, thinks, and feels in ways that are life supporting because it feels right, because it works, because it's wonderful! It is not because we're fearful that someone will reject us if we jiggle or wrinkle as we age.

There are just as many life and health enhancing foods, things to do, resources to use, thoughts to think, emotions to feel, behaviors to enact as there are destructive, toxic, and deadening ones. That is not the issue. The issue is our intentions behind our actions, the belief systems upon which we act, the reasons behind our motivation. In *The Higher Self Integration Process*, THE REAL WORK LIES IN REPROGRAMMING OUR THOUGHTS, FEELINGS, AND BEHAVIORS SO THAT THEY ARE ENTUNED WITH SOUL, WITH GOD/GODDESS, not human mass consciousness and society. CHANGES IN CONSCIOUSNESS are the real nuts and bolts of well-being.

In Soul Consciousness, we don't take care of our bodies in order to try to avoid rejection, disability or loss, pain and suffering. We naturally take care of our bodymindspirit out of love, because of love. We absolutely dig life and if one digs life then there is no other way to live it than in its fullest and with the respect and gusto that life requires.

What we have to REWORK are ALL THE FALSE THINGS WE HAVE BEEN TAUGHT ABOUT LIFE AND OURSELVES, ALL THE FEARS WHICH KEEP US CRAZILY SELF-DESTRUCTIVE, AND ALL THE PARTIAL AND UNTRUTHS THAT HAVE BEEN FED TO US FALSELY AS EVERLASTING FACTS. Then, and only then, will self-control issues no longer wage war within us. Then and only then, will we constantly and consistently listen and follow our all-knowing Soul's Voice.

**THE ISSUE IS OUR INTENTIONS BEHIND OUR ACTIONS, THE BELIEF SYSTEMS
UPON WHICH WE ACT, AND THE REASONS BEHIND OUR MOTIVATION . . .**

ACTIVITY: TOXIC ATTITUDES

Our bodymindspirit doesn't function well running toxic attitudes. TOXIC ATTITUDES are negative mindsets that sabotage, harm or defeat our Beings. Most of us have more destructive preset attitudes concerning our physicality than we can effectively handle if approached one by one. Fortunately, many of these sickening mind dispositions can be grouped under several major categories: physical appearance, physical needs, and sexuality. If we can get a handle on one or two of our major dysfunctional thinking patterns in each category, it will have a cleansing domino affect on all the others.

Learning and applying effective <u>ATTITUDE ADJUSTMENT SKILLS</u> will prove to be one of the healthiest things you can do for your bodymindspirit. This package of skills includes:
<u>RECOGNITION</u> that you are "running attitude" and how it specifically restricts and harms you and your life,
<u>DISCOVERY</u> of the mindsets causing you harm and how they were programmed into you,
<u>LINKAGE</u> between these mindsets and your daily behaviors,
<u>DISCERNMENT</u> and perceiving the differences in your destructive automated behaviors stemming from toxic attitudes and how you would prefer to think, feel, and behave,
<u>INSPIRITING</u> which is inspiring, envisioning, affirming, motivating yourself to think, feel, and behave in those preferred ways, and
<u>PRACTICING</u> or reworking over and over again until the health-inspired mindset becomes as automatic and natural in your life as the toxic attitude had been.
A FEW EXAMPLES OF:

TOXIC ATTITUDES = UNHEALTHY BEHAVIORS

*I'll never really be accepted/loved since I'm not very pretty/handsome = Attracting and staying in destructive relationships because "who else would have me?"
*Anyone can get cancer for no real reason = Eating junk food, smoking cigarettes, not getting enough sleep since "It doesn't matter anyway."
*A man's got to get his needs met but a womyn doesn't = As a man, lacking self control and demanding that another tend to your needs. As a womyn, neglecting own needs in order to please, therefore keeping your man.

ADJUSTED ATTITUDES= HEALTHY BEHAVIORS

*I'm worthy of being loved and treated with respect = Having the self-confidence necessary to wait for a committed relationship that's based on love and respect.
*There are ways of living one's life that help one to be/stay healthy = Enjoying eating organic fruits, veges, and grains, getting the rest and meditation time one needs, positive and joyfilled thinking and feeling patterns.
*Each person's needs are just as important as the next person's = Taking good care of oneself and helping one another for "the best of all concerned."

1. Once in your open and relaxed state, take one of the above categories, such as physical appearance, and begin listing all the general toxic attitudes you have been taught concerning that area. Use BRAINSTORMING, MEMORY FLASHBACK, AND LIFE OBSERVATION, including filmwatching and reading, for focus and stimulation.

2. Read through your list and pick one or two major toxic attitudes that you know negatively influence your life. Then, APPLY the above ATTITUDE ADJUSTMENT SKILLS. Your goal is to be able to change the specific destructive ways you treat and run your life that are based on toxic attitudes you were taught. There will be plenty of practice material in the above bodymindspirit categories. Don't be surprised by the volatility of the sexuality category; just take it slow and easy, one step at a time.

Loving and respecting our bodymindspirit has everything to do with accepting and understanding what it is (what we are), what it is saying to us (what we are saying to ourselves) as we journey through life's passages, and what it individually needs (what we need) in order to function in all its creative glory.   PLANT INTO YOUR CONTINUOUS AWARENESS THAT WE ARE ENERGY BEINGS, WHO NEED CERTAIN VARIETIES AND QUALITIES OF ENERGIES IN ORDER TO STAY ALIVE ON THIS PLANET.   All the energy around us interacts with the energy we are through our bodymindspirit.

What we look and feel like, and how we function has everything to do with the receiving, distribution, transformation, regeneration, and creation of energy within/around our being. The energies we choose to incorporate make us who we are. They can be easily read and understood in order to consciously and purposefully form, balance, or change aspects of ourselves.

Energies that our Beings need in order to thrive and flourish in our Earthly environment have to be in BALANCE. If there is ever a word that needs to be implanted in our brain/mind, it is BALANCE. BALANCE is the keyword that goes hand-in-hand with health.

For example, our bodies need a certain amount of the natural body-produced chemical, adrenaline. However, too little produced for our chosen lifestyle leaves us depressed and immobile, while too much can create havoc with our nervous systems, contributing to immune dysfunction, heart disease, cancer, hyperactivity and other boogabears of the bodymindspirit. And this is the case with every form of energy; too little sunlight means vitamin deficiencies, seasonal affective disorders and more while too much can mean skin cancer and premature aging - too much sleep can be just as damaging in its own way as too little sleep- one can go bananas from people isolation as much as from people overstimulation.

The secret of your own unique BALANCE NEEDS lies in the proverbial KNOW THYSELF. Everyone needs fresh air, a continual supply of oxygen, water, sunshine, vitamin/mineral packed foods, and nature's gifts and lessons. We all need love, people energy, Divine Energy, one's own abundant life force energy often looked upon as sexual energy, and one's own Soul energy.   We all need restful relaxing states, sleep, activity, movement, and exercise. All of us need to detox and clean both physically and etherically. Everyone needs to be touched, to laugh and have fun, to be joyful, to feel fulfilled.   We all need Self-Expression and Cocreation.

The specifics of what each one of us needs to feed ourselves energetically for balance and health in each day of our lives depends on many factors. These factors include how many toxic energies we are daily ingesting into our bodymindspirit systems through our environment, including: the air we breath and the food we eat, the people we spend time with, our thoughts, feelings, beliefs, attitudes, activities, and behavior patterns. The more toxic foods we eat, the more toxic chemicals we both ingest and produce within our bodies, the more toxic people and situations we choose to interact with, and the more toxic emotions and thinking patterns we run, the harder it is to live and be IN BALANCE.   The more we live in separation from God/Goddess and Soul, the harder it is to be whole and healthy. The more self and other dislike, hatred, anger, resentment, and frustration one runs, the harder it will be to be happy and healthy. And the beat goes on and on.

But remember, that the happy news is that EVERYTHING IS INTERCONNECTED. It's not a separate body-from a separate mind-from a separate spirit. It's bodymindspirit, all together, all one, all influenced, balanced and imbalanced together. If your physiological biochemical imbalance is off, then so is your thinking and the energy that makes up your spirit or etheric body. Work on getting all those prostaglandins and hormones balanced and your thinking, feeling and energy will also shape up. It's not as hard as the old Newtonian "man is a machine" misbeliefs would make it out to be.

The old ricocheting domino affect that through ignorance can quickly send us into a painful abyss, can also through knowledge, wisdom, and consciousness, send us directly Into The Light. It's a matter of choice. It's a matter of Yin and Yang. It's a matter of BALANCE.

THE QUALITY OF ENERGIES WE CHOOSE TO INCORPORATE WITHIN OUR BEINGS MAKE US WHO WE ARE AND CAN BE EASILY READ AND UNDERSTOOD IN ORDER TO CONSCIOUSLY AND PURPOSEFULLY FORM, BALANCE, AND CHANGE ASPECTS OF OURSELVES . . .

ACTIVITY: __INTO THE LIGHT__

As important as it is to recognize the toxic/dark ways one lives, thinks and feels in order to start consciously choosing one's life, it is as equally important to recognize the healthy/light thoughts, feelings, and behaviors that have quite literally kept you alive and kicking in positive ways. LOOK FOR THOSE "I CAN, IT'S WORKING, IT FEELS SO GOOD TO BE ALIVE" MOMENTS. What are you doing? What are you thinking? What are you feeling? Who and what is around you? What has worked for you? Those times when you felt balanced, how did you get that way? Search for the light, figure it out, and allow it to happen. THE BALANCE IS UP TO YOU. It's yours, you just need to be able to KNOW IT!

WHAT IT IS SAYING . . .

Our bodymindspirit continuously shows us directly what is and is not working well about our ways of **living, expressing, and thinking.** It constantly gives us clues as to how we are out of balance, including what chakras are blocked and which life issues we are struggling with. If we don't listen, look, feel and then change, these clues will move into full-blown symptoms, dis-eases, accidents, life crises' and traumas. It is our responsibility, each and everyone of us, TO BE AWARE, TO LISTEN, AND TO WORK WITH OUR INNER AND *HIGHER SELF* in order to maintain or become in balance with what we need to be "Holy Healthy."

One of our biggest obstacles to self-listening is being scared of finding out about something within ourselves and our lives we'd rather not know about or have to change. However, our most damaging behaviors are those that not only proclaim ignorance as far as self-listening skills are concerned, but are designed to keep us in such a whirl wind that we can't even begin to HEAR AND SEE THE SOUL'S TRUTH about our lives.

Many of us are workaholics and professional distracters, hung up on being busy and productive, slaves to goals and end products. We fill our lives so full of things to do, people to see, and so much noise that we don't have a spare moment in which to tune in.   We're so busy taking care of our kids, our family members, our friends, our houses, our cars, our things, our society that we neglect the only thing that is immortal and really matters, our Soul.

For *The Higher Self Integration Process*, one has to find and MAKE TIME for one's bodymindspirit, for one's Soul.   One's children, work setting, home, volunteer work, recreational adventures, religious or spiritual support group, etc. can all serve as classrooms and laboratory's for Soul Work. But one has to be consciously aware of ones' Soul Plan. If you are not even aware of what class you are taking, there's no way for you to be prepared to learn your best or do the necessary homework. TUNE IN, FIND OUT WHICH COURSE OF STUDY YOU ARE TAKING, AND THEN GO FOR IT. You'll be amazed at how much more sense and smoother your life makes and goes when you are in your SOUL'S FLOW.

Tuning In to Soul has everything to do with TIME, RELAXATION, A DISTRACTION FREE ENVIRONMENT, CLARITY AND QUIET OF THOUGHTS AND FEELINGS, READING ENERGY, and LOVE AND TRUST.   In order to allow oneself to begin listening to Soul, one has to begin trusting in DIVINE ORDER AND IN A DIVINE PLAN. The fears and distractions of your lower self have got to be dealt with through kind awareness. You also have to incorporate an alert knowledge that there's more to you/your life than scurrying around to fill the demanding and incessant desires of your automatic and mass consciousness conditioned self.

Soul Knowledge is comprehensive and whole. It makes great practical as well as intuitive sense. It includes past, present, and future relevant information. It's a whole package deal that unfolds rather nicely if allowed to. But until you are advanced enough in your Soul Belief System and the SKILLS OF THOUGHT AND FEELING CONTROL along with DEEP FOCUS, CONCENTRATION, SPIRIT LISTENING, and ENERGY READING, your own physical body can tell and show you how you are in or out of balance in thought, form, and spirit.

Your physical body is constantly sending you messages from your mind, spirit, and Soul. You only have to use your senses (to see, hear, feel, smell, taste, and touch) these messages, in order to be aware of them and to know their interpretations. There are several interpretive systems available to you that once learned can specifically pinpoint what's working or not working in your life. Through learning massage, reflexology, acupressure, and chakra diagnoses, we all can know exactly what's off in our physical systems, which life issues are causing us grief, and where and what our energy blocks are. Not only that, but each of these systems provide skills/tools that we can use to help ourselves unplug our blocks and realign our energies.

Through learning to listen to the sensations of our bodies, the thoughts and feelings of our minds, and the energies of our spirit, we can get a clear and comprehensive picture of what is really happening in our lives. It takes LEARNING AWARENESS, because most of us have learned to block out, ignore, disregard, and rebel against our most accessible and valuable teacher, our very own bodymindspirit, our self, our Soul.

> **OUR BODYMINDSPIRIT CONTINUOUSLY SHOWS US DIRECTLY**
> **WHAT IS AND IS NOT WORKING WELL ABOUT OUR WAYS**
> **OF LIVING, EXPRESSING, AND THINKING . . .**

ACTIVITY: __AWARENESS LOG__

On a regular basis at first, date a page in your HSI notebook under AWARENESS LOG, and record what you discover under the following categories:

1. WHAT OBVIOUSLY HURTS . . . Where are you experiencing pain, achiness, stiffness, and tightness? What have you noticed in your everyday functioning? Relax and tune in. Get into an open and relaxed state by doing a few relaxation and breathing activities and then do a MENTAL BODY SCAN. Look and listen for even more areas of tightness and pain. Pay attention to where you feel cold and heat, pins and prickles, numbness, and nervous activity.

2. Go to a full-length mirror and thoroughly CHECK YOUR POSTURE, face, skin, eyes, etc. Really look at yourself. Work through your fear of facing yourself straight on. As you stare at yourself, let any emotion that needs to surface be released. Be aware of your thoughts and reactions as you look intensely at yourself. Check out your weight, balance, flexibility, strength, and stamina. Check your body alignment. Pay attention to yourself as you simply stand, sit, and walk. Record what you see, think, and feel.

3. Do series of STRETCHING AND MOVEMENT EXERCISES that involve every muscle, joint, body organ, chakra, etc. of your being. Maintain a focused awareness on what each body part feels like as it moves, and how your body as a whole unit handles each activity or exercise. As you do physical activities such as swimming, hiking, skiing, etc. check for tightness and for breathing, for comfort and discomfort levels, for fear, worry, and distractions, and for relaxation, confidence and en-joy-ment. Maintain body, thought, and feeling consciousness as you do various physical activities, recording your awarenesses.

(continued on page 80)

4. Using **LIGHT TOUCH**, gently squeeze all of your major muscles, belly areas, and skin all over your body. Scratch, rub and pull your scalp and hair, checking out how your head feels. Take your thumb and fingers and press all over your body discovering all the points that are tender, tight, and sore or painful. There will be points on your thighs, forearms, hands, feet, indeed in every area of your body, which will make their discomfort known to you if you'll just pay them some touching and purposeful attention. Thoroughly cover your entire feet and hands, point by point; they have a lot to teach you. Record what you've discovered.

Then, using the systems and charts available in the next few pages and in other books that specifically cover massage, accupressure, reflexology, chakras, and physical body complications, figure out what all those aches and pains indicate. For example, using the reflexology system, you can find out that the granular and very painful lump on the bottom of your foot a couple of inches below your big toe indicates overactive adrenals. That's a very important bit of awareness to know so that you can get hold of how and why you are overworking those adrenals. Then you can choose to make the lifestyle changes necessary to getting those adrenals back into balance!

5. Become aware of **THE FLOW OF YOUR ENERGY LEVEL** in everything you do and in each day as a whole. Look for correlations between what you are doing, thinking, and feeling and how much energy you do or don't have. Become aware of what happens to the quality of your energy with what you eat, drink, and breathe. Look at the quality of your thoughts and feelings in relation to your energy level. Record your discoveries.

6. Having studied the chakras, become aware of which **CHAKRA AREAS** are feeling bound or displaying symptoms of imbalance and pain through the organs and tissues it affects. Learn to listen to your thoughts and feelings, figuring out which chakra issues you seem to be spinning around and around in. Record your chakra related awarenesses. Add these more minor, yet very important, chakra information areas to the seven major ones you have already studied:

FEET CHAKRAS-

Location: 2 of them, one in the bottom of each foot at the arch.
Function: To bring in Earth Energy.
Healthy/Balanced Functioning: To make the body real by bringing Earth Energy into the body, to dance, run, skate, ski or any creative movement of the feet, good balance.
Imbalance/Blocked: Foot problems, trips easily, left-right imbalance, cold feet, not feeling connected to the Earth or grounded, to shake or fidget nervously with one's feet.

HAND CHAKRAS-

Location: 2 of them, one in the palm of each hand.
Function: To manifest creativity on the physical plane, healing, reading energy.
Healthy/Balanced Functioning: To express oneself through art, music, building, healing, manifesting, ideas, creating.
Imbalance/Blocked: To hurt someone with one's hands (too much energy) or not to use one's hands for creative expression (too little energy), to fidget nervously with one's hand.

7. Conscious awareness of one's thoughts and feelings as they are being run is a bit trickier to learn and be skilled at than one might think. **A THOUGHT AND FEELING REVIEW** of each day, relying on your memory to become aware of what you had been thinking and feeling, works to a degree. Although the average person only stays with a thought for less than 15 seconds, it is usually a part of limited and stuck thought and feeling patterns that get repeated or played over and over throughout the course of a day and as the days go by.

(continued on page 81)

It takes determination while establishing a type of CHECK IT OUT system in order to remember to tune in at first. Meditative and other concentration skills really help in learning instant thought and feeling awareness. Take some moments, throughout your day, to ask yourself what you just thought and felt. Look for repeated patterns. Use quick one word labels for identification purposes such as: anger, planning, remembering, confusion, etc. Record what you are learning about yourself.

For the *Higher Self Integration Process*, becoming AWARE OF the seemingly random and automatic THOUGHT AND FEELING PATTERNS that flit in and out at hyper speed AS THEY ARE HAPPENING is very necessary for the level of awareness one needs in order to know oneself, to know what one is creating, and to consciously change. Purposeful practice will eventually program into your being a natural and automatic ability to know what you are thinking and feeling and the reaction it is having on your being all at the moment it is happening. That's when true choice becomes your moment-to-moment reality.

When we are committed to *Higher Self Integration*, we MAINTAIN A FOCUS ON ENERGY MANAGEMENT. As we have learned, tension anywhere in our physical beings represents blocked energy. We get energetically bound up and out of balance through a variety of ways including emotional stress, improper nutrition and chemical contamination, physical impact or trauma, and negative thinking including misbelief and disbelief patterns. Not only can certain types of massage, including reflexology and acupressure, help us in becoming aware of and understanding the impact of our tension or energy blocks and imbalances, but these systems also help us to release our blocks and heal or balance our energetic flows.

Receiving a relaxing full body Swedish Massage can be quite a pleasurable, nurturing, and healing gift to give ourselves or someone else. Getting certain types of MASSAGE and DEEP BODY WORK, such as rolfing, and ACUPUNCTURE from licensed professionals often proves tremendously helpful, especially at certain stages in our *HSI Journey*. These stages include when we have manifested diagnoseable injuries, illnesses, and dis-eases, when we are learning and starting to do deep memory and emotional release work, and when we are uncovering our darkest fears that have been solidly imbedded in our psyches from our different incarnations. When we are first learning how to do deep work, it is helpful to have a body or energetic worker who knows how to move through intense emotional and physical release.

However, as your work continues through the various stages and levels, you will need to be able to be there for yourself whenever you need it in terms of using touch for release and energetic realignment through the use of SELF-MASSAGE TECHNIQUES, including SELF-REFLEXOLGY and SELF-ACUPRESSURE. Balance and maintenance of harmony depends on a free and unimpeded circulation of energy through the bodymindspirit's organs and energy centers. These self-help techniques may be needed on a daily basis at times.

The following information and techniques covering general massage, chakra massage, reflexology, and acupressure need to be an essential part of one's *Higher Self Integration Program*. Consider taking workshops on various massage techniques that emphasize self-energetic massage. Study the following information and read other books on massage, reflexology, and acupressure or shiatsu, such as:

> *Self-Massage*, Jacqueline Young, Harper Collins, 1992.
> *Hand And Foot Reflexology A Self-Help Guide,* Kevin and Barbara Kunz,
>> Prentice hall, 1984.
> *The Complete Guide to Foot Reflexology*, Kevin and Barbara Kunz, Prentice Hall,
>> 1982 (with a section on anatomy and table of disorders).
> *Do It Yourself Shiatsu*, Wataru Ohashi, E.P. Dutton, 1976.
> *60 Second Shiatsu*, Eva Shaw, Mills and Sanderson, 1986.
> *Chakra Energy Massage*, Marianne Uhl, Lotus Light Publications, 1988.

**WHEN WE ARE COMMITTED TO HIGHER SELF INTEGRATION,
WE MAINTAIN A FOCUS ON ENERGY MANAGEMENT . . .**

MASSAGE is a healing art that is the practice of rubbing and pressing specific areas of the body to relieve pain, prevent illness, ease muscular tension, open up energy blocks, dispel tiredness, and reinforce depleted or unbalanced energy. The various massage techniques usually employed are finger and/or thumb pad pressure, slapping, kneading, squeezing, raking, gripping, cupping, fisting, tapping, chopping, limb rotation, palm press, hand and elbow press and digging.

REFLEXOLOGY (or ZONE THERAPY) is the study of the reflexes in the feet and hands corresponding to parts of the physical body. The feet and hands are worked to break down deposits that build up in them. These deposits consist of uric acid crystals and other waste products. Through massage techniques used on the feet and hands, reflexology causes relaxation responses and energy flow in the corresponding body parts. All of the reflex buttons or points in the feet and hands are connected to all glands, organs, and the endings of the nervous system. There are 10 longitudinal zones running the length of the body from the top of the head to the tips of the fingers and toes. By stimulating a certain zone button, you will affect the entire zone.

REFLEXOLOGY ZONE CHART (ILLUSTRATION # 2)

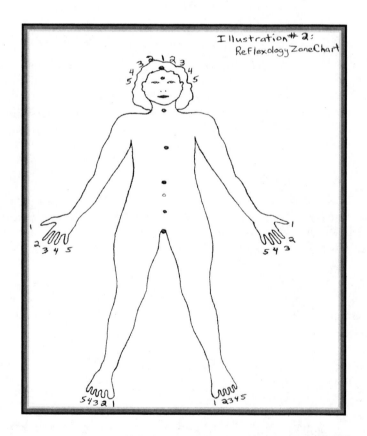

REFLEXOLOGY FEET CHARTS (ILLUSTRATION #3 on page 83)

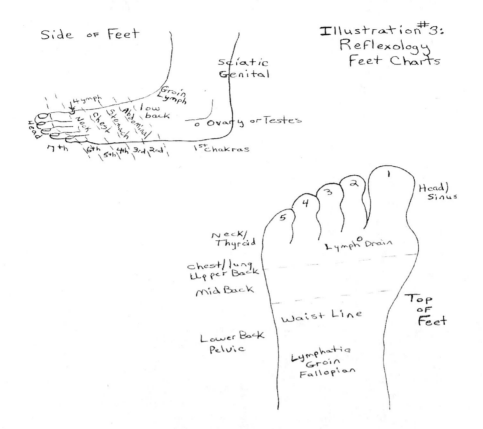

SIDE AND TOP OF FEET

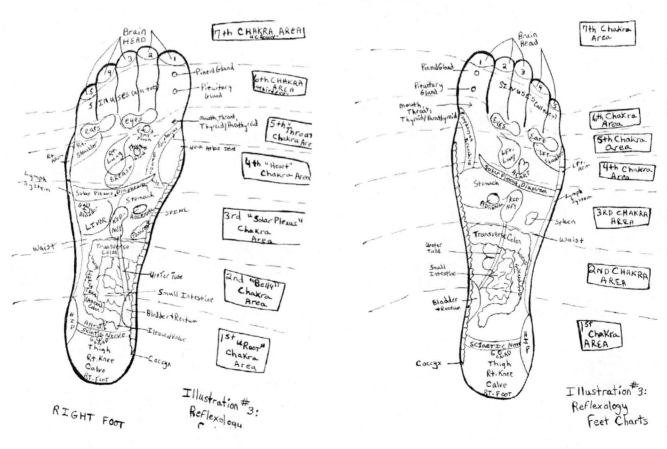

REFLEXOLOGY HAND CHARTS (ILLUSTRATION #4)

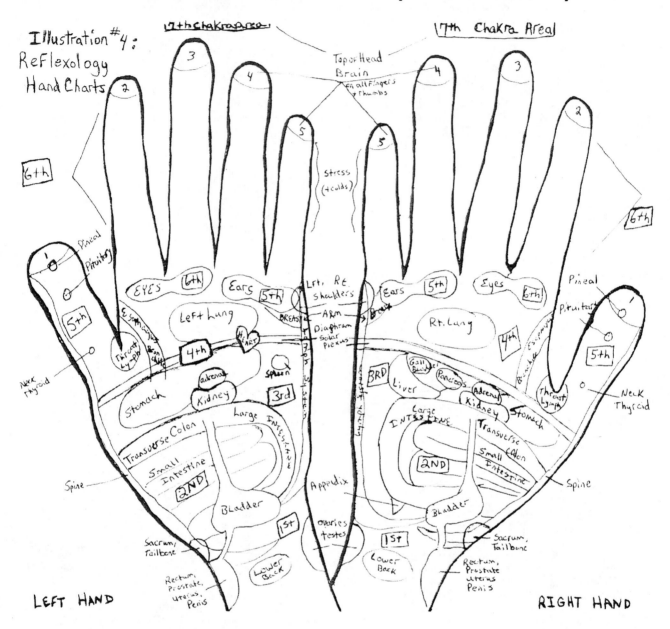

ACUPRESSURE/SHIATSU ("Acupuncture Without Needles") is an oriental massage where the fingers are pressed on particular parts of the body (or points) to ease aches, pains, symptoms of dis-ease, tension, fatigue, and blocked energy flow. These points, called Tsubos/Nadis, are specific places in the body's skin and muscular system, where nerves hurt or feel uncomfortable when the flow of energy through the body is blocked. There are 14 channels or Meridian Lines that our 361 Tsubos are along, through which the essential life force energy of our beings flow.

In order to work a point, one presses each Tsubo, one at a time, with a thumb or finger pad. The ball or flat part, not the tip, is used. The point is pressed and/or rotated, without rubbing or jiggling. Pressure is applied, coordinated with an exhale of breath. The timing of the pressure applied can range from 3 to 20 seconds and up to five minutes depending on the need and area. One will feel comfortable pain as pressure is applied to the plugged up energy point or minor chakra.

ACUPRESSURE/SHIATSU POINTS HELPFUL FOR HIGHER SELF INTEGRATION
(ILLUSTRATION # 5)

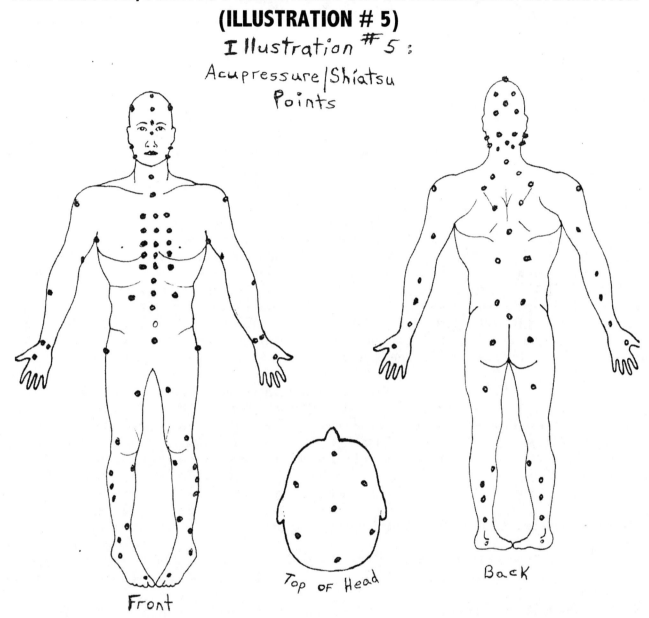

CHAKRA MASSAGE can be accomplished through reflexology, physical movement or exercise that specifically presses, works, or massages the areas where our chakras are located, and imagery that parallels the benefits of massage. Since our seven major chakras or energy centers are the points of connection at which energy flows from our etheric/spirit/energy body into our physical body, they are the links between our bodies. What affects our chakras, affects our physical body and vice versa.

The relaxing, healing, and rejuvenating powers of massage have been recognized and recorded throughout human history. Unblocking and increasing the flow of energy in our beings is of primary importance to well-being. It is also impossible to attain *Higher Self Integration* without clearing out our blocks in order to be able to run the higher vibrating energies associated with Soul and The Divine. REGULAR MASSAGE, INCLUDING REFLEXOLOGY AND ACUPRESSURE, not only helps us to keep up to date with what energies we have been running, but also helps to clear our energetic passage ways and centers for the purer, healthier, lighter energies of The Cosmos.

**IT IS IMPOSSIBLE TO ATTAIN HIGHER SELF INTEGRATION
WITHOUT CLEARING OUT OUR BLOCKS IN ORDER TO BE ABLE TO
RUN THE HIGHER VIBRATING ENERGIES OF SOUL AND THE DIVINE . . .**

ACTIVITY: <u>LET THE JUICES FLOW!</u>

On a regular, if not daily basis, check out your being and help yourself clear out the tensions of being human, unblock your energies, relax, and rejuvenate through self-massage. There are several ways you can go about this. You can do: whole body massages, certain programs related to symptomatology, concentrated chakra massage, and/or specific areas for maximum energetic release and flow. Some helpful tips are:

♦   Always WARM YOUR HANDS by rubbing and shaking them, and using mental imagery or visualizations to turn on and get the healing energies flowing through them.

♦   There are OILS for all reasons. Seek and you will find. In the meantime, don't forget about peanut oil, Tigerbalm, an Edgar Cayce formula named Penetrol, and an Ayurvedic Almond Oil Formula. AROMATHERAPY (using smells and scents of the oils from plant essences to help move and harmonize our energies) can be used by rubbing different therapeutic plant essences into our body's energy points and centers.

♦   Remember to APPLY PRESSURE ON your EXHALE. In using acupressure, try asserting pressure on the point moving your thumb counterclockwise for relaxation and clockwise for stimulation.

♦   Make sure that what you do to one side of your body, you also do on the other. WORK BOTH SIDES OF YOUR BODY.

♦   If one has limited time, yet wishes to affect the whole being as quickly as possible, thoroughly massage, using reflexology methods, both your feet for the "THE ZONE AFFECT."

♦   A FOOT ROLLER is a quick and effective way for working those foot points. Rolling one's feet right before going to sleep is a helpful thing to do. There are also back rollers of various sizes, tennis balls, golf balls and the like that can be used in various ways for those hard to reach areas. Rubbing or pressing various areas of one's back along a corner wall/door edge also works. Be sure to include around the wings where we tighten with negative pressure thoughts. Several times throughout your day, use a PALM PRESS for your eyes, pull and twist your hair for your scalp/head/brain, and use acupressure on both your right and left hand's HOKU POINT (located in the webbing between your thumb and the finger right next to it).

♦   On your head, make sure that you vibrate those ears and PULL those ear lobes. Stretch open your mouth and stick out that tongue as far as they will go. Make your eyes move side to side, up, down and all around.

♦   While massaging your throat, keep on breathing through your nose and swallowing. Really work that neck and those shoulders. Make sure you apply acupressure to all those chest points and DISCOVER those certain OUCH SPOTS of the arms. WORK ON THE BACK . . . Got a friend who can help? If not, go to the corner and collect back rollers. Do not pass go until you loosen up that back.

♦   THE HARA (area between the rib cage and pelvis) is very important for energy flow, relaxing and health. Rub clockwise with your palms, finger poke, squeeze and knead all that skin and those organs.

♦   POUND those buttocks. JIGGLE those thighs on down to your little twinkies. PRESS AND POKE. Make sure you use acupressure on those sexual organ foot and hand correspondents. We're talking hormones here and the difference between biochemical hysteria and harmony.

♦   Learn more about your bodymindspirit and Beingwork, including bodywork. Have fun. Be creative. MARVEL AT THE WONDERS OF YOUR BEING.

Enjoy!

WHAT IT NEEDS . . .

The more we go for Soul Attunement through discovering and developing our *Higher Selves*, recognition of our being's particular needs becomes clearer and more easily attainable. What we need in each moment is very much connected to where we are at in our individual Soul Development or Level of Soul Consciousness. As Earth-based human-bodied Souls, our beings need our daily conscious attention directed towards three areas: FUELING, CLEANSING, AND CONNECTING. To reach our highest potential, to live a lifestyle where we not only access but become our *Higher Selves*, we have to ingest energies that vitalize our beings, clear out those energies that weigh us down, and connect with the energies that lift us up.

◆ FUELING

One of the primary ways we manage our energetic beings is through the fuel or energies we ingest or allow to interpenetrate our physical, mental, and spirit bodies. Our physical bodies need the vitamins, minerals, and other substances that are a part of the foods available on our planet. It is also real important to know and understand that the foods we ingest affect our minds (feelings and thoughts) and our spirits. In addition, our minds/bodies/spirits have to have the revitalizing chemicals, vibrations, and releases (energies) that only come through sleep, rest and relaxation, sunlight, and the air we breathe. And last but not least, our beings need to energetically feed upon positive and joyful relationships, environments, situations, thoughts, and feelings.

For *HSI*, it is essential to EAT, THINK, AND FEEL CONSCIOUSLY: with full attention on and recognition of what you are ingesting (eating, thinking, and feeling), why you choose to eat/think/feel those substances (energies), and how they are affecting you. Sure, organic whole foods with a focus on low fat, high fiber make a lot of sense if one is oriented towards health and wholeness. But if you are into using foods to "stuff your feelings," to hide your power by destroying yourself with foods (and thoughts/feelings) that help create dis-ease, artificially and harmfully control your energy (as one does with caffeine, alcohol, nicotine and other plant drugs), and overeat or starve because of self-hatred, then your food-sabotaging habits have to be addressed first. You are out-of-control and need to LEARN NEW ENERGY-MANAGEMENT SKILLS, as you REWORK your offending and destructive habit-forming thoughts, feelings, attitudes, and behaviors, including the foods/substances you feed your being.

As one reprograms oneself with life-affirming and loving thoughts, feelings, and behaviors, the natural desire to eat or consume what is best for one/you becomes your moment-to-moment reality. At the same time, spontaneous, fun, playful energy and behaviors are just as important to our well-being as is disciplined, stable and regular lifestyle patterning. When one isn't running addictive behaviors to cover-up one's spiritual/cocreative yearnings, then eating a little chocolate icecream, once in a while, is cool. Remember that balance is the key!

Also know that our human bodies have incredibly powerful recuperating and healing abilities, if supported by our thoughts, feelings, and the energies we run. If we can get our body chemistry out of synch by the foods we eat, we can also get it back-in-the-groove. The bottom line is that your Soul and your Spirit Guides all know what will work best for you in the short and long run of your journey. Tune in! Listen! Feel! Watch! Your body, let alone mind and spirit, tells you when you are blowing it and when you are nurturing it wisely. The choice is yours!

TO REACH OUR HIGHEST POTENTIAL, WE HAVE TO INGEST ENERGIES THAT VITALIZE OUR BEINGS, CLEAR OUT THOSE ENERGIES THAT WEIGH US DOWN, AND CONNECT WITH ENERGIES THAT LIFT US UP . . .

******** *HELPFUL HINTS* ********

***In the PLANT NUTRIENTS DEPARTMENT**, there are many different diets that are proselytized as the healthiest way to eat. Again, we are each unique Beings all going through different combinations of events, stages, needs, resources, and intentions. YOUR SOUL KNOWS BEST WHAT YOU NEED TO EAT and not eat. However, if you are at the stage where your lower self out-screams your *Higher Self*, then these suggestions, that take into account the different stages of *The Higher Self Integration Process* (Levels of Soul Consciousness) and the realities of humanity's industrial pollution and modern stress, could prove helpful.

In general, the more fresh, uncooked, organic, whole fruits, veges, nuts, and seeds one can include on a daily basis the more vital lifeforce energy one will be consuming. Whole grains and legumes are also an energizing Earth-gift worthy of appreciating on a daily basis. BE SMART ABOUT WHAT YOU INGEST in your precious body. Go for immune enhancement, not immune destruction. Plant drugs (such as caffeine, nicotine, and alcohol), chemical preservatives, additives, dyes, and various other carcinogens easily imbalance the delicate biochemical balance that is required for health and real vitality.

LOOK AT HOW VARIOUS FOODS AND SUBSTANCES AFFECT YOUR ENERGY LEVEL, which includes your chakras. Adjust your consumption to an eating program that vitalizes you in a way that doesn't lift you up just to send you crashing down, as do white sugar and caffeine. Be attentive to how the energies and realities of animal, bird, mammal and fish or seafood consumption affect you attitudinally, physically, etherically, energetically, and environmentally. Due to interconnectedness, we cannot abuse the critters of our world without abusing ourselves.

Our planet's "SUPERFOODS" (grasses, fungus, sprouts, algae's, seaweeds, and others) and natural pharmaceuticals (its bountiful and diverse HERBS AND SPICES) often prove energizing, therapeutic, and helpful to a particular focus we are centered on. For examples: If one is consciously working on expanding one's mental capacity through various mind techniques, the herb Ginkgo Biloba, which increases our brain's oxygenation process, could go hand-in-hand with one's other efforts. Many people find a Microbiotic Diet helpful when they have manifested cancerous dis-eases, but find it unhealthy to eat Microbioticly once they are back in balance.

What works best is for you to find out what energizes and vitalizes you in the various stages of life you experience. AS YOU CHANGE, SO WILL YOUR NUTRITIONAL OR ENERGETIC NEEDS. In *The Higher Self Integration Process*, you will need to eat differently depending on where you are in your Soul Consciousness and Integration realities. If you are in a stage of going into deep trance/meditative states, undereating alive fresh foods may be just the thing for you while you may need to overeat some heavier foods in order to get more earth-grounded for visiting with your childhood family.

Be aware that Earth's Herbs, nature's drugs a-la-natural, can be dangerous and unhealthy if improperly used. The use of herbs is covered in various books and workshops, so please INVESTIGATE AND TUNE IN, before you turn on either naturally or chemically. Know that herbs work in a more whole way when used in combination or compounded. Remember that although herbs and other plant substances can prove helpful biochemically, it's up to you to CHANGE THE STRESS FACTORS THAT ARE CAUSING YOUR ORIGINAL IMBALANCE. What we eat is only a part of the whole. It is not the be-all end-all by itself to balance, wholeness, and higher attunement.

A few specific resources which have proven helpful for *Higher Self Integration*-oriented others are as follows: The information in the *Naturopathic Handbook Of Herbal Formulas: A Practical & Concise Herb User's Guide* by Herbal Research Publications, Inc.-and- *Spiritual Nutrition And The Rainbow Diet* by Gabriel Cousens, M.D. The most comprehensive superfood formula (which also works ethericly) that I have found is a product called "Pure Synergy" put out by The Synergy Company, Box 2901 CVSR, Moab, Utah 84532, www.synergy-co.com. It blends over 60 of nature's most potent superfoods.

*** **In the REST AND RELAXATION DEPARTMENT**, each person's needs will be different depending on all the various factors that are involved in an individual's life. At the same time, THE FUNDAMENTAL LAW OF NATURE that speaks to the need for BALANCED REST AND ACTIVITY applies to us human animals, no matter what level of consciousness or development we are at. If you want to pump, then also chill out. Ebb and flow. It is crucial that we REENERGIZE THROUGH SLEEP, MEDITATIVE STATES, DO-NOTHING (QUIET) TIMES, LIVING RELAXED, AND JUST HANGING OUT WITH OUR SOULS, NATURE, SPIRIT GUIDES, AND ALL THAT CONNECTS US DIRECTLY TO THE DIVINE.

For most of us sleep is essential, not only because it is a state that rebalances us biochemically, but because it is a state where our lower personalities take a back seat to our Souls. It is in the sleep state that our Soul's and Higher Guidance can help us to therapeutically work through and learn from our daily Earthly happenings, even if we are protesting our lessons while in a waking state. Through dreams, whether we remember them or consciously understand them or not, and through nightly Soul Travels to different dimensions and Soul Realms (whether we recall them or not), we are all given information and energies which can help us in our daily lives, if we so let them. It is also in the dream state that other Souls, that are in spirit form only and Souls that we live with in human form, can work with us on a mental Soul-to-Soul level.

Since many of us live our Earthly lives consciously cut off from these contacts and learning opportunities, THE SLEEP STATE BECOMES MUCH MORE IMPORTANT TO THE CONNECTION OF OUR SOUL. However, we can do some of the Soul Sleep State Work in our daily awake-state lives by UTILIZING CONSCIOUSLY CHOSEN MEDITATIVE AND TRANCE STATES. Likewise, if we use our daily awake hours to do the EMOTIONAL CLEARING AND BELIEF RECONSTRUCTION work that keeps us clear to run Higher Energies, then our sleep states become more of a CREATIVE OUTLET FOR OUR SOULS in connection with other Souls and The Higher Source. Our sleep states then evolve into wisdom oriented happenings that energize us thoroughly and are more easily remembered and carried over into our awakened states.

Most beneficial to our Souls is LEARNING AND INCORPORATING THE ABILITY TO DO EVERYTHING NECESSARY FOR OUR EARTHLY LIVES WHILE IN A RELAXED STATE. The relaxed state is one in which we do not resist what is happening but instead flow from an awareness that we have everything we need to do what we need to do for the best of all concerned. Calmness and the ability "to lighten up" comes from trusting in Divine Order. Living relaxed provides us a steady source of vitalizing and cocreative energy that is far more powerful than a hyper-anxious-adrenaline-driven state.

We feed and fuel ourselves through our emotions, thoughts, and behaviors. Negative thoughts stimulate negative emotions and energies that keep us disconnected from our Soul and the Higher Energies of The Holoverse. The fuel our Beings need in order to run our Higher Self Energies and be Holy Healthy come from love, joy, devotion, confidence, peace-of-mind, wisdom and knowledge, enthusiasm, appreciation, wonder, rejoicing creativity, and other POSITIVE ENERGETIC DOERS AND CONNECTORS.

The most enduring energies we can load our systems with are those of Higher Connection. TRUE LOVE, NATURE ATTUNEMENT, SPIRIT CONNECTION AND DIRECT CONTACT WITH GOD/GODDESS can make and keep us higher than any food, drug, material success, toxic emotion-moving scenario, or adrenaline-pumping activity. And all these healthier and higher energies are more accessible through a relaxed and rested state of mind, body, and spirit.

***In the SKY ENERGIES DEPARTMENT**, it's a given that we all refuel through sunlight and the air we breathe. Concerning sunlight, there again, your individual balance level has to be sought. In general, some SUNLIGHT taken in daily, directly through our eyes and skin for biochemical health and energetic refueling, is necessary. Take care to use the sun's nurturing energizing aspects and not its frying burnout potential.

How we breathe is directly connected to relaxation, brainpower, healthy cell stimulation, and the energetic fueling of our bodybeings. For us humans on Earth, BREATH IS LIFE both figuratively and literally. In *The Higher Self Integration Process*, one cannot separate the quality of one's breathing with the quality of one's Higher Abilities and Attunement. Most of us learned to breathe shallowly. To aid in the revitalization of our energies and the connective life force necessary in Higher Communication, we must LEARN TO BREATHE AND TO USE OUR BREATH RELAXED, DEEPLY, INTENTIONALLY, AND WITH POWER.

LEARN AND PRACTICE DIFFERENT BREATHING EXERCISES AND SKILLS. Become conscious of your breath and breathing ability. Use your breathing to help yourself enter deeper states of consciousness and Divine Awareness. Use your breath in synch with your bodily movement. Use your breath while in meditative, trance, and prayer states. Use your breath to help move blocked energies/emotions. Use your breath and breathing as an energy mover and enhancer in order to ease up, lighten up, go deeper, stretch, release, let go and flow.

YOUR   SOUL   KNOWS   BEST . . .

ACTIVITY: THE BREATH OF LIFE

Many of the books in *A Soul's Delight's* bibliography contain various breathing exercises, activities, and uses necessary for whole health and active spirituality. The Yoga/Yogic systems stress various breathing styles and practices. The three breathing exercises listed below are helpful for energy movement, expansion, transformation, and attunement if applied on a daily basis:

1. **THREE-TIERED BREATHING:** Very attentively and consciously, breathe deeply in and out at a slow pace. While taking in a long full breath, breathe through your nose allowing your belly, ribcage and chest to move out as your Being fills with air. This will automatically lift and straighten your back and spine. Hold this full breath and body position for a few seconds. As you slowly and gradually exhale through your nose, allow your belly, ribcage, and chest to naturally cave back in. Build up your ability to breathe deeply in this particular way to five-minute sessions.

2. **TIGER BREATH:** While kneeling on the floor, move your body forward so that you are on all fours, with your knees and feet evenly behind you and your shoulders aligned above your hands, which are flat on the floor. Your hands and knees/feet are all about 12 inches apart. As you exhale, allow the breath to move your head in towards your knees, rounding and arching your back, emptying and sinking in your belly and chest. As you inhale, allow the breath to move your head back out and your back and head to arch into a swayback position as your tongue also hangs out. Your belly, ribcage, and chest will inflate. Do these two inhale-exhale movements in a slow, continuous rhythm, building up to between 5-10 minutes, allowing your body to bend and dip as you move from position to position, becoming fluid in both breath and movement.

(continued on page 91)

ILLUSTRATION #6 TIGER BREATH

   3. FIRE BREATHING: This one is a real energy mover and builder, so start out doing
it for a minute leading up to 3-5 minutes at a time. Watch for your own dizziness factor and adjust
accordingly. While kneeling on the floor, safely bend backwards until your knees are in front of you, your feet
tucked in back beside you, your head is on the floor behind your knees, and your hands are grasping both your
feet. Your elbows are holding you steady on the floor, helping to arch your chest up as your head is resting on
the floor. Holding this position, you will breathe very deeply and rapidly through the nose, allowing your chest
and back to naturally move up and down as you fire-breathe away. Expect to make breathing noises and to get
hot!

ILLUSTRATION #7   FIRE BREATHING

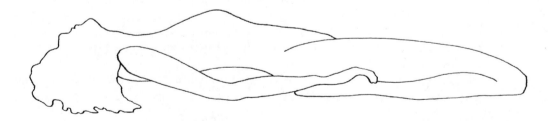

OUR BEINGS REQUIRE CLEANSING ON ALL LEVELS: BODY, MIND, AND SPIRIT . . .

♦   CLEANSING

Earth living can be more than a little dirty and congesting for our Beings. We can accumulate toxins from the body processes we go through and from the negative and poisonous thoughts, emotions, reactions, substances, and pollutants that are a part of our environment. OUR BEINGS REQUIRE CLEANSING ON ALL LEVELS: BODY, MIND, AND SPIRIT. Our Souls have a hard time being felt and heard through slimy clogged chakras, the distracting pains of our bodies, and the crazy self-destructive thoughts and behaviors of our minds. TOXIC THOUGHTS, EMOTIONS, ENERGIES, AND CHEMICALS HAVE TO BE CLEANSED.

Tears are an essential part of the cleansing required in *The Higher Self Integration Process*. Not only do they biochemically release toxins, they are a primary emotional release that helps to wash away the accumulative effects of negative thoughts and feelings. Learn to be able to cry when doing heavy emotional release work. Work with the rhythm required for sobbing as well as for sniffling. THERE IS A FINE ART AND SKILL TO RELEASING THROUGH TEARS, which is necessary for real release and transformation.

There are particular HERB COMBINATIONS that act as real cleansers to our body organs, such as our liver. Be prepared that facilitating seasonal cleansing efforts can stimulate emotional and behavioral releases. On a daily basis, our bodies need to DRINK LOTS OF CLEAN WATER for natural flushing of toxins.

The more transformational work you are involved in the more your body will require in daily liquid consumption. Remember our motto: FLUSH, FLUSH, FLUSH!

FASTING is a real cleanser both physically and etherically. There are many different types and lengths of fasting. Here again, you have to pick a type of fast that will work specifically for you. Be aware of the first 48 hour mega-irritation and halitosis reactions that come pouring out of your Being along with the chemical toxins. Take special care and attention of yourself before, during, and after your fast. Gradual is the key word when it comes to breaking one's fast.

SWEATING is a wonderful way to let all those waste products or overconsumed nasties come pouring out. Saunas, hotubs, mineral baths, aromatherapy, massage, chiropractic exercises, skin brushing, and natural herbal skin care products are not only oriented towards toxin release, they can also be a lot of fun and feel good all at the same time. Remember another one of our motto's: RELEASE AND NURTURE.

MOVEMENT, and lots of it, is essential for our beings. It's all about energy flowing in, around, and out: ENERGETIC MOVEMENT. And there's nothing quite like the movement of our physical body to stir up stagnant and blocked energy.   Movement creates change and transformation. All of our energetic parts, such as our chakras and our auras, as well as our hearts, brains, and nervous systems, need movement, both mentally and physically induced. It is very important to the *Higher Self Integration Process* to USE MENTAL SKILLS REGULARLY, SUCH AS VISUALIZATION AND AFFIRMATION, TO KEEP OUR ENERGY FLOW IN A HEALTHY STATE.

It is as equally important to MOVE OUR PHYSICAL BODY REGULARLY IN WAYS THAT PROVIDE AEROBIC STIMULATION TO ALL OF OUR BODY PARTS. WALKING, HIKING, SWIMMING AND THE LIKE not only help our bodies to flow healthier and to release unwanted toxins, they also help readjust a lot of our mental/emotional uptightness. In addition, these types of activities help clear out our etheric systems and pour revitalizing energies into our beings.

Where physical movement is involved, remember to always WARM UP, STRETCH, GO FOR THE BALANCED GUSTO, KEEP YOUR THOUGHTS CONNECTED TO WHAT YOU ARE DOING, AND COOL DOWN GRADUALLY.   As you heat up, become aware of the irritations, frustrations, and negative thoughts and feelings that resurface as a result of toxic activation. And then move beyond that release into the state that activated endorphins help to stimulate. Coast into the natural high of movement and of connection with your body and the medium you are using or moving in. Sweat, human, sweat!

Afterwards, go back and WORK THROUGH ANY NEGATIVE THOUGHTS AND FEELINGS that were stimulated as you first began to heat up. You'll be much more able to make progress on any mental and emotional stuckness after a physical workout. Our human bodies can move vigorously without having to be pounded into injury. Once the mind releases its fear of movement, it can really hit a groove. Every muscle and organ, and even every single cell of our body needs to be worked. If we let it, our human body will move and flow quite naturally on its own when set free. Visualizations and affirmations help to give it permission and guidance to move as it was meant to be moved. Remember our motto: MOVEMENT IS MARVELOUS!

ACTIVITY: **DANCE OF THE SOUL**

Our bodies need to move and OUR SOULS LOVE TO DANCE. One of the most delightful and productive activities of *The Higher Self Integration or Soul Attunement Process* is uninhibited, freeform, inspirited dance. It not only works every part of your body and etheric systems, it also in-spirits your Being. We're talking about a blood and heart pumping, muscle stretching and building, joint lubricating, chakra clean out, mind liberation celebration of life or Soul Dancing.

1. Do what you have to do to WORK THROUGH YOUR FEARS, INSECURITIES, AND DISPARAGING THOUGHTS ABOUT YOUR BODY AND MOVEMENT. Release emotionally, reprogram your misbeliefs and dis-beliefs, find a supportive dance environment, take dance classes, and gradually build up your body to be able to do freeform, ecstatic movement. Do whatever it takes to get into the state of mind and body in which it doesn't matter what others think about your body and its movement. Inspirited dance cannot happen if you are bound by put downs and I can'ts.

2. The type of music you use to help free your body and Soul to move is very important. Look for rhythms that make your body want to jump and jive, spin and shake. There may be times when it is necessary to move through an anger buildup you've held on to before being able to feel the joy of life once again. Rock and Roll works well in moving from a depressed energetic state into releasing the anger that's bound one up. World beat music with lots of drumming and percussion really allows our bodies to tap into an ancient freeing rhythm that can lift us higher. If the music has lyrics, for the most part they need to be joyful, uplifting words.

3. In a safe space, allow your body to move naturally to the rhythms you are listening to. Your body will build upon that movement if you allow it. As you heat up, ENCOURAGE YOUR BODY TO MOVE IN WAYS THAT WORK ALL YOUR CHAKRAS, ORGANS, MUSCLES, ETC. Make sure you move both sides of your body. Use the floor and air. Bend and shake, leap and squat, sing and make noises. Vibrate, stretch, twirl. Kick, shimmy, and BREATHE. Let your sweat pour, your mind stop thinking, and your spirit soar.

**WHEN OUR SELF-EXPRESSION IS OUR SOUL-EXPRESSION,
WE ARE LIVING IN AND CONNECTED TO THE LIGHT FROM WHICH WE CAME . . .**

♦ CONNECTING

In order to be whole, to be *Higher Self Integrated*, one has to be CONNECTED: with one's Soul, with Earth and nature, with other Souls both in human form and those only in spirit body, and with The Divine Creator. Connection, or being plugged in energetically with whole forms of energy, is even more important to us humans than is food. There have been a few documented cases of humans existing healthily without food, feeding directly instead on The Divine Light, God/Goddess.

WE NEED LOVE, and real love is connection. When our self-expression is our Soul-expression, we are living in and connected to The Light From Which We Came. And that DIVINE LOVELIGHT is our true energy, fuel, and fire. We are unable to truly connect with our Souls if we come from a personality orientation of disrespect. Connection cannot occur without respect, to HONOR WITH CONSIDERATION AND APPRECIATION. Our Beings need to live in WONDER AND THANKFULNESS for life and everything it contains. The vibration of appreciation feeds our Soul and lifts us higher. Add CONSCIOUS INTENTION WITH APPRECIATION and you have care-filled connection.

That honoring has to be towards our Planet Earth and all its critters, our human world, and the dimensional world (the realm of spirit). It is just as important and necessary to be DIRECTLY CONNECTED TO NATURE AND TO SOULS EXISTING IN THE HIGHER REALMS, as it is to have LOVING RELATIONSHIPS WITH OTHER HUMANS AND WITH OURSELVES. Our Beings need TIMES OF PRAYER, MEDITATION, AND THE SILENCE in order to achieve the states of mind necessary for direct connection with Beings or energies that vibrate at a purer and higher frequency than we do.

Learning to enter into the mental pathways that enable us to communicate with the world of spirit is not only necessary to being whole and Soul Attuned, but is also a real help in juggling all the elements of earth living for the best of all concerned. Land Devas are so much more aware of the needs of our planet and all its species and can help us to manage better that which we are CO-STEWARDING. Our Guardian Angels know us a hundred times better than we know ourselves and can help us to stay safely on our Higher Path. Spirit Guides and Teachers are the spirit world's cream of the professors and can help fill us in on information in a flash that might take lifetimes to access rationally on our own.

There are certain energies especially available to Souls while we journey on and with Planet Earth. The ability to TRAVEL THE PLANET, being exposed to its abundant POWER PLACES, life/energetic forms, and with Souls at all the various levels of development, is quite a learning vehicle. Rigidity in personality restricts the amount of Soul energy/connection it is possible and necessary to make. TRAVELING WITH AN OPEN HEART AND MIND is one of the most valuable learning tools there is in *The Higher Self Integration Process.*

The mind and body altering substances that living on this planet provides can also be useful in helping one to open up and to change what has not worked for us in terms of health and creativity. However, the personality pattern of addiction, which is taught most of us, very much gets in the way towards balanced and healthy usage of The Earth's Energies, which include mind and body altering substances/drugs. INTENTIONALITY is extremely important concerning this area of choice. Using an Earth substance to open up one's vision and thinking processes gives an entirely different experience and outcome than if we are using that substance to escape the life we have manifested.

The bottom line is that we all need to BE VERY CAREFUL AND DISCRIMINATING ABOUT THE ENERGIES WE RUN AND BRING INTO OUR BEINGS. We need to learn to run from or off of Soul and Divine energy, not the energies of a mind/body altering plant/chemical substance. Opening up and transforming our thought, emotional, and behavioral processes works clearer and with less traps when we do it through the power of our own minds, not the power of a plant or chemical.

DIRECTLY CONNECTING TO NATURE, the Earth's world of plant, mineral and animal kingdoms, etc. is accessible through FOCUS AND INTENT, AN OPEN MIND AND HEART, THE SKILLS OF LISTENING, OBSERVING AND SENSING, AND WONDER, APPRECIATION, AND THANKFULNESS. Our Soul's feed off of our contacts and connection to and in nature. Surrounding ourselves with nature's energies and opportunities is vitally important for *Higher or True Self Integration.*

Another opportunity for learning which Earth living provides is available to us all through the energies of sexuality. These procreative, evolutionary, and cocreative male and female energies can help ignite the sacred, spiritual be-all-you-can-be fire that lies within us all. The problem is that most of us are taught a very ego oriented, self indulgent, negative, if not frightening, view of our sexual energies. And it is highly important to the welfare of our Beings to be very CAREFUL ABOUT WHO WE DIRECTLY EXCHANGE OUR SEXUAL ENERGY WITH IN THE MOST INTIMATE WAYS.

Most of us have kept our sexual energies bound or under the control of our lower personality. As a result, we abuse and/or neglect these energies, often living in confusion and fear of the outer desires that come out warped from our inner desire for spiritual reconnection. Sexual energy is a potent life force energy which houses creation and manifestation. Understood and used consciously with true connection-awareness, it is quite a useful current which helps lead us to true Earth prosperity and wholeness. LIFT THESE ENERGIES OUT OF THE DOMAIN OF THE LOWER SELF PERSONALITY where it is interwoven with power, control, and self-esteem issues involving others and ourselves. Then they can be used cocreatively by our Soul in our journey home to The Infinite Intelligence/Light/Love.

THE VIBRATION OF APPRECIATION FEEDS OUR SOULS AND LIFTS US HIGHER . . .

ACTIVITY: __TAKE ME HIGHER__

Wonder, thankfulness, and appreciation are energies or thinking, feeling, and behaving processes that bring the JOY vibration into our beings and life. They are essential Soul qualities that need to be a daily, if not moment-to-moment, part of our Earthly Lives.

1. Rigid, judgmental ways of seeing things are a hindrance to appreciating all that surrounds us. Every time you are not in appreciation, wonder, and thankfulness towards what you see (be it a human, the weather, a painting, a plant, an insect, etc.), FIGURE OUT WHAT THINKING AND FEELING PATTERNS ARE BLOCKING YOUR ABILITY TO GRACIOUSLY TAKE IN WHAT IS HAPPENING. Behind your negativity or sarcasm, do you find fear, competition, not-good-enough judgments, and opinionated projected protection? Learn to release these chains on your life so that you can take in all the beauty around you. We're starving ourselves energetically when we refuse to enjoy the life we are given.

2. Take time as often as you can to SLOW DOWN, DEEP BREATH, RELAX, AND REALLY GET INTO WHAT YOU ARE DOING OR SEEING. Open all your senses to that honeysuckle bush, to the baby in your arms, to the cat upon your lap, to the strawberry entering your mouth, etc. Deeply look, smell, taste, touch, hear, feel and sense. Enjoy every moment.

3. LOOK FOR THE GOD/GOOD SELF THAT IS IN EVERY HUMAN BEING, even if it seems to be deeply buried under a lot of garbage. Find the parts that sparkle, the moments of truth, the glow of life that is still within them. LEARN TO CONNECT WITH THEIR SOUL, bypassing the lower-self personality. Yes, I know that this is easier said than done. However, the entire *Higher Self Integration Process* is about learning how to do this. So hang in there, keep trying, and stay aware of what you are doing. Ask yourself, "Am I relating Soul-to-Soul?"

4. Keep on expressing your thankfulness on a daily basis for everything that comes your way: for the food you eat, the clothes you wear, the nature you see, the appliances you use, the people you communicate with, the body that works for you, etc. There are tons of things to appreciate and be thankful for in each day of Earthly Living. PRACTICE THANKFULNESS and it will soon become a natural way to think, feel, and live. And you'll have a much better time.

5. BE AWARE OF AND CONSCIOUSLY THINK ABOUT THE INTERCONNECTEDNESS OF EVERYTHING IN YOUR LIFE. For instance: Take a piece of food such as cheese or an apple. In your mind, trace all the people, things, processes, etc. that were involved in making that one piece of food a part of the nourishment you require in order to be alive on Earth. And be thankful for that sunlight, that soil, that water, that farmer, that plow, that packaging, etc. If you practice this with many of the objects, people, and places that are a part of your life, you're guaranteed to see things in a much more appreciative mode. Allow yourself to get a real kick out of life. Allow yourself to be naturally lifted higher. ALLOW YOURSELF TO "BE HIGH ON LIFE"!

CHAPTER SIX

ENERGETIC CHOICES

WE BECOME SO FAMILIAR WITH ENERGETIC THINKING, FEELING, AND BEHAVING PATTERNS THAT WE GET STUCK IN THEM, LOOSING THE AWARENESS THAT THESE ENERGY PATTERNS ARE STILL A CHOICE . . .

RECOGNIZE

Again, an all-encompassing concept to take hold of in *The Higher Self Integration Process* **is expressed in these two words: ENERGY MANAGEMENT.** As Souls in human bodies upon The Earth Plane, our health, happiness, and wholeness is interdependent on the types or vibratory rates of the energies we take in, produce ourselves, and give out or release. We will just keep spinning a web of confusion and pain, unless we take conscious control of the energies we choose to run. Yes, the word CHOICE is our energetic lightning rod.

We take in energy through the air we breathe, the food we ingest, the places we live, work, and recreate in, and the Beings we come in contact and are intimate with. Our other primary sources of energy are the things we do, the thoughts we think, the beliefs we operate from, the intentions we run, and the emotions we feel. Through time and repetition, we all form HABITUAL ENERGETIC PATTERNING of various types that interact with all the elements in our daily lives. We become so familiar with these energetic thinking, feeling, and behaving patterns that we get stuck in them.

We then loose the awareness that these energy patterns, through which we literally and figuratively feed or fuel ourselves, are still a choice. We can run them. We can choose not to run them. We can release them. We can choose to change and transform them. We can run others instead. And we can choose to rework the combinations.

The first step towards incorporating our freedom of conscious choice involves one's READINESS FACTOR. If one is caught in a cycle of negative thinking, intense emotional dramas, and addictive behavior, then a "a crack in the egg" has to happen. At those crucial moments in our lives, we cry out "There's got to be more to life than this!" We then begin to reach through the crack that has split us open. And our Soul starts to speak.

The yearning for light, love and God/Goddess starts searing our consciousness, whether our lower or mass consciousness conditioned self wants it to or not. It is at this point that learning about our real life choices involving the energies we can choose to run is of utmost importance. We have to not only reload our intellect with the truth about life, but we have to rework, step-by-step, bit-by-bit, the way we have chosen and been programmed to think, feel, and behave.

PERSONAL PROCESS WORK or becoming aware of (RECOGNIZING), letting go of (RELEASING), and consciously reprogramming (RECONSTRUCTING) our thoughts, feelings, and behaviors is absolutely essential. This takes longterm commitment, focus, persistence, and patience. For most of us, it will be the intensest and hardest part of the *Higher Self Integration Process.* Thankfully though, Personal Process Work has many stages and levels that, when acknowledged and understood, help to keep us clearing out and moving on. We have to be able to RECOGNIZE (which is simultaneous with readiness), RELEASE, and RECONSTRUCT our emotional, thinking, and behaving patterns we carry: 1. FROM THE PRESENT MOMENT, 2. FROM ALL OF OUR PRESENT LIFE, and 3. FROM THE CULMINATION OF OUR PAST EARTHLY LIVES or THE WHOLE OF OUR SOUL.

Many of our lower self thinking, feeling, and behaving patterns are self-perpetuating, entrenched within us. Taking off our blinders and being able to not only see but UNDERSTAND WHAT WE ARE DOING AND WHAT WE COULD BE DOING instead requires continual blasting of our energies through AWARENESS, CONFRONTATION, AND DELIBERATELY LETTING GO OF OUR OLD WAYS, HABITS, AND PERSONALITY PATTERNING. Most of us have learned well how to resist truth and change. We will cling to what we know (our blocks or stuck energy), even if it is self-destructively full of pain. We do this by utilizing forms of resistance such as: repression, refusal, rebellion, sabotage, projection, scape-goating, and blame.

Most of our blocks or stuck energy come from our present and past life experiences in which we reacted with strong, negative emotions that we held on to, fed off of, repressed, or denied. When outside patterns do not fit with our inner-programmed patterns (our expectations and illusions), we tend to respond with negative feelings/emotions such as anger, jealousy, shame, frustration, irritation, and resentment thus creating our experience of unhappiness. EMOTIONS ARE CURRENTS OF ENERGY WITH DIFFERENT FREQUENCIES THAT PASS THROUGH US IF WE ALLOW THEM TO. If held on to, either consciously or subconsciously, these energies attract to us circumstances and experiences that run on the same frequencies.

If you are not aware or conscious of the emotions, intentions, and personality parts you run, then those that are the strongest (or so programmed that they are unconsciously, automatically triggered) will win out over the other parts. Our emotions are the most magnetic part of ourselves when it comes to getting what we want. Becoming aware of and comprehending the emotions, or energy currents, we run is a necessary step in understanding how we attract, manifest, and are responsible for everything in our lives.

The first step in consciously choosing which emotions to run for Soul Attunement or *The Higher Self Integration Process* involves KNOWING AND UNDERSTANDING WHAT AND HOW EACH SPECIFIC EMOTION INFLUENCES, ATTRACTS, AND ENERGETICLY REPRESENTS IN OUR LIVES. Yelling at someone is a reaction that looks like anger (an emotional response stimulated through a sense of unfairness or wrongness), but it could also be frustration, irritation, shame, or jealousy. Each of these emotions or energies affect our bodymindspirit and life in different ways.

When we are watching someone have an emotional reaction on the outside, we are guaranteed that the specific type of energy they are running is also affecting them on the inside. Often, what you think you are seeing is not what is really going on or the whole picture. With intense emotion, the present reaction is usually caught up in unresolved issues from the past.

STUDY EMOTIONS! Certain emotions have behind them certain memories and beliefs. Each different emotion affects the physical body and well being in its own way. Every emotion we run has its own intent, its own purpose, its own energetic signature, and its own end result.

Take the emotion frustration. Frustration comes from, represents, and warns us of the feeling of being stuck. It isn't a real mover like pure anger fueled by injustice can be. It's not an energy strong enough to blow the stuckness apart, yet it is not weak enough to be able to just ignore. It is a spinner. Frustration sets in the mind and joints, freezing one's ability to move. It causes one's immune system to attack itself because it doesn't have a clear powerful outlet. Running frustration towards oneself is a way to hold oneself back, to limit and restrict one's own power and abilities. Running frustration towards others means being hooked into a blame pattern that is based on feeling powerless and lacking control. Frustration tells us that we are holding back on our Soul's abilities.

Hurt represents feelings of unworthiness and low self-esteem. It drains us of our vital life force, depressing our energy. Over time, it slows us down, causes toxins to build up, and damages our heart. Running hurt is based on the belief system that we're not good enough and unworthy of being supported and respected in our lives. It holds us back and keeps us powerless, unless we change the self-annihilating beliefs and behavior patterning behind our hurt. Hurt tells us that we have issues of love.

> **BECOMING AWARE OF THE EMOTIONS, OR ENERGY CURRENTS, WE RUN IS A NECESSARY STEP IN UNDERSTANDING HOW WE ATTRACT, MANIFEST, AND ARE RESPONSIBLE FOR EVERYTHING IN OUR LIVES . . .**

ACTIVITY: <u>WHAT YOU SEE IS NOT WHAT YOU GET</u>

1. After you have achieved an open and relaxed state, pick an emotion you wish to STUDY. Then OBSERVE, RESEARCH, AND ANALYZE the following characteristics of that particular EMOTION:

A. What it LOOKS AND SOUNDS LIKE in behavior. . .. (Is the face red? Are the lips pursed? Is the voice screaming or whispering? Is the heart pounding? Etcetera.)

B. What it REPRESENTS. . . (What are the thoughts and belief systems that are triggering the emotional energy? What is its essence or crucial element that identifies it?)

C. What it CREATES, ATTRACTS, and MANIFESTS . . . (What dis-eases does it cause? What is usually the result of running this emotion? What is it really telling us? What are the real issues involved?)

D. What HAS TO BE CHANGED in order to not need to run this emotion in the future . . . (Thoughts, intentions, beliefs, feelings, behaviors, patterns, and situations)

2. Keep on observing and learning to see the DEEPER MEANINGS AND PATTERNS BEHIND EACH AND EVERY EMOTION that is a part of your life, including but not limited to: your different types of anger such as hate, sadness and grief, anxiety and worry, guilt and shame, confusion, resentment and jealousy, irritation, frustration, enthusiasm and excitement, joy, connectedness and oneness, confidence, courage, compassion, peace and serenity, harmony, appreciation, and inspiration.

Essentially, there are two basic elements involved in the whole spectrum of human emotion: LOVE and FEAR. Real or Divine Love is the highest energy current there is. This high frequency produces joy, lightness, radiance, unity, and wholeness. The lowest energy current is fear. This low frequency produces depletion, weakness, stuckness, separation, and sickness. Anger, frustration, resentment, regret, embarrassment, shame, and sorrow are all lower-frequency currents or expressions of fear. Fear is of the personality, while love is of the Soul.

Fear is the result of not knowing that, as Souls, there is nothing to fear. In becoming human, our consciousness becomes Earthbound. The knowingness that we are not separated from God/Goddess is repressed, denied, and blocked. Divine Consciousness, Divine Love, Divine Abilities, Divine Order, and Divine Safety become hidden behind a fear-based illusion of a limited and painful human existence.

If one has not CONSCIOUSLY AND PURPOSEFULLY WORKED ON REOPENING AND REDEVELOPING ABILITIES AND POWERS OF SOUL, then one lives in a state of self-produced powerlessness which gets further muddled in the illusion of mass consciousness and personality. These illusions are then sustained by the emotions or energies that follow fear. Suppressed negative emotions, such as anger, hatred, jealousy, loneliness, despair, grief, envy, greed, guilt, alienation, self-pity, and feelings of inferiority or superiority lead to corresponding negative behaviors towards ourselves, others, and The Earth and its creatures.

ADDICTIONS, SELF-SABOTAGING BEHAVIORS, AND DESTRUCTIVE CHOICES ARE ALL CONNECTED TO SUPPRESSED NEGATIVE EMOTIONS. Suppressed emotions often run our lives without us even being aware of it. If one is not aware of what one is feeling (feelings are emotional reactions) or unaware that we have both a conscious and subconscious choice in which feelings we run as related to the thought processes we engage, then that feeling-reaction pattern gets locked into the bodymind becoming a habitual response. However, by BECOMING AWARE OF WHAT ONE IS FEELING, RELEASING THE EMOTION, AND CHANGING THE THOUGHT PATTERNS THAT PUSH THAT PARTICULAR ENERGY BUTTON, ONE IS REGAINING CONSCIOUS CONTROL OVER ONE'S PERSONALITY, LIFE, AND SOUL.

Over time, we have each created emotional patterning based on a combination of issues, experiences, belief programming, and emotional reactions we have both witnessed and run ourselves in this and other lifetimes. We have collected SOUL CORE ISSUES, understandings and knowledge of life we are working on learning as Souls who have been journeying through time, not as just this lifetime personality. Soul Core Issues are our particular, individual lessons about life we are working on. In addition, we have particular emotional patterns that are ours throughout our various lifetimes unless we consciously choose to transform them. These SOUL EMOTIONAL PATTERNS, based on beliefs and experiences we have collected as Souls taking on various personalities, are the energies that attract to us our circumstances.

An emotional or energetic pattern of angrily exploding at someone when they are not doing what you want them to, because you feel out-of-control based on your past experiences, does not have to remain a theme in your life. Anger can be used as a mover and transformer. Emotional or energetic choice has everything to do with BECOMING AWARE OF WHAT LIFE LESSONS YOU ARE CURRENTLY ENGAGED IN and using the energy of your emotional reaction as an INDICATOR OF WHERE AND HOW YOU NEED TO LEARN/CHANGE.

Every emotion based on fear, whether it be anger, jealousy, sorrow, etc., can be either hurtful/sickening or helpful/enlightening. It's all up to you. IT'S YOUR CHOICE: WHAT YOU FEEL, HOW YOU REACT, AND THEN WHAT YOU DO WITH THE SITUATION YOU HAVE HELPED CREATE. We've really put the word CHOICE back into our vocabulary and reality when we consciously choose how we feel and react. Our Soul then has a clearer chance of being heard over the din of personality. And we are in more conscious control over what we are attracting and creating in our lives.

EMOTIONAL OR ENERGETIC CHOICES HAVE EVERYTHING TO DO WITH BECOMING AWARE OF WHAT LIFE LESSONS ONE IS CURRENTLY ENGAGED IN AND USING THE ENERGY OF ONE'S EMOTIONAL REACTIONS AS AN INDICATOR OF WHERE AND HOW ONE NEEDS TO LEARN AND CHANGE . . .

ACTIVITY: <u>THE CHOICE IS MINE!</u>

1. After you have entered into your relaxed and open state of mind, body, and spirit, allow a SPECIFIC MEMORY to come up in your thoughts of an emotional reaction you had to something happening in your life in which you wish you had responded differently. PICTURE in your minds eye THE WAY, with hindsight, YOU WISHED YOU HAD REACTED AND BEHAVED. Then begin SORTING through:

    A. What PAST MODELING/PATTERNING programmed you to respond that way . . .

    B. What UNNECESSARY BAGGAGE FROM THE PAST OR OLD, UNFINISHED BUSINESS you need TO BE AWARE OF, RELEASE, AND TRANSFORM in order to respond more appropriately in the present . . .

    C. What MISBELIEFS AND DISBELIEFS you are hanging onto that CAUSED YOU TO SABOTAGE your circumstances (to defeat, obstruct, or do harm to yourself, an endeavor, or situation) . . .

    D. What you can do to REWORK YOUR BELIEFS, FEELINGS, AND REACTIONS so that you can respond to a similar situation in a very conscious and positively appropriate response-abled manner . . .

    E. Figure out and IMPLEMENT a practical PLAN using your old emotional reaction to BECOME AWARE OF THE LIFE LESSONS YOU ARE CURRENTLY ENGAGED IN, LETTING GO OF YOUR OLD WAYS OF FEELING AND RESPONDING, AND DEVELOPING NEW CREATIVE, LIFE-AFFIRMING REACTIONS BOTH EMOTIONALLY AND BEHAVIORALLY . . .

2. Look over your memories of this and other lifetimes with the purpose of SEEING WHICH ISSUES AND EMOTIONS KEEP HAPPENING TIME AND TIME AGAIN. As you learn to recognize which specific emotions you run, do a DAILY CHECK IN to see HOW OFTEN YOU RUN EACH EMOTION THROUGHOUT THE DAY. As you open your ability to observe/witness your present lifetime and uncover your Soul memories of your past lifetimes, your key SOUL CORE ISSUES and SOUL EMOTIONAL PATTERNING will become obvious. Your Personal Processing Work then becomes more effective and important to you as a Soul. As you CONSCIOUSLY FOCUS IN ON YOUR SOUL CORE ISSUES AND EMOTIONAL PATTERNING, your Soul's Evolutionary Growth advances more smoothly and rapidly.

RELEASE

Intense negative emotions are a signal to us that we are not following the path and guidance of our Soul or *Higher Self*. If repressed or denied, the energy of these unexpressed emotions affect us ethericly, causing an ENERGY BLOCK that eventually manifests itself in our bodies as pain, discomfort, illness, and dis-ease. If expressed in verbal complaining, blaming, and attack without releasing and working through the energies of the programmed belief and thinking patterns, then the emotional pattern will continue to repeat. This repetition blocks our life flow resulting in struggle, unhappiness, and dis-ease.

Lack of love, healthy relationships, successful work, and the financial/material/human resources we need to be our true, real, or *Higher Self* mirrors the energy blocks within us. When we have suppressed and closed off our feelings, we can not contact the Holoverse and its Spirited Beings (angels, spirit guides, devas, Infinite Intelligence), we cannot hear our own intuitive or Soul voice, and we deaden ourselves to the fullness and joy of life. When our thoughts and feelings remain in a cyclical pattern of negative emotion, either denied/repressed or exploding from us in hostile interactions, we have in essence given our Soul Power away.

Lack of self-love and trust manifest blocked energy patterns that restrict us from running the type and amount of healthy life-force energy we need. As a result, we often use some form of addiction to pace ourselves, providing the energy we have blocked. Addictive energy usually comes from a drug, such as caffeine, nicotine, and alcohol or adrenaline pumping crises, traumas, adventures, relationships, and thinking patterns. We have to be WILLING TO RUN OUR OWN BALANCED LIFE FORCE ENERGY, TO EXPERIENCE OUR OWN POWER AND ENERGY THAT COMES FROM BEING connected to The Divine or A CHILD OF GOD/GODDESS.

Emotions are like moving force-fields which we can choose to experience by LETTING THEM FLOW THROUGH US WITHOUT HANGING ON TO THEM AND USING THE GIFT OF NEEDED CHANGE AND GROWTH THEY INDICATE. If we do not pay attention to our feelings or the energies we run, we manifest aches, pains, problems, accidents, unpleasant situations, illness, and dis-ease without even being aware of what we are creating. All these are messages telling us that we are blocking our life force energy by not paying attention to and taking care of what is really happening within our beings mentally, emotionally, and spiritually.

AWARENESS, RELEASING, AND REPROGRAMMING of negative thoughts and emotions unblocks our energy allowing us to heal and run our life force as we need to in order to be our *Higher Selves.* When we are willing to FULLY EXPERIENCE A PARTICULAR FEELING, our blocked energy releases and the feeling dissolves. But first, all our EMOTIONAL AND BELIEF PATTERNS HAVE TO BE BROUGHT TO THE LIGHT OF CONSCIOUSNESS. To move energy we have to FOCUS on it. In order to focus on something, we have to be AWARE of it. In moving emotional energy, AWARENESS is the first key in UNLOCKING OR RELEASING OUR BLOCKS, STUCKNESS, PAIN, AND CONFUSION.

Many of us, in going through childhood, were taught to repress the emotions that flowed through us instead of being aware of them and supported in letting them out in helpful, healthful, and constructive ways. Neither were we taught how to change our thinking and feeling programming if we chose to not have the same emotional reaction again. At the same time, we learned to repress, along with our emotions, our memories of events and communications that programmed these emotions into our thinking and feeling patterns. As a result of this multilayered blocking-out pattern, we also learn to block out or forget things we say and do that are intertwined to our repressed programming.

Repressed emotions can be stimulated in a variety of ways. READING OR EDUCATING OURSELVES ABOUT THE PSYCHOLOGY OF BEING HUMAN, in particular about HUMAN EMOTION AND INTERACTION, can often bring a particular issue in focus for us individually. PERSONAL MEMORY WORK will also trigger unresolved emotions. If our feelings are hanging out just underneath the surface of our consciousness, then we will often get HOOKED IN BY SOMEONE ELSE'S SIMILAR EMOTION, STORY, OR EXPERIENCE, WHETHER THROUGH A REAL LIFE EVENT, IN PERSON, OR THROUGH A FILM AND BOOK.

When repressed emotions have been hooked by a spontaneous or deliberate inner or outer stimulus, do what you can to allow them to flow if it is safe and valuable to the situation. If it's not safe to let them go, then GO FOR A THOROUGH RELEASE AS SOON AS YOU CAN. BODY PAIN AND TENSION if FOCUSED ON can often become so intense that the repressed emotions pop right out. Your BODY will help you IDENTIFY your EMOTIONS, especially if CORRELATED TO THE MAJOR CHAKRAS. HEATING AND SHAKING up the body through AEROBIC MOVEMENT, SPECIFIC CHAKRA MOVES, AND PUSH/PULL RESISTANT ORIENTED MOVEMENTS can also bring repressed emotions up for viewing.

LISTENING TO AND FOCUSING IN ON YOUR OWN THOUGHT PATTERNS is very helpful in becoming knowledgeable about the emotions you run. Allowing yourself to REMEMBER YOUR DREAMS is important because our dreams expose our repressed emotions. Become aware of your emotional state upon waking and USE YOUR DREAMS AS A PROCESSING TOOL.

Strong negative emotions, if allowed to take over our thoughts, cloud clarity and creativity. Thus, they are self perpetuating if allowed to percolate. In *The Higher Self Integration Process* learning to be aware of and recognizing the emotions we run and the things we and others say and do in that emotional context and particular belief patterning is essential. For it is with awareness and recognition that we then have the reality of choice. Awareness and CONSCIOUS RELEASING go hand and hand.

WE HAVE TO BE WILLING TO RUN OUR OWN BALANCED LIFE FORCE
AND TO EXPERIENCE THE POWERFUL ENERGY THAT COMES
FROM BEING A CHILD OF GOD . . .

ACTIVITY: I KNOW WHAT I FEEL, THEREFOR I CHOOSE HOW I RELEASE

1.   After you have gotten into a relaxed and open state of mind, start IDENTIFYING YOUR PARTICULAR BODY AND MIND SIGNALS THAT POINT OUT TO YOU WHAT YOU FEEL OR EACH DIFFERENT EMOTION YOU RUN. Your body, mind, and spirit is a mirror directly showing you the energies or emotions you run, both repressed or underneath the surface and those that just can't help but come screaming out of you. Righteous indignation looks, sounds like, and feels real different than poor-pitiful-me shame. It is up to you to KNOW TO THE NTH DEGREE WHAT YOU ARE FEELING AND RUNNING EMOTIONALLY so you can make the most appropriate-to-the-situation response.

2.   RECALL MEMORIES of you having an emotional response to something. In your mind, notice how you look and act.   WRITE DOWN THE EMOTION YOU WERE RELEASING AND ALL THE SYMPTOMS OR PARTICULAR BODY, THOUGHT, AND BEHAVIOR CHARACTERISTICS AND SENSATIONS that were caught up in your emotional response. These could be anything from dry mouth to an overabundance of saliva, remembering everything that was said to missing big pieces of the conversation, slamming your fist down on a table to remaining stonily still, etc. Over time, KEEP ADDING to these lists ANALYZING what you discover by:

        A. Looking at your most frequent emotional responses BECOMING FAMILIAR with WHAT TRIGGERS THEM and WHAT THEY DO to your body, mind, and behaviors.   RECALL similar past experiences that have helped to PROGRAM your present emotional reaction. Become aware of WHAT YOU HAVE BEEN TELLING YOURSELF that produces these emotions. Get in touch with WHAT YOU ARE FEARFUL OF or your fantasy of the worst case scenario which fuels your reactions. Then play out within yourself HOW YOU WOULD RATHER REACT, FEEL, THINK, BEHAVE, OR RELEASE that addresses your real issues that are involved in a honest and healthy manner.

        B. Figure out HOW each of these emotions and emotional behavior PATTERNS play out or ARE RELEASED in and around you, using this for a guide:

EMOTION/PATTERN: (Work with all of these, adding any others you are aware of running)
Fear, Anger, Hatred, Righteous Indignation, Disgust, Resentment, Blame, Jealousy, Greed, Competition, Envy, Alienation, Arrogance, Disappointment, Irritation, Anxiety, Frustration, Hurt, Sorrow, Grief, Loneliness, Hopelessness, Despair, Self-pity, Guilt, Shame, Confusion, Separation, Doubt/Distrust, Depression, Stuck/trapped, Betrayal, Rebellion, Inferiority, Superiority, Judgmentalness, Martyrdom, Victimhood, Pleaser, Not-good-enough, Rescuer, Controller, Aggressor, Abuser . . .
YOUR INDICATORS:
YOUR FEARS:
YOUR PAST PROGRAMMING:
ITS LESSON/MESSAGE:
YOUR NEW REACTION/RELEASE PLAN:

3.   BRAINSTORM NEW AND CREATIVE WAYS of releasing and reacting emotionally and behaviorally in your life.

The real human issues most of us face during modern lifetimes can be lumped into two categories: 1. Knowing who we are and what life is really about, and 2. Taking responsibility for our interactions in the worlds in and around us. Issues of self-esteem (particularly in feeling good and worthy enough and in judging others with that criteria), life purpose, personality projection, responsibility and communication with others, getting our human needs met, completing our present and past life karma or lessons, and reconnection with Spirit/Soul/The Divine all make more sense and are more easily understood and completed when worked with from the level of Soul.

Since coming from Soul requires emotional clarity, it is essential to not only KNOW HOW TO RELEASE AND REWORK INDIVIDUAL EMOTIONS but to be able to RELEASE AND REWORK THE MORE COMPLEX PERSONALITY AND SOUL PATTERNS that have evolved from choosing to be human. We've each got to RELEASE THESE VERY PREVALENT FEAR-BASED, LOW SELF-ESTEEM PERSONALITY PATTERNS or energetic signatures of: self-absorption/separation, victim/martyr/rescuer, unworthiness/approval-motivated/shame/guilt, self-dislike and hatred, resistance/rebellion/procrastination, distrust/blame/scape-goating/judgmentalness, provoking/punishing, and the intertwining of all the above which develops today's codependent/addictive personality epidemic. Running any combination of these is a solid block to Soul Attunement. MAJOR BLOCK BUSTING IS REQUIRED.

One area that often gets overlooked in its influence on each of us individually are the emotions or energies we take on from the world around us. Most of us do not know how to not take on or absorb the intense negative (whether hidden below the surface or blaring in our face) emotions or energies of others, particularly of those we are emotionally involved and attached to. Most womyn, worldwide, are directly programmed to take on the energies and characteristics of the men they are involved with. And as young children, we automatically absorb the energies of those we live and are parented by.

However, the three areas of PEOPLE ENERGY that are the hardest to release and rework are: 1. Emotions and ENERGIES that are FORCED on us IN REPETITIVE ABUSIVE SITUATIONS, 2. Emotions or ENERGIES EXCHANGED DURING SEXUAL INTIMACY, and 3. BIRTH EMOTIONS or those ENERGIES, emotions, and resultant chemical programming that a fetus absorbs while in the womb of its birth mother.

In addition there are certain patterns that we carry lifetime-to-lifetime that transcend issues of individual personality. These can be labeled SOUL PATTERNS. Soul Patterns, or energetic emotional complexes that tie in directly on the Soul level, all come from SOUL SEPARATION. Soul Separation is when we inhibit our conscious awareness of being Soul, connected to all living beings throughout the multidemensions of life. Soul Separation breeds: SEPARATION SADNESS, HUMANITY RAGE, HUMANITY ACHE, AND SOUL FRUSTRATION…

> **SEPARATION SADNESS** is the intense emotional pattern of loss, separation, and disconnection we feel when we have enough awareness of the beauty of The Divine and the realization that we have consciously disconnected from that Beauty, Love, and Light…

> **HUMANITY RAGE** is the anger we feel when we begin taping into our own Soul memories, actually reliving our personal involvement with human pain and suffering. We're advanced enough to know how wonderful life on Earth could be, yet we haven't released our own Soul pains collected on our Soul Journey. Consequently, we're mad at everything…

> **SOUL FRUSTRATION** is when we have reconnected enough to have higher visions of the potential of life here on Earth as a human, but still lack the know-how in order to create it…

> **HUMANITY ACHE** occurs when we are advanced enough to read and feel the energies of all of humanity throughout history. The heaviness of those energies weighs on us until we have moved into the next level of nonjudgmentalness and full acceptance of all aspects of life. In order to be able to handle the emotional depth and intensity of these Soul Patterns, we have to BE EXPERIENCED AND CONFIDENT IN OUR ABILITIES TO RELEASE GREAT AMOUNTS OF EMOTIONS OR EMOTIONAL ENERGIES…

**SINCE COMING FROM SOUL REQUIRES EMOTIONAL CLARITY,
IT IS ESSENTIAL TO RELEASE AND REWORK MORE COMPLEX PERSONALITY AND
SOUL PATTERNS THAT HAVE EVOLVED FROM CHOOSING TO BE HUMAN...**

ACTIVITY: <u>LET IT ALL HANG OUT</u>

EXPERIMENT, PRACTICE, AND DEVELOP YOUR OWN EFFECTIVE AND CONSTRUCTIVE WAYS TO RELEASE YOUR FEELINGS/EMOTIONAL ENERGY. Work with each of the following categories over time, LEARNING THE SKILLS REQUIRED IN USING THE RELEASE TECHNIQUES individually or in unique combinations that work well for you and the different intensities of the emotions, situations, and moods you will be involved with.

Remember that the more intense and repetitive your programming and reacting situations were and are, the more emotional energy you will have to release as you focus on reworking your life reactions. Be aware that there are many available workshops, retreats, books, and therapists/counselors who can help you learn to trust yourself with emotional release processes and techniques .

1. PHYSICAL RELEASE... Those emotions sit in that body of yours. Your body is and has to be involved in releasing emotionally:

A. TEARS- Ah blessed tears! Learn to water, to sniffle, to sob, and to wail. And don't forget to breathe! Uninhibited crying washes one out quicker than anything else. Let them flow! Fill up that hanky and be sure to rest afterwards . . .

B. NOISES- Sighs, growls, groans, and screams in the safety and privacy of one's own Personal Process Sessions also get those emotions ripping out. Air molecules really don't mind if you yell! Just rest those cooperating vocal cords afterwards . . .

C. LAUGHTER- Jiggle those emotions away through an unabashed sense of humor. Turning those serious negative thoughts and feelings around into the humorous aspects of running emotional energies, like how you look like a frog's face when you are angry, does wonders on getting you cleared out and back into the lightness of being. Laughing so deliciously that you are all drained and happily worn out will rework those stuck circuits . . .

D. PHYSICAL ACTIVITY- Physical movements that heat you up and let those emotions clear out are activities such as dancing/running/mountain climbing/hiking/wood splitting, etc. Do these activities safely with a focus on emotional release and you'll sweat and grind your way to tension relief. Working out tight emotions through physical activity really helps . . .

E. BODY POSITIONING- All our emotions have different ways of expressing themselves. Use body positioning to help stimulate their release. Move or place your body in a position that best expresses the emotion. Sadness often flows better if we lie down on our sides, curl up in a ball, and hug a stuffed animal. Anger flows out easier as we pound pillows. . .

F. BODY WORK- Focused deep massage and manipulated body movement can really jolt those under-the-surface emotions outward. Through touch and the energy transfer and stimulation of an energetic healer, we can often get our body's armor freed up enough that the tightening energies or emotions that are causing discomfort can surface and be released . . .

G. FACIAL AND BODY EXPRESSIONS AND GESTURES- Let your old gremlin out through grimaces, repeated over and over again. Let your fist shake angrily in the air over and over again. REPETITION is the key to move beyond awareness and recognition into an energetic release. There's nothing quite like sticking your tongue out at someone to release a mild irritation. Study children if you've forgotten how to safely let it all hang out in order to move on foot loose and fancy free into the next adventure.

(continued on page 105)

2. WORD RELEASE . . . Expressing one's feelings with language can often awaken us to our repressed energies. As we focus on using words to express feeling, and write or say those words with expression, the repressed feelings will often come leaping out along with a change of rhythm and tone:

      A. TALKING- Sharing in words what we are going through to a good listener will often stimulate unresolved emotional energies. We just have to listen to our Being's signals, give ourselves a quiet moment to focus on what feelings are being stimulated, and use words to heighten those feelings so they can really reveal themselves. We can do the same with the technique of **SELF-TALKING** if we have developed the skills of **SELF-WITNESSING** (being able to watch and be in tune with what we are going through while it is happening)...

      B. WRITING- As someone else's written story can stimulate our emotions to rise and release, slow and focused reading of an issue you are currently learning to release and rework can often help. When using writing as a way to get your plugged-up emotions flowing, writing uncensored, withholding all judgment as to the form and content of your writing, is necessary. Writing, while purposefully stimulating one's right side of the brain through writing in prose, being in a relaxed and open state, or writing with your left hand if you are right hand dominated and vice versa, works well in trying to stimulate repressed emotions. The release also tends to flow more smoothly and at a deeper level . . .

3. RIGHT BRAIN RELEASE . . . In more whole brain engagement for the sake of smooth and thorough emotional releases, working with images through one's imagination and dreams, and the use of art and music are helpful techniques:

      A.   **ART-** Focused drawing, coloring, painting, and working with clay can help reveal and release emotions we've been too scared to let go of. **ART AS MEDITATION** and as a **SPIRITUAL PROCESS** is very powerful and so natural to our very artistic life process.

      B.   **MUSIC-** If we are listening to music whose lyrics, tones, and rhythms match our emotional energies, we can often achieve a synchronized release. Angry oriented music stimulates and releases angry oriented emotions if they are there for the taking . . .

      C.   **IMAGES-** Images that pop into our minds through either day and night dreams usually get fed and developed by our unreleased and still active emotional energies. Pay attention to these images, the buttons they push within you, and the accompanying emotions that will soon be on their way. You can further increase the level of release by purposefully exaggerating your images with fantasy . . .

RELEASING ON THE SOUL LEVEL AND OVERTIME YOU NOT ONLY TRANSFORM YOUR PRESENT LIFE'S NEGATIVE PATTERNS, BUT THROUGH YOUR SOUL'S CLARITY BECOME COMPASSIONATE AND CREATIVE WITH THE WORLD...

◆ THE THREE STAGES OF RELEASE

SOUL RELEASE happens in layers and stages. The tools and techniques, skills and abilities necessary in releasing our deeper and highly complex Soul Patterns, such as Humanity Rage, take awhile to really grasp, be effective, and safe when intense and complicated patterns of emotional release and mental reworking are required.

To move forward in one's Soul Evolution it is necessary to LEARN, CONSISTENTLY USE, AND MOVE THROUGH THREE DIFFERENT STAGES OF RELEASE. As you learn each one, you will get quicker and more skilled at becoming aware of, releasing, reworking, and understanding deeper and more complicated issues and patterns. What may now take you weeks to be aware of, release, and work through will only take you moments in the future. What helps is to SLOWLY LEARN AND PRACTICE THE THREE STAGES OF RELEASE:

+++<u>STAGE ONE-IN THE MOMENT RELEASE</u>

Stage One In The Moment Release is when we learn a first level awareness of what we are feeling or running and handle the situation as if it were an isolated event and feeling. We do MOVE OUT OF UNAWARENESS, actually ALLOW THE EMOTION TO SURFACE, LEARN HOW TO RELEASE IT, and USE COMMUNICATION SKILLS TO WORK IT OUT WITH OTHERS.

An example of Stage One-In The Moment Release is: You are in a public line, someone cuts in front of you, and you feel anger. Instead of simmering and remaining out of control, you become aware of and acknowledge your anger. You take a couple of deep breaths visualizing the anger releasing from you and step up to the cutter saying, "I'm uncomfortable with your cutting in line. I don't think it's fair to the rest of us." The caught cutter mutters under their breath but leaves. And you are fine for the moment because you got your immediate needs met.

This first stage release takes care of the moment which is healthier than denial, repression, and simmering (The Squelch of Self), but is not transformative. When another line cutting incident occurs, you'll be running the same energy all over again. You are aware of the emotion you run, release it, take care of the supposedly isolated situation as best you can, but continue to run the emotion in the future. You are still feeding off of the emotion in order to take care of yourself. Your concern is focused only on your need of and in the moment.

+++<u>STAGE TWO-CONNECTED TO YOUR LIFE RELEASE</u>

Stage Two Connected To Your Life Release acknowledges that you have the human choice as to whether or not you run anger towards the line cutter and that choice of reaction is based on your thought and belief patterns. So, once you are in a safe place, you UTILIZE MEMORY WORK AND HOOK STIMULATION TECHNIQUES, discovering a huge amount of anger, frustration, righteous indignation, and sarcasm not only towards the line cutter, but towards all those who step on others in order to get what they want. As you ALLOW THE TEARS of hurt and frustration TO FLOW, you SEE IMAGES of family members and fellow workers who have pushed you back ruthlessly in order to get ahead. You recognize that your anger towards the line cutter is only the tip of the iceberg.

It's now time to do some REAL TRANSFORMATIVE WORK, RELEASING THE OLD TOXIC EMOTIONS, LETTING GO OR FORGIVING THE PEOPLE AND SITUATIONS INVOLVED IN THOSE OLD SETUPS, AND REWORKING YOUR OWN ENERGETIC PATTERNS THROUGH BELIEF REPROGRAMMING. That way you become free from the craziness of being a victim and harboring frustration, righteous indignation, and other negative and sickening emotions.

StageTwo really delves into and releases all the emotion of the moment and the connected past. It allows the past emotional and behavioral programmed patterns to be revealed. Connections and choices are made. Techniques such as MEMORY WORK, HOOK STIMULATION, DEEPER RELEASE METHODS, ESSENCE AND SYMBOLIC CONNECTION, BRAINSTORMING, BELIEF REPROGRAMMING, THE FORGIVENESS PROCESS, VISUALIZATION, AFFIRMATIONS, AND ROLEPLAYING all are part of the transformative change process that enables you to move out of your old stuck emotional and behavioral patterning.

You are aware of what you are running, release it in the moment taking care of the situation the best you can and then you work on it more later. You choose to move the process further by doing DEEPER RELEASE WORK RECOGNIZING THE PERSONALITY PATTERNS YOU NEED TO CHANGE IN ORDER TO NOT RUN THE SAME EMOTIONS IN THE FUTURE. You work hard at making some thinking, feeling, and behaving changes so that you flow and feel better with what's happening around you. You are focused on what's best for you in this lifetime. However, you still run a separation energy between others, your personality, and your Soul. You are still self-absorbed.

+++STAGE THREE-CONNECTED TO SOUL

Stage Three Connected To Soul Release takes it all one level further where you are aware of, understand, and work with each pushed-back, stepped-on, discounted line-cutting type of situation from the level of Soul and not personality. You become aware of and release another level of emotion that comes from a deep, multiple lifetime history of situations and feelings stemming from human-to-human selfishness and meanness that you have witnessed and been a part of for what seems like forever. You release tons of Humanity Ache, that cell-level witnessing that you have held on to throughout your Soul's journeys.

Through PAST LIFE MEMORY WORK you not only rewitness and feel being abused by others, but you also tap into abuse you gave to others. You are able to READ YOUR OWN SOUL'S ENERGY AND THE SOUL ENERGY OF OTHERS you are involved with. You learn the deepest level of FORGIVENESS through seeing how all you have been working on is connected to all your interactions with others. You and the line cutters of the world are one and the same, with your individual life lessons interacting in a Divine right-on-the-target dance.

You release on the Soul level, and over time, you not only transform your present life negative patterns but, through your clarity, BECOME COMPASSIONATE AND CREATIVE WITH THE WORLD's line cutters. You are able to know where you and the others you interact with are at concerning the lessons the moment is initiating. As a result your response to the situation is not based on emotional/personality-oriented reaction but on SOUL LEARNING.

You are working on the level SOUL-TO-SOUL irregardless of what level other people are at. You have built AN INNER SECURITY AND SELF-ACCEPTANCE BASED ON AN UNDERSTANDING OF YOUR (AND OTHERS) REAL ORIGIN: a solid inner psychic structure that cannot be taken or destroyed by emotion, characteristic, or circumstance. Therefore, you are now able to FOCUS ON THE BEST FOR ALL CONCERNED. You are ORIENTED TO THE RESOLUTION OF KARMA AND THE JOY OF LIVING.

YOU ARE ABLE TO KNOW WHERE YOU AND OTHERS ARE AT IN RELATION TO THE LESSONS EACH MOMENT IS INITIATING AND, AS A RESULT, YOUR RESPONSE IS NOT BASED ON PERSONALITY-ORIENTED REACTION BUT ON SOUL-TO-SOUL LEARNING . . .

♦ WHAT YOU NEED TO KNOW ABOUT SOUL WORK

SOUL WORK IS A MULTIPLE LIFE-LONG PROCESS, REQUIRING ONGOING DEEP EMOTIONAL RESTRUCTURING. In other words, you have to run your emotional energies differently for *Higher Self Integration* than you do as your lower self personality. The following GUIDELINES can help make the time and energy consuming adventure of "PERSONAL PROCESS WORK" a lot less scary and a whole lot more fun:

*** *AGAIN, AND AGAIN, AND AGAIN* –

Put a dollar in a jar every time you think you are finished reworking or learning a particular issue, process, pattern, and/or lesson. And then go out and do something fun with the money before you once again head back to the drawing board! Soul Work comes in layers, and lots of them. All your issues and lessons are interconnected with one another. Work a layer, get a little rest and a chance to integrate the resulting changes into your daily life, and then plunge (or be plunged) into another layer.

*** *DEEPER, AND DEEPER, AND DEEPER* –

Learn to RIDE THE WAVES of deep personal and Soul Work with respect, honoring both your button pushers and your pushed buttons. Every negative emotional reaction you have bespeaks of issues/lessons you are a part of. Learn to quit resisting the classes your Soul is enrolled in. Become open to each one and at the same time, don't grasp hold of the current layer tightly for you'll miss the full joy of the next. Learn to suspend your judgment of an experience or situation from the shallowness of good or bad. Time is your friend, not your enemy. It takes time for transformation. All your life is a circle, but if you do your Soul Work you'll be on THE SOUL SPIRAL: coming back around over and over again from a higher, more conscious, and more whole place.

*** *FLOOD WATERS* –

Be aware that when you begin to consciously work on an issue or energy block that has been spinning and stuck for quite awhile in your Soul's journey, then you will more than likely experience THE DAM EFFECT. The emotions and situations involved may feel like they are exploding in and all around you. Don't fight it. Just get through your white water experiences through deep breathing (relax for this too shall pass), using your paddle (working the techniques of transformation towards the direction or path you consciously choose), and getting by with a little help from your friends (those humans that know and the Higher/Divine help that comes from turning within). Once the flood has subsided, roll up your sleeves and start cleaning up (clearing out and reconstructing).

*** *HEAD ON* –

The energetic patterns, issues, and lessons that will require the most time, energy, and skill to transform and integrateare those that are or were deeply and intensely planted within your psyche. Suppose, that you were repeatedly told you weren't good enough by someone who demonstrated it through using their own negative emotions to blast your sense of self away, along with setting up situations where they could prove your supposed inadequacies over and over again. Then it is going to take a lot of COUNTER-BLASTING, reworking of the implanted energetic blocks, to transform the emotional, thought, belief and behavior patterns. The more stuck something is the more effort it will take to get that something unstuck. If you really feed off of negative thoughts and their anger, then it's going to take an equal amount of positive thoughts (harmony) to counteract the negativity and SWITCH YOUR SYNAPSES AND HABITS.

*** *GOING BEYOND* –

Past Life Exploration is necessary in the *Integration of Our Higher Self* due to the reality of karma, or cause and effect, and because we come into each current life with whatever unresolved/stuck energies we have taken on in our other personalities. If we don't consciously discover, release, and rework our old energetic patterns, we carry them life-to-life. These energies, in turn, attract to us characteristics, people, and situations that can help us to remove our SOUL BLOCKS, if we so choose to use the gifts of life for our SOUL'S EVOLUTION. We are often scared of developing our Higher Powers if we have misused them in previous lives and have not completed the release/forgiveness/reworking program that is necessary in FREEING OUR SOUL.

PAST LIFE EXPLORATION (memory work and emotional release) can often be real intense because of the amount and type of memories and emotions that have been stored in the recesses of our mind for so long. PAST LIFE THERAPY brings to us the memories and direct body and emotional pains that another has been through; Only that other is ourselves and we are directly experiencing what it was like to be that other personality and body in our present personality and body. We may not have a conscious-this-lifetime association or way to deal with the past life trauma. In addition, we may use our present life judgments towards our actions in other lives that don't fit modern life's illusions of how things should be.

As a result, it is possible to get in way over your head or in deeper than your ability to process and positively work through past life memories and emotions. You could open up your memory banks quicker than developing and practicing the skills and abilities that enable you to safely and effectively process those memories. Learn well the first two stages of Soul Release before you try the third. PROCEED WITH CAUTION as you develop your skills to go deeper into your Soul's past. Allow yourself the time, safety, and support necessary in PAST LIFE WORK and in completing each process involved. Work through your negative judgments of yourself and do whatever work is necessary in this lifetime to complete your lessons hanging on from your previous lives.

*** TRANCING OUT –

Learn to do your Personal Process Work while in a TRANCE: a relaxed, aware, and very focused state. The various LEVELS OF TRANCE one can achieve through body relaxation, deep breathing, and mental imagery are very useful for: memory work, deep emotional release, changing one's perspective about a stuck issue, moving through a state of immobilization where you are not functioning at the level that relaxation/trance are conducive to, and receiving Higher energies and guidance. It is easier for your Guides, Teachers, and Angels of the spirit world - and your own Soul's Voice - to work with you when you are relaxed and open. It is also easier to work through your fears while in trance, to turn your fears into your allies.

*** REFORMING –

Know that, because of the deep Soul Work you will be doing, your body will experience all sorts of strange releases, sensations, symptoms, changes, and movements. You might cry more tears than you ever thought could be produced, for tears are the quickest way to release and be cleansed of old energy leftovers. Huge mouth stretching yawns, one right after another, will appear in the middle of a processing session as your brain tries to regulate itself. Over time, your joints will snap, crackle, and pop as they begin to unfreeze. The loud body pops also bring with them a flood of heat that even makes your skin red. You may ache, limp, have skin zits/rashes/discoloration, loose your voice, develop illness patterns you didn't have before, experience a level of exhaustion that you didn't know was possible, and "feel like shit." SoulWork is not easy. However it is very real. As we move the energy through our chakras in ways that we couldn't before and get unblocked, OUR BODY'S HOLDING AND CHEMISTRY PATTERNS WILL START TO CHANGE. We will be changing on a CELLULAR LEVEL. Sometimes the process feels a whole lot crazier than the end result, which will give a reworked and wholer/healthier body, mind, and spirit.

As we free up to directly run our HIGHER SOUL POWERS AND ABILITIES, our bodies would fry if they didn't get RECIRCUITED. It's hard to run Soul energy through slumped shoulders and hunched over backs that became that way through limiting our Soul energies, powers, and abilities via negative emotions, thoughts, and conditioning. With Soul Work, it's a guarantee that your thinking processes and physical body will change. Watch yourself with great care. Take care of each symptom that becomes a part of your transformation process holistically. Stay calm and unattached to the wild sights and sensations you will experience. Humor helps!

*** SELF CARE –

You will require special care throughout your *Higher Self Integration Process and Journey*. What that care specifically needs to be is dependent on the stages, levels, and types of Soul Work you are currently undergoing. You, and therefore your physical, mental, and spiritual bodies, will be moving out of the patterns of the lower-self and as a result, LIFE STYLE CHANGES are necessary. You will need to be positively attentive to your own personal needs, LEARNING TO MAKE THE DISTINCTION BETWEEN REAL SOUL NEEDS AND ADDICTIVE LOWER-SELF DESIRES.

In addition, the two areas listed below require constant attendance. You will need to:

1. <u>Pay attention to getting the human-to-human, human-to-spirit, teacher-to-student support</u> that you need in each leg of your journey. You will be experiencing some unusual, exciting, joyful, confusing, painful and scary thoughts, feelings, behaviors, sensations, phenomenon, and situations. You'll need to: share what you are going through, be questioned, confronted, and validated. You'll also need some reeducating. Remember that your teachers will often come from totally unexpected places.

2. <u>Pay attention to your changing relationships</u> with others, for your relationships are guaranteed to change as you do. Not everyone's going to be thrilled with what you are going through and becoming. Your relationship requirements will also undergo transformation. As one moves along in one's *Higher Self Integration Process*, one moves away from needing others approval and companionship based on the need-to-control. QUIET TIME and NATURE CONNECTION needs increase as one's ability to BE HAPPILY ALONE grows. This affects not only our personal relationships and needs, but also our work/service and public/community involvements.

!!! **HUMOR HELPS** !!!

RECONSTRUCT

Remember that a BLOCK is a place where energy is constricted, not moving or flowing. Blocks are usually caused initially by repressing the emotions of fear, such as resentment, anger, and guilt. These repressed emotions cause a tightening up and closing down spiritually, emotionally, mentally, and physically. When you are ready to no longer deny and repress your feelings becoming willing to let go of the energy block, you must feel and release the emotion. When the emotion has been worked out of your mind and body, you will be able to think clearly enough to start looking at the cause of the emotion: your thinking patterns. For: YOU FEEL WHAT YOU THINK!

Behind every emotion and behavioral reaction we feel and enact is a set of programmed thinking patterns, or ways of looking at and responding to life based on our previous experiences and learnings. And behind most negative emotions and reactions are faulty misbeliefs and disbeliefs about ourselves, how life works, and how people are or "should be." Behind every negative emotion and thinking pattern is fear based on a lack of self and Divine love and trust.

AFTER WE HAVE BECOME AWARE OF OUR FEELINGS, ACCEPTED THAT WE ARE FEELING THEM, AND HAVE RELEASED THEM GETTING THE ENERGY TO MOVE, WE ARE THEN READY TO TAKE A CLEAR LOOK AT THE UNDERLYING BELIEFS AND ATTITUDES THAT IN TURN FORM BEHAVIORAL AND PERSONALITY PATTERNS WHICH ORIGINALLY CAUSE OUR PROBLEMS.

We have to become aware of these misbeliefs and disbeliefs and change their resulting negative characteristics, attitudes, reactions, and emotions concerning the nature of life, people, and reality to something more positive and, therefore, healthy. As we reprogram our negativity to positive, loving, vital, and constructive energy, that energy will in turn attract more positive, loving, creative life-enhancing experiences into our lives.

Becoming a free and healthy *Higher Self Integrated Soul* usually involves learning to think and respond differently than you were probably taught. Part of RECONSTRUCTION is to REEDUCATE OR REPROGRAM YOURSELF IN THINKING, FEELING, AND BEHAVING THROUGH PERSONALITY REFORMATION AND MENTAL/SPIRITUAL PRACTICES (Covered in the following three chapters).

The other part that is pertinent to reconstruction of our lower self into our *Higher Self* involves the ability to let go of our negative, stuck energy through REWORKING HOW WE GIVE/RECIEVE ENERGY TO AND FROM OTHERS. We not only have to RELEASE AND REWORK our own negative emotional energy, but also the NEGATIVE EMOTIONAL ENERGY OF OTHERS THAT WE HAVE TAKEN ON AS OUR OWN.

When we communicate with others, energy is exchanged. Sometimes we get snagged or hooked by someone else's energies or misbeliefs and disbeliefs. We may be really attached to what others think and feel about what we do, finding security in the act of pleasing others. Many times we hang on to these exchanged energies through our thoughts and emotions long after the exchange is over. Some of these hanger-oners are counteractive to running our own energy: to clarity of thought and action based on who we are as Soul, not on what someone else is or wants us to be as a personality.

You will know that you need to return energy to its rightful owner when you find yourself ruminating about what someone else said. Our NEGATIVE RUMINATIONS ARE CAUSED BY NEGATIVE BELIEFS AND EMOTIONAL ATTACHMENTS (based on fear) THAT NEED TO BE REWORKED. We have to release the other person's energy. We can do this through VISUALIZATION AND AFFIRMATION TECHNIQUES BASED ON SENDING THE OTHER PERSON'S ENERGY BACK TO THEM. We then have to let our own Soul's energy fill the space within us where we had run on another's energy.

There are three essential styles in which we receive or EMBRACE THE ENERGY of others and of our situations. They are: 1. RESISTANCE, 2. AFFINITY, and 3. NONRESISTANCE. In the practice and process of *Higher Self Integration* it is very important that you THOROUGHLY UNDERSTAND EACH OF THESE STYLES, so that you can exercise the freedom of choice in how you interact with energies coming from outside of your self. Don't be fooled by the seeming simplicity of these explanations. This lesson usually takes longterm focus because of all the emotional attachments we carry around in our extra baggage bag that often feels strapped with steel on our backs and chests.

1. RESISTANCE:

To resist or to be in resistance means that our energy tightens and becomes rigid in order to use force in actively fighting off or opposing the energy that is coming at us. For some reason connected to our thinking and emotional patterns and our expectations and attachments, we have decided that we don't like what's happening. We put out energy to resist it, trying to make it go away or change to meet our expectations of the moment. This holds the energy near us requiring an enormous amount of our own energy to keep fighting. As a result, this wears us out and is ultimately very destructive.

In *The Higher Self Integration Process*, we have to BREAK DOWN OUR RESISTANCES, ESTABLISHING THINKING AND BELIEVING WAYS THAT EMBRACE LIFE AND EACH OF ITS MOMENTS FULLY AND JOYFULLY. As we become in acceptance of each moment, we are able to rationally and intuitively pick up on the energetic choices and consequences. We can then consciously choose the path that works the best for all concerned . .

2. AFFINITY:

To be in affinity with means that the energy in your Being is in agreement and at one with energy coming to you. To choose to be in affinity with positive energy, such as joy, feels healthy. To be in affinity with negative energy and to run that energy is doubly destructive. One has to KNOW ONE'S INNER SELF WELL in order to have conscious choice when running affinity. Even if it is energy you are in agreement with, it is still allowing outside energy to combine with your own. That makes whatever you are running doubly powerful. Because of this, conscious awareness is very important.

3. NONRESISTANCE:

To be in nonresistance means that there is neither force, nor agreement in regards to incoming energy. You are running in neutral regarding what is coming your way. You do not keep hold of it. You notice the energy coming to you, and you watch the energy flow through you and out the other side. You have no considerations, attachments, expectations, nor judgments on which it can get caught.

You have learned OBSERVATION WITHOUT JUDGEMENT. You can be totally aware and involved in life but not attached or caught up in trying to control it. Nonresistance means being able to TRUST FROM A SOUL LEVEL that everything is as it needs to be for all concerned. You are then free to respond to the moment from the level of Soul, not out of fear of loss.

YOU FEEL WHAT YOU THINK! . . .

There are also three styles of HELPER'S ENERGY, or moving one's energy outward in relation to others. They are: SYMPATHY, EMPATHY, and COMPASSION. It is equally as important in *Higher Self Integration* to THOROUGHLY UNDERSTAND the differences in these three styles of operating in terms of relating to others. The work it takes to live a life of compassion, not running sympathy and empathy, is usually a long journey of reworking one's conditioned emotional, mental, and behavioral programmed beliefs out of the denier/abandoner and rescuer/controller modes. Separation is based on doubt and fear; anxiety and worry on distrust.

1. SYMPATHY implies:

"I feel your problem. It's such a big problem. Let me have it so that I can solve it for you because you cannot. I give you pity." Using sympathy means that you are dependent on or subjected to other's energies and how well they are doing (including moods and whims) in order to feel OK about yourself. When you give sympathy, you pull their problem/energy into your Being, becoming stuck with others negative energy. It is a real set up, for you can not rid another of their energy, or the essence of their difficulty. You can only give them a bandaid; help to patch them up. It is not up to you. Only they can do the emotional, mental, behavioral work it takes to truly change/transform their energy patterns.

2. EMPATHY implies:

"I feel your problem. And because I want to validate you, I will hold up your problem and project it back to you to show you that I understand." When you give empathy, you pull the other's energy or problem into your own being and become a part of it. This takes energy, tires us out, and can create confusion as to the ownership of the problem. It can also lead to a type of misery loves company setup. While it may feel good to share the knowledge and pain we're going through, empathy is not a real mover of energy. It is not a transformer; it is a stabilizer.

3. COMPASSION implies:

"I feel your problem. I understand how hard it is to work out your problem because sometimes it is hard for me to work out my problems. I have confidence that you can resolve your problem because of the natural laws of energy. You can control your energy and your problems created out of your own energy." In running compassion, you are not emotionally hooked into their energy. You have learned to let others go through their own processes without running your own fear of loss. You are unattached to or not running expectations of the outcome. You are not only able to understand their problem, but also their whole Being. You are aware of their Soul's journey and see how they have created their own problem and what they are getting out of it or could be learning from it. You can provide clear and uncontrolling Soul support.

ACTIVITY: <u>**CHANGING STYLES**</u>

After you are in an open and relaxed state, take each of the styles in both receiving and giving energy and work with them in the following way:

1. Put these styles into your awareness and OBSERVE yourself and others use them. FIGURE OUT the: A. EMOTIONS run with each style, B. the BELIEFS that are a part of each style, C. the OUTCOMES of each style, and D. what a person has to RELEARN or RECONSTRUCT in order to change styles.

2. Make up two situations that could happen in your life, one involving the receiving of energy and the other involving the giving of energy. In your mind's eye, ROLEPLAY EACH OF THE THREE STYLES IN BOTH CATEGORIES. Then pick situations that have recently occurred in your life involving the giving and receiving of energy in which you have not run nonresistance and compassion. BRAINSTORM what you can do TO REWORK YOUR PROGRAMMING so that you do respond from NONRESISTANCE AND COMPASSION.

3. READ, OBSERVE, ANALYZE, EXPERIMENT, PRACTICE for however long it takes to be aware in every giver and receiver situation that occurs in your everyday life that you have a choice of which style to run. HEAD TOWARDS THE COMPLETE ACCEPTANCE OF LIFE IN EACH MOMENT AND FOR FULL COMPASSIONATE LIVING.

Another extremely important area in the reconstruction of our selves involves THE FORGIVENESS PROCESS. Forgiveness of ourselves and others releases stuck energy, enabling us to move out of the past. When we do not flow freely with life in the present moment, it usually means that we are holding on to past moments through regret, sadness, fear, guilt, blame, anger, resentment, or revenge. Each of these states comes from a space of unforgiveness, a refusal to let go and come into the present moment.

Forgive is defined as: to cease to feel resentment against - to GIVE UP RESENTMENT. Resentment means a feeling of indignant displeasure at something regarded as a wrong, an insult, or injury. In order to forgive we must LEARN TO ACCEPT THE CORE OF EVERY HUMAN BEING AS THE SAME AS OURSELVES. We must learn to GIVE THE GIFT OF NOT JUDGING BASED ON PERSONALITY. Any kind of resentment or unforgiveness towards anyone or anything, including ourselves, keeps us blocked, stuck, and unhealthy. Since *The Higher Self Integration Process* is all about movement, transformation, and health, PRACTICING AND ACHIEVING FORGIVENESS (letting go of all negativity) is what it is all about on a personality level and deep in one's Soul.

The Forgiveness Process is usually much harder to integrate on every level than we usually think. Remember that old onion and the many layers that can bring tears to the eyes. Forgiveness has to go way deep into our beings. It is A PRACTICE AND WAY OF LIFE that needs to live on eternally. The following are some books which help clarify various aspects of the "recognize, release, and reconstruction" stages of running the energetic choices we are given in our lives:

1. *Emotional Intelligence: Why It Can Matter More Than IQ* by Daniel Goleman, Bantam, 1995.
2. *The Inner Child Workbook: What To Do With Your Past When It Just Won't Go Away,* by Cathyrn Taylor, Jeremy P. Tarcher/Putnam, 1991.
3. *Forgiveness: A Bold Choice For A Peaceful Heart* by Robin Casarjian, Bantam Book, 1992.
4. *Forgiveness: How To Make Peace With Your Past And Get On With Your Life*, by Sidney and Suzanne Simon, Warner Books, Inc., 1990.

WE MUST LEARN TO GIVE THE GIFT
OF NOT JUDGING BASED ON PERSONALITY. . .

ACTIVITY: LETTING GO!

1. CONCERNING FORGIVING OTHERS-

A. Once in an open and relaxed state, list everything and everyone you can think of who has ever caused you indignant displeasure. Go back as far as you can remember and WRITE DOWN EVERY HURT, INSULT, mental/emotional/physical INJURY RECEIVED from someone. Think of the people, places, situations, and conditions that you have disliked and write them down. Think of every experience that has polluted your consciousness with negative energy and add them to your list. When your inventory is complete, start at the top and slowly move down the list, bringing each image into your mind saying: "I FORGIVE YOU COMPLETELY. I hold no unforgiveness back. I am free and you are free!"

B. In time, go back to your list being completely honest and take a long look at those you are resisting letting go of/forgiving. Continue to try to forgive everyone whom you feel has not been released from your emotional attachment by FIGURING OUT WHY YOU ARE HANGING ONTO THE ATTACHMENT: What do you get out of the resentment and what misbeliefs and disbeliefs need reworking in order to let go once and for all? Do your work!

C. With those persons and situations you are having more difficulty forgiving, take each person individually and visualize their image. Imagine them smiling and happy. VISUALIZE GOOD THINGS HAPPENING TO THEM. Hold this image for awhile and gradually let it fade. Next, do the same thing for/to YOURSELF. If you can not get this far without faking, go back to step B. Two helpful affirmations are: "Never again will I knowingly allow this to happen." and "There are many ways I have been wounded, hurt, abused, abandoned, betrayed, and scapegoated by others in thought, word, and deed knowingly or unknowingly. I forgive them."

2. CONCERNING SELF-FORGIVENESS-

Many times we are stuck in negative judgment towards ourselves because we perceive a part of ourselves or something we've done/haven't done as not good enough or bad. We can be harsh in how we think and feel about ourselves, holding on to trashing ourselves for days, months, years, and even lifetimes. These angers, putdowns, and distrusts then become automatic and deeply ingrained in our thinking/feeling/behaving patterns. Many of our self-destructive addictions and behavior patterns arise from a self-dislike based on these old self-judgments. FORGIVING OURSELVES AND THEN CHANGING THE DESTRUCTIVE WAYS WE SEE OURSELVES IS ESSENTIAL IN DEVELOPING THE CLARITY REQUIRED FOR *Higher Self Integration*.

(continued on page 115)

A. Apply the above techniques to yourself. As you sort through your negative judgments about yourself, take one at a time, enter an open and relaxed state, and then focus on your concern. Allow all the negativity you have felt about yourself and your concern to surface knowing that the past or present behaviors or personality characteristics that "got you into trouble" can be forgiven and changed. PICTURE YOURSELF AND THE SITUATION HEALING. Do your work in order to change your destructive patterns.

B. BRAINSTORM WHAT YOU CAN DO TO LOVE YOURSELF unconditionally. Affirm frequently:

"I affirm forgiveness for myself.
I forgive my past and present thoughts, feelings, words, and actions as need be.
I forgive my aches and pains of mind, body, heart, and spirit.
I forgive my feelings of hurt and disappointment.
I forgive my doubts, fears, irritations, frustrations, and resentments.
I forgive my impatience toward myself and others.
I forgive my nervousness about my responsibilities.
I forgive my seeming lack of faith in or love towards others and myself.
I forgive my doubts and fears about life, its challenges and lessons. I accept its incredible
BLESSINGS."

CHAPTER SEVEN

WHICH WHO AM I?

SOUL MASTERY INCLUDES USING TWO OF THE FUNDAMENTAL FREEDOMS
WE HAVE: THE FREEDOM TO CHOOSE HOW WE WILL RESPOND AND THE
FREEDOM TO ACT IN WAYS THAT ELEVATE AND EVOLVE OUR SOUL . . .

PERSONALITY PROPAGATION

At first glance, the old adages "Know Thyself" and "To Thine Own Self Be True" do not seem too confusing. But apply this one simple question - Which self are you talking about? - with an awakening consciousness, and the muddled self of personality will usually rear its various voices in alarm. For most of us, all the different selves of our personality were trained how to outscream the one united voice of Soul. And as far as energy management is concerned THE WAR OF THE SELVES is so conducive to battle fatigue, that the loudest voice or most habitual current of energy running at the time usually wins out.

Soul Attunement or *Higher Self Integration* is all about SELF MASTERY. It includes using two of the fundamental freedoms we have as Souls in human bodies: the freedom to choose how we will respond and the freedom to act in ways that elevate and evolve our energy, our Soul. Through the misbelief that we are our personalities, we allow habits of thought, feeling, and behavior, that we picked up from our environment, rule our lives and shut out who and what we really are: Evolving Soul. Our lower-self personality and all its fragmented parts - including SUBPERSONALITIES, ARCHETYPES, AND MODERN MADNESS MEMENTOS - have to be reformed into a *Higher Self* personality that allows our Soul's true voice a clear channel.

Reread Chapter One, after the Defining God Activity through to the end of the chapter, working some more with the Beginning to Decipher Personality Activity. These specific books might prove helpful in comprehending and integrating this chapter's focus:

John Bradshaw's *Bradshaw On: The Family - A Revolutionary Way of Self-Discovery,*
Anne Wilson-Schaef's *When Society Becomes An Addict,*
Sanaya Roman's *Living With Joy: Keys To Personal Power & Spiritual Transformation,*
Jack Kornfield's *A Path With Heart: A Guide Through The Perils & Promises Of Spiritual Life.*

As you read on, remember that personalities are patterns of thinking, feeling, and behaving that are influenced by: our earthly surroundings or environment, the personality modeling we receive from those who teach us their ways of adapting to Earth Living, our genetic and biological programming of this lifetimes physical encasement, and our previous Soul Journeys on Earth. You are not your personality. You are a spiritual being who has lost contact with your essential self, or Soul, through your habits. You can access your SOUL POTENTIAL by BECOMING FREE FROM FEARS, REPETITIVE ANXIETIES, AND UNCONSCIOUS DRIVES ROOTED IN THE PAST. However, recognizing, releasing, and reprogramming your emotional patterns is only a part of the whole picture.

Another big puzzle part lies in the need to BE AWARE OF, UNDERSTAND, RELEASE, AND REFORM those parts of your personality, or PERSONALITY TYPES AND PATTERNS, THAT CREATE NEGATIVITY, DISHARMONY, AND VIOLENCE, contributing in a huge way to the SQUELCH OF SOUL - SOS. In turn, you have to learn to IDENTIFY, VALUE, AND RUN THOSE ENERGY CURRENTS, THINKING, AND BEHAVING PATTERNS THAT GENERATE CREATIVITY, HEALING, AND JOY which contribute to the SENDING OF UNIVERSAL LOVE - SOUL.

This entails MAKING AN INVENTORY OF THE ELEMENTS THAT FORM YOUR CONSCIOUS THINKING AND BEHAVING PATTERNS AND AN EXTENSIVE EXPLORATION OF THE THOUGHTS AND ENERGIES THAT LIE REPRESSED IN YOUR UNCONSCIOUS. Carl Jung said, "That which we do not bring to consciousness appears in our lives as fate." Remember: CONSCIOUS CHOICE IS FREEDOM!

IDENTIFICATION AND REFORMATION OF YOUR SHADOW OR DARK SELF (the negative, hidden parts of your lower-self) involves facing up to and systematically removing from your thoughts and actions the fears that paralyze you, the ancestral/societal images that obsess or silently dominate you, and the conflicts that waste your energies. TRANSMUTATION OF THE SEXUAL AND COMBATIVE ENERGIES from power and control issues into creative achievements is also a part of working on one's "Booga Bear" side. Along with these, the SELF-WARS we create between the different parts of ourselves living in conflict, which cause us dis-ease and life traumas/crises, have to be brought out and truces drawn.

These BATTLES OF THE SELVES are different from another very significant psychospiritual process called "THE DARK NIGHT OF THE SOUL." The Battles Of The Selves are times when we question everything about our present life usually because of emotional and/or physical pain and loss of some sort. The Dark Night Of The Soul comes as a result of learning and being involved in SOUL EXAMINATION, where one is purposefully tapping into one's SOUL MEMORIES, bringing into consciousness one's thoughts, feelings, and behaviors from other lifetimes as well as this current lifetime. One's SOUL BAGGAGE, all the leftover issues, lessons, and unresolved karmic situations become conscious and therefore added to this current lifetime's particular dance. One has to integrate one's SOUL HISTORY and knowledge consciously into one's present day consciousness.

It is a very intense and advanced process one needs to be well prepared for before undertaking. It is not easy to relive oneself doing things one would never do in this lifetime because of one's current morals and values. The Dark Night Of The Soul takes place when we are face-to-face with all the negative darkness we've carried around for eons. Just like you have to integrate into a whole all the various parts of your present personality, so too do you have to integrate your previous personalities in with your present one.

It is a necessary part of SOUL WORK, because without it one's real SOUL SHIFT cannot occur. A Soul Shift happens when one has accepted, forgiven, and reworked what one has been and done in various incarnations. This includes recognizing and reliving when one separated from one's SOUL KNOWLEDGE in one's present lifetime. The shift is an evolutionary move from SOUL SEPARATION TO DIVINE RECONNECTION.

In working with your present personality, you have to SHED OUTGROWN MORALS, OUTMODED AND DYSFUNCTIONAL FAMILY AND SOCIETAL STRUCTURES, AND OUTGROWN RELIGIOUS THINKING which was based on man's need to control one another. You have to IDENTIFY YOUR REFLEXIVE FALSE SELVES OR SUBPERSONALITIES, REINTEGRATING THEM BACK INTO A CONSCIOUS WHOLE WHERE THEY SERVE AND ENRICH THE WISDOM STORED IN YOUR SOUL. Your LOWER-SELF personality's negative THOUGHTS/FEELINGS/BEHAVIORS HAVE TO DIE – be given no energy, time, or power - so that you can REFORM those CHARACTERISTICS INTO *Higher Self* THOUGHTS/FEELINGS/ BEHAVIORS/ENERGIES that are aligned with Soul.

Experience, revelation, tradition, scripture, culture, and reason shape our world view. Our lower-self has been formed largely from our assumptions based on that outer world view or the opinions of others. THE NEED TO HAVE APPROVAL FROM OTHERS HAS TO BE REWORKED. Lower-self personality directed activity is often based on "shoulds" and not done to benefit your Higher Purpose, while *Higher Self* or Soul-directed activity is always done with your Higher Purpose in mind. Through working with Soul using *Higher Self* personality thoughts/feelings/behaviors, you can evolve without creating crises.

BE AWARE OF, UNDERSTAND, RELEASE, AND REFORM THOSE PERSONALITY PARTS AND PATTERNS THAT CONTRIBUTE TO THE SQUELCH OF SOUL – SOS . . .

ACTIVITY: <u>MY MOTHER/FATHER MYSELF</u>

So many of our automatic reflexive energies and feeling reactions, thinking patterns, and behaviors were programmed into us by the person(s) who parented or were around us as we began learning about life. If there was a particular person you were around the most, or identified with more, or who was more intense than others, then you probably have more of their mannerisms, beliefs, emotional reactions, and energies. Whether negative/lower or positive/*Higher Self* characteristics, you need to know what they are so you can make a conscious choice whether to run them or not.

1. WOMB ENERGIES- After you have achieved an open and relaxed state, focus on the energies you directly received from your mother while in her womb. These are some of the most subtle yet significant energetic patterns you have run ever since you were born and they don't have to be yours. You can release and reprogram them through doing "DEEP CELLULAR WORK."

Whatever energetic patterns your biological mother was running while you were in her womb were directly transferred to you through body chemicals and cellular vibrations. If she was nervous and fearful, then you more than likely run an energetic pattern that is also nervously anxious, only you have developed your own slant to it. Not only will you need to BECOME AWARE OF THESE DEEPSEATED ENERGETIC PATTERNS, YOU WILL ALSO NEED TO KEEP RELEASING THEIR ENERGIES, REWORKING THE FEAR-BASED THINKING SEQUENCES YOU ASSUMED AS YOU GREW UP, AND CHANGING THE AUTOMATIC REACTIONS. USING SPECIFIC VISUALIZATIONS AND BODYWORK ORIENTED TOWARDS CHANGING THE CELL/BODY ARMORING YOU DEVELOPED IN ORDER TO RUN THAT PATTERN(S) is also necessary. And you will have to do this over and over, until you have proven to yourself that the energetic pattern is no longer a part of you.

Use yours (and others if helpful) MEMORY WORK, VISUALIZATION, and CONNECTIVE ANALYZATION to recognize the pattern/s. In order to release the pattern's energies/emotions, use EMOTIONAL RELEASING TOOLS, such as: physical movement, writing, self and other talk, artwork, etc. Work with the FORGIVENESS PROCESS. DISCOVER THE MISBELIEFS AND DISBELIEFS that are tangled up in that pattern, using PROGRAMMING TECHNIQUES (such as role-play, repetition, affirmations) to begin establishing the thoughts that run the energies you choose instead. WITNESS or become consciously aware of the BEHAVIOR REACTIONS the old pattern runs, purposefully TRYING OUT NEW AND DIFFERENT REACTIONS that work out better for you. And CELEBRATE when you are no longer caught up in emotions, thoughts, and behaviors that don't serve well the unique Being/Soul that you are now!

(continued on page 119)

2. PARENTAL ENERGIES- These are the emotions, beliefs, thoughts, and behaviors you were directly taught concerning how to manage in the world at large by your parenting models, whether your mother and/or father. Focusing in on both if applicable (one at a time), use memory work, visualization, and connective analyzation to discover and comprehend the ways your parents taught you to be. You can keep those that work well for you: the ones that allow your Soul to shine through. You can also release and change those that do not work as well. GO BEYOND COMFORT LEVEL, because we often hang onto something that needs to be let go of simply because we are familiar with it.

3. RELATIONSHIP ENERGIES- Your parent(s) taught you ways to feel, think, and behave in regards to relationshiping with others, including lover to lover, marriage partnerships, child to parent, sibling to sibling, and worker to coworker to boss. Using your techniques and tools of RECOGNIZE, RELEASE, and RECONSTRUCT, sort through these many and often confusing patterns. HEAL what needs to be healed within you. Let their relationship patterns be their own. LEARN NEW COMMUNICATION SKILLS. REDEFINE YOUR OWN RELATIONSHIPS, EXPERIMENTING WITH HEALTHIER WAYS OF BEING.

In the SELF-CHANGE process, don't forget about these strategies:
1. Move STEP-BY-STEP, one day at a time,
2. Study EFFECTIVE MODELING,
3. Use SELF-OBSERVATION, and
4. Always apply SELF-REINFORCEMENT. Self-change takes lots of time, effort, and motivation. You need to make sure you keep yourself going by noticing and enjoying the positive movements you make.

Also bear in mind that there are several conditions where it is easier to slip back into habitual (or lower-self) ways of responding. These are:
1. When our hormones/body chemistry are not in balance, such as when we are fatigued,
2. When we are hooked into another's game-playing due to our emotional attachments, assumptions, and expectations,
3. When we are running any of our more negative subpersonalities, and
4. When our Soul Core Issues and Energetic Patterns are being stimulated. It's a guarantee that you'll spin, slip back, and sink at times. It's also a guarantee that your self-change processes will take more time, energy, effort, motivation, techniques, skills, and reinforcement than you could ever fathom in this present moment.

FIND PEOPLE WHO ARE ABLE TO ENCOURAGE YOU, INSPIRATIONAL READINGS THAT CAN LIFT YOU, AND FUN THINGS TO DO THAT BLAST YOU FULL OF INVIGORATING ENERGY. Then dust yourself off, use your self-change techniques, and TAKE SOME MORE RISKS. Risks are whatever scares you.

Working on and in *The Higher Self Integration Process* is A CALLING: your Soul is calling you to go beyond the limits of your lower self. That means that you/we have to risk getting to know the fears of rejection and failure, the fear of being a beginner, and the fear of change. Fear is a denial of the reality of God and Soul. Our Soul's Calling means that you/we have to learn COOPERATION AND COLLABORATION instead of competition and dominance. We have to reorient ourselves from product orientation to PROCESS ORIENTATION, and to moving from shallow understanding to the symbolic representation and the energy ESSENCES which are behind and a part of everything here on Earth.

The Higher Self Integration Process is about moving out of Separateness Thinking to WHOLE SYSTEM THINKING and from an emphasis on external authority to TRUST IN INNER KNOWING/INNER WISDOM/DIVINE AUTHORITY. It's about SHEDDING all the OUTGROWN PRETENSES AND GAMES our addictive-oriented society has given us, about LETTING TOXIC THOUGHTS, FEELINGS, BEHAVIORS AND

RELATIONSHIPS GO, and about LEARNING NEW ONES that are healthy, whole, and from The Soul. It is about IDENTIFYING AND REINTEGRATING into a conscious whole our SUBPERSONALITIES and about STUDYING OUR PERSONALITY TYPES. The point in studying our personality types is to recognize our habitual perceptual and relationship strategies and to grow beyond them.

We can grow beyond the influences of Society and instead bring forth the influences of Soul. As John Bradshaw writes, "Soul-murder is the basic problem in the world today." The Higher Self Integration Process is all about SOUL-RETRIEVAL or SOUL-RESURRECTION.

> **THE HIGHER SELF INTEGRATION PROCESS IS A CALLING: YOUR SOUL IS CALLING YOU TO GO BEYOND THE LIMITS OF YOUR LOWER SELF . . .**

ACTIVITY: <u>DO AS I SAY NOT AS I DO</u>

The messages, beliefs, behaviors, and patterns of emotions and reactions we pick up from our environments (from society) are often very confusing, hypocritical, destructive, and Soul-annihilating. Mixed and contradicting messages abound from every direction. And all this craziness gets mixed-up within the thinking, feeling, and behaving patterns that become our personality. The difficulty in being able to really see through society's teachings to TRUE TRUTH is: We often believe that which we have been taught and are familiar with.

In the *Higher Self Integration Process* an essential skill is the ability to see and understand beyond that which others have taught us. We have to BECOME AWARE OF ALL THE DIFFERENT MESSAGES CONCERNING EVERY AREA OF OUR LIVES THAT WE HAVE PICKED UP FROM SOCIETY, BE ABLE TO SEE WHERE RUNNING EACH PARTICULAR ENERGY TAKES US, AND DECIDE WHETHER WE REALLY WANT TO GO THERE. Then we have to know how to ACCESS AND PROGRAM, INTO OUR DAILY LIFE, ENERGIES that are not deadening and which do not rob us of OUR NATURAL SOUL POWERS AND ABILITIES. RECOGNIZING and then REPROGRAMMING all the hundreds of separating and scared, dependent-forming and dysfunctional messages we have received goes hand-in-hand with desired behavior and energetic change.

1. After you are in an open and relaxed state, use BRAINSTORMING, FREE ASSOCIATION, and MEMORY RECALL in order to start listing in your notebook all the different messages/teachings/beliefs/sayings you have been taught over the course of your life about each of the following areas: womyn, men, children, animals/pets, earth/nature, people of different sizes/ages/skin color/countries/religions/abilities/disabilities/economic-class/professions/work-skills, sexuality/hetero- sexual /homosexual/bisexual relationships, marriage, parenting, money and money management, jobs and the working environment, and any other areas you can think of where society's mixed messages have influenced you. Over time, your lists will become long.

2. Then take all the messages you have thought of in one category (doing all the others later) and list them under these titles: A. Contradicting Messages, B. Messages I believe, C. Messages I Am Confused About, and D. Messages I Think Are Full Of _____ (Untruths based on fear). Be aware of any of your thoughts that run defensiveness, embarrassment, shame, guilt, anger, and other negative emotions because these messages will require the most reworking effort. Put a star by them.

(continued on page 121)

3. For every message you have received, put beside it the feelings and behaviors that would be or are a result of running the energy of that message.   For examples: "Everybody is just out for themselves" = Fear, insecurity, competition, jealousy, aggressiveness,   or repression of one's needs... "Money is the root of all evil" = Confusion, conflict, deprivation, shame, money mismanagement...

4.   Take another look at your lists and categories focusing on which messages are still directly influencing your thoughts, feelings and behaviors today. Are the results of your incorporated messages what you really want in your life? All of this DECODING WORK takes Soul-baring honesty and determination to get beyond the narrowness and rigidity of Judgmental Thinking that is based on fear.

5. One at a time, focus on each message you do not want to continue to influence your life- such as "I'm responsible for my mate's/children's happiness" which results in pressure and stress, denial of one's own needs, the need to control others - and begin reworking/reprogramming.   What different messages do you need to program into your thinking processes through the use of affirmations, bibliotherapy, and roleplay? Remember that you, first, want to develop the awareness that the old programming is being ticked off. Then you have the choice to not react/respond in the habitual ways that bring forth the old emotional and behavioral results.

Life's events will bring you plenty of practice once you decide to focus on something. Your daily systems, which became entrained by the old messages and beliefs you ran by, will show resistance. That's when PATIENCE AND PERSEVERANCE go hand-in-hand. Remember to release those old emotions and keep working with yourself towards mental, behavioral and, sometimes, situational change.

PERSONALITY PATTERNS

Since the *Higher Self Integration Process* encompasses changing lower-self (energetically negative) characteristics into *Higher Self* (energetically positive) characteristics, it helps to study PERSONALITY PATTERNS AND TYPES. Personality Patterns are particular composites of various thinking, feeling, and behaving traits or features. ARCHETYPES are the original types over which others are patterned, modeled over and over again by society. Personality Types are groups of people who share common traits and characteristics.

It is helpful to become aware of and to understand your own personality and the personalities of those whom you interact with. There are many systems of personality patterning that humans have come up with throughout our history/herstory in order to make the quest of knowing and being with one another a little more simplified and accessible. Many of the books listed in *A Soul's Delight* include information on various systems of personality types. STUDY THE SYSTEMS YOU ARE DRAWN TO. However, bear in mind that most people are a unique conglomerate based on their individual life and Soul stories, defying strict one-category or one-system classification.

When you are past your intellectually oriented study stage of understanding personalities and into conscious and active personality change, it will be important to UNDERSTAND AND WORK WITH and/or through THE FOLLOWING:

1.   THE ARCHETYPES we have all witnessed and learned,
2.   THE   DUALISTIC   ENERGETIC   PATTERN   known   as   MASCULINE/YANG   AND
        FEMININE/YIN energies,
3.   OUR SOCIETY'S ADDICTIVE SYSTEM,
4.   MODERN MADNESS MEMENTOS such as stress, disconnection, and technology-terror, and
5.   THE SUBPERSONALITIES we form.

COUNSELING AND ASTROLOGY can be two very helpful personality or Personal Process Work tools, both of which STRESS EMOTIONAL INTELLIGENCE, PROBLEM SOLVING, CONSCIOUS CHOICE, AND APPROPRIATE TRANSITIONING AND TIMING. *The Higher Self Integration Journey* is not a lightweight kind of adventure. If you choose to incorporate counseling and astrology into your program plan, align yourself with holistic, in-depth helpers, information, and other resources.

Karma is the set of circumstances that you have chosen to inhabit in this lifetime in order to find and work on areas of yourself that are not yet in truth nor aligned with Soul. Learn to use your everyday situations as the change agents they really are in cosmic actuality. Make the best use of your internal compass: your bodymind complex or entrained system. If you will incorporate the skills of ATTENDING/ CONNECTING/ EXPRESSING and RECOGNIZING/RELEASING/RECONSTRUCTING, then your personality change process will go quicker, smoother, and be a lot more fun.

Relying upon the guidance of your own BODYMIND FEEDBACK SYSTEM will help you in learning which paths to take in terms of all the daily tasks your personality is involved in. You can discover how much work is too much, how much support you need, how much sleep you require, how much time you need to grieve a loss, etc. Then you can take the expressive action to correct the present imbalances that weaken you and the personality characteristic - such as pressuring yourself unrealistically to do more because you are scared you're not good enough - that has set you up or sabotaged your wellness.

MOST PEOPLE ARE AN UNIQUE CONGLOMERATE BASED ON THEIR INDIVIDUAL LIFE AND SOUL STORIES, DEFYING STRICT ONE-SYSTEM OR ONE-CATEGORY PERSONALITY CLASSIFICATION . . .

ARCHETYPES are habitual themes that are stored in the great group mind of the whole human race that are rehearsed again and again in individual lives. They are types of energies that can teach us certain lessons which will further our evolution/reconnection if we so allow. If we don't play out a particular archetype or theme this lifetime, then we have either learned all the lessons involved in previous lifetimes or will engage it again in future lifetimes. Some of us will work with a few or even all of the themes over a lifetime and others will stay with just one.

Listed here are four archetypes, although there are others: The Victim, The Prostitute, The Child, and The Saboteur. You can figure out certain things about these archetypes just by their titles. However, OBSERVE, READ, DISCUSS, AND STUDY each one and as many as you become aware of. FIGURE OUT an archetype's: 1. general pattern of behavior, 2. the emotions and beliefs that fuel the theme, 3. all the possible results of running the archetypes particular energies, thoughts, and behaviors, 4. what one gets out of running that particular theme, 5. the lessons available for learning, and 6. ways/tools/skills necessary in order to complete the archetype's lessons and move out of the theme's energetic grasp.

If you discover an archetype that you are currently running and would rather not, then do your PERSONAL PROCESS WORK focused on that particular archetype. Archetypes are potent. Don't underestimate their hold on your subconscious. If you are caught up in playing The Victim, for example, you not only have to become aware of what you are doing but you have to BE WILLING TO GIVE UP THAT THEME. And that's where it gets a little tricky, for you are engaged in being a victim because it feeds you in certain ways.

In letting go of your attachment to being a victim, you may have to move out of a major relationship, leave your home, quit your job, or a variety of other LIFE STYLE CHANGES. The lessons of the victim, summarized as learning Soul Safety and Soul Power, if sincerely sought will definitely put you on a different path than the one where it was necessary to play the victim.

THE DUALISTIC ENERGETIC PATTERN is not one you want to move out of. Here your focus is on BALANCE. You want a balance in the energies where both male/yang and female/yin work towards a unified goal of *Higher Self Integration or Soul Attunement.* YIN, or FEMININE, ENERGY is the receptive aspect of energetic flow. YANG, or MASCULINE, ENERGY is the active aspect of energetic flow. Both have to be in synch in order to achieve their united purpose and complementary function, which is to reach a balanced state of creation.

Shakti Gawain in her book, *Living In The Light,* has a short and clear chapter on "The Male And Female Within." She points out that the female aspect is the deepest wisest part of ourselves being our intuitive self and that the male aspect is the potent ability to act or to express in the world. It might also be spoken of in terms of the mind and body. It takes both intelligence and form to be human on the Earth Plane.

As Carl Jung pointed out all men have a feminine side (anima) and all women have a masculine side (animus). It is just that most of us were taught to repress certain energies within us so that we would fit into society's current mold. The truth is that both currents run within us and all that is around us. Furthermore, most of us have been both male and female in physical form throughout our Soul journey's various human incarnations. Whatever remained unresolved in our previous lives is animated in some way in this one. Therefore, whichever physical sex we chose to take on this lifetime reminds us to focus on healing that particular energetic patterning.

Our male side is our protector, our risk taker, and our do-er or action. Our female side is our nurturer, our guide/empowerer, and our be-er or light. You need to FOCUS ON AND BRING INTO YOUR LIFE THE CONSTRUCTIVE ASPECTS OR QUALITIES OF BOTH YIN AND YANG. Let the more destructive qualities rest or recede without any momentum or direction. Constructive qualities move towards Soul, wellness, wholeness, and joy. Destructive qualities are oriented toward the lower-self, dysfunction, separateness, and pain.

Often our male and female energies are not functioning naturally in the healthiest way, which is to use our Yin or feminine energies as our consultant and guide and our Yang or masculine energies as our worker and accomplisher. Most of us have been taught dysfunctional ways of using and repressing our Yin/Yang energies and qualities. And that is when the qualities come out twisted. Yang/masculine distorted gets expressed as egotistical, patronizing, chauvinistic, separating, controlling, and annihilating. Yin/feminine distorted gets expressed as dependent, manipulative, seductive, catty, whiny, and needy. Each one of us can end up running a real mixture of both the masculine and feminine destructive qualities. Who hasn't known a needy, manipulative, and controlling egotist?

In *The Higher Self Integration* Process, our goals in working with this dualistic energetic pattern are to:

1. HEAL AND BALANCE OUR YIN/FEMININE AND YANG/MASCULINE ENERGIES AND QUALITIES WITHIN US,

2. RUN THE CONSTRUCTIVE AND LIFE SUPPORTING QUALITIES or CHARACTERISTICS OF THESE ENERGIES.

That means that OUR SPIRIT NEEDS TO MATCH OUR FORM. We need to PURPOSEFULLY DEVELOP OUR INTUITIVE, INNER, GUIDING VOICE AND OUR ABILITY TO RESPOND/ACT WITH MINDFULNESS, PASSIONATE STRENGTH, CLARITY, AND COMPASSION.

BOTH OUR YIN/FEMININE AND YANG/MASCULINE ENERGIES HAVE TO BE IN SYNCH IN ORDER TO ACHIEVE THEIR UNITED PURPOSE AND COMPLEMENTARY FUNCTION WHICH IS TO REACH A BALANCED STATE OF CREATION . . .

ACTIVITY: <u>BALANCING/HEALING YOUR YINYANG</u>

1. These sayings (quotes and clichés), whether they speak of truth or not, concerning modern men's and womyn's general uses/abuses of our masculine/feminine energies, may help stimulate your own thoughts, visions, memories, and plans:

~ Womyn have lost the feeling of power and men have lost the power of feeling ~
~ Men are taught to substitute anger for fear/womyn are taught to substitute dependence for fear~
~ Men are one-minded focused and womyn are whole focused ~
~ Womyn think in relational terms and men think in situational terms ~
~ Womyn are compulsively neat and men are compulsively messy ~
~Men want to do it and womyn want to feel it~
~ Men want their needs met now and womyn want to meet others needs first ~
~ Boys forget and girls won't forget that boys forget ~
~ Boys yell while girls whine ~
~ Macho Men stuck in Cynical Controlling shouting about Self-centered Stunts ~
~ Woozy Womyn stuck in Frumpy Fear telling Toxic Talltales ~
And more . . . LIST OTHERS you have heard or run up against . . .

2. After you have reached an open and relaxed state, think about and LIST YOUR PERSONAL CHARACTERISTICS which you consider running FROM MASCULINE ENERGY AND those you consider FEMININE ENERGY. Ask others you trust what they think. Then taking your list and examining each characteristic, think about whether each one acts in a constructive or destructive way in your life.

3. Now, put the lists aside, preparing to go into visualization. On the mental screen inside your head, allow yourself to PICTURE HOW YOU WOULD ACT AND WHAT YOU WOULD BE DOING USING BALANCED FEMININE/MASCULINE ENERGY. Go into detail using examples or pictures from everyday life. An example would be picturing yourself being able to take responsibility for both the healthy running of your automobile and the preparation of healthy meals, whether you are in a male or female body. Another example is picturing yourself setting a particular goal, taking the action to make it real, and nurturing yourself afterwards. BE THOROUGH, SPECIFIC, AND REAL. You want to program a balanced healing that can work out well for you.

4. Returning to your lists, focus on any imbalances in how you run your masculine and feminine energies. Look for even more destructive uses of these energies within the imbalances themselves. Then discover how you can CHANGE THESE IMBALANCES AND UNHEALTHY USES OF THE DUALISTIC ENERGETIC PATTERNING.

First, USE YOUR RATIONAL, ANALYTICAL (MASCULINE) SIDE to formulate which characteristics and areas of your life are imbalanced in masculine and feminine energy and the constructive/destructive uses of these energies, and how you can change. Use connective analyzation, organizational skills, brainstorming, and free association.

Second, USE YOUR INTUITIVE, RELATIONAL (FEMININE) SIDE by employing prayer, meditation, trancework, dreamwork, and/or art/music/dance to open up to your inner guidance.

Finally, COMBINE ALL YOU'VE LEARNED INTO A PLAN/PROGRAM ORIENTED TOWARDS BALANCING AND HEALING YOUR FEMININE AND MASCULINE SIDES/ ENERGIES. Remember, this is a long, ongoing process, so make sure you have some fun discovering and using the wonder-full parts of being both Yin and Yang, or YinYang!

OUR SOCIETY'S ADDICTIVE SYSTEM AND OUR RESULTING ADDICTIVE AND CODEPENDENT PERSONALITIES AND CHARACTERISTICS are one's that, hopefully, you have already started healing within your own life, because *Higher Self Integration or Soul Attunement* does not go hand-in-hand with addictive ways and means. Not in the least! Rather, Addictive Personalities/Systems are designed for separation not connection, for disempowerment not empowerment, and for fragmentation not wholeness.

Our society is one that is based on ADDICTIVE BEHAVIOR. An addiction is any pathological relationship to a mood-altering experience that has life-damaging consequences. They are designed to keep us unaware of what is going on inside of us, to keep us separated from Soul. Addictions are the wants of our lower personality (programmed by society) that lead us into obsessive and compulsive behavior inconsistent with Soul Values. We use both SUBSTANCE AND PROCESS ADDICTIONS to alter our moods in an attempt to ease or manage the painful feelings, thoughts, and relationships we are running.

Instead of working through all our fears in and of life, most of us use a wide variety of addictions in an attempt to ease our pains. Addictions keep us afraid, out of touch with ourselves, and too busy to challenge the societal/familial system that has learned to spin in painful dysfunctional ways of being. Working through your addictions, through your dependence on our addicted society, and through your addictive personality or thinking/feeling/behaving patterns is working directly with the healing and realignment of and to your Soul.

One can use food (particularly sugar and fat), adrenaline, alcohol, nicotine, caffeine and many other legal/illegal, natural or synthetic drugs in an addictive relationship where one becomes dependent on the substance in order to feel temporarily better. There are many process addictions which are specific series of actions/interactions of thinking and feeling patterns that we've learned can, for the moment, get us away from acknowledging and confronting the negative and fearful feelings/thoughts we have learned to run. Many of our process addictions stimulate the body's chemical adrenaline. As a result, there are many unacknowledged adrenaline junkies experiencing physical ailments due to the chemical imbalances kicked off by excess adrenaline.

Multiple addictions are the norm in today's world. Remember that an addiction is any process in which we are caught up in order to manage our fears and discomforts. Many of us are addicted to money, gambling, adrenaline-pumping risk-taking experiences, work, sex, relationships, and religion. Most of us (particularly men because of society's extra dose of sexual addictive conditioning permeating the learning of the male species) are addicted in some way to sex, or more accurately stated, to power or controlling others behaviors for the fulfillment of one's own needs and desires. Addiction to drama and trauma, to worry and hysteria (to intense emotions), to one's own and other people's problems, to being right/perfect, to busyness and distractions such as noise and speed/time (time-sick people) are also quite prevalent.

WHICHEVER COMBINATIONS OF ADDICTIONS YOU ARE RUNNING THIS LIFETIME SHOW YOU WHICH ASPECTS OF YOUR PERSONALITY HIDE YOUR GREATEST LESSONS AND HEALING NEEDS. After you have been able to ACKNOWLEDGE YOUR ADDICTIONS and DO YOUR PERSONAL PROCESS WORK required to move out of those addictions, you can then FOCUS ON THE PERSONALITY CHARACTERISTICS that are a part of the addictive process and system. One of the most prevalent ADDICTIVE PERSONALITY PATTERNS is CO-DEPENDENCY. Beneath the addiction or dependence to another person or persons and their problems, or to a relationship and its problems, is a mixed-up mess of low self-worth and its resulting Suffering Martyr and Manipulative Server Syndromes.

Many of the negative personality characteristics that we all have to work out of or change in order to *Higher Self Integrate or Attune to Soul* are part of the Addictive Personality and perpetuate what many in the addiction field call "STINKIN' THINKIN'." Negative and catastrophic thinking, confusion, frozen feelings, tunnel vision, making assumptions and having expectations based on selfishness, feelings of deprivation, denial and dishonesty, forgetfulness and spaciness, blame and irresponsibility, critical judgmentalness and pickiness, and the all-pervading defensiveness are all real Soul Stoppers.

WORKING THROUGH YOUR ADDICTIVE PERSONALITY CHARACTERISTICS IS WORKING DIRECTLY WITH THE HEALING OF YOUR SOUL . . .

Our addictive systems, over time, have helped to create some modern societal and personality patterns that appear to be increasing in intensity. These **MODERN MADNESS MEMENTOS** require our personal and societal attention in order to transform their focus of pain and destruction to compassion and healing. The patterns of ONLY ME AND MINE MATTER, SUPER STRESS, and TECHNOLOGY TERROR steer us toward a world full of fatal accidents, maxed-out economies, putrid politics, and cancerous epidemics of body, mind, and spirit.

The Higher Self Integration Process focuses on MOVING THE PERSONALITY OUT FROM THE GREAT LEVEL OF DISCONNECTION AND ITS ACCOMPANYING SELF-ABSORPTION that so permeates our present human condition. Disconnection and self-absorption are the precipitators of The KILLER STRESS most of our cultures have moved into and the wide-spread FEAR AND DESTRUCTIVE USE OF MODERN TECHNOLOGY. The process of CONSCIOUSLY, PURPOSEFULLY, AND PERSISTENTLY RECONNECTING WITH SOUL AND THE GREAT SPIRIT gradually moves one out of THE PLAGUES OF ME-ME-ME and US-AGAINST-THEM into HANDLING EACH MOMENT INTUNED AND INTRUST OF DIVINE PLAN AND ORDER.

In using Personal Process Work for moving out of the addictive cycles, traps, and Modern Madness Memento patterns, it is very important to remember that your task is not to get rid of all your problems, but to LEARN HOW TO DEAL WITH THEM EFFECTIVELY THROUGH USING LOVE, WISDOM, AND COMPASSION. Problems are messages you need to hear. FIND THE ENERGY ESSENCE of what you are working with, for your focus needs to be on FINDING THE DIVINE LIGHT that is BENEATH OUR HUMAN-CREATED DARKNESS.

THINK DEEPLY ABOUT EVERY LOWER-SELF CHARACTERISTIC YOU ARE AWARE OF, ASCERTAINING WHAT IT REPRESENTS, WHAT IT TEACHES, AND WHAT IT CAN BE TRANSFORMED INTO. Contemplate, but don't limit yourself, on the following lists:

Defense Mechanisms- denial, compensation, displacement, dissociation, identification,
    projection, introjection, rationalization, reaction formation, regression, substitution

Emotional & Behavioral Patterning - worthlessness, lack/deprivation, anger, blame, greed,
    frustration, irritation, jealousy, rebellious, rigidity, righteous, judgmental, selfish, competitive,
    war with time, quick-fix thinking, distorter, overwhelmer, controller.

Here are some glimmers of truth about various emotions and personality characteristics/ patterns to help you get started in seeing and thinking beyond the nose:

---- CONTEMPLATE THAT----

~ E-motion is energy in motion: Fear is the energy of discernment. Sadness is the energy of completing.
    Guilt is the energy of conscience. Shame is the energy of limitations.
    Joy is the energy that all is well . . .

~ Anger is a signal and a message that you are being hurt, that your rights are being violated,
    that your needs/wants are not being adequately met, that something is not right.
    Your anger can motivate you to say "no" to the ways in which you are defined by others and
    "yes" to the dictates of the inner self. Anger tells you to think more clearly about yourself.
    Why do you need anger in order to stand up for yourself? . . .

~ Having expectations, and therefore resistance and resentment when expectations aren't met,
    produce hurt, a type of anger . . .
~ Pure sadness without anger is clean and refreshing. Sadness with hurt is toxic . . .

~ Sarcasm is an overload warning signal of anger . . .

~ Procrastination is an escape from living present moments as fully as possible . . .

~ Blame is used whenever we refuse to take responsibility for/of our life . . .
~ Dishonesty is a by-product of fear . . .

~ Shame is "there is something wrong with me" and guilt is "I've done something wrong" . . .

~ Doing things automatically isn't creative. It is functional and a past process . . .

~ Needing to control makes one uptight & tense. Change the neediness and fear that reside
    within your psyche, so each moment can be a wondrous event seen through eyes and
        thoughts that celebrate the learning going on and the chance to grow/change . . .

~ Whenever you compare yourself to anyone else, you are playing the "it's not fair game,"
        shifting from self-reliance to other-directed external thinking . . .

~ Denial is when we refuse to see what we see and know what we know . . .

~ Betrayal comes from not recognizing where someone is at and putting expectations on them that they
    are more advanced than they actually are . . .

~ Not feeling good enough or not having enough sets us up for being used, violated, betrayed, attacked,
        abandoned, neglected, scapegoated, and rejected by others . . .

~ A major reason we're so speeded-up as a society is because of discomfort with our feelings.
        Effectiveness in life happens when we come into our own rhythm . . .

~ Competition causes anxiety and is inefficient, redundant, aggressive, undermines intrinsic
        motivation, destroys self-esteem, and poisons relationships . . .

~ We worry when we see life from a limited perspective, not realizing that life is an evolving process.
    Worry is an activity of the mind in which we dwell on things from a pessimistic point of view.
    It involves preoccupation with and concentration on life's experiences, people, and oneself
    from a dismal perspective. Worry can involve anticipation of dire possibilities or a review
    of past experiences with an eye on destructive, morbid elements. Worry can include thoughts
        of obstacles, delay, or failure to attain one's dreams or goals . . .

THE PROCESS OF CONSCIOUSLY, PURPOSEFULLY, AND PERSISTENTLY RECONNECTING WITH SOUL/THE DIVINE GRADUALLY MOVES ONE OUT OF THE PLAGUES OF ME-ME-ME AND US-AGAINST-THEM INTO HANDLING EACH MOMENT INTUNED AND INTRUST OF DIVINE PLAN AND ORDER . . .

The bottom line is: DON'T LET YOUR PERSONALITY GET IN THE WAY OF YOUR SOUL ANY LONGER! And in order for that to happen, you have to become aware of and work with all the various **SUBPERSONALITIES** you have formed. Your subpersonalities were created by your subconscious in reaction to: the Earthly environment you were raised and lived in, archetypes, dualistic energetic patterning, addictive personality patterns, including Modern Madness Mementos, and your own Soul's history and karma.

Subpersonalities are different patterns of characteristics, behaviors, temperaments, emotions, and mental thoughts/traits that form sub or less intact personalities within one's larger personality configuration. They usually emerge or take over our interactions through a learned automatic stimulus-response reaction. Just like the characteristic- stubborn - can be used both positively and negatively, each of our subpersonalities, formed out of survival and Earthbound needs, have their positive and negative sides. When consciously working with integrating one's various subpersonalities, remember that YOU HAVE FORMED EACH ONE IN PROTECTION OF YOUR LIFE: to survive/be accepted in the environment under which they were formed.

In *Beyond Belief Into Knowing,* my autobiography, the first few pages of Chapter Twenty One go into a detailed description of how I named, got to know, and reworked my various subpersonalities, such as Ms. Critical, The Overwhelmer, Ms. Wanna Be, and Peacekeeper. Perhaps you have a Mr. Perfect, a Devil's Advocate, a Happy Helper, and/or World's Best Lover lurking within you, just waiting for their chance to shine or muddy things up a bit.

Your task is to RECOGNIZE, NAME, AND GET TO KNOW EACH ONE OF YOUR SUBPERSONALITIES. You want to FIGURE OUT WHEN, HOW, AND WHY EACH ONE FORMED AND WHAT IT TRIES TO DO FOR YOU. It is also important to KNOW THE CONDITIONS UNDER WHICH EACH ONE'S VOICES AND MANNERISMS COME INTO THEIR OWN. As you CONSCIOUSLY WITNESS your various subpersonalities do their thing, you are then able to OBSERVE THE EFFECT running that particular brand of reactive energies has in your current life. That's when CHOICE becomes your tool once again.

Will it work out better, will you feel more comfortable, is it now more appropriate to run Mr. Compromiser when your life's partner wants to do something a certain way, rather than Mr. Know It All? Perhaps Mr. Compromiser got you nothing and nowhere with your childhood Bully Brother, and back then Mr. Know It All at least got your foot in the door. But unless you are mated to your childhood Bully Brother, perhaps your adulthood Sensitive Spouse would work better with Mr. Compromiser. So, you work hard at STOPPING THE OLD AUTOMATIC REACTION, work harder at STRENGTHENING Mr. Compromiser, and NOTICE that Mr. Know It All starts ceasing and desisting when he's no longer needed in order to survive.

Make no mistake about the fact that reworking/transforming one's personality is not a simple, quick, easy thing to do. However, it can be fascinating and fun if you will let it be. Once you've turned the tide on Stinkin' Thinkin' and all those outdated automatic reactions/patterns, it is quite a blast to consciously choose and become the wonder-full being you are as Soul.

And don't forget to not only let go of those outmoded and destructive ways of feeling, thinking and behaving, but to "LET GO AND LET GOD…"

The following AFFIRMATIVE PRAYER for reprogramming one's personality is helpful when used on a regular basis:

Holy Spirit,
    I release to you all thoughts, intentions, beliefs, feelings, attitudes, habits, energy patterns, and subpersonality parts that bind me to negative and nonproductive experiences.
    All my _____ (fear, doubt, frustration, anxiety, harsh criticalness, etc.) is released from me. I am surrounded in Divine Love Light.
    I let go all concerns knowing that your miracle-working power is manifesting _____ (harmony, guidance, freedom, safety, prosperity, order, etc.) in my life.
    I give thanks in advance for my good . . .
        Amen… So Be it… And it is so… Blessed Be…

ACTIVITY: <u>BECOMING ONE</u>

     1. After you have gotten into an open and relaxed state, use various techniques to focus your mind on **BECOMING AWARE OF THE DIFFERENT SUBPERSONALITIES** you run. Recall how you have responded in the past to various types of situations. Start recognizing patterns of feelings and behaviors you run at different times. Recall in detail what you felt like, the expressions and mannerisms you used, and the results of the interpersonal and emotional patterns you ran. Once you have become aware of the differences in who you were or acted like at various times and situations in your life, begin naming them. You want to use descriptive names that parallel the overall feel of that particular pattern. **MAKE THE NAMES TO THE POINT**, so they act as visual as well as mental comparisons to your subpersonalities.

     2. Once you have become aware of your subpersonalities, write their names down in your journal with lots of space under each one. As time passes by, **USE YOUR TOOLS OF AWARENESS AND OBSERVATION TO DISCERN AND WRITE DOWN FOR EACH SUBPERSONALITY:**
     A. What you look, act, and feel like while running each one,
     B. What stimulates/triggers each,
     C. How and why each subpersonality was formed in your life,
     D. What it does or attempts to do for you,
     E. The misbeliefs and disbeliefs each of your subpersonalities run on,
     F. How it regulates your energy,
     G. What the results of running each subpersonality today are,
     H. What other characteristics or patterns it employs, and
     I. What life lessons you can learn from it.

     3. When you have the above sorted out for all of your subpersonalities, it is time to **CHOOSE WHICH PARTS OF CERTAIN ONES ARE APPROPRIATE FOR YOU TODAY.** What does each of your subpersonalities need in order to transform its negative or unfulfilled energy and purpose into its higher form? Which of your more destructive or inhibiting subpersonalities have outrun the others? What can you do to bring out the more constructive, loving subpersonalities? What specific reworking and developing of characteristics do you need in order to integrate your subpersonalities into a more functional whole? Which skills and tools will lead you into being one whole, complete, and appropriate-to-the-moment personality, instead of various fragmented, imbalanced subpersonalities?

DON'T LET YOUR PERSONALITY GET IN THE WAY OF YOUR SOUL . . .

PERSONALITY PRIORITIES

    Higher Self Integration **is about aligning our personality with our Soul.** In so doing, we not only have to become aware of and rework our lower-self personality characteristics and patterns we took on, but WE HAVE TO VERY CONSCIOUSLY, PURPOSEFULLY, AND KNOWINGLY LEARN AND INTEGRATE INTO OUR DAILY LIVES *HIGHER SELF* PERSONALITY CHARACTERISTICS AND PATTERNS THAT ENABLE US TO LIVE FROM, WITH, IN, AND AS SOUL. Our task as CONSCIOUS BEINGS is to experience our uniqueness while staying in conscious alignment with Soul/Oneness/The Divine.

In regards to personality, the fields of psychology, psychoneuroimunology, and metaphysics are all starting to beat the same drum. It turns out that those who learned HIGH SELF-ESTEEM are the same ones who are more successful in/with life and healthier than others. Psychologist Daniel Goleman in his book, *Emotional Intelligence*, explains that success in life depends a lot more on emotional skills like SELF-AWARENESS, SELF-MOTIVATION, AND USING ONE'S INTUITION (characteristics of high self-esteem) than it does on either intellectual prowess or technical-know-how.

Henry Dreher, a leading writer in the fields of health and medicine, alerts us to the fact that there is a particular personality pattern that strengthens the human immune system, thus enabling that person to be healthy. In his book, *The Immune Power Personality,* he points out that people using the immune power personality, who also have high self-esteem, handle stressful events not with denial, but with ACCEPTANCE, FLEXIBILITY, AND A WILLINGNESS TO LEARN AND GROW. In *The Future Of The Body*, Michael Murphy proposes that most instances of significant human development are produced by activities such as DISCIPLINED SELF-OBSERVATION, VISUALIZATION OF DESIRED CAPACITIES, AND CARING FOR OTHERS. All of those activities can be linked to high self-esteem, emotional intelligence, and the immune power personality.

Dan Wakefield, in his book*, Creating From The Spirit*, points out that we are also seeing a new paradigm or model of positive/enlightening creativity arising from every walk of life, with these similarities among the creators:
~ They cultivate their natural senses to stimulate their creativity, use their dreams as an initiator of ideas and knowledge, and develop clarity as their source of creativity . . .
~ They live rich lives sharing themselves with others, find nourishment in community, feel connected to the whole of life, and express their gratitude for their time on the planet . . .
~ They recognize the body-mind-spirit connection, practice inner silence and guidance in their daily lives, and take full responsibility for all that they are, have, and do . . .
~ They see obstacles as an opportunity to create new solutions/techniques/skills, regard age as an opportunity to apply the wisdom of experience, find surprising new ways to perform routine tasks, and use their creative gifts in all areas of their lives . . .

Attuning to Soul requires developing high self-esteem, and all the characteristics listed above for the SOUL'S REAL TRUE IDENTITY IS CONSCIOUSNESS, WISDOM, AND LOVE. In order for our Soul's voice to be heard it has to be tuned into the energy frequencies created by such qualities as OPENNESS, PEACEFULNESS, PLAYFULNESS, WONDER, AND COURAGE. Soul ignites through the energies and forms of LOVING KINDNESS, RELAXED AFFILIATION, MINDFUL TALKING, THOUGHTFUL LISTENING, CONSCIOUS ACTIONS, PASSIONATE PATIENCE, CARING DETACHMENT, AND EASY-GOING FERVOR.

Being *Higher Self Integrated or Soul Attuned* is synonymous to being labeled as both a HERO AND AN ECCENTRIC. The hero is the growing edge of humanity/community, the part that explores the unknown to uncover mystery, discovering new information and skills, gaining new assets or allies and then bringing all these things back for the benefit of the whole. Forming skills and abilities, qualities and traits (A *Higher Self*) that provide one's Soul thought and voice, is both revolutionary and evolutionary in connection to the overall human condition. As philosopher William James puts it, "Ignoring our spiritual need to connect with a higher form of consciousness is the equivalent of limiting one's mind to a small percentage of its potential." In accessing Soul, opening up and developing one's mind goes hand-in-hand with connecting with higher forms of consciousness.

Living Soul through your *Higher Self* means that you will be beating your drum in a rhythm that doesn't fit or even placate mass consciousness's drone. As a result you will often appear as eccentric to others, and indeed you will be. Eccentrics show a lack of social conformity, often deviating from established norms. They display strong curiosity, intuition and inner inquisitiveness, playfulness and humor, and a high-level of creativity. Being aware even in childhood that they are different, they have a tendency to be outspoken about their particular focus using their "make the world a happier place" idealism to keep on breaking through barriers.

Speaking and acting from a level of integrity that reflects Soul can only be channeled through *Higher Self* characteristics, thought patterns, and emotional energies. Soul's naturally positive, joyful, wise, and loving energies that spark intuition, creativity, and healing have to have thinking, feeling, and behaving pathways and traits that match in frequency. IT IS UP TO EACH ONE OF US TO CONSCIOUSLY DEVELOP A PERSONALITY, A HIGHER SELF, THAT EXPRESSES SOUL. SOUL SELF-EXPRESSION IS WHAT IT'S ALL ABOUT.

> **SPEAKING AND ACTING FROM A LEVEL OF INTEGRITY THAT REFLECTS SOUL CAN ONLY BE CHANNELED THROUGH HIGHER SELF CHARACTERISTICS, THOUGHT PATTERNS, AND EMOTIONAL ENERGIES...**

ACTIVITY: <u>EXPRESSING SOUL</u>

1. **BRAINSTORM** all the *Higher Self* characteristics and abilities that are attuned to Soul. Write them all down. Once you've reached the end of one wave, get in an even deeper and more relaxed state and go again. Come back to this at different times because there are a lot more *Higher Self* abilities and characteristics than you thought there were. Positive Soul energies greatly out-weigh the negative human ones, although you were probably taught, through mass-consciousness, the opposite. Review this book for more "AH-HA'S."

2. Over time, think about, **RESEARCH, AND STUDY** each of the *Higher Self* abilities and characteristics one-at-a-time. They have much more complex, whole, and Soulful meanings and uses than you were taught through society's socialization process. Their real Soul or Divine meanings are often very different than what human society teaches. For example, we've been taught that humility is being meek, modest, and submissive when it really means being open. In order to be open, one has to have high self-esteem, an inner Soul security that enables one to be willing to see, hear, and be with others without the need to compare, compete, or squelch. Since there's a lot more to humility than usually meets the eye, you take it from there. Just remember: When you think you understand a *Higher Self* characteristic and ability, more levels, meanings, and opportunities will be brought your way if you remain humble, or open to truth.

As a deeper meaning of each *Higher Self* characteristic and ability comes your way, **EXAMINE IN DETAIL EACH PART OF THE DEFINITION** you are discovering, because in so doing you will uncover more and more of life's truths. For example, in this definition of joy you would also spend a lot of resources delving into love, inner peace, appreciation, gratitude, compassion, and connection, all Soul qualities in and of themselves:

> Joy is an attitude. It is the presence of love, for self and others. It comes from a feeling
> of inner peace, the ability to give and receive, and appreciation of self, others, and life. It
> is a state of gratitude and compassion, a feeling of connection to your *Higher Self*, Soul.

3. At the same time you are discovering, researching, and studying each Soul quality and ability, look for ways to specifically integrate that quality/ability into your daily happenings. **AWARENESS, FOCUS, AND PRACTICE HELP TO MAKE IT A REAL PART OF YOUR LIFE.** To live life as Soul is to live life in a state of enthusiasm and joy. If you are working on the quality enthusiasm, use enthusiasm wherever it's appropriate, for you will learn so much more about a quality, ability, or characteristic as you experiment with it. Real integrated learning is all about knowing and becoming, for doing turns into Being. And in The Being State, expressing is naturally unstoppable. In The Becoming Process, remember:

A. **AWARENESS** B. **FOCUS** C. **RELEASE ANY FROM-THE-PAST EMOTIONAL BLOCKS** D. **REWORK ANY MISBELIFS AND DISBELIEFS AND OTHER BLOCKING THOUGHT PATTERNS** E. **STUDY AND PROGRAM THE TRUTH ABOUT THE SOUL QUALITY AND ABILITY INTO YOUR MINDCOMPUTER** F. **MAKE OPPORTUNITIES TO SAFELY PRACTICE AND EXPERIMENT WITH NEW WAYS OF BEING** G. **REINFORCE, CELEBRATE, AND BE THANKFUL FOR WHAT YOU HAVE LEARNED ...**

Spiritual joy and wisdom come through our capacity to open, to love fully, and to move/grow/be free in life. Outward activity propelled from within is the essence of creative existence. These Soul capacities are applied on the Earth plane through *Higher Self* personality characteristics, abilities, and thinking/feeling/behaving patterns. Soul-directed activity is always oriented to helping Soul-center and magnetize to you those resources and experiences that can teach you to be in alignment with your inner being, Soul. The choice to attune to them as such is yours.

Even so, Soul is always watching over your lower-self personality's gyrations, monitoring to see if your attitudes, who you are at the personality, emotional, and physical levels, are ready for your next step in the quest to become all you can be, or Soul Attuned. It is only waiting for YOUR CONSCIOUSLY COMMITTED, "ALL SYSTEMS GO" SIGNAL. Your Soul is ready to speak and create, but you have to allow it to get through.

You have to not only be aware of and stop all lower-self negative thinking, feeling, and behaving patterns, you have to consciously choose thoughts, emotions, behaviors, and activities that align you with Soul, enabling you to COCREATE each moment of your life.

CONSCIOUSLY CHOOSE TO RUN:

** APPRECIATION & BLESSING FOR EVERYTHING YOU HAVE...
Thankfulness, gratitude, awareness, unity, softness, peacefulness, pleasure . . .

** ENTHUSIASTIC VITALITY ABOUT ALL YOU ARE ENGAGED IN...
Excitement, optimism, goal setting, organization, commitment, happy-to-be-alive . . .

** BLESSING AND PRAISE FOR FAMILY MEMBERS, FRIENDS, SERVICE WORKERS...
Respect, love, appreciation, friendship, support, acknowledgement, recognition . . .

** POSITIVE ACKNOWLEDGEMENT OF YOURS & OTHERS SKILLS AND ABILITIES...
Self-knowledge, attention, pleasantness, communication, sharing = giving & receiving . . .

** AWARENESS & UNDERSTANDING OF OTHERS PERSPECTIVE/DEVELOPMENT...
Broad-mindedness, compassion, discernment, kindness, kinship, thoughtfulness . . .

** THOUGHTS ABOUT: HIGHER SELF INTEGRATION, SHARING RESOURCES & GIVING TO OTHERS (THE EARTH AND ITS CRITTERS), HIGHER ABILITIES, THE DIVINE, LEVELS OF SPIRIT, THE BEAUTY AND HEALING OF NATURE/ART/ MUSIC/MOVEMENT, WHAT YOU CAN TEACH OTHERS, AND THE LIKE...
Whole thinking skills, creativity, growth energy, stimulation, motivation, wonder . . .

** PHRASES/QUESTIONS THAT EXPAND YOU: "I AM AND RADIATE DIVINE LOVE." "I LET GO AND LET GOD." "HOW CAN I INCREASE MY LOVE/JOY ENERGY?" "AM I OPERATING FROM SOUL CONSCIOUSNESS?" AND THE LIKE...
Positivity, expansiveness, discovery, blossoming, breaking-through energy, insight . . .

** CONSCIOUSLY RUNNING HIGHER SELF PATTERNS OF THOUGHTS WHICH ARE FILLED WITH POSITIVE WAYS OF LOOKING AT THINGS...
Joy, happiness, Soul consciousness, upliftment, flexibility, unfoldment, renewal . . .

** CALM, JOYFUL, RELAXED THOUGHTS THAT AFFIRM DIVINE ORDER THAT ALL WILL WORK OUT GREAT, THAT YOU HAVE CONSTANT CREATIVE EXPRESSION, AND CAN OPERATE AT A RELAXED, HEALTHY PACE ALL THE TIME...
Success, safety, can-do energy, hope, acceptance, nonresistance, smoothness, enjoyment . . .

** SILLY, HUMOROUS, HAPPY THOUGHTS...
Giggling, laughter, lightness, humor, fun, wit, merriment, delight, spontaneity . . .

** TUNING IN, ASKING, AND RECEIVING HIGHER GUIDANCE (LETTING THE GREAT SPIRIT BE A CONSCIOUS PART OF YOUR EVERY MOMENT AND COMMUNICATING WITH THE SPIRIT WORLD/EARTH'S SPIRIT DIMENSIONS)...
Faith, wisdom, learning, trust, knowledge, perception, understanding, exploration . . .

** CREATING NEW IDEAS/WAYS OF DOING EVERYTHING IN YOUR LIFE...
Positive change, adventure, creativity, progression, advancement, inspiration . . .

** MANAGEMENT OF YOUR RESOURCES FROM VIEW OF SOUL/HIGHER SELF: THE HIGHEST AND BEST FOR ALL CONCERNED...
Honesty, connectedness, calm, confidence, community, goodness, caring, concern . . .

Make the above thinking/feeling choices a part of your moment-to-moment every day reality and you will be acting as, with, and from Soul. You will dance your way through life, sparkling and spinning in delight instead of drowning in confusion and fear. You will attract to you those things that bring out the vital aliveness that is inside you, for you refuse to deaden or stifle your Soul any longer. And most of all, you will model happiness and wholeness, something our Earth World could use a whole lot more of!

OUTWARD ACTIVITY PROPELLED FROM WITHIN
IS THE ESSENCE OF CREATIVE EXISTENCE . . .

ACTIVITY: <u>SWITCHING CIRCUITS</u>

You have to make *Higher Self* characteristics and abilities a real part of your life in order for the integration component to realistically set in and switch those negative, mass consciousness aligned energies into positive Higher Consciousness energies and circuits. It's not possible to truly praise and appreciate your life and others if you still run critical judgmentalness because you believe that others are out to get you. Compassion is unattainable if you still operate out of a definition of love that centers around self-absorbing sacrifice with its resulting rescuer and martyr patterns. Switching circuits is a complex process. Get the steps set in your mind. Work them well by taking it one characteristic, ability, step, and day at a time. Faking doesn't cut the mustard here.

1. Apply all the steps you practiced under the activity "Expressing Soul" which are:

A. AWARENESS   B. FOCUS   C. RELEASE ANY FROM-THE-PAST EMOTIONAL BLOCKS D. REWORK ANY MISBELIEFS AND DISBELIEFS AND OTHER BLOCKING THOUGHT PATTERNS   E. STUDY AND PROGRAM THE TRUTH ABOUT THE SOUL QUALITY AND ABILITY INTO YOUR MINDCOMPUTER F. MAKE OPPORTUNITIES TO SAFELY PRACTICE THE NEW WAY OF BEING   G. REINFORCE, CELEBRATE, AND BE THANKFUL FOR WHAT YOU HAVE LEARNED.

2. Make sure that your new circuits, which are ingrained over time, can handle the type and amount of voltage or energy you will be running as your *Higher Self* in direct attunement to Soul and God/Goddess. Consciously and purposefully WORK ON ALL THE AREAS/ thoughts/feelings/abilities that are LISTED UNDER "CONSCIOUSLY CHOOSE TO RUN." (continued on page 134)

3. Learn to BECOME INSTANTLY AWARE OF YOUR EVERY NEGATIVE ENERGY CURRENT, thought, feeling, and behavior that even flits through your consciousness. Your body will tell you through its intricate feedback system, even if you miss your own nasty thought. You will find that as you get more advanced, your body will tolerate less negativity. You'll bind up and hurt a lot more much quicker and by running a lot less ca-ca than you use to. Don't get discouraged, because this will help to naturally increase your awareness.

4. FIGURE OUT WHAT WOULD BE HEALTHIER AND HOLIER, and a whole lot more helpful and pleasant, TO RUN INSTEAD. And then try your best to "SWITCH CURRENTS". The more planned practice sessions you do while in a light trance or relaxed and open state of consciousness concerning learning to run the thoughts/emotions/abilities/behaviors listed under "Consciously Choose To Run," the easier it will be to switch into running them in the moment. If you find yourself hanging on to the old negative, dysfunctional thoughts and energies, then go back to the drawing board and work on: your attachment to letting them still control your life. What are you getting from or out of your old ways of being? And what can you do to get out of that attachment or system?

5. BE CREATIVE about ways you can remind, reprogram, be aware of the old stuff and reinforce, strengthen, entrain switching into the healthier, more conscious modes of being. Put up appropriate signs throughout your living quarters. Use key words that you write on your hands, sew into your clothing, paint on your mirrors, tape into your mind. Ask others to point out when you are falling back into a particular pattern. Brainstorm, free associate, get ideas from your dreams, seek inner guidance from your specially-assigned spirit guides, etc. etc. etc., for there are many techniques you can use. Visualize, affirm, sing, shout, paint, pray, and boogie into your new ways of being. Heal and cultivate your INNER CHILD, so that your natural need to explore with excitement, joy, and wonder will once again shine forth.

6. This affirmation, used over time, is very reinforcing. Fill in the blanks with what you wish to incorporate, integrate, and be, such as:

   FAITH, PROSPERITY, HEALING, WISDOM, DIVINE ORDER, etc.

   "I HAVE _____. IT IS A PART OF MY BEING. IT IS WHAT I AM. I AM THE
         POWER OF _____. AND I EXPRESS THAT POWER NOW!"

CHAPTER EIGHT

OUR ETERNAL MIND

OUR MINDS ARE CAPABLE OF KNOWING EVERYTHING THERE IS TO KNOW, EVEN BEFORE IT HAPPENS . . .

THOUGHT CONTROL

Mind, **or intelligence, being of spirit and Soul, exists forever and in every dimension of The Holoverse.** It is eternal, without a beginning or end, existing outside of time. There are not any limits to the power of mind, except those we place on ourselves when in human form. Get over or beyond one of the biggest misbeliefs and myths you were taught by mass consciousness: "Because the mind and the human brain are the same thing, when our brain ceases to function our intelligence dies." This is a big NOT SO! When our brains/bodies cease to function, our mindspiritSoul moves on into other dimensions.

In human form, our mind appears to work through our brain in order to manipulate within the material world. However, even man's limited science is starting to prove that intelligence, or mind, exists in every cell of our bodies, in every leaf of a tree, and indeed, in everything. Essentially, our brains are our communications headquarters. For our Souls in their spirit form to be able to inhabit a human body, a functioning brain and a functioning body coexist in a totally and intricately connected dance. In life here on Earth in human form, our mind (intelligence) communicates to its body, and the rest of the material world, through its brain.

Mind or consciousness manifests through the brain in terms of thought, perception, reason, intuition, feeling, will, memory, and imagination. Our capacities to acquire and apply knowledge and to communicate to ourselves and others our thoughts through language enable us to consciously explore everything and anything we are willing to focus on. However, the majority of us have greatly limited our vast abilities and potential, willing only to acknowledge a limited and narrow part of total existence.

Our minds are capable of knowing everything there is to know, even before it happens. We don't even have to speak in order to communicate because we have the capacity to read minds: to read energy. We can move material objects, heal our dis-eases, and create things that have never been created before directly through the power of our minds.

Even the brain researchers say that we humans only use from 1/10th to 1/4th of the potential of our brain. Our brains were built to channel or communicate the awesome power of mind. Yet, we still use fear, insecurity, distrust and a whole barrel full of negative, destructive thoughts that reek of restrictions based on tons of crazy misbeliefs and disbelief's in order to limit ourselves.

Thoughts are how our minds move energy into the Earth Plane. Thoughts all vibrate because they are full of energy. These vibrations transmit information making communication possible. Each thought vibrates/pulses to a beat or rhythm of its own. Positive thoughts vibrate at a rate that is life enhancing and affirming. Negative thoughts vibrate at a rate that is deadening and destructive. Thoughts then produce emotion, which are even more energetically charged with either a negative or positive pulse. Negative pulses don't do nice things to our bodies. They pump imbalanced chemicals that make us feel and act nasty. Thus, our body mirrors our thoughts.

The Higher Self Integration Process is all about learning to be in contact with, channel, use, and enhance the power of our minds. In order to do that we have to:

1. THOUGHTCONTROL- Be aware of and choose thoughts that are based on life-affirming and Soul-evolving energies.

2. BRAINWORK- Heal, balance, and expand our physical brains so that we can communicate the power of our minds and the energy of our Souls.

3. MIND TRAIN- Consciously train our mind/brain complex to operate smoothly together and open up our Beings to the abilities and powers that are ours as Souls.

4. METAPHYSICALLY RELATE- Allow our minds to interrelate with the various dimensions of life in its totality, whether they are of material, Earthly form or beyond physicality.

In moving from mass consciousness programming into Soul Expression, one of the first places to start in relation to opening up to the powers of MIND, is to GET CONSCIOUS CONTROL OVER THE THOUGHTS YOU RUN YOUR LIFE WITH AND ON. Clarity of thought is essential to clarity and openness of mind. If you think thoughts that generate negative emotions, these emotions will block one's ability to communicate with Soul. Remember, YOU FEEL WHAT YOU THINK. Thoughts produce emotions, or energies. That lower-rated emotional energy has to be consciously tended to or it stays in the body/mind/spirit complex, blocking the higher vibes that are available and our ability to be in touch with our Souls.

THE FIRST PLACE TO START IN OPENING TO THE POWERS OF MIND IS TO GET CONSCIOUS CONTROL OVER THE THOUGHTS YOU THINK . . .

ACTIVITY: <u>TWISTED THOUGHTS</u>

1. After you have achieved a relaxed and open state, review your last 24 hours looking for the TWISTED THOUGHTS you have run: thoughts that are negative, emitting uncomfortable feelings and destructive behaviors. LIST ALL that you recall. Then choose one to focus on.

(continued on page 137)

2. Relax further by taking several deep, slow breaths. RECALL THE EXPERIENCE of running that particular twisted thought, or series/spiral of twisted thoughts since they are famous for feeding upon one another. Allow yourself to revisit the scene in your head, and as the negative emotion rearises within you, CHOOSE A HEALTHY RELEASING ACTIVITY and let it go.

3. After you are clearer, ask yourself what really bothered you about the situation, or what ticked off the negativity. Remember all the feelings and words that were happening inside of you. Why did you think and feel that way? Take a LOOK AT THE PROGRAMMED ATTITUDES OR MODELS you have had that showed you how others (or yourself) "should have" behaved. FIGURE OUT YOUR EXPECTATIONS that weren't fulfilled AND YOUR PERCEIVED INJUSTICES that stimulated twisted thoughts based on fear. Through all this exploration, your intent is on BRINGING INTO CONSCIOUSNESS THE MISBELIEFS AND DISBELIEFS YOU ARE OPERATING SUBCONSCIOUSLY FROM which set you up for twisted thoughts. Write down each belief that obviously doesn't work out so well in your life and EXPLORE WHERE THEY CAME FROM AND WHERE THEY LEAD TO.

4. Now, take another look at the original incident that ticked off your twisted thoughts you have been working on. If you had consciously chosen positive and clear thoughts and feelings to run, WHICH THOUGHTS BASED ON WHAT BELIEFS COULD HAVE LED YOU THERE? USING A VARIETY OF YOUR CREATIVE CHANGE SKILLS AND TOOLS, such as affirming and humor, REFRAME your experience for yourself. Reframing means learning to perceive things from the eye of Soul, not from the fickle way mass consciousness has dictated life should be. How can you move from a "that jerk hurt me" to an "I'm free from his/her personal pain" frame of mind and experience?

Just because you have been stuck in a particular mode of automatic, twisted response doesn't mean that you have to stay there. Find the thought path that led you to unhappiness and discomfort, and rework it! Figure out the thought path that can lead you to comfort and joy and program it into your mindbrain complex! REFRAME YOUR THOUGHTS! REPROGRAM YOUR PERSONAL BIOCOMPUTER/BRAIN!

5. Continue EDUCATING/REPROGRAMMING yourself to thinking and feeling more positive through spiritual and mental studies and practices. Every time you fall back into a negative belief, thinking, feeling, and reacting pattern, go back to the drawing board and keep on reworking. Remember that your old ways of thinking took years to form and were reinforced over and over again. There will be huge time gaps between your awareness of the need to change and your ability to make those reworked thinking and feeling patterns a real part of your daily behavior. So, STAY FOCUSED AND CELEBRATE when you get there!

In order to reach your Soul Level, you have to be able to CONTROL BOTH THE CONTENT AND THE SPEED OF YOUR THOUGHTS. The average human usually takes less than a second to run a single thought. A thought pattern takes less than 7 seconds, with our minds flitting off in another direction within 15 seconds. Yet, the more we focus on something, the more that thing will happen as it was addressed.

The "as it was addressed" part is not to be denied or underrated, for THIS IS HOW WE ARE RESPONSIBLE FOR SHAPING THE COURSE OF OUR LIVES. It is a truth to be reckoned with, for the power of negative emotions often keep us focusing or obsessing about something longer than most things if, due to an untrained mind, we have not learned thought control. For *Higher Self Integration*, you have to CHOOSE THOUGHTS THAT ARE SOUL-ALIGNED AND DEVELOP THE ABILITIES TO SUSTAIN DEEP AND LONG PERIODS OF CONCENTRATION AND FOCUS.

You also have to be able to EMPTY YOUR THOUGHTS, OR QUIET YOUR MIND, so that even higher energy, or Divine Wisdom and Guidance, can get through the denseness of living on the Earth Plane. And this, for most of us, is much easier said than done. To be in the state of "having no thoughts" is a high level skill.

One of the most helpful states you can achieve and incorporate into your daily life is called MINDFULNESS. It is the art of living in the present moment, the BE HERE NOW state. Mindfulness involves paying attention on purpose and deliberately, with all one's thoughts remaining on and only about the present moment. It also involves nonjudgmentalness: not placing value judgments, bad or good, on what and how you (others, and/or the circumstances) are doing something in that moment. Mindfulness is all about appreciating and accepting each moment in life as it is in, of, by, and for the moment.

Mindfulness takes most of us oodles of effort because it goes against the grain of many of the society's we live in. Yet, IT CAN BE PRACTICED IN RELATION TO MOST THINGS WE DO IN DAILY LIFE. Try taking a shower with all your thoughts being focused on you in the shower. Wash your dishes with mindfulness. As your hands are only washing dishes, make your mind focus only on the same. Allow all your thoughts to only be about what you are doing in that very moment and act of cleaning plates and pots.

A helpful book about Mindfulness is Jon Kabat-Zinn's, *Wherever You Go There you Are: Mindfulness Meditation In Everyday Life.* Other books that can be helpful in reiterating the concepts covered in this chapter are: Roger B. Yepsen Jr.'s *How To Boost Your Brain Power: Achieving Peak Intelligence, Memory, and Creativity,* Marilee Zdenek's *The Right Brain Experience,* Janet Burr's *Awaken Your Intuition,* and Petey Stevens's *Opening Up To Your Psychic Self.* And don't forget about those suggested at the end of this book's Chapter Two.

Practicing mindfulness helps in learning TO THINK BY CHOICE. TRAINING ONE'S ATTENTION AND ONE'S SENSES INTO EXPANDED, YET CONSCIOUSLY CONTROLLED, PERCEPTION provides a doorway into higher knowledge and wisdom. We don't want our increased ability to image and visualize to result in confusion and terror because we're automatically running negative energies through preprogrammed thoughts and feelings. It's a smart move to get a grip on your lower-self negative thought, feeling, and behaving patterns before you focus on entering into deeper and more expansive states of meditation, trance, and spirit journeys.

In addition to mindfulness, SHAPESHIFTING/TIMESHIFTING is another set of skills that provide a protective foundation for attaining advanced knowledge and Soul Experiences. Shapeshifting involves the ability to control and utilize your energy to the fullest to meet whatever the particular life situation of-the-moment requires. Let go of your assumptions, expectations, and preconditioned set ways, so that you can allow your being to interact clearly with what is going on at the present time. Attention and thought control are necessary. NONRESISTANCE, along with WHOLE THINKING application, are also necessary in order to respond to each event in life in a way that makes true sense to what is happening on all levels, including the energetic domino future effect. You have to be able to be fully in-the-moment in order to respond from Soul and not from lower-self automatic patterning.

Every single moment has its own energies and rhythms to it. In order to expand or contract an individual moment, we have to be able to shift our own personal rhythm and energies to truly meet and be present in it. This is what allows us to create our life the way our Soul knows it can be instead of how other humans, operating from their lower-selves, want it to be or programmed us to think it should be. If you are clearly in the moment, its energies will be able to register in your mindbrain complex, and a more whole-based response will be stimulated.

Mindfulness and shapeshifting allow you to ACTUALLY EXPERIENCE CONCEPTS OR BELIEFS, instead of just intellectualizing them. Really experiencing beliefs is what moves us into change and makes things real. For example, once you have actually reexperienced (images, thoughts, and emotions together) a past life while in this current life, the belief in reincarnation changes into knowing. In the mental processes that churn between the belief and knowing stages, all the interconnected thoughts, feelings, and reactions will get reworked. You will never be the same again, for you will have evolved. Just remember that all that rewiring takes time.

Consciously controlling your thoughts is choosing which energies you run in your life, which in turn, choose the situations or energies you attract. Your thoughts control the pace and rhythm of your life. If you are in the midst of a "war with time," then you are still battling with your lower self. And as the old *Yes* song *"Your Move"* so eloquently sings to us: "Quit surrounding yourself with your self and move on back to square."

**CONSCIOUSLY CONTROLLING YOUR THOUGHTS IS CHOOSING
WHICH ENERGIES YOU RUN IN YOUR LIFE, WHICH IN TURN,
CHOOSE THE SITUATIONS OR ENERGIES YOU ATTRACT . . .**

ACTIVITY: <u>I WANT PEACE OF MIND</u>

1. After you have become relaxed and open, read each line of the quoted paragraph below these instructions, line by line, very SLOWLY AND DELIBERATELY, taking three long, deep breaths between each line.

2. After you have gone all the way through this three separate times, spend five minutes FOCUSING, CONCENTRATING, and CONTEMPLATING on each and every line. Be aware of any blocking thoughts and feelings. If your mind drifts, find it and gently bring it back.

3. After you have completed that second process, allow yourself to VISUALIZE what your life will look like once this paragraph has been moved BEYOND A CONCEPTUAL RECOGNITION INTO A FUNCTIONAL, DAILY REALITY. Repeat all three steps, as often as appropriate, changing all future tenses into present tenses when you are emotionally ready:

> **"I want genuine, constant peace of mind through running loving and
> joyous thoughts/thought processes. That means pleasant and imaginative thoughts
> and feelings, coming from the ability to control my thoughts, only choosing those
> that feel good, that are clear, and that solve problems. Through running Soul trust
> and faith, I stop all angry judgment, fear, self-doubt, and other putdowns or disbelief.
> Attaining peace of mind means stopping all uncontrolled thoughts from past
> programming, choosing what I want to think instead when those old patterns have
> clicked off. When I have consistent peace of mind, it will feel normal, naturally
> pleasurable, productive, fulfilling, and fun. Life will feel and be calmly exciting
> with each day a positive, creative adventure with lots of wonderful choices!"**

BRAINWORK

A **fit brain, or biocomputer, is a prerequisite to** *Higher Self Integration* **and being able to access the higher mind powers of Soul.** We all shape our brain by our eating, drinking, sleeping, exercising, and thinking habits for all have their effects on the brain's chemical and physical makeup. In fact, according to Roger B. Yepsen, Jr. in *How To Boost Your Brain Power,* "Research shows that the brain feels the effects of certain nutrients within minutes of a meal."

To expand your mental powers and abilities while on Earth, you have to STIMULATE AND CHALLENGE YOUR BRAIN so that it will keep up with and grow new synapses or circuits. To do that, you need to INCLUDE RELAXATION AND EXERCISE, MEDITATION AND CONCENTRATION, MULTI-TRACKING AND WHOLE-THINKING, and a whole lot more in your life's routine. If you want to maximize your brain, STAY AWAY FROM NICOTINE, CAFFEINE, AND ALCOHOL. WATCH OUT FOR LEAD, NOISE OVERLOAD, ALLERGIES, AND STRESS. BALANCE YOUR SUGAR INTAKES AND YOUR REST/MOVEMENT EQUATION. MAKE SURE YOU GET ENOUGH B/C/E VITAMINS, TRACE ELEMENTS, ESPECIALLY IRON AND ZINC, SUNLIGHT, AND FRESH AIR.

Other areas to concentrate on balancing are the brain waves you stimulate and the use of different parts of your brain. Our brains need these four types of brain waves: 1. ALPHA WAVES occur when the mind is turned inward, still alert yet relaxed, 2. BETA WAVES occur when we focus on some aspect of the outside world (and which get overstimulated with emotional anxiety), 3. DELTA WAVES occur during deep sleep, and 4. THETA WAVES occur in the drowsy state immediately preceding sleep. Our brains also need a healthy balance between working its parts or hemispheres in order to enable us to function with the maximum power of our whole brain. In brain research terms and for purposes of simplification, it is called WORKING WITH BOTH SIDES OF THE BRAIN, THE RIGHT AND THE LEFT. Doing so enables us TO ACCESS not only OUR CONSCIOUS and SUBCONSCIOUS, but also our SUPERCONSCIOUS LEVELS OF MIND (See Index Glossary for definitions).

Fortunately, many of the techniques, skills, and abilities that stimulate our brain hemispheres, also stimulate our various brain waves, and the different levels of mind. It isn't a matter of the right brain, alpha waves, and superconscious mind being better than the left brain, beta waves, and conscious or ordinary mind. It is all about the fact that we need all portions of our brain, all brain waves, and all mind levels in order to function as conscious Souls in human form on this planet. Once again, it is all about BALANCE.

You need to WORK WITH AND DEVELOP BOTH YOUR LOGICAL AND INTUITIVE PARTS OF YOUR BRAIN so that all mental processes, levels, and realities can get through and be expressed. You need your (left brain) logical, verbal, analytical, literal, linear, and mathematical abilities *and* your (right brain) intuitive, non-verbal, holistic, spatial, musical, metaphoric, imaginative, artistic, emotional, and spiritual abilities. Since many of our educational and societal experiences have really stressed the analytical, verbal, and logical ways of working our brainmind complex, you may have to put in some overtime awakening and strengthening your intuitive, emotional, and imaginative ways of being.

Your goal is to have all awakened, strengthened, understood, and accessible whenever it is most appropriate. Using only logic can run you into some brick walls and using only intuition can make you impractically spacey in this material world we live in. Using both logic and intuition moves one into the realm of the optimistic realist and the grounded creative genius.

STIMULATE AND WORK YOUR LOGICAL BRAIN and thinking modes through: reading and learning about new subjects, developing advanced problem solving skills, using the various styles of reasoning, enhancing your ability to communicate with words/languages, increasing your ability to store and retrieve information within your biocomputer, and challenging yourself in your mathematical and organizational skills. Advancing your use of your logical capabilities will be of the utmost importance when you have also advanced your abilities to feel, hear, and see into nonphysical dimensions through your intuitive parts of your brainmind complex. Your logical abilities will help to keep you grounded and serve as a way of making the metaphysical world a harmonic part of your material world.

There are many ways you can STIMULATE, WORK WITH, AND ADVANCE YOUR INTUITIVE BRAIN and thinking modes. However, one the of the first things recommended is to DO YOUR EMOTIONAL OR PERSONAL PROCESS WORK and clear out the mindfogging and numbing portion of your negativity and programming. As you do so, you will also be learning some of the tools and skills that are helpful in accessing ones intuitive brain, mind, and self: relaxing and RELAXATION exercises, EMOTIONAL AWARENESS along with the logical brain skill of identification, tuning into GUT FEELINGS, placing things in new and WHOLER PERSPECTIVES, and developing/using IMAGERY AND VISUALIZATION skills.

From there, you can have more fun PLAYING in the vast realms of VISUAL ART, STORYTELLING, CREATIVE WRITING, MUSIC, AND DANCE. RITUALS you've incorporated into your life that align your consciousness with your intentions and provide you sacred space in which to focus are also helpful. Learning to enter into and work within TRANCE STATES OR ALTERED STATES OF CONSCIOUSNESS will open up the vast worlds of the intuitive, spiritual, or metaphysical. Purposefully developing and advancing your abilities to IMAGINE, FANTASIZE, AND PERCEIVE VISIONS/IMAGES, to remember and use your DREAM STATES/IMAGES, and to SEE THE INTERRELATIONAL, INTERCONNECTED, AND WHOLENESS of all you are involved in will help you in seeing and working hand-in-hand with Soul Processes and Essences.

WE NEED ALL PORTIONS OF OUR BRAIN, ALL BRAIN WAVES, AND ALL MIND
LEVELS IN ORDER TO FUNCTION AS CONSCIOUS SOULS IN HUMAN FORM . . .

ACTIVITY: <u>UNITED WE STAND</u>

In this activity, you will incorporate a variety of techniques that enable one to reach and work with the various states and parts of one's brain waves, brain areas, and states of consciousness. These techniques include:

RELAXATION EXERCISES, TRANCE INDUCTIONS, WORKING IN ALTERED STATES, FANTASY, GUIDED IMAGERY, PERCEPTION, FREE ASSOCIATION, USE OF TRANSITIONAL OBJECTS, MEMORY RECALL, SENSORY STIMULATION, AND AFFIRMATIONS.

Work this activity often. Over time, keep being open to the issues and realizations that come up for you while doing your United We Stand sessions. Watch for some added help coming through your night dreams.

1. Get into your open and relaxed state, and then go deeper by using a traditional "COUNTING DOWN" process along with visualization. In your mind's eye, watch yourself slowly descend down a 20 step staircase. With every step, you will take a deep slow breath, silently saying to yourself, "I am moving into a deeper more expansive state of being."

2. Once you are on the bottom step you will see four fuse boxes representing your four brain-waves (alpha, beta, delta, and theta), a computer and a music box representing your logical and intuitive brain areas, and three doorways representing your three mind levels of the conscious, subconscious, and superconscious. One at a time, take these objects, boxes, and doors exploring what is inside each.

You can use your sight, taste, sound, smell, and even touch senses working entirely through mind. Your memory, emotions, joys and hang-ups can all be stimulated by the images occurring in your mind's eye. You can be taken on journeys, go places you've been and not been, meet people you know and don't know, talk with animals, spirits, and nature forms all in your mind. You can learn great wisdom and knowledge, witness great fear and turbulence, and dance and sing all at the same time within your mind.

If your mind drifts from your task at hand, bring it back and work on relaxing and going deeper. Then, start again. Don't worry if not much comes through your mind's eye and thoughts, for it will over time and with relaxed effort. Just let the images and thoughts come, without getting hung up on their origin. You may not get images, thoughts, memories, and realizations from every one of the objects, doors, and boxes each session. Simply ACCEPT WHAT YOU DO RECEIVE.

3. After you have explored all that presents itself through your boxes, doors, and objects, thank them for their gifts. Ask them to present to you now or in the near future how all these things work together and how you can help in their United We Stand Campaign.

4. As you climb your staircase up, in your mind's eye, affirm "I open myself to the knowledge of the whole as all my brainwaves, brain parts, and mind levels become synchronized and balanced." When you are at the top of your staircase, open your eyes and record your experiences in your *HSI* notebook.

CREATIVITY is a real buzz word for both the brain and *The Higher Self Integration Process.* Becoming attuned to Soul takes a highly creative journey, producing an advanced COCREATOR (a creative person who is consciously working with and directly through The Divine, or The Creative Source). Being creative is about having the ability or power to create things that are original, expressive, and imaginative. It expands the brain, heats it up, makes it move and groove. When we are creating, we're causing something new to exist. *Higher Self Integration* is about creating, recreating, and cocreating and then giving form to that creation, which requires unique, creative SOUL EXPRESSION.

To become the Creative Cocreator that you are as Soul, you need to CULTIVATE YOUR SENSE OF WONDER, CURIOSITY, AND PLAYFULNESS. EMPHASIZE THE JOY OF CREATION (THE PROCESS) instead of the achievement of results (THE PRODUCT), because the most creative of states involves being both TOTALLY INVOLVED AND TOTALLY DETACHED at the same time. For then, you are free to EXPERIMENT. You want to be IMMERSED, FASCINATED, AND ABSORBED IN THE PRESENT CREATIVE MOMENT because to be creative means to OPEN YOURSELF UP TO THE UNKNOWN AND ITS ADVENTURES. MAKE CHOICES THAT STRETCH YOU.

You have to find it acceptable to not know for that is the natural state which is the beginning of all creative acts. Learn to move back and forth freely between plan and play, so that you can REGAIN THE ABILITY TO COMBINE THINGS AND IDEAS IN NEW WAYS. Changing perspectives is what creating is all about. It requires DIRECTING YOUR ATTENTION OVER A WIDE FIELD OF EXPERIENCE and BEING FLEXIBLE AND OPEN to absorbing different information and insights. Narrow mindedness and rigidity are hindrances in the world of creation.

The act of creation takes TRAINING AND EDUCATION. It takes SELF-DISCIPLINE, DESIRE AND MOTIVATION, DETERMINATION, PERSISTENCE, PATIENCE, AND PERSEVERANCE, all qualities necessary for *Higher Self Integration.* CHANGE AND RISK are normal aspects of the creative process. True creative people relish the discovery of ideas, new directions and challenges, and the belief that there is another wonderful adventure just around the corner. They also experience a wealth of feelings and images in their daily lives.

The blocks to creativity are lack of self-discipline, lack of time, physical pain and fatigue, stress, fear of failure and criticism, and not knowing how to work effectively with the various stages that are a part of the creative process. To achieve the high level of creativity that is a part of an awakened and integrated Soul, you must loose the fears that bind you so that you can free your vision by changing your consciousness.

One of the joys and wonders of the creative process is The Flow State. THE FLOW STATE occurs when one is so completely engrossed in an activity that they loose track of time, going into an altered state. In this altered state, you will TRANSCEND YOUR EVERYDAY SELF AND PERCEPTIONS. It is a highly concentrated and highly focused state that in order to be achieved requires that negative and agitated emotions be under control. Positive emotions have to dominate and even produce elation.

In THE COCREATIVE STATE, you will feel more like you are channeling information and ideas from a Higher Source, and indeed you will be, whether from your Soul, other Spirit Guides, or The Divine. Therefore, you will be stunned at the results, for they will be far more whole and unique than you ever fathomed could "come out of me." The Cocreative State is achieved through CLARITY OF THOUGHT AND FEELING, MOVING PAST ALL FEAR AND ATTACHMENT, KNOWING ONE'S CREATIVE MEDIUM, AND THEN INVITING SOUL/SPIRIT TO CREATE THROUGH YOU. It is a fascinating and joyful process.

TO ACHIEVE THE HIGH LEVEL OF CREATIVITY OF AN AWAKENED AND INTEGRATED SOUL, YOU MUST LOOSE THE FEARS THAT BIND YOU, SO THAT YOU CAN FREE YOUR VISION BY CHANGING YOUR CONSCIOUSNESS . . .

ACTIVITY: **CREATIVE EXPANSION**

Expanding one's ability to create is essential to *Higher Self Integration*, for one of our Soul Powers is Causation/Cocreation. If you already have some areas of creativity in which you are involved, you will want to PURPOSEFULLY OPEN AND DEEPEN THEM FURTHER. If you have already uncovered what appears to be a natural talent in a certain area (or more accurately, you have somehow tapped into directions/skills you developed in previous lifetimes), then ALLOW IT TO TAKE OFF AND FLY IN NEW AND DIFFERENT DIRECTIONS. However, your main FOCUS needs to be ON DEVELOPING THE GENERAL CREATIVE/ COCREATIVE ABILITIES, SKILLS, AND ATTITUDES, because then you will be able to express your Soul through any medium that is appropriate to each stage and situation in your life.

1. One of the first things in opening and expanding your creativity that has to be tackled is your outdated and destructively negative misbeliefs and habits concerning the act of creating and cocreating. DO THE WORK NECESSARY IN DISCOVERING YOUR PARTICULAR BLOCKS OF ATTITUDES, BELIEFS, MEDIUMS, AND HABITS REWORKING THEM. Then, PROGRAM INTO YOUR BRAINMIND THE ATTITUDES, BELIEFS, MEDIUMS, AND HABITS WHICH WILL ENABLE YOU TO BE THE AWESOMELY JOYOUS CREATOR THAT YOU CAN BE! Use your right and left brain skills of relaxation, trance, memory recall, connective analyzation, free association, brainstorming, affirmations, belief reconstruction, and whatever else works for you in a light-shedding way. Work with that EGO of yours! CHECK YOURSELF IN THESE AREAS:

A. YOUR GENERAL VIEWS ABOUT THE CREATIVE PROCESS: Have you fallen for those old destructive misbeliefs: that you have to suffer in order to create, that very few of us are creative geniuses, that singing/painting/writing/dancing is a gift only bestowed on certain people? Etcetera . . .

B. YOUR SPECIFIC VIEWS TOWARDS YOUR OWN CREATIVITY: Have you labeled yourself a Creative Dummy, a Creative Disaster, a One-Time/Area Creator, a Better Than The Best, etc.? What limits and boundaries have you placed on your creativity? What expectations and attachments have you placed upon your creative process? Etcetera . . .

C. YOUR VIEWS CONCERNING COCREATING: Are you caught in a disbelief and/or worthy-unworthy battle concerning working with and through Soul, Spirit, and Divine? Do you know how to "Let Go And Let God?" Etcetera . . .

D. YOUR CREATIVE HABITS: Do you hold your breath and are tight or tense when trying to create? Do you get angry at yourself and put yourself down for not creating the perfect whatever? Do you quit your projects before they are through? Do you forget to take the breaks your body needs? Etcetera . . .

2. READ books and WATCH videos on developing and expanding one's creativity. TRY and PRACTICE activities and techniques designed to develop and enhance one's creative abilities. GO TO and USE classes, workshops, retreats, conferences, specific teachers/guides on the creative process in general and creating with specific mediums. VARY THOSE MEDIUMS. If you already sing, but think you can't paint, then purposefully set off to learn to paint.

3. JUST DO IT! Color, doodle, sing nursery rhymes, dance the twist, be dramatic as you are relating a personal story to a friend, let any word or sentences just roll off your pen, take a paint brush and your favorite colors and just papersplash. Freeform! Spontaneous! Make the time! No expectations! Suspend judgement! Play! Try everything! Be a child again! No limits! You can use everything and anything in your daily life routines in helping you to be creative.

MINDTRAIN

It **is through MIND that we connect, integrate, and become our** *Higher Selves* **as expression of our Soul.** Training your mind to be able to comprehend, perceive, and express the infinite knowledge, wisdom, and multidimensional realities of The Holoverse and of The Divine or Infinite Intelligence starts with controlling and expanding one's abilities to work with and on The Earth Plane. Being able to use the following four types of skills at advanced levels will enable you to realize and be your fullest potential: 1. CONCENTRATION,   2. VISUALIZATION,   3. SENSORY STIMULATION,   and 4. INTUITIVE PRACTICE.

Along with developing *Higher Self* personality characteristics, these form the foundation of creative genius, of advanced mental functioning, and of being able to work with levels of Spirit and Soul while being stabilized and healthy on The Earth Plane. Be very aware and forewarned that one can develop higher mental abilities (ESP or more accurately Higher Sense Perceptions), such as prophecy and long distance seeing, and still attract destructive relationships, experience poverty, and be miserable, unhappy, and even cruel. That is why attention has to be paid to removing one's negative and destructive habits of thinking, feeling, and behaving and to consciously developing QUALITIES OF SOUL.

If you are running and therefore attracting negative energies, then having developed the ability to travel on the astral level, to know what someone else is thinking, or even to create new things becomes yours and others nightmare-in-living-color. Multiplied or deeper levels of awfulness is a real drag of the most deadly kind. As you are developing and training your higher mind abilities, be sure to notice any and all negativity that rears up and hisses. Slow down your mental training until you have dealt with, released, and reworked those deep dark dragons.

What is super important for you to thoroughly understand is the IMPLICATIONS AND RESPONSIBILITIES you are creating when you develop any, a few, most, or all of your inherent Soul powers and abilities. As you develop and use in your daily life your Higher Abilities or Higher Sense Perceptions - in other words running and opening up more powerful energy - consequences for misusing those energies are also more powerful, intimate, and dramatic. You need to have developed Soul Ethics/Values, along with *Higher Self* Characteristics. You want to be plugging into Divine Order and Safety, not human turmoil and chaos.

For example, when opening up one's ability to read minds, one enters more deeply into ethical and social dilemmas. What then do you do with that information? What if you picked up on a passing stranger's thoughts that they were on their way to kill The President? Think about it... There are as many considerations and influences to bear in mind as there are possible outcomes. Opening up one's Higher Abilities and Powers can be like placing yourself without any protection in the eye of a hurricane, if you haven't done your Personal Process and Soul Work.

You need to open up and train your mind in the light of and with the help of Higher Guidance. That is why SPIRITUAL (not necessarily religious) PRAYER AND MEDITATION, and *Higher Self* qualities have to be the basis of your *Higher Self Journey*. Every step of the way you will need to deeply think about and consider the physical, mental, spiritual, and ethical implications of what you are learning and developing. ARE YOU READY TO HANDLE THEM? That is the BIG QUESTION you will need to honestly search your Soul for every step of the way.

This Readiness Checklist might prove helpful in your Journey:

READINESS CHECKLIST

1. WHAT IS MY MOTIVATION IN LEARNING THIS SKILL, ABILITY, AND POWER? Look into your thoughts, feelings and behaviors. If you are interested in an advanced mental skill for any of the reasons listed here, you had better rethink what you are doing: Out of or for revenge, anger, fame, fortune, despair, addiction, avoidance, control of others, and/or to prove someone wrong. Motivation for greater mental powers needs to come from love, connectedness, natural rights, compassion, and Soul awareness.

2. AM I BEING GUIDED BY HIGHER GUIDANCE TO DEVELOP THESE ABILITIES? Are the resources you need coming to you easily? If you are trying your hardest to make something happen, then you are probably not in the flow of Divine Order. Then, it is time for a reassessment on your part. When you are in the Soul Zone, your life is full of coincidence, syncronicity, and direct guidance. If it's full steam ahead in your Soul, then everything you need will be there for you. It's your task to be open to it, recognize it, go with the flow, and do it!

3. DO I HAVE AN IDEA OF WHAT I AM GETTING MYSELF INTO? Research, question, study, and contemplate. Play If-Then. Rotate your view in and around all angles of what you are interested in. Look at cause and effect. Do you need to change any misbeliefs and disbeliefs for yourself? Do you need to stretch or adhere to any of your own personal boundaries? How will you know if you are getting in over your head? What is your safety net? Sttrreettcchh your thinking.

4. HOW DOES THIS POWER/SKILL/ABILITY FIT INTO MY OVERALL SOUL PURPOSE AND LIFE? Why do you need to develop this ability? Are you prepared for how it will change your life? Do you have a reliable and trustful support system? How can you get help in learning this ability? Where else will developing this ability take you? And are you prepared to go there?

ALONG WITH DEVELOPING HIGHER SELF PERSONALITY CHARACTERISTICS, CONCENTRATION, VISUALIZATION, SENSORY STIMULATION, AND INTUITIVE PRACTICE FORM THE FOUNDATION OF CREATIVE GENIUS, OF ADVANCED MENTAL FUNCTIONING, AND OF BEING ABLE TO WORK WITH LEVELS OF SPIRIT/SOUL WHILE HEALTHY AND STABILIZED ON THE EARTH PLANE...

ACTIVITY: <u>FUN DA MENTAL</u>

In developing and advancing your abilities to concentrate, visualize, and use your sense of sight, smell, taste, hearing, touch, and sensation (using your various body tingles, etc. to sense what's going on in and around you), you can use many things within your daily life to practice with. **LEARN THE BASICS OF CONCENTRATION, VISUALIZATION, AND SENSORY STIMULATION AND THEN BE CREATIVE WITH YOUR PRACTICE.** Here are a few suggestions. Remember, that what helps in learning to train and control one's mental faculties, abilities, and skills is to make mind-expansion fun!

1. CONCENTRATION:
STAY WITH YOUR FOCUS! CONTROL YOUR ATTENTION AND THOUGHTS!
A. Get quiet and stare at a lighted candle, watching only the flame. Try not to think about anything else but the flickering flame. Gently keep bringing your thoughtfocus back to the flame if it wanders.
B. Relaxed and breathing deeply, focus your attention on a particular body part of your own. Allow your thoughts to explore only that body part. Concentrate on how it feels, what it means to you, how you feel about it, and how you would like to feel about it. If your thoughts take off in other directions, gently bring them back.
C. Walk slowly step-by-step, outside or inside, concentrating on seeing and thinking only about what is directly around you. Notice everything with a mental note around, above, and below you before moving on. Keep your mind right there.

(continued on page 146)

D. Use whatever you are doing in your everyday life to increase your concentration skills. If you are vacuuming the floor, focus only on vacuuming the floor. If you are noticing a flower, take three to five minutes to observe and think of only that flower. Notice details, and then look for more details. Be aware of RIDING MIND WAVES. Just when you think you have concentrated enough on something to know everything you could possibly know about it, take a few deep breaths and go again.

E. Combine your imagination with deep focusing and concentration. Take a simple object such as a pencil. As you concentrate on it, notice everything it is made of and how it is and could be used. Write it all down. And then, try again. And again. And again. No censoring is allowed because you are mentally brainstorming. Watch that list grow and be awed at how much more you have thought of than you had before, even if it is only about a pencil. LEARN TO MINDWAVE IN REGARD TO CONCEPTS, RELATIONSHIPS, AND WORLD PROBLEMS. Yes, you are on your way to WHOLETHINKING through concentration, focus, and imagination/visualization.

2. VISUALIZATION:
FOCUS & CONCENTRATE ON IMAGES! PERCEIVE! INVENT MINDMOVIES!

A. Look at an object in your room. After you have stared at it for a while concentrating on it, close your eyes and visualize the object in your mind's eye as clear as you can. Next, do this with a section of the room and then with the whole room.

B. In your mind's eye, picture an uninflated red balloon. Mentally blow it up until it is half full. Knot it. Throw the balloon up in the air. When the balloon gets near the ceiling, stop it. Make it rotate faster and faster. Make the color change to yellow. Watch the balloon transform into a canary that flies from your outstretched hand. There are many reasons and types of GUIDED IMAGERY that are helpful in the *Higher Self Integration Process*.

C. Think of someone you know very well. Visualize what they look like. Go over all the details about them physically. Recall one of your favorite places you like to go to in nature. Visualize all the details of the place including temperature, sounds, smells, feelings, etc.

D. Relaxed and breathing slowly and deeply, imagine a living space in which you would feel completely comfortable. Notice the walls, furniture, view out the window, etc. Walk around the various rooms noticing or seeing small details like knickknacks, flooring, and the like. Notice the feel, smell, and sound of the place. Eventually wander outdoors, again noticing everything. Your mind is "making this all up." INTENTIONAL FANTASY WORK can tell you a whole lot about your feelings, hopes, and fears. In this case, it is your unique and special mental space that you can return to anytime no matter where you are in body.

E. LEARN TO REMEMBER AND REVIEW THE INCREDIBLE IMAGERY AND VISUALIZATIONS THAT YOUR MIND PRODUCES WHILE YOUR BODY IS SLEEPING- YOUR DREAMS. There are many ways to interpret or use one's dreams in transformative work and many different books, teachers, and workshops that can help. However, learn to remember and concentrate on the feeling state you wake up in from your dream and what the dream means to you. You are your own best interpreter since your dreams are your subconscious - and sometimes superconscious - messages, thoughts, and images performed by you. You can also learn to dream purposefully and to even consciously change your dreams, called LUCID DREAMING. Focus on learning how to work with myths, images, and symbols for then you will be able to use your dreams, visions, and visual guidance in the ways that are most appropriate to your unique being.

3. SENSORY STIMULATION:
BE IN THE MOMENT! CONCENTRATE! VISUALIZE!

A. SEEING- Observe things around you without judging and categorizing . . . Learn to observe things as if you were an artist and would need to draw whatever you are looking at, noticing great detail, space, form, color, texture, movement, emotion, and essence . . . Learn to feel what you see . . . Learn how to soft focus and see energy forms, auras, and past life images . . . Develop your visualization skills. . .

(continued on page 147)

B. HEARING- Listen to sounds around you without judging . . .   Listen to your own body sounds inside and out. . .   Listen to your own thoughts . . . Really listen to music . . . Learn to compassionately listen to others. . .   Develop your ability to listen beyond human voices and physical sounds . . .   Consciously expand your hearing . . .

C. SMELLING AND TASTING- Try tasting and smelling many varied and different foods, really concentrating on their smells and tastes . . . Concentrate on distinguishing smells and tastes from one another . . . Let your feelings be aroused by different smells and tastes learning to work with those feelings . . . Allow memories to be recalled through smells and tastes . . .

D. TOUCH- Touch unknown things with your eyes closed, trying to figure out what they are without sight . . .   Let yourself feel different textures allowing any feelings to arouse . . .   Move your hands within a few inches of each other, concentrating on feeling the energy between your palms . . .   Concentrate on feeling the different types of energy you can pick up from things around you and the human body . . .

E. SENSATIONS- Become aware of all your different bodily sensations . . . Figure out when, why, and how they are stimulated . . . Concentrate on various bodily sensations learning to both increase and decrease them one-at-a-time and simultaneously . . .   Learn to read your body sensations in the context of feelings stimulated and energies being perceived or picked up by your body, before your mindthoughts register them in words . . .

WHAT HELPS IN LEARNING TO TRAIN AND CONTROL ONE'S MENTAL FACULTIES, ABILITIES, AND SKILLS IS TO MAKE MIND-EXPANSION FUN . . .

Through mind, you are capable of:

CONNECTING THROUGH COMMUNICATION AND SELF EXPRESSION –
Communicating (listening, receiving, sharing and talking) with self, others, animals, spirits, God/Goddess, Highly-evolved Souls, Extraterrestrials, nature devas and elementals including Elves and Fairies, plant and mineral life . . . Expressing self through how you live your life and how you manage your energy, through words and language, writing, dancing, singing, drawing/sculpting/painting, organizing, creating, and what you do . . . Channeling spirits (mediumship) . . .   Praying or talking with The Divine . . .   Mental Telepathy . . . Performing inspirational or charismatic speaking and writing . . .   Hearing a variety of sound levels . . .

KNOWING THROUGH PERCEPTION AND READING ENERGY –
Seeing things of the material world directly around you, seeing things of the spirit dimensions, imagining things that don't exist . . .   Knowing the past, present, and future . . .   Predicting the future . . .   Visiting and comprehending the energetic recording of all time or The Akashic Records . . .   Seeing and knowing what auras mean . . .   Knowing information about people by reading their objects (Psychometry), sensing their energy, reading their minds . . . Knowing what's out of balance physically, mentally and spiritually in regards to yourself, others, animals, nature, and other aspects of life/world . . .   Picking up on things that are happening all over this planet, be it natural or manmade disasters . . .   Long Distance Viewing (seeing places, events, etc. in your mind's eye that are taking place miles away) . . .   Seeing lights, colors, and spirit forms . . .   Feeling sensations that give you information about other things . . . Soul Reading which is being able to know someone else's Soul Journeys . . . Great memory recall . . .

CHANGING THROUGH TRANSFORMATION AND HEALING –

Making changes and helping others to change . . .   Transforming yourself, your thoughts, feelings and behaviors, your lifestyle, your energy . . .   Healing yourself, others, animals and plants and our Planet Earth . . . Using mind over matter to transform or heal matter . . .   Using your dreams in order to change, transform, or heal . . .   Heal through touch or transmit healing energies to others through touch and directed thought . . .   Being able to cleanse and repair your own and others energy force fields, including auras and chakras through consciously developed mental and spiritual or metaphysical skills and abilities . . .   Using Divine Protection and healing, and the transformational shield of The Divine White Light . . .

ATTRACTING THROUGH MANIFESTATION AND DEMONSTRATION –

Attracting or repelling human, nature, spirit resources . . .   Manifesting everything from poverty to full prosperity . . . Demonstrating all aspects of being human and advanced levels of Being including Soul and Higher Sense Perceptions of a really wide variety . . . Traveling in the Astral World while your body sleeps on Earth . . .   Time Traveling . . . Being able to use all of your sensory modes in order to run, manifest, and demonstrate who you are becoming as an equal seer, hearer, feeler, toucher, taster, smeller, intuiter . . .   Advancing both your short and long term memory processes . . .   Levitation . . .   Demonstrating psychokinesis which is the production of motion . . . Finding missing objects . . .

CREATING THROUGH COCREATION AND CAUSATION –

Inventing new things, forming new words, composing new tunes, building new bridges (literally and figuratively) . . . Consciously choosing who you want to be, going where you want to go, doing what you want to do . . .   Consciously choosing when and how you pass on (die) . . .   Being a part of birthing Souls in human bodies on the Earth Plane consciously and recognizing that you are enabling a Soul to have a human experience and the Soul responsibilities inherent in your Soul agreement . . .   Causing material things to form and materialize . . .

Remember that you are not just a five-sense type of person, but a MULTISENSORY AND MULTIDIMENSIONAL BEING. Learning advanced skills in concentration, visualization, and sensory intunement will be useful in every one of the above powers and abilities. However, opening up, developing, and advancing one's INTUITION is the area that will be of incredible benefit! Knowing advanced levels of focus, imagery, and sensing make Intuition Practice much easier.   And being able to WHOLETHINK, which includes the ability to MULTITRACK, enables you to then take all your intuitions and integrate them smoothly and effectively in your daily life.

Multitracking is the skill of being able to do, think, and feel on multiple levels all at one time. We really can use all our senses and abilities all at once. Deep concentration skills enable us to concentrate on multiple levels, if we so choose to. An attuned Soul is a Multitracker. We have to be in order to comprehend and effectively deal with the complexity of living as a Soul in human form on this material dimension while staying in touch with the worlds of spirit.

TO TRAIN ONESELF TO BE A MULTITRACKER, PRACTICE VARIATIONS OF THESE ACTIVITIES. Remember, the key is to DO THEM EACH WELL, ALL AT ONE TIME, for a significant period of time:

While on your back making continual biking motions with your legs, pat your head and rub your belly (and then switch after two minutes), whistle your favorite song and at the end of a verse, sing a verse (then whistle, then sing, etc.), all the while you are noticing what is happening in the room around you, *and* remembering and feeling in detail a joyfully high experience you had in the past . . .

OK, if you can't be a one-person vaudeville act all at once, do one skill at first, adding all the others one at a time. As your abilities improve, change and add to your routines. For example, once you have accessed your Spirit Guides, throw them into your juggling equation. And don't forget to look at yourself in the mirror, for you are guaranteed to crack yourself up.

WHOLE THINKING is the ability to use both logical/intuitive and situational/relational modes of thinking in order to know the best for all concerned. It is looking at things from a perspective that includes: 1. past, present, and future,   2. you, others, and the Earth, and   3. essence, process, and product.   It is an interconnected, multi-dimensional way of thinking that requires involved detachment and compassionate awareness. It takes a while to become the natural primary mode of thinking, so keep working at it.

REMEMBER TO ASK YOURSELF THESE QUESTIONS, WHICH CAN HELP IN MAINTAINING ONE'S AWARENESS IN WHOLE THINKING ORIENTATION:

❖ Do I know all the facts and feelings involved in this situation or problem?

❖ Is there a history to this that would be helpful to know or remember?

❖ Have I looked at different ways or perspectives concerning this other than my own primary automatic one?

❖ Have I looked at all the possible processes and outcomes that could be involved?

❖ What is the best for all concerned for everyone and everything involved, the present and future, and for the Earth, all of its creatures and lifeforms?

❖ Have I included the Spirit and Soul factors?

❖ Have I been open to Divine Guidance?

INTUITION is the all-observing, receptive, free, spontaneous, open, and truly knowing part of our thinking. It is those gut-feelings, hunches, insights, and inspirations that we experience that seem to come from out of nowhere, yet are right on. Intuition is an inner-knowing, an ability to tune into knowledge in a nonrational way that happens from within oneself. It provides a greater comprehension from the heart level than our lower-self or mass-consciousness programmed personality can because intuitions come from the Soul. The more we develop our *Higher Self,* the more we are able to acknowledge and smoothly integrate into our daily lives these Soul Messages. As Gary Zukav puts it, in *The Seat Of The Soul*, "Intuition is a walkie-talkie, so to speak, between the personality and the soul which happens through the *Higher Self.*"

INTUITIONS OFTEN COME IN VISIONS AND FEELINGS, SYMBOLS AND METAPHORS. They are experienced through mind-body communication and are always felt by us in some way. That is another reason why we must be aware of, understand, and obtain clarity on an emotional level. In enhancing one's intuitive communications, it is necessary to be able to DISCERN BETWEEN PAST CONDITIONING, NEGATIVE ATTACHMENTS AND PRESENT SOUL SIGNALS designed to propel us forward with compassion and grace.

Intuitions feel very different than fears, parental voices, and ego. They don't feel mired in the mud like other thoughts that run through our heads. They don't repeat the past, but add to our present knowledge in ways that are fresh and real. Intuitions don't come from logical, rational thought processes. They just happen when the moment is right from the level of Divine Timing and Order. Intuition serves survival, creativity, inspiration, and higher spiritual communications.

Hindrances to receiving intuition are: being scared of and not trusting your intuitive voice, having expectations and attachments that things be a certain way (including wishful thinking and wild guesses), filling your life with noisy distractions, social and cultural bias, and arrogance or other egotistical characteristics designed to dictate and separate, divide and conquer. The major thing we all tend to do that greatly confuses true intuition is our need to interpret what we have perceived or intuited. Placing humanoid interpretations on Soul Messages usually miss their mark because we are filtering the messages through our own biases, ignorances, desires, and fears.

PRACTICE USING YOUR INTUITION IN EVERYDAY LIFE BY PAYING ATTENTION TO PEOPLE AND EVENTS AROUND YOU, BEING RECEPTIVE TO INFORMATION COMING TO YOU ABOUT THEM NON-VERBALLY. Learn to sense moods and feel energies. Try your best not to analyze or interpret, but just allow yourself to know. The use of IMAGERY or VISUALIZATION, including a wide variety of GUIDED VISUALIZATIONS, are often fun, creative, and expansive ways to practice receiving intuitively. Developing one's intuitive abilities leads into even more direct communications between us humans, our Souls, and the multidimensional or metaphysical worlds of spirit.

> **ALWAYS REMEMBER THAT YOU ARE NOT JUST A FIVE-SENSE TYPE OF PERSON, BUT A MULTISENSORY AND MULTIDIMENSIONAL BEING . . .**

ACTIVITY: TRANSFORMATIONAL TAPES

There are many different audio tapes available today that could prove helpful in reprogramming and developing a wide variety of physical, mental, and spiritual goals and skills for you. However, DEVELOPING YOUR OWN TRANSFORMATIONAL TAPES, with your unique set of goals, intentions, needs, and techniques that fit for you in your own voice is recommended as part of the *Higher Self Integration Process*. SORT THROUGH WHAT YOU KNOW, WHERE YOU ARE PRESENTLY, AND WHAT YOU NEED TO LEARN AND DEVELOP NEXT IN TERMS OF SOUL ATTUNEMENT, AND ESPECIALLY MIND DEVELOPMENT AND TRAINING. FILTER IN YOUR INTENTIONS AND FOCUSES, using this as a guide:

1. Structure Of The Tape: Make sure it is a quality audio cassette so that both your voice and music are clear, not distracting. Make your session length anywhere from 20 to 120 minutes, depending on what works best for you with all things considered. Regardless of length you will need a move-down/relaxation time at the beginning of your tape and a come-back/awakening time towards the end of your tape. Design your tape ahead of time, selecting readings and activities that will help to program your mind towards your goals and intentions. Use music that enables you to relax, deepen, and heal your everyday state of mind. Then, use your tape regularly.

2. Contents: BRAINSTORM, LIST, AND FOCUS ON THE SPECIFICS OF WHAT YOU ARE WISHING TO PROGRAM OR TRAIN YOURSELF IN OR TOWARDS, for example: prosperity, developing concentration skills, communicating with God/Goddess, opening up to Spirit Guidance, using intuition, quitting junk food, healing a weak bladder, etc. WITH YOUR LIST IN MIND, SELECT PARTICULAR TECHNIQUES AND VERBALIZATIONS THAT FOCUS ON ALL THAT YOU WANT INCLUDED IN YOUR TAPE.

Make your guided transformational tape as experiential and real as you can using: relaxation techniques, focused word and body part attention, progressive muscular relaxation, breathwork and various breathing activities, self-hypnotic/trance techniques, affirmations, visualizations, guided imagery, guided prayer, memory recall, personal process work, various healing techniques, inner guidance activities, inspirational readings, poetry, music, meditative techniques, biofeedback training, fantasy work, free association, patient perseverance, compassion, unconditional love, and a lot more! Have fun creating!

METAPHYSICALLY RELATE

W**e are fully equipped through body, mind, and spirit to relate to and interrelate with the metaphysical realities that are a part of Soul.** Physical form does not and cannot exist without energetic form, without the infusion of spirit. When we talk of working with the metaphysical world, we are consciously involving ourselves with the energy, spirit, and Soul that is a part of everything. WE EACH HAVE THE ABILITIES TO READ/PERCEIVE, TRANSFORM/HEAL, MANIFEST/DEMONSTRATE, COCREATE/CAUSE, AND COMMUNICATE/SELF-EXPRESS WITH ENERGY (SPIRIT AND SOUL).

Being able to read energy is the category many of the Higher Sense Perceptive Abilities (popularly called ESP), that we all have, fall under. Reading energy is such a natural thing to do that we all do it at times whether we want to or not. It is a part of us whether it is undeveloped, hidden, and even buried out of fear, misunderstanding, misinformation, doubt, and distrust. If we haven't educated ourselves nor consciously set about to develop and control our natural abilities of sensing energy, then what manages to get through our barriers and ignorance, is often such a jumbled mess that we don't even know what we are doing. As a conscious and attuned Soul working through your *Higher Self,* it is wise and very practical in terms of Earth living to FREE UP YOUR NATURAL ABILITIES OF READING ENERGY.

Since you are a SoulSpirit, it is not healthy nor prudent to have cut off your natural abilities to interrelate in your worlds of spirit and Soul. Each one of us is equipped with a mind and a brain that enables us to be aware of and work within levels of spirit/Soul at the very same time we have chosen to be in human physical form upon Earth. The Earth Plane itself is so highly energetic that it is full of spirits/Souls that reside here in various forms. STEP OUT OF YOUR SELF-IMPOSED ISOLATION AND LEARN TO RECONNECT! This reconnection occurs through the powers of mind and the abilities that we can purposefully develop.

There is a GUIDANCE PROCESS that is basic to life. Each and everyone of us is equipped to be in touch with, perceive, and receive all the information and knowledge we need in order to live lovingly prosperous lives. We all have intuition and the abilities to tune inward to the abundance of help that comes from the world of spirit and Soul, or the metaphysical realms.

When we have closed off these natural abilities and haven't consciously developed them, then using other systems of guidance, can prove helpful. Seeking guidance from those who have developed their psychic and mediumistic (channeling) abilities and tarot card/palm/astrological readings and the like, are interesting at the very least when one is operating from a one or two Soul Evolution Level. However, DEVELOPING YOUR ABILITIES TO CONNECT WITH INNER AND HIGHER/DIVINE GUIDANCE YOURSELF IS REALLY WHERE IT'S AT. The basis for *The Higher Self Integration or Soul Attunement Process* lies in accessing and utilizing Higher Guidance in order to live a wonderful Earthly life while evolving on a Soul level.

THERE IS A GUIDANCE PROCESS THAT IS BASIC TO LIFE . . .

ACTIVITY: <u>WHAT'S RIGHTFULLY YOURS</u>

To read energy and thus know all things . . .
To communicate beyond the physical and thus connect with all of life . . .

(continued on page 152)

In developing your Metaphysical Abilities, it is important to not only understand what they are but to know how they can help you take good care of your life and move you forward in your Soul's Evolution. If you are going to step beyond mass consciousness's power paranoia and obsessive need to control human behavior within rigid boundaries, then it is very important for you to DO YOUR HOMEWORK in order to move past the mystiques and fears. Below are many of the Higher Sense Perceptions and Metaphysical abilities, skills, techniques that are rightfully yours as SoulSpirit in human form. Taking each of those categories one-at-a-time, RESEARCH the answers to this series of questions:

1. What is this/are these all about?

2. How is it/are they best developed?

3. What are the possible dangers or misuses of this/these?

4. How can it/they be of positive, loving, helpful use to our planet's inhabitants?

5. At what stage or level (of my life passages and Soul Evolution) can it/they fit in and how can it/they help with my daily life?

Here are the categories:

*Using objects in seeking information and symbolic quests, such as crystal balls, tea leaves, tarot cards, the positioning of the planets, Ouija boards, etc. –
*Dowsing with rods, pendulums, hands -
*Inspired, charismatic, and/or automatic writing, speaking, and creating -
*Superperformance or accomplishing something way above normal, breaking previously recorded accomplishments -
*Psychic/Spiritual Healing, including long distance (absent) and local healing through mental means and energetic hands-on-touch, and prayer for self and others -
*Using God/Goddesses protective, healing, and transformational shield of Divine White light -
*Mind-over-matter including pain control, changing your physical functioning, bodily temperature control, levitating, and psychokinesis (the production of motion) through the power of mind -
*Great Memory Recall -
*Finding missing objects (yours and others, local and long distance) -
*Consciously setting out to manifest something in your life through your mental powers and abilities, such as attracting/manifesting a Soul mate or all the money you need to be free -
*Accessing The Akashic Records -
*Out -of-body, mind, time, and Astral World travels -
*Psychic and Lucid Dreaming -
*Prophecy, to predict something is going to happen before it happens through Divine Inspiration -
*Precognition, knowledge of something in advance of its occurrence -
*Long distance viewing, watching something happening in your mind's eye at the same time it is happening a long distance away physically -
*Seeing and understanding Auras -
*Being able to cleanse and repair yours and other's energy force fields, including auras and chakras, through mental powers -
*Metal Telepathy, reading minds (human, other animals and lifeforms) and communicating mentally, without physical form and words –
*Soul Reading, being able to know someone else's Soul journeys, lessons, purpose, karma -
*Spontaneous Past Life Recall, being able to recall, process, resolve your own Soul's journeys –

(continued on page 153)

*Self Guidance, accessing or being able-to-know all kinds of subconscious and superconcious (beyond ordinary) information about yourself/oneself -

*Life Forms Communication, tuning into the energies of animals, plants, trees, minerals, etc. -

*Sensing Earth Traumas, such as hurricanes, fires, earthquakes, etc. -

*Clairaudience, hearing things that are out of the ordinary range of human hearing –

*Clairvoyance, seeing things that are out of the ordinary range of human sight -

*Clairsentience, feeling things that are out of the ordinary range of human sensing – *Direct contact and communication with your own Soul's Voice -

*Spirit Contact, communicating with and sometimes seeing nonphysical entities including those you have known in this lifetime who have passed on before you, spirit guides and teachers, angels, devas, elves and other elementals -

*Direct contact/connection/communication with Advanced Souls, such as Buddha and Jesus -

*Direct contact, connection, and communication with God/Goddess, The Divine, including being bathed in Divine White Light –

The above may look like a long and intimidating list, but there is good news: If you DO YOUR PERSONAL PROCESS WORK, TAKE GOOD CARE OF YOUR WHOLE BEING, AND DEVELOP YOUR MENTAL POWERS AND ABILITIES OF CONCENTRATION, VISUALIZATION, AND SENSORY STIMULATION/ENHANCEMENT, you will be well on your way to being a Modern Metaphysical Talent, and as a side benefit, a Problem Solving Genius. You will also want to MASTER BEING ABLE TO GET INTO AND OUT OF ALTERED STATES OF CONSCIOUSNESS smoothly by will and choice, and to become a MASTER OF THE QUIET MIND.

There are SPECIFIC TECHNIQUES AND SKILLS that apply to some of the abilities you may choose to develop, such as learning to "soft focus" in order to see auras and elves. There are also particular skills you will want to have developed in order to successfully and safely navigate in some of the dimensions you are opening up to. An example of that involves learning the ability to control your mindthoughts before you adventure in the astral worlds, for whatever you think while in the astral world gets immediately realized. It can be quite disconcerting if your thoughts are flying all over the place because, in an astral world, your spirit body will have to go along for the ride. Let yourself be guided to the particular books, teachers, and experiences you need in your quest to developing your higher abilities and the dimensions they enable you to be aware of while physically living on the Earth Plane.

You will be opening up on many levels and it will be ultra important for you to DEVELOP YOUR SENSITIVITIES SLOWLY. Don't push and pressure yourself. Patience needs to be your constant companion. At first, the various metaphysical abilities may spontaneously pop out of you. You will need to recognize that those very abilities need to be focused on and dealt with in an ORGANIZED LEARNING PLAN. Then you will be able to control them so you won't be suddenly dropping into a trance while driving, or direct voice spirit channeling when your mother calls for a simple "how's the weather" chat.

CONSISTENTLY MONITOR YOUR PROGRESS, checking and rechecking that you are going STEP-BY-STEP and not trying to play "leaps and bounds" out of either eagerness or frustration. Stay away from "the crash and burn syndrome" by: CONTINUALLY CENTERING YOURSELF THROUGH PRAYER AND MEDITATION, RELEASING THE EXCESS EMOTIONS YOUR JOURNEY STIMULATES, NOT HOOKING INTO OTHERS NEEDS TO KEEP YOU DISEMPOWERED, AND MAKING SURE YOUR INTENTIONS AND GOALS ARE BASED ON LOVINGLY SERVING FOR THE BEST OF ALL CONCERNED.

LET YOURSELF BE GUIDED TO THE PATICULAR BOOKS, TEACHERS, AND EXPERIENCES YOU NEED IN YOUR QUEST TO OPEN UP TO YOUR HIGHER ABILITIES AND THE DIMENSIONS THEY ENABLE YOU TO BE AWARE OF WHILE PHYSICALLY LIVING ON THE EARTH PLANE . . .

In opening up and developing your Higher Powers, make sure you are not trying to escape from life. Instead, you can use your Higher Sense Perceptions to TRANSFORM YOUR EVERYDAY LIVING into the quality of life available to us all as Awakened Souls. Do what you can to KEEP GROUNDED. Spaciness doesn't work out well. Always remember that YOUR EVERYDAY LIFE IS THE BEST LABORATORY available just for you. BE AWARE OF WHAT IS GOING ON AROUND AND IN YOU, for the metaphysical world isn't located a trillion light years away. It's all around you in every present moment.

When you first start developing, you will run up against BARRIERS IN THE FORM OF DISBELIEF, TENSION CREATED BY FEAR, AND SELF (LIFE) DISTRUST. You do not need to leap blindfolded. You do need to WORK STEP-BY-STEP THROUGH YOUR FEARS, DISBELIEFS, AND DISTRUSTS. Once you have done your research and studying, having decided to develop certain metaphysical skills and abilities with intentions steered by the qualities of love and wholeness, then you need TO ASK. Yes, asking your Soul and your helper team of angels, spirit guides and teachers, and The Divine is something you'll need to do over and over again. You have to BE OPEN TO RECEIVE! It's one of the prerequisites and there is no faking or pretending to The Powers That Be.

When you are honestly ready for each step in your journey, your Spirit Helpers and Soul will help orchestrate the most appropriate form, event, experience, lesson, teacher, etc. for you in relation to where you really are. They'll often know way before you do, because they know and see you clearer than you know and see yourself. And they aren't hung up on the fact that you, being raised in the human world, need and, indeed have to have PROOF. Proof isn't hard to materialize since it's real. When you are ready, you'll get all the proof you need.

OTHER BARRIERS YOU WILL NEED TO WORK THROUGH ARE: YOUR TRICKY NEED TO INTERPRET WHAT YOU ARE TAPPING INTO, OTHER PEOPLES NEED TO CONTROL AND TRY TO STOP YOUR GROWTH, AND YOUR LOWER-SELF THROWING UP ALL ITS EGO-BOUND TRICKS AND TRAPS. Understanding and appropriately applying what we perceive through our metaphysically connected Higher Sense Perceptions is an area that requires enormous attention and practice. It hangs up most of us, creating a lot of uncomfortable and confusing times when we have obviously misinterpreted what we have perceived. Misinterpretation is more than likely going to be the thing that slows you down and gets you in more jams than any other issue concerning the accessing of metaphysical knowledge and worlds.

We misinterpret what we receive from metaphysical realms because we filter those images, sensations, voices and words, etc. through our lower-self's ego needs, our past experiences, our present misbeliefs and disbeliefs, our fears, and our emotions. SEEK TO BE A CLEAR CHANNEL FOR HIGHER COMMUNICATIONS. Learn to BE AWARE OF YOUR OWN BODYMIND SIGNALS that tell you that you are blowing the message through being hooked into the outcome or product. Systematically watch yourself over time, ANALYZING both what you did to misinterpret a message and what you did when you obviously worked the message appropriately to its true meaning. Over time your statistical average of being right-on will improve if you keep doing your clearing work.

Many of our planetary people are intimidated by others that are empowered by and through Spirit. Your mere joyful and prosperous existence will push buttons in others. SELF-TRUST AND CONFIDENCE, as well as TUNING INTO YOUR CENTER, inner and *Higher Self*, will help you to get through the push and pull of changing relationships. Your task is to BE TRUE TO WHO YOU ARE AS SOUL WITHOUT NEEDING OR TRYING TO FORCE OTHERS TO GROW WHEN THEY ARE NOT SOUL-READY. And there is quite a difference between personality-stuckness and Soul-Readiness.

Many times the potential you will be picking up in others is their Soul's energy. However, that doesn't necessarily mean that they will develop that potential in this lifetime, for they will have to do the hard work of getting their lower-self personality out of the way first. They were given will and choice just like you, and they may choose to stay stuck and in pain, indefinitely. IT IS A GREAT MISUSE/ABUSE OF YOUR POWERS TO TRY TO FORCE SOMEONE ELSE TO CHANGE FOR YOUR OWN SELFISH NEEDS. The bottom line is that it just doesn't work.

Your lower self personality will be threatened by your own changes let alone by others who are fearful of you. Your ego - in the form of "I'm better than . . ." "I'm so cool nothing can knock me down. . ." and quite a few other distortions - will rage during different parts and stages of your metaphysical quest. These EGO SNARES/TRAPS will attract negative energies from people and other dimensions. You don't want to draw to you angry, negative, lower spirit beings, anymore than you do angry, negative human beings as your metaphysical abilities are starting to be a normal part of your daily life.

PSYCHIC SELF-DEFENSE has everything to do with being aware of what you are attracting and why, and then doing your Personal Process Work to close the circuits within you that are attracting negative conflicts. CLEANSE THOSE CHAKRAS. SURROUND YOURSELF WITH WHITE LIGHT. PRAY AND ASK FOR DIVINE PROTECTION AND GUIDANCE. RUN INSPIRITING, JOYFUL, LOVING ENERGY. GET THE REST AND REVITALIZATION YOU NEED. TAKE EXTRA GOOD CARE OF YOURSELF as you are consciously, deliberately, purposefully, and lovingly developing all you can be!

YOUR TASK IS TO BE TRUE TO WHO YOU ARE AS SOUL WITHOUT TRYING TO FORCE OTHERS TO GROW WHEN THEY ARE NOT SOUL-READY . . .

ACTIVITY: <u>WHO'S TALKING NOW?</u>

As your metaphysical abilities really start blossoming, you may experience the "Who said that?" phenomenon. In becoming an Attuned Soul, you will become aware of the many ways or channels that thoughts and images occur within your brainmind complex. It is essential in becoming a clear messenger that you LEARN TO DISCERN THE ORIGIN OF THE MESSAGE.

These "voices" could be the collective voice of your present life lower-self personality, your various subpersonalities, a programming tape you received from your parents and other people, or even an unresolved past life influence. You could be taping into a memory, an energy reading, a thoughtform, a previously read fact, or someone else's emotions and thoughts that are strongly projecting. It could be the energy and voice of your Soul, a nature spirit, or any one of the numbers of angels and spirit teachers and guides that are there for you.

Being able to immediately know when, who, and what is getting through to you will come through LOTS OF PRACTICE, DIRECT EXPERIENCE, AND DELIBERATE AWARENESS AND ASSESSMENT of what occurred. At first, always ASK YOURSELF "WHERE DID THAT COME FROM?" In time you will recognize when you have made something up through your own imagination fueled by human neediness and desire, attachments and expectations. As you get to know the various components of your personality, you will also start recognizing them when they insist on having their say. When you have become aware of the influences you picked up from your parents, others, and your past experiences, you will recognize when you are speaking or seeing through their voice and eyes. (continued on page 156)

When you aren't sure from where your knowledge came, SCAN YOUR MEMORY BANKS for possible times, places, events you may have learned something similar from. If you are picking up on things while around other people, check and make sure that, through your opening and developing sensitivities, you haven't just tapped into the energies they are running. Each energetic being, including angels and spirit guides, have their own ENERGETIC SIGNATURE that you need to get very familiar with.

Your bodymind is very sensitive to energy signatures. Over time and with much experience, you need only focus on listening and feeling for these each time you are receiving or perceiving on a metaphysical level in order to be able to instantaneously know who is talking now.

BE AWARE!
LISTEN!
WATCH!
FEEL!
SENSE!
RECOGNIZE!
ASK!
TEST!
NOTE!
EXPERIMENT!
CONTEMPLATE!
ANALYZE!
STUDY!
CONFIRM!
PROVE!

CHAPTER NINE
SOARING IN SPIRIT

> **WE HAVE TO LIVE OUT OUR SPIRITUAL NATURE**
> **RATHER THAN OUR HUMAN CONDITIONING . . .**

DIVINE CONSCIOUSNESS

Soul is manifested in spiritual dimensions through our spirit body just like Soul is manifested on Earth through our spirit that resides in a physical human body. It is through our *Higher Self* that Soul, or the God-aspect individualized, is expressed here on Earth. And through developing our *Higher Self,* we can contact any other consciousness in the Holoverse. This includes messengers/helpers known as angels (Souls higher up on the evolutionary ladder) and direct communication, without any mediators, with The Divine/God/Goddess/Infinite Intelligence.

Developing Divine Consciousness means that one is opening up and learning to COMMUNICATE ON HIGHER LEVELS. Learning to see the larger picture of life is learning to think like God. Learning to relate from a STATE OF UNCONDITIONAL LOVE is learning to feel like God. Learning to run our lives in cooperation with Holoversal Truth or Divine Universal Laws/Principles is learning to live like God.

Earth living is not about trying to make things happen. It is about cocreating through allowing it to happen. Cocreating and, indeed, whole living takes a natural, constant tuning into Higher Knowledge, along with Earthly know-how. Guidance comes from one's Soul by way of *The Higher Self's* ability to intuit and read energy. When we do not use our natural energy reading and intuitive abilities, then spirit can still get through to us by speaking directly within our minds or helping to orchestrate synchronicities. Spirit voice within our mind is different than intuitive action, which is sensing and knowing.

We come back to Earth again and again in order to complete the special learning Earth's unique environment initiates, which includes bringing spirit into this world and helping Divine Consciousness open up within the minds of we Souls who still assume human bodies. In terms of reincarnation, we cannot place an average number on the years inbetween our incarnations, for Soulspirit doesn't choose according to human-imposed time lines. Soulspirit (we) choose to reincarnate upon Earth according to what we need to experience (karmic needs) in terms of the current earthly conditions and when karmic-appropriate Soulgroups will be on Earth: in other words, when conditions are ripe for our up and coming lessons and growth opportunities.

We come back in order to EXPRESS OUR SPITITUALITY THROUGH OUR HUMANITY, to bring "heaven here on Earth." To do that, we have to live out our spiritual nature rather than our human conditioning. God/Goddess needs to be expressed in this Earthly World through you and me. We are wired for God, so to speak.

We have body parts and chemicals, mind abilities and expressiveness, and spirit connections all oriented to expressing Divine Consciousness here on Earth. Indeed, we are capable not only of replacing disbelief with Divine Knowing, but we can REPLACE CONCEPTS OF GOD WITH ACTUAL AND REALISTIC EXPERIENCE. We can be filled with Divine Light and guided by God/Goddess through every experience in our lives.

To regain that COSMIC CONNECTION, we've got to REMEMBER: we've got to uncover our Soul's touch and voice from the trappings of humanity. Spirituality is all about feeling and living with and by the presence of God's energy and power. We've got to reconnect with Soul/Spirit in order to remember why we're really here on Earth. Clearing out the human psychospiritual garbage we've piled on ourselves, of course, is essential. *And* at the same time we have to OPEN UP OUR COMMUNICATION LINES TO THE DIVINE AND THE VARIOUS LIFE FORMS THAT MAKE UP THE ALL OF LIFE, THAT ARE A PART OF GOD. It's not enough to just weed your garden. It's all about bringing yourself into full bloom.

UTILIZE THE GIFTS OF ALTERED STATES that are inspiration, new perspectives, insights, connection, healing, and extraordinary faith. Developing your inner life requires learning to ENJOY SOLITUDE, REST YOUR BODY, QUIET YOUR MIND, and CALM YOUR EMOTIONS. Prayer, meditation, contemplation, witness consciousness, Soulspirit connection and communication, shamanic journeying including chanting/toning/drumming, and praising and giving thanks and blessing are all techniques and abilities which can lead to Divine reconnection.

All the above can increase our Soul energy enabling us to have the peak experiences which are so much a part of Soul: self-realization, fulfillment, the cocreative state, illumination, peace, joy, elation, and ecstasy. Other ways to increase Soulspirit energy are by running white light, working with your chakras and other subtle energies, and consciously increasing and moving your Kundalini (Evolutionary Energy). As your abilities increase and you are able to work directly and consciously with the spirit world, you will recognize and experience that you also receive energy from those realms, including directly from The Divine. Consciously receiving the very real, multi-leveled DIVINE RAYS is an experience that is beyond words. It's an instant and eternally lasting "beyond belief into absolute knowing" energetic blast that catapults Soul Movement.

A few books that cover more details on this chapter's focus are: John Randolph Price's *Practical Spirituality*, Genevieve Lewis Paulson's *Kundalini And The Chakras*, Catherine Ponder's *The Dynamic Laws Of Prayer* and *The Dynamic Laws Of Prosperity*, Bruce McArthur's *Your Life: Why It Is The Way It Is And What You Can Do About It,* and Charles Fillmore's *Prosperity.* In opening up to and developing SPIRIT, all of the categories listed below are important to have as tools, techniques, and abilities. Each will change and expand as you do. They are all quite dynamic in form and result, so allow yourself to feel and move through their different levels.

1. MEDITATION:
In their book, *The Life We Are Given,* George Leonard and Michael Murphy define meditation as "The disciplined observation of thoughts, feelings, impulses, and sensations, as well as the spontaneous turning of heart and mind towards a presence beyond the ordinary self." There are many forms of meditation to practice that will change as your abilities and attentions deepen. The forms of meditation that allow you to learn how to control your thoughts, how to have no thoughts, and how to hear beyond your own thoughts work best for *Higher Self Integration* and in opening your abilities to communicate with Spirit/Soul/Divine.

QUIET, PEACEFUL, UNINTERRUPTED SPACE ALONG WITH BODY STILLNESS AND POSTURE STRAIGHTNESS HELP ONE TO FOCUS ON SUCH MEDITATIVE TECHNIQUES AS COUNTING ONE'S BREATH AND USING A MANTRA (significant word), CHANTING, OR FOCUSED PHRASE. Some focused words and phrases are: Love - Om - Namaste - Oneness - I am and radiate Divine Love Light - I let go and let God express with, as, through me - God's healing light and love radiate through me and throughout all creation . . .

2. PRAYER:
Prayer is a method of thought that links you with God/Goddess. As Catherine Ponder puts it in her book, *The Dynamic Laws of Prayer*, "When you pray, you stir into action an atomic force. You release a potent spiritual vibration that can be released in no other way. Through prayer you unleash a God energy within and around you that gets busy working for you and through you, producing right attitudes, reactions, and results. It is your prayers that

recognize and release that God power." Just like with meditation, which can be considered a form of prayer, there are many different prayer techniques that will be appropriate for you as you evolve as a Soul growing on Earth.

Constant communion with The Divine is a part of Level Seven of the Soul Consciousness levels that are achievable in this Earthly dimension. But until prayer becomes your way of thinking, it is helpful to SET ASIDE REGULAR PRAYER TIMES where you can focus beyond your Earthly life. Prayer is not about telling God what to do. Higher Intelligence knows the whole picture in a way our lower selves wouldn't ever be able to comprehend. Prayer is about asking for the Soul Essence of what you (or someone else when you pray with others in mind) need in order to be fulfilled as your Higher Self. It is also about being open to receiving from The Great Spirit. In order to do so, you have to move through any remaining unworthiness issues.

AFFIRMATIVE PRAYER is a technique and tool that is very helpful to *The Higher Self Integration Process.* Here are a few examples:

* * *

God/Goddess, go before me this day, preparing my way and prospering me in all that I do. I place my needs in your care and I trust you to guide and prosper me. Fill my mind with rich ideas and lead me in the way of success and prosperity. My life is in Divine Order. I live each day thankful to God for light, inspiration, and the courage to follow Divine Direction/Guidance.

* * *

I pray that peaceful solutions to world challenges influence the thinking of all world leaders and citizens.

* * *

The light of God surrounds me/you. The love of God enfolds me/you. The power of God protects me/you. The presence of God watches over me/you. Wherever I am/you are, God is.

James Dillet Freeman

* * *

SPIRITUALITY IS ALL ABOUT FEELING AND LIVING WITH AND BY THE PRESENCE OF GOD/GODDESS ENERGY AND POWER . . .

3. WITNESS CONSCIOUSNESS:

Essentially, this is the skill and ability to BE AWARE OF YOUR HIGHER SELF OR SOUL COMPASSIONATELY AND KNOWINGLY, (AND WITHOUT JUDGMENT) WATCHING YOUR LOWER-SELF DO ITS TRICKS OF THE TRADE. It requires that you run a couple of awareness tracks at the same time. Doing so makes switching out of the energy path of the lower self easier, quicker, and smoother.

You can stop yourself in mid-spurt, ask yourself if you really choose to think/feel/act this way, answer yourself, and then make the change. Running Witness Consciousness means that you are entuned to Higher Consciousness and enables Spirit/Soul/Divine to communicate directly with the parts of you that aren't quite there yet, while the action is happening. At first, find a way to remind yourself to break into your ordinary consciousness to purposefully check yourself out. After a while, it will start occurring naturally and *Higher Self Integration* will be another step closer to your daily Earthly reality.

4. SHAMANIC JOURNEYING (INCLUDING CHANTING/ TONING/ DRUMMING):

Learning things on the metaphysical level through altered states of consciousness has been a technique of growth and spirituality since Souls first came to Earth in human form. It is all about EXPLORING NONORDINARY REALITIES WHILE MAINTAINING CONTROL OF YOUR OWN CONSCIOUSNESS. The purposes of Shamanic Journeying are: diagnosing and treating dis-ease, prophecy/divination/path-direction clarity, and interaction with spirits, power animals, and non-ordinary teachers and guides. Shamanic Journeying can include: communicating with nature and spirits, traveling in other dimensions, and metaphysical healings.

It incorporates such techniques as Vision Quests, the use of symbols/rituals/power-places, music, dancing, and imagery. Toning, chanting, and drumming are the use of sound and rhythm to enter deeper and clearer states of consciousness. In TONING, you let a self-generated vocal sound and rhythm move from within you, focusing on it for a while. In CHANTING, you pick a mantra or chant to focus on for an extended period of time. And in DRUMMING, you repeat a rhythm for a long while. If you feel that you are not quite skilled enough to initiate your own non-ordinary journeys, there are different books, tapes, videos, and workshops you can use until you are ready to fly on your own.

5. PRAISING/GIVING THANKS/BLESSING:

These three thought and feeling forms help to open us up and magnetize more positive/higher energies to us. Learning to TRULY APPRECIATE EVERY COMPONENT OF LIFE and the Beings who travel with us on our journey is part of living in nonresistance and with compassion. EMOTIONALLY AND VERBALLY EXPRESSING APPRECIATION THROUGH PRAISE AND THANKSGIVING moves us in positive and life-affirming directions. BLESSING, or honoring and conferring well-being and prosperity on all that is a part of our lives, brings Divine Energies into our daily affairs. Besides helping to move us out of binding and destructive self-absorption and selfishness, praise, thanksgiving, and blessing help to open the gateway of our Soul's and God's Love. Two simple and brief, yet effective, blessings are:

I bless with Divine's Love and Light _____ . . .
-and-
I bless all of creation . . .

6. RUNNING WHITE LIGHT AND KUNDALINI:

Along with consciously working with your subtle energies in the form of your aura and chakras through visualization, movement, and affirmative thought focus, you also have to work with two other forms of energy from both the inner and outer realms. THE USE OF WHITE LIGHT FOR PROTECTION IS USING THE POWER OF VISUALIZATION, AFFIRMATION, AND PRAYER TO INVOKE DIVINE ORDER AND SAFETY. Use this powerful form of intervention towards your house, family and friends, your own Being, your travels, etc. Surround whatever you think needs a little extra juice to stay the course with WHITE LIGHT VISUALIZATIONS AND AFFIRMATIONS.

KUNDALINI (a Sanskrit word meaning circular power) is an individual's basic evolutionary life force. It is the energy available that helps us to move forward in awakening our consciousness to the higher awareness and energy of each chakra. Spiritual Kundalini is the all-pervading cosmic energy (Shakti) which condenses to create our physical form. After the creation of our physical form, residual energy is left in the body waiting in a potential energy state.

There are many layers of Kundalini waiting to be released. The Kundalini releasing process is a dynamic, self-directed, self-limited process of mental and physiological purification, leading to a healthier and more developed state than what we usually consider normal. Awakened Kundalini moves through our physical and subtle bodies removing blocks and spiritualizing our consciousness. You must learn to feel, know, and use what you have and to awaken the much greater amount waiting at the base of your spine, for this energy transmutes into healing, inner strength, creativity, joy, and enlightenment.

In the *Higher Self Integration Process*, we learn to use Kundalini in a conscious way in order to cleanse and refine the body, even on a cellular level, so that our higher mental and spiritual energies can operate in our system. Anything that moves and cleans your energy system will work with your Kundalini. THESE ACTIVITIES ARE GENERALLY RECOMMENDED FOR THE KUNDALINI RELEASE PROCESS: MEDITATION, FREE-FORM DANCE AND EXERCISE, CONSCIOUSLY THINKING HIGHER THOUGHTS, TIME IN NATURE, CREATIVE PURSUITS, DEEP BREATHING, MASSAGE, AND VISUALIZATION ALL WITH THE FOCUS AND INTENTION OF SPECIFICALLY CLEANSING AND OPENING YOUR CHAKRAS AND RAISING YOUR KUNDALINI ENERGY.

It is important that you are informed about the Kundalini Awakening Process and that you obtain whatever support you need as you work on deeper and deeper levels. Usually the raising of Kundalini Energies is part of what one can call the Initiation Phase of Higher Consciousness. It includes a burning-out of some of our darkest energies and can be quite overwhelming if one is unprepared. The Kundalini Jeanie is one of the mysteries with which you will need to become personally intimate. Take your time, study up on this area, and utilize visualizations that are specific to and for this particularly fiery Soul Energy.

AWAKENED KUNDALINI MOVES THROUGH OUR PHYSICAL AND SUBTLE BODIES REMOVING BLOCKS AND SPIRITUALIZING OUR CONSCIOUSNESS . . .

---

7. CONTEMPLATION:

Deep CONTEMPLATION, in a spiritual sense, means using one's whole brainmind complex to go further in one's comprehension than had been done before. It is striving to be of like mind with The Divine, of tapping into Soul knowledge and wisdom. In order to move through your stuck or preprogrammed thinking, you have to quiet your body and automatic thought patterns through meditative practices and emotional clearing. You also have to consciously and purposefully set aside your expectations, old assumptions, bias, and prejudices.

Once in an open, relaxed, and focused state, pick a topic or question that you would like to know The Divine Truth about. YOUR INTENT IS TO ACCESS UNDERSTANDINGS THAT COME FROM BEYOND HUMAN CONDITIONING AND ILLUSION. Make sure that you clearly ASK FOR GUIDANCE from your team of spirit helpers: your Soul, spirit teachers and guides, angels, and even The Akashic Records. One of the ways you will know that new realizations and energies are reworking you is that your brain will literally heat up and your head, if not other parts of your body, will get hotter than usual. You will also startle yourself at how profound or what interesting directions your thinking moves into.

You are not trying to regurgitate your old thoughts. You are allowing fresh ideas and more information about all the aspects of your chosen topic or question to present itself to you. If your focus strays, bring it back. Keep breathing deeply and slowly, taking each contemplation session as far as you can go. Deep contemplation takes practice. In your different sessions, keep going back to the same topics and questions in order to see a definite progression in your ability to comprehend the essences and whole meanings of life.

These topics make for interesting and vigorous contemplative sessions: Divine Order, Divine Safety, Divine Solutions, Unconditional Love, Humility, Faith, Grace and other Soul qualities. Another way to approach a contemplation session on a specific topic is to work with a definition of the topic that already stretches you, such as: GRACE is God's love in action - and - FAITH is the perceiving power of the mind linked with the power to shape substance . . . Be aware that once you have opened yourself to the truth about something, you will be presented lessons on that topic throughout your normal consciousness and daily affairs. So, be on the look out!

YOUR INTENT IS TO ACCESS UNDERSTANDINGS THAT COME FROM BEYOND HUMAN CONDITIONING AND ILLUSION . . .

ACTIVITY: <u>REACHING BEYOND</u>

1. STUDY, PRACTICE, EXPAND, AND INCORPORATE into your life each of the above categories of techniques, skills, and abilities. Keep a record of your concerns, changes, and experiences. Pray, meditate, contemplate, and ask for both inner and outer guides or teachers in their various forms to help you in your step-by-step journey with The Divine. Use this AFFIRMATIVE PRAYER daily:

* * *   I invoke the love, wisdom, and power of my Higher Consciousness: to guide me to the right activity in the plan, to illuminate, inspire, clarify, and expand my mind, to transform, transmute, and stabilize my feelings and emotions, to energize, vitalize, and heal my physical and vital body so there is a Divine Flow of energy through my being today and everyday, to attract to me all those I can truly help and all those who can help me in anyway, and to provide me with all the material and monetary resources I need in order to be my *Highest Self* here on Earth. I have been created for a life of health, joy, prosperity, and Divine Unity.

Amen…   * * *

2. The meditative level called "THE SILENCE" usually takes disciplined practice before it becomes an easily attainable state. It is very important to achieve it through gently loving and caring for yourself, combined with perseverance and patience. Those qualities make the word discipline quite palatable and the consistent, long-term process it needs to be in ACHIEVING HIGHER CONSCIOUSNESS. The following activity is helpful in attaining The Silence:

Sitting in a meditative pose, use your breath to relax letting go of all tension.
Focus on surrounding yourself with White Light.
Then concentrate your mind on your breath with the words:
"Let go and let God"
"Be still and know that I am God."
When it happens naturally, allow the words to stop and your thoughts to be silent.
Listen!

3. Every time you deeply and lovingly communicate with another energy form, be it human, nature, spirit, etc., you are in communion with The God/Life Force. THE LIFE FORCE is everywhere and has various energetic degrees with which it is projected onto the material and spiritual realms. As you become wholer and more fully integrated, you can healthily work with higher and more potent levels of this ultimate energy and light.

An aspect of this work is when one experiences "SITTING IN DIVINE LIGHT."   One cannot force these higher experiences, but one can become open to them and prepare one's being to receive them. Many people will see God's Light in their mind's eye during an altered and healing state.   That is a different experience than sitting in God's Light or DIVINE RAYS, but you can use your skills of visualization to practice, until the actual experience occurs. The actual experience of sitting in God's Light will occur in Divine Timing, but you will at least be prepared:

Enter into a meditative and altered state of consciousness.
Visualize a magnificent light coming towards you and shining upon you.
Sit perfectly still and keep your mindthoughts as focused as you can.
Imagine God's Lovelight filling you with love and joy.

Knowing The Divine and working with spirit also means knowing and understanding how life really works. There actually is a reason and a rhyme for everything in life as a result of "THE UNIVERSAL LAWS." Universal Laws are unbreakable, unchangeable principles of life that operate inevitably, in all phases of our life and existence, for all human beings and all things, everywhere, all the time. Spiritual laws, nature's laws, laws of mind/body/spirit, and all of the principles which man divides into laws of science are actually Universal or Holoversal Laws.

We are all subject to Universal Laws. These laws are also guideposts to a basic path of spiritual development, for they are the keys by which we can transform our lives. As you become aware of The Universal Laws and consciously use them effectively to transform yourself and your life creating joy and success in everything in which you are involved, your life will become a fulfilling one because your actions will be in accord with the purpose of the Universe.

For *Higher Self Integration* purposes, BECOME AWARE OF, STUDY, INTEGRATE, AND WORK CLOSELY WITH THESE UNIVERSAL LAWS IN YOUR DAILY LIFE:

The laws of cause and effect, of attraction, of increase, laws of transformation and attunement of self and in relation with others, of guidance and correspondences, of consciousness and manifestation, laws of balance, of belief, and the laws of love and enlightenment . . .

These can also be named The Spiritual Principles of Wholeness. As you become graphically aware of how these principles of life influence everything that you do, you will also start feeling a connectedness and responsibility that comes from Soulspirit. Everything in your life will start making sense, and we're talking about COSMIC OR SOUL SENSE.

As you explore these principles of life, the Universal Law of "like begets like" is one of the most important to comprehend and consciously integrate on every level possible. The ultimate reality of this basic UL is: "The spirit in which I act will create and return to me in the same spirit." We're talking about the power of intention here. Or as Bruce McArthur wrote in his book that demystifies these laws, *Your Life-Why It Is The Way It Is And What You Can Do About It or Understanding The Universal Laws*: "If you use, work, or manipulate The Universal Laws for selfish purposes, that spirit or purpose will come through and you will reap detrimental results."

Consciously working with The Universal Laws is about empowerment. BE VERY CLEAR AS TO WHAT YOU ARE SEEKING TO CREATE OR BECOME THROUGH THE POWER AND ENERGY OF WORKING THE UNIVERSAL LAWS. The Universal Law of - "That which we hold in consciousness will be made manifest for us." - on a daily basis teaches us that we should not hold the thought of anything that we do not wish to see appear. Therefore, learning attitude adjustment, reframing, affirmations, visualizations, and other reprogramming techniques are necessary aspects of living in Soulspirit as a part of humanity.

Many of these basic principles to all of life are sentences you have probably heard before, such as:

"Know the Truth and the Truth shall set you free . . ."
"For every effect there is a cause . . ."
"What we give our attention to expands and grows . . ."
"Seek first the spirit within and you will find. Ask the spirit, with faith, and you will receive.
Knock with faith, in spirit, and the door will be opened . . ."
"As you give, so it is measured to you again . . ."

Your long-term task is to fully understand each individual law, how they are all connected working hand-in-hand with one another, and how they influence everything in your life from the most significant to the very least. Study life and its basic principles or Universal Laws. USE YOUR DEVELOPING ABILITIES AND SKILLS of detailed observation, suspended critical judgmentalness, connective analyzation, visual imagery, roleplaying, and many others in order to jump into the center of how life really works.

The ability of deep CONTEMPLATION works well in exploring Universal Laws. Be prepared that knowledge, comprehension, and application of these basic principles of life put a stop to any pity-parties, blame, and "I'm not responsible" excuses you still employ in order to stay the same. Wait until you really learn and experience (be and live) the truth that "Nothing happens by chance: There is a purpose to everything that happens." Your life cannot remain the same for you will have lost your ability to run your old pity-party routines.

**THERE ACTUALLY IS A REASON AND A RHYME FOR EVERYTHING
IN LIFE AS A RESULT OF THE UNIVERSAL LAWS OR PRINCIPLES OF LIFE . . .**

ACTIVITY: <u>IN THE FLOW</u>

The more you consciously work with The Universal/Divine Laws in a life-affirming manner, the more your life will flow in spirit and in Soul. Take the Universal Laws already mentioned and the ones listed below, later adding anymore you have been made aware of, and gradually **FLUSH THEM OUT:** Study and apply them in your own daily life. Contemplate, talk about, and creatively work with them. **TAKE EACH ONE INDIVIDUALLY, FIGURING OUT HOW EACH ONE, APPLIED APPROPRIATELY, WOULD INFLUENCE THESE AREAS OF YOUR LIFE:** Your intimate and familial relationships including children, your life's work or service and your Soul's purpose, your economics/finances, your relationship with God/Goddess/a Higher Source of guidance and wisdom, your self-change program of body/mind/spirit, and your problem solving skills in general.

Here are more Universal Laws for your conscious study and application:

* As you honor, respect, and love your own unique individuality,
     so you honor, respect, and love the individuality of others . . .
* All exchanges balance . . .
* Your Soul needs and their fulfillment are as important as those of any other Soul . . .
* You must first serve, help, care for, love, and know your self if you would serve another . . .
* As you put the God within first in your life, so you manifest the God you are . . .
* Spirit is the life, mind is the builder, physical is the result . . .
* Love transforms . . .
* Life is the experience of your choices . . .
* As you believe, so it becomes for you . . .
* As you know your purpose and apply Universal Laws in accord with it,
     you will know what the results will be . . .

SPIRIT CONSCIOUSNESS

In the process of becoming and integrating your *Higher Self*, **your abilities to work with and in other spiritual realms and with other spiritual energies/Beings will gradually open and expand.** As you practice activities and skills that enable you to communicate beyond this material plane on which you presently live, bear in mind that you will also need to keep on doing, if not increasing, your emotional and etheric energy clearing and cleansing practices. In addition, you must find and implement ways that help keep you grounded on Earth and that allow you to be clear about integrating what you experience on spiritual planes with Earth Plane realities.

Levels of spiritual communication that are yours to consciously explore are: your own Soul's energy *(Higher Self* Communication), the spiritual energy of other nature forms on this planet (Nature's Connection), other Spirits (Spirit Guidance) from the Spiritual Dimensions, and the original Life Force Energy (The Divine Light/God Communion). Spirit Guidance can come in many forms, existing in a type of hierarchy based on the Soulspirit's developmental stage. Not only are there Evolutionary Levels of Soul Consciousness possible for we Souls who choose human form upon the Earth Plane, but there are also Spiritual Levels of Soul Consciousness in regards to the Spiritual Realms.

As you open and develop your abilities to read energy and communicate spirit-to-spirit and Soul-to-Soul, you will be connecting with the worlds of trees, plants, animals, birds, and insects in ways that you probably thought were impossible. Other Earth-based nature spirits in the spirit forms of Devas (the organizing spirit in charge of a particular group or area), elves, and fairies are quite an interesting group to experience. They are also called Elementals.

You can learn to communicate with Souls you had a human relationship with before they left their physical form and passed on into the spiritual dimension. Spirit Guides and Teachers are more advanced Souls who no longer need to take human form, although they have in the past, and who can become as much, if not even more, of a family member to you than your human family. There are also different levels of angels, Souls that have never lived real human lives, who vibrate energetically closer to The Divine.

We all have a "Spirit Family" we can learn to get to know who are there for us, whether we are consciously aware of them or not. Remember the Universal Law of "Like Attracts Like." When we pass on into the Spiritual Dimension, we carry with us the energy state we developed while here on Earth. That energetic state or Energetic Signature is what attracts to us our experiences in the Spiritual Realms. It operates the same way in regards to the types of Spirit Guides and Teachers we attract while we are still in human form. Therefore, you will be able to work with more evolved SpiritSouls from the Spirit Realm as you evolve yourself.

Recall the Universal and also Metaphysical/Spiritual Law that "Everything begins in mind." It is the emotion and imagery we give to these thoughts or the energy we pour into them that molds both our outer and inner worlds. If you are fearful of the spiritual worlds and get stuck on dark or "evil" thoughts, you will be creating an energetic sludge that is really hard for the lighter/higher Spiritual Beings to get through. We all have Guardian Angels who are with us every step of our journey, but they can only get through to you if you allow them to. Allowing them to has everything to do with how you run your energy.

As you develop your psychic abilities, including your abilities to see, hear, and touch other worlds or dimensions, YOU HAVE TO BE CAREFUL TO NOT OVERLOAD YOUR CIRCUITS. If you have not learned how to keep grounded and balanced through a wellness program involving diet, relaxation, and emotional stability and are carrying encumbrances such as unnecessary baggage from the past and unfinished business in the present, then working with higher energies than your being can deal with can lead to dis-ease. You will feel like you are frying or killing your body. Pure Divine Energy is usually a bit more than most people have learned to handle. That is why God/Goddesses messages usually come through our thoughts, our circumstances, and other messenger Beings.

WE ALL HAVE A SPIRIT FAMILY WE CAN LEARN TO GET TO KNOW WHO ARE THERE FOR US, WHETHER WE ARE CONSCIOUSLY AWARE OF THEM OR NOT . . .

ACTIVITY: SETTING YOUR ANTENNAE

Some people can access their angels and spirit guides/teachers while in an altered state using guided imagery. As a result, there are various guided visualizations on tape and in printed form that are specific to receiving Spirit Guidance, some of which are included in A Soul's Delight's Bibliography. However, if you DO YOUR PERSONAL PROCESS WORK AND SYSTEMATICALLY OPEN UP YOUR INTUITIVE/PSYCHIC ABILITIES, you will eventually be able to ACCESS SPIRITSOUL AND DIVINE CONTACT WHENEVER YOU SO CHOOSE AND IN JUST A BLINK OF AN EYE. In fact, *Higher Self Integration* is all about learning to believe, know, do, and be in with God's Program 100% of each and every moment.

What's really important is that you properly set your antennae. Follow your ever expanding HSI Program you will form through the concepts and processes outlined in this book. In direct relation to Spirit/Soul/Divine Guidance:

A. WORK THROUGH YOUR FEARS AND IGNORANCES CONCERNING THE WORLDS OF SPIRITSOUL. This includes releasing and not feeding all the crazy untruths that have been fed to you in the form of images/words that speak about horror and evil.

B. GET CLEAR AS TO WHAT YOUR INTENTIONS, GOALS, NEEDS, AND WANTS ARE IN RELATION TO SPIRIT GUIDANCE. Selfishness, self-absorption, greed, envy, jealousy, competition and other such negative emotions and motives will attract to you less desirable spirit contacts and situations. As the popular expression goes: "You don't even want to go there!"

C. If you lack in effective communication skills, then you better TAKE A FEW COMMUNICATION COURSES AND PRACTICE ON HUMANS FIRST. If you lack will power and assertiveness in working with humans, then you better wait before contacting other worlds, for you will need to KNOW WHO YOU ARE AND HOW TO CLEARLY BE AND GET WHAT YOU NEED OR ETHICALLY BELIEVE. Don't forget that it's easier if you just don't set yourself up for attracting underdeveloped SpiritSouls. But if you do, always know that with full intent, you can remove them from your energy field and life, by meaning in every way, "Get out of my space!"

D. Higher SpiritSouls or Angels, Spirit Guides, Spirit Teachers, and God/Goddess, don't use tricks, manipulations, and destructive games for they don't need to control you in any way. They are extremely brilliant, creative, clever, witty, and even unbelievably patient and forgiving once you have declared and have proven that you're ready to go with the program. What is great is that you can have an enormous amount of delight while learning some really cool things with the Realm of Spirit. TALK TO THEM ABOUT EVERYTHING. ASK THEM ANYTHING YOU WANT. You can rage to and even at them, and it doesn't phase them, not in the least. They don't mind that you need a whole lot of proof that they are real. LET GO OF YOUR PRECONCEIVED NOTIONS ABOUT RELATIONSHIPS, for you're in for the most pleasant of all surprises. They make unbelievably wonderful friends, limited only by you and your hangups!

The Divine and all of The Divine's Emissaries are there watching and waiting for you to consciously reconnect. They don't hang out watching TV with you, yet they are only a moment's consciousness away. WHEN THEY SPEAK TO YOU INSIDE YOUR HEAD, IT IS AS IF, INSTEAD OF THINKING THE THOUGHT, YOU HEAR IT. There is a huge difference you will learn to recognize overtime.

Each Spiritual Being, be it Jesus, Buddha, your guardian angel, each of your spirit guides and teachers, or the Deva of the land that you think you "own" but are really just costewarding for a very short time in its history, have their own ENERGY SIGNATURE you will learn to recognize. As you learn to metaphysically see and hear each one, they will appear in a spiritual form and voice uniquely appropriate to the message they are delivering, the lesson they are teaching, and the guidance they are giving.

Angels and spirit guides and teachers are messengers of hope and assistance. Not only can they communicate directly with you if you so allow and open to it, but they also help create SYNCHRONICITIES: when something in the universe seems to swing into place, against the odds, to answer an inner need we have. Another important role they play is in helping to create "GODCIDENCES" which are synchronicities that create validating experiences of The Divine in Earthly life. While they can be a part of these particular energetic collaborations, they can not do anything for you that you can and need to do for yourself.

Angels give unconditional love and help us to hit the groove of Divine Order and Safety. They can pull off safety-type phenomenon on our behalf, if our Soul is on target and our lower self is ready for transformation. Spirit guides provide guidance, not advice. They help us to remember things we've forgotten and to look into things we didn't know we could. Spirit teachers come and go in our life as our life lessons and understandings change and grow. They can teach us very directly about specific things or processes we need to know for our particular life's stages, developments, and situations. And they do so without human ego involvement, often making much clearer teachers than humans do, if we are willing to do all the work necessary in order to be able to communicate with them. The different types of Nature Spirits make fun playmates, increasing our knowledge of how best to work with Earth and all its critters and life-forms.

It is also possible to communicate with humans who have died within your present life, but who keep hanging out in the Earth's ethers in their spirit forms. Commonly called "ghosts", MAKE SURE YOU ARE CLEAR AS TO WHY THEY ARE MAKING SUCH AN EFFORT TO COMMUNICATE WITH YOU. Sometimes they can help you in your own spiritual journey, especially if you shared a real loving karmic bond with them. However, there are some who are resisting having made their transition and who only want to feed off of your energy, to use you as a battery to keep hanging out on The Earth Plane. IF YOU WANT NOTHING TO DO WITH THEM, BE FIRM ABOUT DEMANDING THAT THEY LEAVE YOU ALONE.

In addition to being able to connect with Souls in the Spirit Dimensions, we also have strong ties/bonds with individual Souls and SOUL GROUPS who we journey with here on Earth in human form at various times throughout our incarnations. As your abilities to sense your inner feelings and read energies enhance, you will know who these Soulfolks are because of the intensity of feelings you feel for them as soon as you are in physical contact with them. Your SOUL COMPANIONS AND SOULMATES and you not only have karmic lessons to complete, but you are also linked or wired energetically. That means you use each other as a type of battery, to give and take, share, contract, expand, and transform energy. These are ties you can't run away from because sooner or later they have to be reckoned with.

It can be helpful to TUNE INTO ONE ANOTHER ON SOUL LEVELS, even remembering specific karmic ties from other lifetimes, so you can complete those energies and concentrate on the here and now part of your involvement. One of the areas many of us get caught up and confused in, concerning those we feel are our Soul Companions and Soul Mates, is in trying to place them in a certain role based on lower-self and addicted needs.

Although these SoulSpirits are in human form, it doesn't work out well to relate to each other with a shallow "just another humanoid" mentality. Soul Companions or Soul Mates need to be related to on a spiritual/Soul level as well. You'll have to get beyond personality issues in order to set each other free and truly love one another unconditionally. For that's the bottom line: We're all here, in whatever form we take, with the opportunity to INSPIRIT or inspire one another, to liberate our Souls, and reunite as One.

AS YOU LEARN TO SEE AND HEAR ADVANCED SPIRITUAL BEINGS,
EACH WILL APPEAR IN A SPIRITUAL FORM AND VOICE UNIQUELY
APPROPRIATE TO THE MESSAGE THEY ARE DELIVERING, THE
LESSONS THEY ARE TEACHING, OR THE GUIDANCE THEY ARE GIVING . . .

ACTIVITY: ATTUNING TO NATURE

All the abilities and skills one needs to have in order to communicate deeply with our Natural World are the same ones that help in communicating with the other dimensions of Spirit. Below are a few activities to HELP YOU LEARN, THROUGH NATURE, ABOUT DEEPER LEVELS OF LIFE, THE SPIRITUAL PRACTICE OF ONENESS, AND TRAINING ONE'S BODY, MIND, AND ENERGY TO BE STILL AND LISTEN, SEE, THINK, AND COMMUNICATE BEYOND ORDINARY AWARENESS WITH OTHER DIMENSIONS:

+ Go on a discovery walk. Walk very slowly noticing the ground, the sky, and everything all around you, stopping to explore what you see, hear, and sense. Close your eyes and listen. Close you eyes and touch. Walk without categorizing. Look at everything as though you were seeing it for the first time in awe and wonder . . .

+ Close your eyes, walk into a tree, explore it without sight, walk away, and then spin. Open your eyes to see if you can find your tree . . .

+ As you slowly walk, feel yourself in every sound and movement of nature by observing, hearing, realizing how you are like what you are watching. Feel that kinship with all you see around you. Feel the essence of life in a particular form of nature. See how that essence fits into the whole. Enjoy the harmony of the many forms of life. Keep your awareness of your unity with all life foremost in your mind as you walk . .

+ Find a place to sit. Sit absolutely motionless, waiting for nature to return to its normal routine (20 + minutes). Try to melt into the landscape mentally and energetically as well as physically. Free your mind from expectation. Pay attention to every thing you see. Later, pick a critter you would like to get to know within your eyesight. Clear your mind. Slowly, simply, and silently try to communicate a clear thought. Watch and listen. Gently keep trying . . .

+ Sitting quietly with your thoughts as clear as they can be, ask to hear what the river, tree, etc., have to say. Practice feeling its essence and being as one, tuning deeper into their sound and ways of communicating . . .

+ Train your mind to watch one detail of what is around you for minutes at a time before you switch to another. Develop your powers of observation, awareness, and concentration while out in the natural world. Look for the life force energy in the sky by letting your eyes soft focus or by looking at space instead of detail. As you become better at this, try seeing The Universal Life Force Field (Aura) around trees, rocks, plants, animals, and other things . . .

+ In communicating with Devas, Elves, and other mystical beings, practice all the various nature attunement activities to develop your attitude, mind, and body skills so that you can enter a level which can attract, hear, and see other dimensions of life. Generate as much love and clear-access feeling as you can. Keep trying to raise your vibration level. Remember to keep calm. Getting excited about a contact changes the vibration level and breaks the communicado . . .

PROSPERITY CONSCIOUSNESS

PROSPERITY CONSCIOUSNESS incorporates all aspects of Divine and Spirit Consciousness in a system of wholeness that can make Earth Living a really transforming and joyous adventure. It leads to full *Higher Self Integration* because it is the result of DELIBERATE HIGHER THOUGHT AND ACTION. It is the study and practice of The Universal/Spiritual Principles or Laws of Wholeness.

True prosperity is having all the time, energy, financial, material, spirit, human, and nature resources your Soul needs in order to be, do, and express as Soul here on Earth. Whole health, true place success, joyful relationships, peace of mind, and a spirit-filled lifestyle and environment are by-products of incorporating Prosperity Consciousness into your life. Manifesting financial independence/freedom, so that you have all the financial and material resources you need in order to be free to give, express, and cocreate as your *Higher Self,* is a part of being Holy Prosperous.

To prosper means to flourish, succeed, thrive. Prosperity's roots mean well-being and wholeness. You are prosperous to the degree that you are experiencing peace, health, and plenty in your world. Just think of any area you are experiencing lack, struggle, pain, and discomfort in as a direct indicator of NEEDING TO INSPIRIT, LETTING SPIRIT BE AN ACTIVE PART OF. It's a flashing light with sirens screaming, "Help me!" And you can HELP YOURSELF BY:

1. STUDYING AND APPLYING THE SPECIFIC UNIVERSAL LAWS THAT HAVE TO DO WITH SPIRITUAL WHOLENESS/PROSPERITY,

2. WORK THROUGH YOUR FEARS, PAST RESTRICTING AND LIMITING PATTERNS, MISBELIEFS, AND DOUBTS, and

3. CONSISTENTLY USE THE WIDE VARIETY OF ABILITIES, SKILLS, TECHNIQUES, AND ACTIVITIES THAT ENABLE YOU TO ACTIVATE YOUR POWERS OF COMMUNICATION, PERCEPTION, TRANSFORMATION, COCREATION, AND IN PARTICULAR, MANIFESTATION.

Know that there is no lack of time, energy, money, material resources, ideas, vision, knowledge, motivation, joy, skills and abilities, real friendships, and health. Infinite Intelligence has abundantly provided everything we need. It is up to each of us to access it according to the Universal or Holoversal Principles and Laws of Life.

> **PROSPERITY CONSCIOUSNESS LEADS TO HIGHER SELF INTEGRATION BECAUSE IT IS THE RESULT OF DELIBERATE HIGHER THOUGHT AND ACTION . . .**

ACTIVITY: HELP YOURSELF!

Help yourself to all the abundance of love, wellness, creation, and material resources living on Earth has to offer you as a Soul. It is all here for you.

1. BECOME CONSTANTLY AWARE of the fact that whatever you center your attention upon, steadily and deliberately in thoughts, feelings, and clear intentions, form the experiences in your life. Study

(continued on page 170)

and apply the Principles of Prosperity. Catherine Ponder in her book, *The Dynamic Laws Of Prosperity*, states that the basic Universal Law that operates directly with Prosperity is: "What you radiate outward in your thoughts, feelings, mental pictures and words, you attract into your life and affairs." If you really work-this-law, you will also be learning intimately about a lot of the other how-life-really-works principles and techniques. You are guaranteed to change the aspects of your Being that are keeping you from your Highest Good.

2. WORK THROUGH your fears, blocks, limitations, restrictions, misbeliefs, and doubts that you have placed upon yourself or were convinced by others and past circumstances were real. Let go of fixed ideas, attitudes, opinions, and judgments. Utilize the freeing and opening up results of forgiveness. Let go of what you don't want in order to make room for what you do want. Vision! Find out who you really are and what you really need as Soul. Go to work in your thinking to mentally choose, accept, and radiate what you consciously wish to experience in life.

3. USE enthusiasm, belief, faith, understanding, organization, joy, love, compassion, discipline, commitment, and inspiration. Apply visualizations, prayers, meditations, brainstorming, affirmations, and inspirational study. Remember to focus, concentrate, bless, give thanks, and appreciate. Stimulate creative ideas. Make sure you do deep mental cleansing. Work with your subpersonalities and your *Higher Self*.

Use your Higher Abilities of telepathy, clairvoyance, clairaudience, and clairsentience. Don't forget about the all-important need for effective Energy Management. Move through ego-involvement and learn nonattachment and nonresistance. Think higher thoughts. Bless with Divine White Light. Open up your abilities to both give and receive. Make the connection that money is a form of God's love and energy. EXPLORE HELPFUL, INSPIRITING WAYS YOU CAN USE YOUR MATERIAL AND ENERGETIC RESOURCES FOR THE BEST OF ALL CONCERNED.

To manifest means to reveal, show, or demonstrate plainly. It is one of your basic Soul Powers and the power with the biggest "umph" in the area of Prosperity. YOU ARE HERE ON EARTH TO REVEAL, SHOW, AND DEMONSTRATE SOUL. Manifesting all you need in order to truly express your Soul, allowing The Divine to work through, with, and as you, is a natural Soul Right and ability. You are a DIVINE DEMONSTRATOR!

In order to demonstrate or manifest, you have to be aware of and KNOW WHAT YOU WANT TO MANIFEST. What wonderful things can you attract/demonstrate/manifest in your life? Then, WORK THROUGH YOUR OPPOSING INTENTIONS AND UNDERLYING FEARS AND DOUBTS that are keeping you from being a Manifestor. You have to SYSTEMATICALLY BUILD UP YOUR BELIEF AND KNOW-HOW concerning what you are choosing to manifest. Don't forget about WORKING THROUGH ANY ANXIETY/ NEGATIVITY about your up and coming demonstration and its guaranteed changes in your life.

Continuing on with the manifestation process, you then have to ACCEPT AND APPLY YOUR HIGHER ABILITIES and energies towards your desired manifestation or demonstration. This means connecting with your Higher Guidance and working with Divine Order. There are two processes, MAGNETIZATION and QUANTUM LEAPING, that you can engage if your desired manifestation requires a lot more energy/ability than you have previously accomplished.

Magnetization means increasing your powers to attract. This involves RAISING YOUR ENERGY LEVEL by working with your chakras and auras, inspiriting your intentions, aligning clear vision with Sacred Will, invoking compassionate wisdom, engaging the voice of affirmation, and, last but not least, much diligence. True desire while praying that "God's will be done" helps to keep that interfering ego at bay. Charles Fillmore, in his book *Prosperity,* writes:

"Everything we touch mentally or physically represents God-substance. It is limited only by ourselves in our thought and capacity. We cannot ask God for more substance, for the Universe is full of it. We can and should ask for understanding to lay hold of it with our mind: that is for an increase in our capacity."

To Quantum Leap, or to jump from one energy level to another while absorbing both, you have to move completely out of the "just put up with it" mentality. It involves believing that: "I have the faith in the substance of God/Goddess working in and through me to increase and bring _____ abundantly into my world!"

IMAGE, VISUALIZE, PERCEIVE, AND AFFIRM:
1. BEING YOUR HIGHER SELF
2. OPENING TO RECEIVE
3. IMAGING A WHOLE LIFE…

You have to be willing to make changes. Let go of old outdated images. The process and essence of what you are trying to manifest have to be your directional focus. Your emotions have to be calm, yet charged with joy, for you have to move "BEYOND BELIEF-INTO-KNOWING" that it is all for the manifesting. Your motivation must be great, tied in with your life's purpose. Specific steps toward your goal need to be taken every day, for you have to keep the energy steadily flowing in and out.

Go for Whole Prosperity! The Earth could use a lot more TLC (Tender Loving Care) from those who have the resources to take real care of themselves and all of the Earth's critters. Just remember to BE CAREFUL IN CHOOSING WHAT YOU ASK FOR. Always ask Higher Guidance,
"IS THIS SOMETHING THAT NEEDS MY ATTENTION AND RESOURCES BEING THE BEST FOR ALL CONCERNED?"

Be prepared for the increased energy that comes along with the manifestation process. Crashing and burning is no fun, so make sure you prepare your foundation well for the new structure and uses you are being reconstructed for.

Affirm:

"The drawing power of Divine Love, the constantly active magnet that attracts unfailing supply, is active each moment in my life!"

"The Infinite Intelligence of my Higher Consciousness attracts to me all the financial, material, human, nature, spirit, time, energy, abilities, and skill resources I need to do everything I am here to do!"

"God/Goddess, I release all financial and material restrictions and limitations to you, giving thanks in advance for my good."

"To be fully prosperous is to fully express My *Higher Self.*"

"I give thanks for the immediate complete Divine Fulfillment of these desires. This and more comes forth with perfect timing according to God's rich good for me and all concerned."

MANIFESTING ALL YOU NEED IN ORDER TO TRULY EXPRESS YOUR SOUL, ALLOWING THE DIVINE TO WORK THROUGH, WITH, AND AS YOU, IS A NATURAL SOUL RIGHT AND ABILITY . . .

ACTIVITY: <u>SEEK, ASK, AND KNOCK</u>

" Seek and you will find. Ask and you will receive. Knock and the door will be opened . . ." really do work if you seek, ask, and knock with faith while listening to the spirit/Soul within. These are the activities you need to do in order to allow Seeking, Asking, and Knocking to help you manifest the specifics of what you need as a Soul during your journey here on Earth:

A. "SEEK AND YOU WILL FIND" - Become aware of a need, idea, or desire that is dancing in your conscious mind and then get into an open and relaxed state. Ask yourself, "Where does this idea come from? What does it mean for my world and me? Is it nonhurtful and "the best for all concerned?" Listen and watch for information and understandings to come both in the moment and as time passes.

Pray that this idea will be developed for the highest good. Work through any negative reasons involved in your desires and channel your energies into reasons that feel good, that make sense in your life as a whole. Remain open to all images, thoughts, and feelings that then arise. Utilize activities, such as brainstorming, free association, and dreamwork as you explore your idea, need, or desire. Always look at the essence behind your desire. Seek to clarify your intent and motivation. Once you can maintain a motivating level of enthusiasm for your idea or desire, you are ready for the next step.

B. "ASK AND YOU WILL RECEIVE" - Now, focus on picturing and wording your idea, need, or desire in a way that is clear as to what you want, leaving the details of how it comes into your life to the Higher Energies/Spirits/Divine. You might make a collage or draw what represents your desire, journal about what you want, sing and dance your intentions, and practice affirmations. Do a variety of things that put your idea or desire out into your life and the Holoverse. Asking includes using meditative prayer to remain connected with the clarity and positive intent of your Higher Self/Soul. If you stumble upon any doubts and fears, release them. Rework the misbeliefs that keep you feeling limited or unworthy.

C. "KNOCK AND THE DOOR WILL BE OPENED" - Wait, watch, and listen for information and help that may come through a variety of ways. When you feel and see a clear direction, knock by doing what you are guided to do. If you are following God's Guidance, then your way will be relatively smooth. If you are trying to control the situation based on lower-self expectations, then running up against proverbial brick walls is commonplace. Inner guidance provides you far more choices and creative ways to get things done than just your rational or logical mind, with or without negative emotions to throw in some ugly twists.

Keep tuning inward to receive the knowledge of new doors to knock upon using your outward abilities to follow through. Following through or the doing is essential. If you have gotten this far and are still dragging your feet, then you better figure out which remaining blocks within yourself and your life that you have created need to be busted. Go for Block Busters. And then get ready to reap what you have sown!

CHAPTER TEN
GO FOR IT!

ATTUNING TO SOUL, OR INTEGRATING YOUR HIGHER SELF,
IS THE MOST PRACTICAL AND REALISTIC WAY YOU CAN
HELP YOURSELF IN BEING HUMAN . . .

BEING YOUR HIGHER SELF

As you continue to learn about Soul and the fuller, wholer, and deeper realities of this multidimensional life, all aspects of your daily routines, situations, and affairs undergo transformations. When any of us move past the level of marking time into actively exploring further what life can be, it is hard to comprehend all the stages and changes our thinking, feeling, and behaving patterns will move through. However, what you need to be aware of is the fact that once you have actually experienced the realities of spirit, it is impossible to try to go back to a way of thinking and living that excludes spirit/Soul/The Divine. THE NEEDS OF THE SPIRIT, OF THE SOUL, ARE A PART OF EVERYDAY LIFE.

Once the shell of mass consciousness starts cracking around and in you, the spiritual emptiness which comes from having shut down the ways you are connected to Soul and to The Divine starts being "in your face" as the expression goes. You will be DRIVEN BY AN INNER PUSH to know, do, and be that which is once again consciously connected with spirit, with Soul, and with God/Goddess. One of the tasks of being Soul in physical, human form is to EXPERIENCE YOUR UNIQUENESS WHILE STAYING CONSCIOUS OF YOUR ONENESS WITH EVERYTHING. Life on Earth is really about BRINGING FORTH THE SOUL POTENTIALITIES that exist in everyone of us. And we obviously cannot do that without spirit.

Operating from Soul, being *100 % Higher Self Integrated*, means that you will be TUNING IN FOR HIGHER GUIDANCE IN EVERY AREA, CONCERNING EVERYTHING, ALL THE TIME. You will be functioning from Soul Knowledge, integrating spiritual or Divine Wisdom with the practicalities of living and working in a material world. As John Randolph Price says, "... moving from theoretical to practical spirituality." Becoming a SPIRITUAL PRAGMATIST is about bringing Soul into all aspects of one's life. Using intuition to find a parking space on a busy city street is just one of many examples where developing one's Soul Abilities make the realities of modern Earth living doable. Attuning to Soul, or integrating your *Higher Self,* is the most practical, realistic way you can help yourself in being human.

THIS MEANS COMING TO EACH MOMENT IN YOUR LIFE OPEN TO DISCOVERY, PARTICIPATION, AND GROWTH. Remember, that what you experience as real is simply a reflection of your belief system, your mind thoughts and feelings. The consciousness behind the word is the real power, mover, and groover. And the greater the changes in your consciousness the greater the changes in your outer world. As you grow to understand and directly experience how The Soul System really works, how you relate to each and every moment, event, and area in your life will gradually move into Soul Rhythm and Reality.

Acting upon the knowledge that we each live multiple lives upon this Earth in the course of our Souls' journey, and are responsible for all that we attract to ourselves in this current life, takes awhile to integrate in each moment, event, and area of our daily affairs. If one hasn't been raised in and with these facts of life, then changing from victim-consciousness and only-one-life consciousness will take quite some time and deliberate effort.

What confuses most of us is that it often takes a lot more time and effort than we had imagined to change our consciousness to the degree that the new energy moves into and then changes our outer world. As a result, there are often huge gaps between our awareness and our experiences, between our conceptual reality (what we think) and our functional reality (how we act and attract). In closing those gaps, it helps to PROGRAM INTO OUR MINDS WHAT IT REALLY MEANS TO BE FUNCTIONING AS OUR HIGHER SELVES, AS SOULS.

Here are the major areas in our lives on Earth and how LIVING FROM SOUL CONSCIOUSNESS affects each one in general:

***EARTH'S ENVIRONMENT –

As an Attuned Soul, one is very much aware of the intimate connection between Earth in all its aspects (including all its various creatures) and being human. An altruistic need to have it healthily preserved for future generations of Souls who will choose it (again) as "a classroom" and a "blessing" (which might include you!) overrides the selfish need of the ego or lower self to take and do whatever one so desires without regard to others or the future. A heart connection and appreciation for all that the Earth gives, in turn, stimulates a need TO TAKE CARE OF, NURTURE, AND LOVE OUR PRECIOUS EARTH.

Through the abilities and awarenesses of one's *Higher Self*, everything one does while on Earth is filtered through consideration of how this affects the Earth and all of its various inhabitants. One sees oneself not as an owner, but as a COSTEWARD for a relatively short period of time (relative to the Earth's history). As a result, one respects the Earth's powers. THE PLANT, MINERAL, AND ANIMAL WORLDS ARE TREATED WITH WONDER, APPRECIATION, AWARENESS, AND RESPECT FOR THEIR NEEDS, INTELLIGENCES, AND RIGHTS. By tuning into the natural world's spiritual energies, one's *Higher Self* can OPERATE FROM THE KNOW-HOW OF "THE BEST FOR ALL CONCERNED."

With Soul Consciousness, one experiences continual joy in being alive on Earth. All of the Earth's wondrous processes and incredibly diverse environments are fully and intimately experienced. Their offered lessons/learnings are acknowledged and incorporated. The interconnectedness of all life forms is fully realized.

***HOME ENVIRONMENT –

Our home becomes AN EXPRESSION OF OUR *HIGHER SELF*. As we change from lower self ways of functioning to Soulfullness, how we live changes. We move from what others expect of us and material desires to what most fulfills our needs for peace and harmony, beauty and connection with nature, expressed creativity and spiritual alliance. Making one's shelter more Earth-friendly, more conducive to quietly alone meditative times, and A REFLECTION OF WHAT IS IN THE HEART, instead of the pocket, are all characteristics of the Attuned Soul's home while on Earth.

The home environment becomes more holistic, healthier for the body, mind, and spirit. LESS TOXINS in both the foods served and the household materials used become a focus. RITUALS that invoke one's joyful, loving, and sharing spiritual nature are established. Parts of the home set aside for SACRED SPACE, where one can spiritually cleanse and revitalize, are often found. The concepts of energy usage and management (or Feng Shui - see Glossary and Bibliography) within one's buildings are explored and utilized. Family time becomes important SOUL SUPPORT, with the focus on HELPING EACH OTHER TO DEVELOP FURTHER, REACH HIGHER, AND COMMUNE FREER.

***MATERIAL AND FINANCIAL RESOURCES –

These become AN EARTHLY MEANS TO EXPRESSING SOUL PRACTICALLY AND REALISTICALLY ON THIS MATERIAL PLANE. Keeping up with the Jones and using financial/material means as power and control over others and even our own lives falls to the wayside. Money/things do remain a part of our lives, as long as they are useful in helping us to live consciously aligned with Soul. Remember that money is a reflection of your consciousness. You can attract all the financial, material, human, nature, and spiritual resources you need to fulfill your Life's Purpose and to express your *Higher Self* when cocreating. Manifestation is easier and quicker when it is something directly initiated and guided by spirit/Soul (infused with spiritual energy).

As Souls, expressing on Earth through our *Higher Selves*, we see and realize the INSPIRITING AND SOULFULLY HELPFUL WAYS MONEY AND MATERIAL THINGS CAN BE USED IN TAKING CARE OF THE EARTH AND LIFTING UP HUMAN CONSCIOUSNESS. "Random acts of kindness and senseless acts of beauty" are only the beginning. What about joyful acts of rejoicing and breakthrough acts of cocreating?

> **AS SOULS, EXPRESSING ON EARTH THROUGH OUR HIGHER SELVES, WE SEE AND REALIZE THE INSPIRITING AND SOULFULLY HELPFUL WAYS MONEY AND MATERIAL THINGS CAN BE USED TO HELP TAKE CARE OF EARTH AND LIFT UP HUMAN CONSCIOUSNESS . . .**

***RELATIONSHIPS –

Whether it be living partnership, marriage, family, social, and/or community relationships, operating from Soul Consciousness means that you will need to come from a COOPERATIVE AND COLLABORATIVE space instead of a competitive and dominance-oriented approach. Soul-to-Soul, we're all here to help one another to achieve our Soul Goals. TRUE RELATIONSHIPPING IS USING THE ABILITY TO MOTIVATE, LOVE, SUPPORT, AND HELP OURSELVES, AND ONE ANOTHER, TO RECOGNIZE WHO WE ARE AS SOULS AND TO DEVELOP OUR HIGHER SELVES.

As your Soul evolves, being in a living partnership or marriage for convenience and for addictive and social needs doesn't work out, for your Soul will yearn for SPIRITUAL PARTNERSHIP. This is a commitment between partners to assist each other's spiritual/Soul growth. The deeper reason for people being together is to resolve karmic lessons and help in the evolution of each other's Soul.

At first, a major task in living partnerships/marriage is to find a compromise between each one's family of origin's House Rules. As Soul evolution takes place, the task becomes COCREATING HOUSE RULES THAT WORK FOR THE SOUL AND THAT HELP *HIGHER SELF* EXPRESSION. In living partnerships, we function as each other's mirror, which becomes a real sticky situation to be in if ego is still raging. Spiritual Partnerships are all about HELPING ONE ANOTHER TO LET GO OF EGO, OR LOWER SELF PERSONALITY CHARACTERISTICS, AND TO BUILD UPON SOUL.

Our family, social, and community relationships reflect our internal changes and how they are fulfilled in action. Not all of us will choose the paths of spiritual partnership or birthing/parenting children as a way to grow and transform. However, SOUL CANNOT HELP BUT LOVE, INTERACT WITH, AND INSPIRIT THE WORLD AROUND IT.

Our auras or energy fields are electro-magnetic and exchange energy with people and places. We need these exchanges, although as our Soul evolves, we move out of addictive, desirous lower-self needs. When we are in direct touch with our Soul's energy, higher spiritual energy, and The Divine, we are not around people because we'll starve if we aren't energetically fed by them. Nor are we there to attempt to change them or rescue their Souls. We are around them to send "the juice" on, to spread the love. The rest is up to them, their choice. This radically changes how and why we choose to interact.

Here are TWO PRAYERS FOR OUR LOVED ONES:

"Dear One: I love you, I bless you, and I behold you surrounded by and enfolded in God's loving light. I trust God to help you, to inspire you, to lead you on your own unique journey in life. I will always do what I can for you, but I know that God and you will do so much better. In all you do, I know that you are being blessed . . .

***

"I hold all people who are dear to me in my prayers today for light, love, and wisdom. I pray that they are fulfilled in heart and mind. I pray that they continue to know the peace and love of God in everything they do and in all that they aspire to be. God, bless my loved ones with the energy they need to complete every task, with prosperity enough to meet every bill, with strength enough to face every situation. I know that you are protecting and guiding them every day of their lives. And, God, I thank you for the blessing of their companionship and friendship in my life . . .

***

Having developed Soul Consciousness puts one in the position of being able to remember one's past lives, of knowing this lifetime's Soul Purpose, tasks, goals, mission, and lessons, and of being able to read where others are at and what the Earth needs. This makes the choice of whether to experience birthing/parenting this lifetime a bit more complex than being mass consciousness programmed that everyone does it. HONORING/RESPECTING BOTH OUR CHOICE TO BIRTH AND NOT TO BIRTH HELPS US ALL TO HAVE THE FREEDOM TO EXPLORE WHO WE REALLY ARE AND TO FIND OUR TRUE PLACE OF SERVICE AS SOULS. "Does birthing/parenting fit in with my Soul's needs, karma, and evolution?" is a question that could prove beneficial for the whole world if we would each but ask it.

CONSCIOUS BIRTHING involves acknowledging the individual Soul that we are intimately inviting into our lives and on Earth. Being aware of what we are offering this Soul or Souls means making our responsibility upfront and clear. In a Soul's journey, agreeing to help bring another Soul into the Earth Realm and/or to teach it ways to work with being alive on Earth is a very serious commitment. Whether we are female or male, we are still giving our essence, a part of our Soul's energy, to another Soul creating an unbreakable link between our Souls. If we do not carry it out in love and wisdom, the karma we will have created is intense.

***WORK/SERVICE –

When living from Soul Consciousness through your *Higher Self*, your work or the services you can share and give to the Earthly World needs to come from the knowledge of who you are, not from fear of lack. KNOWING WHO YOU ARE AS SOUL, MEANS HAVING DONE THE WORK IT TAKES TO DISCOVER YOUR SOUL'S PURPOSE AND YOUR NATURAL AND LEARNED ABILITIES. It involves following what is alive in you, what moves you, what brings you joy. When you love doing something, it means you have a gift for it. Carry it through and it, in return, will gift you further.

The more you can separate your lower self or ego needs from the services you provide, the easier it is for the world to receive your gifts. Your unique Soul offerings to the world will change as you evolve, so it is important to MAINTAIN AN AWARENESS OF THE REASONS AND LESSONS OF WHAT YOU ARE DOING. When operating from Soul Consciousness, when the reason, lesson, or karmic need for what you are doing has been completed, another door will open as the old one is shutting. Soul energy, once opened, will bring some unique and powerful knowledge, creations, and surprises to our temporary planetary home.

KNOWING WHO YOU ARE AS SOUL INVOLVES FOLLOWING WHAT IS ALIVE IN YOU, WHAT MOVES YOU, WHAT BRINGS YOU JOY . . .

ACTIVITY: <u>A HIGHER SELF DO-BE</u>

You've got to DO before you can BE. Integrating your *Higher Self* into your daily affairs starts with consciously ARRANGING YOUR DAYS TO INCLUDE WORKING THE TECHNIQUES AND ACTIVITIES THAT BRING FORTH YOUR SOUL ABILITIES, SKILLS, AND POWERS. Once you purposefully do something long enough, it then becomes a natural part of your life without scheduling. That's when being your *Higher Self* comes into its own.

These four books could prove helpful to you as you establish your lifestyle to match your Soul's energy: Shakti *Gawain's Living In The Light,* Dan Millman's *The Life You Were Born To Live: A Guide To Finding Your Life Purpose,* Marsha Sinetar's *Ordinary People as Monks, Mystics,* and Naomi Stephan's *Fulfill Your Soul's Purpose: Ten Creative Paths To Your Life Mission.* Keep working on the activities from Chapter Two of this book. Also, work frequently with this visualization:

Relaxing and breathing deeply, imagine that your Soul, a Being Of Light, an All Knowing Intelligence, has awakened within you. Allow your Soul's vibrations to slowly penetrate your body, mind, emotional nature, your entire consciousness. Feel the surge of energy as you experience Soul Power. Sense the intense knowingness of its mind as you allow your Soul to be heard within your consciousness.

On your Mind's Screen see these words very clearly,
"I CHOOSE to realize a loving relationship with *My Higher Self,* with my Soul."
Say silently to yourself,
"With all my mind, all my heart, all my Soul, I accept the fulfillment of this desire.
I now have the conscious link in my oneness with my *Higher Self.*"

See yourself awakening in the morning, joyfully greeting your *Higher Self* and enjoying your relationship throughout your day. See yourself keeping in attunement with your Soul through your *Higher Self,* exchanging words and feelings of love, understanding, and of knowing. See yourself moving throughout the rhythms of your days in Divine Safety and Order. TAKE EACH ONE OF THE LIFE AREAS LISTED ABOVE THIS ACTIVITY AND IMAGINE OR VISUALIZE IN DETAIL WHAT EACH AREA OF YOUR LIFE WILL LOOK LIKE WHEN OPERATING FROM SOUL CONSCIOUSNESS. ALSO IN DETAIL, VISUALIZE WHAT EACH DAY OF YOUR LIFE WILL BE LIKE WHEN YOU ARE DOING AND BEING SOUL THROUGH YOUR *HIGHER SELF.* What would you say and do within each situation in your life?

At each days end, review what went on and what you will do differently when 100% *Higher Self Integrated.* Imagination, or stretching one's thinking habits, is a necessary step to creating a Soul Attuned or *Higher Self Integrated* life.

Integrating into your daily life the knowledge that your true essence is Soulfully spiritual and that your physical body and outer life activities are your instruments of expression, will lead you into discovering YOUR LIFE'S PURPOSE/PLAN.
"Why am I living this present life at this time in Earth's history?" is a question that also leads to:
"What have I come to learn?" - YOUR LIFE'S LESSONS/TASKS - and
"In what ways can I best serve?" - YOUR LIFE'S GOALS/ MISSION.

These are all questions that have multiple layers to them. As you discover and develop your *Higher Self*, the answers will gradually become clearer. You will be able to hear and respond to your Soul's and spirit's "CALL TO ATTENTION" or SUMMONS to do something specific that has purpose, lessons, and mission. This summons will call you to work and to serve in ways that will develop something(s) you hadn't known about yourself previously. It will enable you, put you through the test, and give real meaning to your life.

As you meet your Soul, you will learn to integrate your Soul's manifestation into service to others. Your creative voice is your gift to humanity and this Earthly World. Soul expresses itself in loving, committed, and caring ways that are inwardly connected to The Creative Source and outwardly connected to the community. Cocreation is both inspired and practical.

There are many paths that we can take on our "JOURNEY HOME." As you discover more and more about your Soul, you will need to make sure that the current PATH OF CHOICE you are taking matches your Soul's energy. If you have been taught the Path Of Struggle by your parents, once you have begun exploring your own consciousness, it may no longer be appropriate for you. You may need to switch to the Path Of Will while you do your Personal Process Work. The Path of Joy and The Path of Compassion are orientations that well serve the Soul as it spreads its wings and flies. Be conscious of how you are choosing to learn. Make sure that the various pathways you take are congruous with your Life's Purpose, Tasks, and Goals.

Uncovering your Life's Purpose, Tasks, and Goals, that you set as a Soul as you chose a certain time and circumstance with which to be reborn into the Earth Plane, is one of the most important and liberating processes you will undertake in the Higher Self or Soul Attunement process. You will need to clear yourself from much of your emotional baggage and crazy habits of thinking and feeling before you will be able to access your true reasons for returning. You also have to develop your Higher Abilities of mind and spirit. Being able to DEEPLY CONTEMPLATE AND CLEARLY HEAR THE VOICE OF SPIRIT AND SOUL is a prerequisite.

However, in the meantime, discovering the skills you are already good at, the things that already bring you joy, and the people and happenings that you already cherish, can give you a real sense of direction. Look at what you have already created, the lessons you have already learned, and the priorities you have already accomplished. Sum up their symbolism, energetic essence, and value and you'll have a clearer picture of where you are heading. FINDING YOUR OWN UNIQUE DRIVE AND PASSION AND COCREATING WITH SOUL WILL BRING YOU FULFILLMENT BEYOND SUCCESS. Believing in your own Soul and living and loving your Soul's own Life Blueprint or Plan is a glorious part of becoming one, of unitation.

ACTIVITY: <u>RHYME AND REASON</u>

There are reasons and rhymes, or correspondences, as to why you are here on Earth in human form at this particular moment. In fulfilling your Soul's intent, it really helps to bring these out into your consciousness and into the light of understanding. Over time, do the work necessary in clearly knowing:

   1. YOUR LIFE'S PURPOSE AND PLAN,

   2.YOUR LIFE'S LESSONS AND TASKS,

   3. YOUR LIFE'S GOALS AND MISSIONS.

As you access them, your next step will be to implement them. Spend some time with the "HOW TO'S" of each implementation, always weighing your ideas with the balancing act of "the best for all concerned."

(continued on page 179)

In your *HSI* Journal or notebook, use brainstorming, contemplation, trancework, dream work and other techniques you have learned to list your ideas concerning each of the above categories. It may be helpful to use these areas under your Lessons & Tasks and Goals & Missions:

**Body - Mind - Spirit - Emotional Energies - Personality –
Material and Financial Resources - Service Work Career - Relationships…**

Over time, you will add to, delete, rearrange, and rework as your continual growth brings forth new awarenesses and insights.

**LEARNING TO MOVE SMOOTHLY THROUGH THE NATURAL EBB AND FLOW
OF SOUL WORK IS ONE OF THE KEYS TO HIGHER SELF INTEGRATION . . .**

ALL THE INGREDIENTS

The Higher Self Integration Journey **is a lifetime (and beyond) affair.** It requires ongoing commitment, focus, evaluation, and consciousness. You will become aware of more aspects, details, and happenings of life that require management than you ever imagined there were, even in your wildest fantasies. Applying competent ENERGY AND TIME MANAGEMENT SKILLS will become one of your lifelines.

Learning to move smoothly through THE NATURAL EBB AND FLOW OF SOULWORK is one of the keys. The necessity of TRANSITION TIME, the passage of changing from one form, state, activity, or place to another, is often underrated. It is an element of the transformation process with which you need to know your own needs and develop your own personal systems to handling the changes you will be undergoing. At the very least, you will need support, emotional outlets, quiet reflective time, and some fun. Many transitions take a lot more time and effort to move from conceptual to functional reality than we often estimate. Don't try to unnaturally speed up the transition time you need. It will only wear you out and create unpleasant circumstances.

During various phases of your *Higher Self Integration Journey*, you will have more energy than you thought was possible. However, there will also be times that you will experience fatigue that leaves you sitting around in a zombie state drooling. You need to be able to move through these various states without the aid of drugs, including pumping too much adrenaline. REST WHEN YOU NEED RESTING. FIND CREATIVE OUTLETS FOR THE INTENSE BURSTS OF ENERGY YOU WILL BE UNLEASHING.

Don't try to build your Soulhouse without a foundation! Don't skip necessary steps and stages. "ONE DAY AT A TIME - ONE STEP AT A TIME" greatly applies to SoulWork. Do the Personal Process Work that can free you up from fear, deprivation or deficit complexes, and past patterns of misbeliefs and disbeliefs, restrictions, and limitations, no matter how many years it takes. Bust through those energy blocks and rewire your circuits for Divine Love. Cocreate with God. You are not alone in any way, shape, or form! Don't keep yourself out of the Divine Loop any longer! CONNECT AND COMMUNE!

AND YOU CAN DO IT ALL WITH A LOT OF HELP FROM YOUR SPIRIT/SOUL FAMILY AND THE EFFECTIVE SKILLS OF ORGANIZATION. Inner Guidance is a must and so is being organized. Yes, it is more than possible to live a 20th-21st century life *and* "do the Soulthing." However, you won't be able to fly until you stop distracting yourself through being scattered and disorganized. Organization is all about the act and state of putting together, arranging, or systematizing into an orderly, functional, structured whole. Heard that WHOLE word before? Yes, and it goes hand-in hand with BALANCE.

BALANCE! BALANCE! BALANCE! It just can't be stressed enough. As you form your *Higher Self Integration Program*, aligning the practices and techniques that you feel will help you in becoming Soul Attuned, look out for the areas each practice does not cover. Become aware of what Jack Kornfield, in his book, *A Path With Heart,* calls "THE SHADOW AND NEAR ENEMY THAT EVERY SET OF TEACHINGS HAVE." These are the aspects of life that they do not illuminate wisely and the way that particular teaching can be most easily misused. Assess your own strengths and weaknesses along with the strengths and weaknesses of the practices you use. And then BALANCE! BALANCE! BALANCE! And then BALANCE some more . . .

Remember, that EVERY PERSON AND SITUATION IS YOUR TEACHER AND YOU ARE A TEACHER FOR THEM. Sometimes, it is the stranger on the street, a four-legged companion, a family member, or coworker that you are learning and teaching the most with at a particular time in your (and their) development. Bearing this truth in mind at all times will help make the lessons you are both learning and teaching louder, clearer, and realistic.

There will also be particular persons who have more to share with you at certain stages in your/their development. A SPIRITUAL MASTER can be helpful in opening your eyes and heart through their demonstrations of spiritual enlightenment. A MASTER TEACHER can be helpful in showing you how to integrate both your spirituality and humanity on and into this Earth Plane. True Master Teachers are forever "walking their walk and talking their talk", through sharing their own adventures and demonstrations with honesty, compassion, sincerity, practicality, and of course, humor. They help spiritualize our world by showing how to use spiritual knowledge and experience in facing the daily challenges of human living.

However, don't allow your lower-self, who tends towards dependency, addiction, falling off the edge, game playing, and sabotage, to forget that an outer human teacher, by the very nature of their continued humanity, will be limited in their exchanges and teachings. Listen to what is being offered, since you have put yourself in that particular time and space for a reason. But always GO INSIDE YOURSELF SEEKING GUIDANCE FROM YOUR SOUL (not your lower self), as to what you need to do with what you observe and learn.

In *Higher Self Integration*, your most meaningful focus and goal is to OPEN YOURSELF UP TO YOUR INNER AND HIGHER GUIDANCE. Remember, that your Soul knows best. In so doing, you will be able to do, be, and go everywhere your Soul needs to, feeling comfortable and effective. Why? Because you will always be directly connected with the Higher Spiritual Dimension, with Infinite Intelligence.

With every step you take, pull yourself out of any EGO TRAPS you may have set off. Be aware of these self-monsters nipping at your heels: The Better-Than-Thou Critically Angry Judge, The I-can't/Not-Worthy/Not-Good-Enough Fearfully Stuck Wimp, The It-Can't-Be-True Unimaginably Distrustful Cynic, The Which-Excuse-Would-You-Like-To-Hear Obviously Procrastinating But-ter, and The If-I-Were-King-Of-The-Forest Revenging Control Freak. Instead of allowing them to go for broke, nip them in the bud by becoming aware of them, working through the crazy thoughts and emotions they battle with and reforming their personas into energies which form wonderfully exciting and positively-grounded adventurers.

What you have to deal honestly and potently with, in regards to the traps your lower-self has created which hold you back from knowing your Soul, are the conflicting INTENTIONS which scatter your energies/spirit, muddle your mind, inflame your emotions, and dis-ease your body. If you are still operating subconsciously through various different programmings and their resulting subpersonalities, you experience Conflicting Intentions. CONFLICTING INTENTIONS also plague us when what we want is different than what someone else or others want who still have some type of control over our lives and affairs.

PSYCHIC SABOTAGE occurs when conditions, people, and your own mental misconceptions work against you achieving your Soul goals. The energies, will, or intentions flowing in and around you from parts of yourself and others influence the directional flow of the Life Force Energy that forms into material substance here on the Earth Plane through use of intention. Intentions set into motion energetic processes that affect every aspect of our lives. YOU CREATE YOUR REALITY WITH AND THROUGH YOUR INTENTIONS, YOUR WILL. If you are unaware of your conflicting intentions, the strongest one wins.

To create what your Soul wants, it is essential to UNCOVER YOUR MIXED INTENTIONS and to then SORT THEM OUT. You will have to firm up the ones you really want to go with and WORK WITH THOSE INTENTIONS CONSCIOUSLY AND PURPOSEFULLY ON A DAILY BASIS. At that point, affirmations and visualizations will help plant into your consciousness the intention(s) your Soul's energy can run with. Once Soul energy unites with the mental faculty by which we all deliberately choose or decide upon a course of action, WILL, then the cocreation process can take hold in the material world.

**YOU CREATE YOUR REALITY WITH
AND THROUGH YOUR INTENTIONS, YOUR WILL . . .**

ACTIVITY: <u>WILLFULLY INTENTIONAL</u>

1. Anything you say you've set out to do or create, and you haven't been able to make it happen, has conflicting energies messing up the equation and therefore the result. Your willpower cannot create for you situations that require a lot of creative energy if that energy is being scattered or pulled asunder by thoughts, feelings, and behaviors that are not recognized and reworked in order to fit in with the program at hand. AWARENESS IS THE FIRST STEP.

A. Pick something you say you want but have, thus far, been unable to manifest. This could be financial freedom and independence or $100. It could be a new home, the ability to communicate directly with a spirit guide, or a marriage based on a loving, equal, and spiritual life partnership. Whatever. Enter an open and relaxed state and say aloud, as well as write down, what you desire. Then begin looking at all the elements involved in your wants. EXPLORE YOUR SITUATION THOROUGHLY, LOOKING FOR ANY NEW REALIZATIONS.

B. ASK YOURSELF these questions:

What do I have to change about myself in order to get what I want?
In detail, what would change in my life if I manifested my desire?
Is there anyone or anything opposing my desire and why?
How am I sabotaging the fulfillment of this desire and why?

C. USE OTHER TECHNIQUES, such as dreamwork, journal writing, verbal exploration with a knowledgeable and objective person, prayer, guided imagery, to uncover any hidden agendas of your own and the other persons and situations who would be affected by your achievement. Then, write out each Conflicting Intention you have discovered, also figuring out which has the strongest strangle-hold on your will and ability to cocreate and manifest.

D. Figure out and form, through brainstorming and other techniques, a STEP-BY-STEP plan that will help you move out from being crushed by those other intentions. This is an ACTION PLAN: what specifically you need to do in order to change the situations and circumstances, misperceptions and misbeliefs,

(continued on page 182)

thoughts, feelings and behaviors that stand in your way. At the same time you begin activating this plan, you need to use visualization and affirmations to ENERGIZE YOUR ORIGINAL INTENTION or the one you now really want to accomplish.

       E. As you are able to DEVELOP UNWAVERING INTENTION WITH UNIFIED FOCUS, SEEK INNER GUIDANCE about what you need to specifically do now to bring your desire into reality. Follow that guidance as you continue to INSPIRIT YOUR INTENTION.

       2. Take a look at your Life's Purpose/Lessons/Goals. What is the essence of what you are living for? Figure it out and, from there, WRITE DOWN YOUR SOUL'S INTENTIONS. Here are a few examples of other's Soul Intentions:

> "I INTEND to manage my resources with true Soul Consciousness towards the highest and best for all concerned."

> "I INTEND to live each day in a natural flowing rhythm that is harmonic, health oriented, and joyful getting everything done smoothly and efficiently in Divine Order."

> "I INTEND to have conscious control of my mind thoughts ever-expanding my mental, psychic, and spiritual abilities."

> "I INTEND to be wholly prosperous, integrated as my *Higher Self*/Soul."

       You will add to this list as you go along in your *Higher Self Integration Process*. As you do, utilize the above steps (A – E) towards manifesting your Soul's Intentions. Again, remember that these are long-term processes. KEEP YOUR SPIRITS UP!

       Bringing forth your Soul's true or TRUTH VOICE, integrating your *Higher Self*, and consciously reconnecting with spirit, God/Goddess is truly *"the journey of a lifetime and beyond."* You have to realistically and practically become HOLISTIC: deliberately, purposefully, and knowingly working with all aspects of your being, body/mind/spirit/Soul, in every area of your life. You will be developing and advancing your POWERS of communication and self-expression, perception and reading energy, transformation and healing, manifestation and demonstration, and cocreation and causation, as you move through the various LEVELS OF EVOLUTIONARY SOUL CONSCIOUSNESS that can be attained while here on Earth.

       NEW WORLDS will be opened to you as you free yourself by doing your PERSONAL PROCESS WORK. As you consciously CHOOSE TO RUN ENERGIES that vibrate attuned to Soul/The Divine and develop your HIGHER SENSE PERCEPTIONS, PROSPERITY becomes a reality. This includes true-place success, love-filled relationships, and all the resources you need in order to BRING YOUR HIGHER SELF INTO FULL CREATIVE EXPRESSION. You will learn about so many different areas of life and living that will totally EXPAND YOUR PERCEPTIONS as to who you are and what you are doing here. Boredom will not be an illusion you will recreate. It will be impossible to separate from THE JOY OF LIVING ever again.

       Your journey will be long and intense, feel pretty crazy at first, and then later on, absolutely incredible and right on. Your life will change, perhaps a hundred times over. You'll spin and spiral, leap ahead and fall back, be ridiculed and exalted by others, and cry buckets just before you turn around and laugh so much your belly will ache. Most of all, you will fall deeply in love with life. And in, through, with and as love you will spread your wings and fly home to The Divine as you bring your soulfulness to light here on Earth.

There are so many aspects to *The Higher Self Integration or Soul Attunement/Mastery Process* that most of us feel quite overwhelmed when we are first trying to establish a HIGHER SELF INTEGRATION PROGRAM into our daily lives. It helps tremendously to be aware of all the components and ingredients involved, even though it will take much time and effort to really get what it is all about. The most important, effective, and indeed crucial place to start is just exactly where you are.

**IN, THROUGH, WITH AND AS LOVE, YOU WILL SPREAD YOUR WINGS
AND FLY HOME TO THE DIVINE AS YOU BRING YOUR SOULFULNESS TO
LIGHT HERE ON EARTH . . .**

ACTIVITY: <u>**INGREDIENT CHECKLIST**</u>

Below is a word list or summary of the concepts, techniques, skills, and abilities that are all a part of *The Higher Self Integration Process*. This list is here to serve as a reminder and guide for the process as a whole. You can also use it as a checklist concerning what you are actively working on, need to learn more about, and/or incorporate in the future. Check in with this list every once in a while. It will serve you well.

H S I CHECKLIST

♦ CONCEPTS TO LEARN AND APPLY

<u>*Higher Self Integration*/Soul Attunement & Mastery</u>

<u>Earth-Based Levels Of Evolutionary Soul Consciousness:</u>

Level One - Marking Time	Level Two - Exploring Further	Level Three - Circling 'Round
Level Four - Standing In The Doorway		Level Five - Lifting Up
Level Six - Communicating Truth		Level Seven – Transcending

<u>Soul Powers:</u>
CONNECTING = Communication/Self Expression
KNOWING = Perception/Reading Energy
CHANGING = Transformation/Healing
ATTRACTING = Manifestation/Demonstration
CREATING = Cocreation/Causation

<u>Energy Management:</u>

Aura	Kundalini	Chakras	Grounding Cord
Block Busting	Toxin Release	Emotional Releasing Methods	
Whole Health	Integral Practice	Yin/Yang	Balance
Flow States	Three Energy Styles- Resistance/Affinity/Nonresistance		Transitions
Time Management/Organization	Divine Order/Divine Safety		Energy Patterns
Communication/Energetic Cords	Energetic Neutralization		Recircuiting

Personality:

Higher Self   Subpersonalities   Battle of the Selves   Attending/Connecting/Expressing
Self-Sabotaging   Psychic Sabotage   Shadow/Dark Self   Study Emotions
Nonattachment   Logical/Intuitive Combination   Transforming Negativity   Fears
Personal Process Work - Recognizing/Releasing/Reconstructing   Lower Self   Addictions
Three Helper Styles - Sympathy/Empathy/Compassion   Parental Energies   Discernment
Relearning Learning Process   Personality System Helpers such as Astrology   Archetypes
Modern Madness Mementos - Only Me & Mine Matter/Super Stress/Technology Terror
Misbeliefs & DisBeliefs   Memory Work   Inner Child Cultivation   Self Healing Skills

Soul Work:

Qualities of Soul   Universal Laws   Prosperity Consciousness   Soul Memories
Past Life Exploration   Dark Night Of The Soul   Soul Core Issues   Separation Sadness
Humanity Rage   Humanity Ache   Soul Frustration   Higher Self Vision
Spiritual Partnership   Soul Companions/Soulmates/Soul Groups   Grace   Soul Baggage
Life Purpose/Plan, Lessons/Tasks, Goals/Missions   Three Stages Of Soul Release   Intentions
Commitment   Cocreative States   Godcidences   Syncronicities
Higher/Inner/Spirit Guidance   Divine White Light   Joy/Unconditional Love   Soul Nurturing
For The Best Of All Concerned   Nature Attunement   The Silence   Divine Rays
Angels/Spirit Guides & Teachers   God/Goddess   Envisioning   Soul Voice/Expression

♦ TECHNIQUES, SKILLS, ABILITIES TO LEARN AND APPLY

Relaxation   Open & Relaxed States   Awareness   Concentration
Focus   Observation   Trance Work/Hypnosis   Breathwork
Journaling/Writing   Brainstorming   Contemplation   Memory Work
Visualization   Guided Imagery   Questioning   Affirmations
Affirmative Prayer   Mental Role Play   Free Association   Self Talk
Connective Analyzation   Conscious Cognizance   Bibliotherapy   Intuitive Practice
Sensory Stimulation   Transformational Tapes   Counseling   Nature Attunement
Thought Control   Mindfulness   Timeshifting/Shapeshifting   Multitracking
Forgiveness   Attitude Adjustment Skills   Witness Consciousness   Fasting
Right/Left Brain Integration   Movement/Dance   Nutrition/Herbs   Massage/Acupressure
Whole Thinking Skills   Appreciation/Thankfulness   Asking   Humor
Learning Physical Anatomy   Dis-ease Connection   Chanting/Singing/Toning/   Drumming/Music
Color/Light Healing   DreamWork   Daily Check In   Artistic Release
Mirror Work   Body Awareness   Yoga/Stretching   Rest/Nurturance
Mindfulness   Giving/Receiving   Aromatherapy   Crystals/Gemstones
Rituals   Soul Dancing   Body Prayer   Art As Meditation
Pain Connection   Hands On Healing   Intentional Fantasy Work   Blessing

♦ METAPHYSICAL ABILITIES TO LEARN AND APPLY

Clairvoyance   Clairaudience   Clairsentience   Spirit Contact
Angelic Association   Nature Spirits Communication   Advanced Soul Communication
Direct Divine Reconnection   Soul Voice Contact   Sensing Earth Traumas   Self/Inner Guidance
Life Forms Communication   Past Life Recall   Soul Reading   Mental Telepathy
Energy Force Field Repair   Prophecy   Precognition   Mind Over Matter
Energetic Reading/Cleansing   Psychic/Spiritual Healing   Out Of Body Travels   Seeing Auras
Superperformance   Long Distance Viewing   Psychic and Lucid Dreaming   Dowsing
Charismatic Writing, Speaking, Creating   Channeling/Mediumship   Soul Memory Recall
Protective Use of Divine White Light   Absent Healing   Levitation   Psychokinesis
Finding Missing Objects   Manifestation   Accessing The Akashic Records

---

**YOUR HIGHER SELF INTEGRATION PROGRAM NEEDS TO FLOW
WITH YOUR NATURAL, YET CHANGING, RHYTHMS AND NEEDS . . .**

MAKING IT VISIBLE

In becoming *Higher Self Integrated*, or Soul Attuned, it is important to KNOW WHERE YOU ARE AT IN THE PRESENT AND AT LEAST A GENERAL IDEA ABOUT WHERE YOU WANT TO BE IN THE FUTURE. Bear in mind, that both will keep on changing for that's what transformation is all about: movement and growth. It is helpful in forming your own *Higher Self Integration Program/Plan*, one that fits your unique development and individuality, to HAVE A FREQUENT REVIEW, EVALUATION, AND ASSESSMENT PROCESS BUILT IN. Your *HSI* program needs to flow with your natural, yet changing, rhythms and needs.

In making your ongoing assessments, go back occasionally to THE DEVELOPMENT ASSESSMENT GUIDE IN CHAPTER THREE. Also, REREAD AND REWORK this book and its activities as needed. As YOUR INNER/HIGHER GUIDANCE abilities open and expand, getting in your open and relaxed state, asking, and listening for truth and understanding about who you are in the present and the directions you need to move in for *Higher Self Integration*, will prove to be your most accurate and valuable assessment tool.

USING THE LEVELS OF EVOLUTIONARY SOUL CONSCIOUSNESS AVAILABLE ON EARTH FOR DIRECTION can also help. Although the levels are more fluid and metamorphic than titles or names would bestow on them, naming the levels the following could prove helpful as a mental reminder and communication tool:

> *Level One - Marking Time,*
> *Level Two - Further Exploration*
> *Level Three - Circling 'Round,*
> *Level Four - Standing In The Doorway,*
> *Level Five - Lifting Up,*
> *Level Six - Communicating Soul Truth*
> *Level Seven - Transcending*

More than likely, Level Oner's will have had a real hard time being attracted to and reading, let alone finishing this book. And Level Sixer's and Sevener's won't any longer need this book, for their Soul's Voice will be singing loud and clear. Below are some recommended areas, skills and techniques to focus on for Levels Two, Three, Four, and Five:

LEVEL TWO - *FURTHER EXPLORATION*:
Relearn how to learn . . . Study holistic (physical, mental, emotional, psychological, spiritual, and metaphysical) information & systems . . . Start learning to work through your emotional difficulties, perhaps through counseling, workshops, and retreats . . . Work with physical fitness concepts, including nutrition . . . Begin working on relaxation, observation, concentration, and meditation skills . . .

LEVEL THREE - *CIRCLING 'ROUND*:
Learn to take good care of/nurture yourself for this level is the hardest and therefor easiest in which to get way out of balance, very stuck, and dis-eased in a heavy-duty way. . . Learn focus, discipline, deeper levels of concentration and meditation, prayer, affirmations, visualizations, dreamwork, breathwork, stretching and movement, massage/various bodywork techniques, and whole thinking skills . . . Become aware of and rework your Addictions and Addictive/ Codependent Personality . . . Start dealing with your Battle Of the Selves and your subpersonalities . . . Uncover, release, and reprogram past, including childhood traumas, and negative emotional and thinking patterns . . . Really work with reprogramming your misbeliefs and disbeliefs. . . Work on and explore forgiveness, self-esteem, nonjudgmentalness, and unconditional love . . .

LEVEL FOUR - *STANDING IN THE DOOR WAY:*

Reach Soul & spirit levels of meditation, contemplation, connection, prayer, and forgiveness . . . Continue to release and transform negative energies, learning all Three Stages Of Soul Release . . . Expand your Energy Management/ Transformation skills . . . Add Soulwork- Are your ready for Dark Night Of The Soul time?- Soul Examination, Past Life Exploration, Soul Baggage. . . Work through Humanity Ache, Humanity Rage, Separation Sadness. . . Discover your Soul Core Issues . . . Expand your Higher Sense Perceptions . . . Reconnect and communicate through Higher Guidance with Angels and Spirit Guides and Teachers . . . Connect with The Natural World Soul-to-Spirit/Soul-to-Soul. . . Study and consciously work with The Universal Laws. . . Make your commitment to *Higher Self Integration* . . .

LEVEL FIVE - *LIFTING UP*:

Access Higher Visions . . . Cocreate . . . Rediscover and work on your Soul's Life Purpose/Plan, Lessons/Tasks, Goals/Missions. . . Establish Soul Qualities in and as you and your life. . . Allow Compassion and Nonresistance to be how you operate . . . Unite your Intentions. . . Bring all parts of your life up to the standard of living that best serves your *Higher Self*/Soul - Whole and True Prosperity . . . Relate to others through the eyes of Soul- Spiritual Partnerships, Soul Mates/Companions/Groups . . . Integration and deepening of The Soul Powers - Communication/ Expression, Perception/Reading Energy, Transformation/Healing, Manifestation/Demonstration and Cocreation/Causation. . . Really integrate your Higher Sense Perceptions/Metaphysical Abilities into your normal everyday affairs . . . Walk with Goddess/God!

ACTIVITY: <u>Where I'm At</u>

In working with the material suggested in this Chapter, Go For It!, and in order to form your own *Higher Self Integration Program*, ask yourself (through inner work and guidance) these questions:

* Is this something that needs my attention and resources?
** What is the best, concerning the past, present, and future, for all concerned?
*** What are my opposing Intentions?
**** What are my underlying fears & doubts that are keeping me from my highest good?
***** What do I need to acknowledge to and for myself?
******Why do I need this _____ that I am trying to attract?
******* Does this choice follow the voice of my *Higher Self* /Soul?
******** Where does this choice lead me and am I honestly ready to go there?
********* How would the God/Goddess of Wisdom and Compassion handle/teach this?
********** Am I in THE FLOW, where it is happening with GRACE, and making both
logical and intuitive sense? DIVINE ORDER

**ALLOW YOURSELF TO BRING FORTH BOTH THE IDEA AND REALITY OF
ALL THE SOULFULLY WONDERFUL THINGS YOU CAN ATTRACT AND CREATE . . .**

What you are working towards is fully supporting and expressing your *Higher Self*, your Soul, in every moment of your life. That means you have to DAILY FOCUS on what you want and how it will feel when you are 100% *Higher Self Integrated*.

AFFIRM:

"I am the person living the life my Soul truly desires to do and be!"

"The drawing power of Divine Love, the constantly active magnet that attracts unfailing supply, is active each moment in my life!"

EVERYDAY, Soul program that biocomputer of yours by   IMAGING,   VISUALIZING,   PERCEIVING,   AND   AFFIRMING:

------------------------------------- IMAGES OF A "HOLY PROSPEROUS" LIFE -------------------------------

-- OPENING TO RECEIVE --

---------------------------------- BEING YOUR HIGHER SELF ALL THE TIME ------------------------------

Allow yourself to bring forth the reality of the Soulfully wonderful things you can attract and create. And then energize and inspirit your Intentions into realizations!   Treat yourself to INSPIRITING/BELIEVING SESSIONS through dance, music, words, nature, and trance.

There are activities you will need to participate in every day. In the morning, do a DAILY CHECK and in the evening do a NIGHTLY REVIEW with yourself. These two times will help you keep on track and focused. After you have gotten in your open and relaxed state of being, these questions/activities are suggested for your Daily Check In and Nightly Review:

Daily Check In:
     Dream Recall and Work ...
     Release of Residue Emotion ...
     Body Scan and Healing ...
     Current Issues Focus (including how you can tie in your Life's Lessons
         and Goals within the context of your planned day) ...
     Higher Guidance/Meditation and Prayer Tune In ...
      -then- Get up, stretch, and move.

Nightly Review:
     Slow down and stretch - then-
     The Day's Examination...
     Current Issues Clarification...
     Release of Residue Emotion (Don't go to bed contorted with negative
        emotion hanging over your head or stuffed in your belly!)...
     Body Scan and Healing Work...
     Set The Stage For Dreaming with Affirmations/Goalsetting...
     Prayer...

MEDITATION,
    PRAYER,
      ENERGETIC CLEANSING,
        AND WHOLE HEALING SKILLS need to be applied daily. Also, focus everyday on catching old, negative, lower-self thoughts, emotions, and behaviors, releasing, reworking, and replacing them on the spot or as soon as you can.   Consciously choose Soul thoughts, topics, emotions, and behaviors throughout the day.   Deliberately run these until they are prominent and coming spontaneously by their own accord or habitually. Practice intuition, whole thinking skills, and mindfulness throughout your normal everyday affairs.

ACTIVITY: __MAKING IT WORK__

Enabling yourself to do all the work necessary in your *Higher Self Integration Program* and keep up with all your daily obligations, that come from living on Earth and having committed relationships, means that you have to become a MASTER INTEGRATOR. To integrate is to make into a whole by bringing all parts together: to unite and unify. You can do this successfully, smoothly, and still have time for vacations by: TUNING IN AND ASKING FOR DIRECTION, USING YOUR WHOLE THINKING AND PROBLEM SOLVING SKILLS, ORGANIZING, CHARTING, COMBINING, AND PRIORITIZING based on daily/weekly/monthly/yearly, and seasonal natural rhythms and needs.

For examples: Most folks have more time for deep inner work during winter. You can make sure you are keeping up with your program or at least know when you need to make your program more realistic to your time schedules by keeping a daily chart. You can design your own workout program that includes the physical stretching and aerobic movement you need along with emotional and energetic releasing and cleansing techniques, ending up with meditation and prayer all in an hour's time!

Designing and applying your own *HSI Program* will be an ongoing adventure. As you do so, REMEMBER:

Start where you are at ...   Figure out where you want to be ...

Look at it from its whole as well as all its parts...   Tune in...   Combine...

Study ...   Organize ...   Use charts...   Prioritize...

Sort out your Intentions...   Check in...   Review...   Explore...   Reinvent...

Create...   Balance ...   Have fun...   Go for it!...

and   INTEGRATE "TO YOUR HEART AND SOUL'S CONTENT" . . .

YES! `ENJOY`   your explorations and, in doing so, watch them turn magical. Be into each stage, phase, and level of your journey with   DE*LIGHT*. Allow NATURE to be one of your most surprising, intimate, and incredible teachers.   After all, you chose to come to Earth.

FOCUS ON YOUR CONNECTION TO THE DIVINE,

so that you can fly high in THE FREEDOM OF HIGHER SELF/SOUL EXPRESSION!

Consciously align with Soul/Infinite Intelligence in everything by asking for guidance,

bringing forth your intuition and Higher Sense Perceptions, and following through.

This will allow you to:

YIELD CREATIVE SOULFUL SOLUTIONS THAT CAN HAVE WIDE GLOBAL IMPACT,

for The Earth and all of Humanity need your Soul . . .

YOU NEED YOUR SOUL!

Higher Self Integration, or Soul Attunement, is indeed

" THE JOURNEY OF A LIFETIME AND BEYOND."

AND TRULY

"A SOUL'S DELIGHT"...

BLESSED   BE!

BIBLIOGRAPHY / RESOURCES

(The following have proven helpful to the writing of this book and other's *HSI* Programs. Please note that catalogs, magazines, and conference centers often change their information and form. There are *many* other books and resources available to help you on *Your Higher Self Integration Journey.* Tune into your own Inner Guidance for those most suited to you . . .)

1. BOOKS:

M.J. Abodie, *Your Psychic Potential*, Adams Media Corporation, 1995.

Ted Andrews, *Animal - Speak: The Spiritual & Magical Powers of Creatures Great & Small*, Llewllyn Publications, 1996.

Roberto Assagioli, *Psychosynthesis: A Manual of Principles & Techniques*, Penguin Books, 1981.

Marcus Bach, *I, Monty*, Island Heritage, 1978.

Richard Bach's novels . . .

Christina Baldwin, *Life's Companion: Journal Writing As A Spiritual Quest*, Bantam, 1990.

John Benson, *Transformative Adventures, Vacations, And Retreats,* New Millenium Publishing, 1994.

Thomas Berry, *The Great Work*, Bell Tower, 1999.

Barbara Biziou, *The Joy Of Family Rituals: Recipes For everyday Living*, St. Martins Press, 2000.
   Joy Of Ritual: Spiritual Recipes to Celebrate Milestones, Ease Transitions, and Make Every Day Sacred, Golden Books, 1999.

Brad Blanton, *Radical Honesty: How to Transform Your Life By Telling The Truth*, Dell Trade Paperback, 1996.

Douglas Block, *Listening To Your Inner Voice*, Hazelden, 1991.

Harold H. Bloomfield & Robert B. Kory, *The Holistic Way To Health & Happiness*, Simon & Schuster, 1987.

Joan Borysenko, *Minding The Body Mending The Mind*, Bantam, 1987.
   Guilt Is The Teacher, Love Is The Lesson, Bantam, 1990.
   Fire In The Soul, Time Warner, 1993   & more . . .

Joan & Miroslav Borysenko, *The Power Of The Mind To Heal*, Hay House, Inc. 1994.

John Bradshaw, *Bradshaw On The Family*, Health Communications, Inc., 1988.

Barbara Ann Brennan, *Hands Of Light*, 1988.   &   *Light Emerging*, Bantam Books, 1993.

Janet Vera Burr, *Awaken Your Intuition*, Intuition Trainings, 1986.

Gillian Butler & Tony Hope, *Managing Your Mind: The Mental Fitness Guide*, Oxford University Press, 1995.

Julia Cameron, *The Artist's Way: Spiritual Path To Higher Creativity*, Tarcher/PutnamBook,1992.

Hereward Carrington, *Your Psychic Powers & How To Develop Them*, Newcastle, 1975.

Mildred Carter, *Hand Reflexology: Key to Perfect Health,* Parker Publishing Co., 1975.

Robin Casarjian, *Forgiveness: A Bold Choice for a Peaceful Heart*, Bantam Books, 1992.

Carlos Castenada's novels . . .

Gloria Chadwick, *Discovering Your Past Lives*, Contemporary Books, 1988.

Deepak Chopra, *Perfect Health,* Harmony Books, 1991.
   Unconditional Life: Discovering the Power to Fulfill Your Dreams, Bantam, 1991.
   Ageless Body, Timeless Mind, Harmony Books, 1993.
   Journey Into Healing: Awakening The Wisdom Within You, Random House, 1995. & more . . .

Alan Cohen, *The Dragon Doesn't Live Here Anymore*, Fawset Columbine, 19981, 1990.
   Lifestyles Of The Rich In Spirit, Hay House, 1987.
   A Deep Breath Of Life: Daily Inspiration For Heart-Centered Living, Hay House, 1996. & more . . .

Joseph Cornell, *Listening To Nature,* Dawn Publications, 1987.

Judith Cornell, *Drawing The Light From Within: Keys to Awaken Your Creative Power*, Prentice Hall Press, 1990.

Gabriel Cousens, *Spiritual Nutrition & The Rainbow Diet*, Cassandra Press, 1986.

Tony Crisp, *Do You Dream: How To Gain Insight Into Your Dreams*, E.P. Dutton, 1972.

Melita Denning and Osborne Phillips, *Psychic Self-Defense*, Llewellyn Publications, 1980.

Alexandra Collins Dickerman, *Following Your Path: Using Myths, Symbols, and Images To Explore Your Inner Life,* Jeremy P. Tarcher/Putnam Book, 1992.

191 SOUL'S DELIGHT 191

Gary Doore, *Shaman's Path: Healing, Personal Growth, Empowerment,* Shambhala, 1988.

Larry Dossey, *Prayer Is Good Medicine*, Harper San Francisco, 1996.

Henry Dreher, *The Immune Power Personality: Seven Traits You Can Develop To Stay Healthy,* Dutton Signet/Penguin Books, 1995.

Wayne Dyer, *Manifest Your Destiny: The Nine Spiritual Principles For Getting Everything You Want,* Harper Collins, 1997.   *Your Erroneous Zones,* Avon Books, 1976.

Marcia Emery, *Intuition Workbook*, Prentice Hall 1994.

Clarissa Pinkola Estes, *Women Who Run With The Wolves,* Ballentine Books, 1992.

Charles Fillmore, *Prosperity,* Unity Books, 20th printing 1987.

Stephen Forrest, *The Inner Sky*, ACS Publications, 1992.

Mathew Fox, *Creation Spirituality*, Harper San Franscisco, 1991.
    Meditations With Meister Eckhart, Bear & Company, 1983.
    The Reinvention of Work, Harper Collins, 1995.   & more . . .

Foundation For Inner Peace, *A Course In Miracles.*

Mara Freeman, *Kindling The Celtic Spirit*, Harper San Franscisco, 2000.

Brian Froud, *Good Faeries Bad Faeries*, Simon & Schuster, 1978.

Shakti Gawain, *Creative Visualization,* Whatever Publishing, 1978.
    Living In The Light, New World Library, 1986.
    Path of Transformation, Nataraj Publishing, 1993.   & more . . .

Richard Gerber, *Vibrational Medicine*, Bear & Company, 1988.

Bruce Goldberg, *Soul Healing*, Llewellyn Publications, 1996.

Daniel Goleman, *Emotional Intelligence: Why It Can Matter More Than IQ*, Bantam, 1995.

Daniel Goleman & Joel Gurin, *Mind Body Medicine*, Consumer Reports Books, 1993.

Richard Gordon, *Your Healing Hands-The Polarity Experience*, Unity Press, 1978.

Jeff Green, *Pluto The Evolutionary Journey Of The Soul,* Llewellyn Publications, 1986.

Robert Hand, *Planets In Transit,* Pararesearch, 1976.

Thich Nhat Hanh, *Living Buddha, Living Christ,* Riverhead Books, 1995.

Andrew Harvey, *The Direct Path*, Broadway Books, 2000.   & more . . .

Louise L. Hay, *You Can Heal Your Life*, Hay House, 1984.

Herbal Research Publications, Inc., *Naturopathic Handbook Of Herbal Formulas*, 1995.

James Hewitt, *The Complete Yoga Book*, Schocken Books, 1978.

Jean Houston, *The Possible Human,* J. P. Tarcher, Inc., 1982.

Bill Hunger, *Clearcut: A Novel of Bio-Consequences*, Hampton Roads Publishing, 1996.

B.K.S. Iyengar, *Light On Yoga, Schocken* Books, revised 1979.

JoyBeth, *Beyond Belief Into Knowing: My Soul's Journey*, Trafford Publishing, 2001.

JoyBeth, *The WE That Is ME: A Creation Spirituality Guidebook For You*, Trafford Publishing, 2004.

Anodea Judith, *Wheels of Life: A User's Guide to the Chakra System*, Llewellyn, 1995.

Jon Kabat-Zinn, *Wherever You Go There You Are,* Hyperion, 1994.

Penny Kelly, *The Elves Of Lilly Hill Farm: A Partnership With Nature*, Llewellyn Publications, 1997.

Ken Keyes, *Handbook To Higher Consciousness,* DeVorss & Company, 1972.

Alix Kirsta, *The Book Of Stress Survival,* Simon & Schuster, 1986.

Jack Kornfield, *A Path With Heart*, Bantam Books, 1993.

Gopi Krishna, *Kundalini: The Evolutionary Energy In Man,* Shambhala, 1971.

Kevin & Barbara Kunz, *The Complete Guide to Foot Reflexology*, Prentice Hall, 1982.
    Hand & Foot Reflexology - A Self-Help Guide, Prentice Hall, 1984.
    The Practitioners Guide To Reflexology, Prentice Hall, 1985.

Irene Lamberti, *Spirit in Action: Moving Meditations For Peace, Insight, and Personal Power,* Ballentine Wellspring, 2000.

C.W. Leadbeater, *The Chakras,* Quest Books, 5th printing 1987.

Harriet Goldher Learner, *The Dance of Anger*, Harper & Row, 1985.

Elen Lederman, *Vacations that Can Change Your Life*, Sourcebooks, Inc., 1996.

Frederick Lenz, *Surfing The Himalayas,* St. Martin's Press, 1995.

George Leonard and Michael Murphy, *The Life We Are Given*, Jeremy P. Tarcher/Putnam, 1995.

Lawrence LeShan, *How To Meditate: A Guide to Self-Discovery,* Bantam Books, 1974.

Genevieve Lewis Paulson, *Kundalini And The Chakras*, Llewellyn Publications, 1992.

Myrna Lofthus, *A Spiritual Approach To Astrology*, CRCS Publications, 1983.

Olivea Dewhurst Maddock, *The Book Of Sound Therapy*, Fireside, 1993.

Al. G. Manning, *Helping Yourself With ESP*, Parker Publishing, 1966.

Bruce McArthur, *Your Life-Why It Is The Way It Is And What You Can Do About It: Understanding The Universal Laws*, ARE Press, 1993.

Dan Millman, *The Life You Were Born To Live: A Guide to Finding Your Life Purpose*, H.J. Kramer, Inc., 1993.

Thomas Moore, *Care Of The Soul: A Guide For Cultivating Depth And Sacredness In Everyday Life*, Harper Perennial, 1992.   *The Re-Enchantment Of Everyday Life*, Harper Perennial, 1996. *Soulmates: Honoring The Mysteries Of Love And Relationships*, Harper Perennial, 1994.

Robert Moss, *Conscious Dreaming: A Spiritual Path For Everyday Life*, Crown Trade Paperbacks, 1996.

Bill Moyers, *Healing and The Mind*, Doubleday, 1993.

Michael Murphy, *The Future Of The Body: Explorations into the Further Evolution of Human Nature*, Jeremy P. Tarcher, 1992.

Caroline Myss, *Anatomy Of The Spirit: The Seven Stages Of Power And Healing*, Harmony Books, 1996.

Michael Newton, *Journey of Souls: Case Studies Of Life Between Lives*, Llewellyn Publications, 1998.

Jim Nollman, *Dolphin Dreamtime: The Art & Science of Interspecies Communication*, Bantam Books, 1990.

Christiane Northrup, *Women's Bodies, Women's Wisdom*, Bantam Books, 1994.

Dennis O'Grady, *Taking The Fear Out Of Change*, Bob Adams Inc., 1994.

Wataru Ohashi, *Do It Yourself Shiatsu*, E.P. Dutton, 1976.

Maggie Oman, *Prayers For Healing: 365 Blessings, Prayers, & Meditations From Around The World*, Conari Press, 1997.

Sheila Ostrander & Lynn Schroeder, *Super-Learning*, Delta Books, 1979.

Stephan C. Paul & paintings by Gary Max Collins, *Illuminations: Visions For Change, Growth, and Self-Awareness*, Harper San Francisco, 1991.

Danaan Parry, *Warriors Of The Heart*, Sunstone Publications.

Robert Pelletier, *Planets in Aspect – Understanding Your Inner Dynamics*, Pararesearch, 1974.

Richard Peterson, *Creative Meditation: Inner Peace Is Practically Yours*, ARE Press, 1995.

Joseph Pizzorno, *Total Wellness*, Prima Publishing, 1996.

Marko Pogacnik, *Nature Spirits and Elemental Beings:Working With The Intelligences In Nature*, Findhorn Press, 1995.

Catherine Ponder, *The Dynamic Laws of Prayer*, De Vorss & Co., 1987. *The Dynamic Laws Of Prosperity*, De Vorss & Co., 1962 revised 1985.

John Randolph Price, *The Superbeings*, Facade Crest, N.Y., 1981. *Practical Spirituality*, Quartus Books, 1985.

Ira Progoff, *At A Journal Workshop*, Dialogue House Library, 1975. *The Practice Of Process Meditation*, Dialogue House Library, 1980.

James Redfield, *The Celestine Prophecy*, Satori Publishing, 1993.   & more . . .

Don Richard Riso & Russ Hudson, *Personality Types: Using the Enneagram for Self-Discovery*, Houghton Mifflin Company, 1996.

Pat Rodegast, *Emmanuel's Book*, Bantam New Age, 1987.

Sanaya Roman, *Living With Joy*, H. J. Kramer, 1986. *Spiritual Growth: Being Your Higher Self*, H.J. Kramer, 1989.

Ray Rosenthal, *Astanga Yoga: An Aerobic Yoga System*, Hart Productions, 1988.

Michael Samuels & Mary Rockwood Lane, *Creative Healing: How To Heal Yourself By Tapping Your Hidden Creativity*, Harper Colloins, 1998.

Mike & Nancy Samuels, *Seeing With The Mind's Eye: The History, Techniques & Uses of Visualization*, Random House, 1975.

Lee Sannella, *Kundalini: Psychosis or Transcendence*, H S Dakin Co., 1978.

Jack Schwarz, *Voluntary Controls: Exercises For Creative Meditation And For Activating The Potential Of The Chakras*, E.P. Dutton, 1978.

Eva Shaw, *60 Second Shiatsu*, Mills and Sanderson, 1986.

C. Norman Shealey & Caroline M. Myss, *The Creation Of Health: The Emotional, Psychological & Spiritual Responses That Promote Health and Healing*, Stillpoint Publishing, 1993.

Todd Siler, *Think Like A Genius*, Bantam, 1997.

Sidney &Suzanne Simon, *Forgiveness: How to Make Peace With Your Past and Get On With Your Life*, Warner Books, Inc., 1990.

Marsha Sinetar, *Ordinary People As Monks And Mystics*, Paulist Press, 1986.

Diane Stein, *The Women's Book Of Healing*, Llewellyn Publications, 1987.

Rudolp Steiner, *The Way Of Initiation*, Macoy Publishing, 1910.   & many more . . .

Naomi Stephan, *Fulfill Your Soul's Purpose: Ten Creative Paths to Your Life Mission*, Stillpoint Publishing, 1994.

Petey Stevens, *Opening Up To Your Psychic Self*, Nevertheless Press, 1984.

Brian Swimme & Thomas Berry, *The Universe Story*, Harper Collins, 1992.

Cathryn L. Taylor, *The Inner Child Workbook: What To Do With Your Past When It Just Won't GoAway*, Jeremy P. Tarcher/Putnam Book, 1991.

Angel Thompsen, *Feng Shui: How To Achieve The Most Harmonious Advancement Of Your Home And Office*, St. Martin's Press, 1996.

Susan Trott, *The Holy Man*, Riverhead Books, 1995.

Marianne Uhl, *Chakra Energy Massage*, Lotus Light Publications, 1988.

Swami Vishnudevananda, *The Complete Illustrated Book Of Yoga*, Pocket Books, 1972.

Dan Wakefield, *Creating From The Spirit: Living Each Day As A Creative Act*, Ballantine, 1996.

Amy Wallace & Bill Henkin, *The Psychic Healing Book*, Wingbow Press, 1978.

Roger Walsh, *Essential Spirituality: The 7 Central Practices to Awaken Heart And Mind*, John Wiley & Sons, Inc. 1999.

Andrew Weil, *Spontaneous Healing*, Fawcett Columbine, 1995.
   Natural Health, Natural Medicine, Houghton Mifflin, 1995.
   8 weeks to Optimum Health, Alfred A. Knopf, 1997.

Sharon Wendt, *The Radient Heart: Healing The Heart Healing The Soul*, Radiant Heart Press, 1995.

Marianne Williamson, *The Healing Of America*, Simon & Schuster, 1997.

Anne Wilson Schaef, *When Society Becomes An Addict*, Harper & Row, 1987.

Anna Wise, *The High Performance Mind: Mastering Brainwaves For Insight, Healing, and Creativity*, Jeremy P. Tarcher/Putnam Books, 1997.

Nancy Wood & paintings by Frank Howell, *Spirit Walker*, Doubleday Book, 1993.

Roger Yepsen, *How To Boost Your Brain Power: Achieving Peak Intelligence, Memory, and Creativity*, Rodale Press, 1987.

Jacqueline Young, *Self-Massage*, Thorsons/ Harper Collins, 1992.

Dhyani Ywahoo, *Voices of Our Ancestors*, Shambhala, 1987.

Marilee Zdenek, *The Right-Brain Experience*, McGraw-Hill, 1985.

Zolar, *The Encyclopedia Of Ancient And Forbidden Knowledge*, Nash Publishing, 1970.

Gary Zukav, *The Seat Of The Soul*, Fireside/Simon & Schuster, 1990.

2. BOOK CATALOGS/MAGAZINES/CONFERENCE CENTERS (Just a little sampling)...

The Association For Research and Enlightenment
ARE Bookstore: A Catalog of Books and Videos
68th Street & Atlantic Ave.   PO Box 656
Virginia Beach, Va. 23451   1-800-723-1112
ARE CONFERENCES & TRAINING PROGRAMS-
67th & Atlantic Ave. PO Box 595,
Virginia Beach, VA. 23451   1-800-333-4499.
ARE's VENTURE INWARD
 PO Box 595, Virginia Beach, VA   23451-0595
1-800-333-4499   FAX 757-422-4631.

Llewellyn's New Worlds of
Mind & Spirit 1-800-THE-MOON
PO Box 64383   St.Paul, MN
55164-0383   www.llewellyn.com

INSTITUTE OF NOETIC SCIENCES - 101 San Antonio Road, Petaluma, CA. 940952-9524 www.noetic.org
            707-775-3500   FAX 707-781-7420

UNITY'S DAILY WORD/ UNITY MAGAZINE - Unity Village, MO 64065-0001   816-524-3550.

COURAGE TO CHANGE – Catalog For Life's Challenges   1-800-440-4003

ONE SPIRIT BOOK CLUB – Camp Spirit, Camp Hill, PA 17011-9576

LEADING EDGE REVIEW – P.O.Box 24068 Minneapolis, MN. 55424

SOUNDS TRUE CATALOG - 1-800-333-9185

NEW DIMENSIONS TAPES - 1-800-935-TAPE

NEW MEDICINE TAPES TO TURTURE YOUR SOUL -   1-800-647-1110

ESALEN INSTITUTE- Big Sur, CA. 93920   408-667-3000.

FEATHERED PIPE RANCH- Box 1682, Helena, MT., 59624   406-442-8196.

KRIPALU CENTER- Box 793, Lenox, MA., 01240-0793   1-800-741-SELF.

NAMASTE' RETREAT & CONFERENCE CENTER- Grahams Ferry Road,Wilsonville, Oregon
        97070-9516   namaste@lecworld.org   www.lecworld.org 1-800-893-1000.

NEW YORK OPEN CENTER- 83 Spring St. (Soho), New York, N.Y.   (212) 219-2527.

OMEGA INSTITUTE FOR HOLISTIC STUDIES- 260 Lake Drive, Rhinebeck, N.Y. 12572-3212, 1-800-944-1001

ROWE CONFERENCE CENTER- Kings HWY Rd. Box 273, Rowe, Ma. 01367 413-339-4216.

_**LOOK FOR YOUR LOCAL AND REGIONAL PAPERS, MAGAZINES,
            AND WORKSHOPS ON BODY MIND SPIRIT SOUL...**_

THE INDEX GLOSSARY
SOUL LANGUAGE

ACUPRESSURE OR SHIATSU: Acupuncture without needles is an oriental massage in which the fingers are pressed on particular points of the body to ease pain, symptoms of dis-ease, tension, and fatigue through helping to unblock blocked energy flow… **33, 81, 84, 85**

ADDICTIONS: Substances, behaviors, and processes used compulsively, abusively, and as a way to distract ourselves in order to deny, hide, escape from our feelings and response-ability… **45, 99, 125**

AFFINITY/ NONRESISTANCE/ RESISTANCE: Three styles of receiving energy… **111, 113**

> AFFINITY- to be in agreement with the energy that is coming your way and to accept it
> NONRESISTANCE- To be neutral towards incoming energy, letting it pass right through
> RESISTANCE- To fight with and oppose incoming energy

AFFIRMATIONS: A strong positive statement that something is already a reality… **41, 159, 171, 187**

AKASHIC RECORDS: An energetic, metaphysical recording of all history from all time… **161**

ANGELS: Advanced or highly evolved souls or spirit beings who do not take on human form but serve as helpers/guiding influences to humans… **166, 167**

ARCHETYPES: Habitual themes which are stored in the great group mind of the whole human race that are rehearsed again and again in individual lives… **121, 122**

AROMATHERAPY: The use of smells and scents to help soothe, balance, and heal … **86**

ASTRAL PROJECTION (TRAVEL): Moving one's spiritbody into spiritual dimensions and other places on The Earth Plane while still keeping life-force-connected in one's human body, appearing to be asleep… **16, 148, 151**

ASTROLOGY: The study of the positions and aspects of heavenly bodies with a view to predicting their influence on the course of human affairs … **122**

ATTACHMENT/NONATTACHMENT: Attachment is a personality need that is dependent on something being a certain way in order to feel OK about one's self and one's life. Nonattachment is the Soul ability to feel and be balanced, whole, and happy regardless of one's outer circumstances (have to have vs. preferences)… **114**

ATTITUDE ADJUSTMENT SKILLS: Mental activities that help repattern our negative thought and feeling programs … **67, 76**

AURA/ENERGY FIELD: Manifestation of Holoversal energy intimately involved with individual humans, animals, etc. Energy that surrounds and interpenetrates the physical body … **19, 49, 58**

AURIC VISION: The ability to see auras … **24, 49**

AWARENESS / TO BE AWARE: To be alert to, cognizant of, to recognize, be mindful, to know something by perception and means of information … **26, 79**

BALANCE: Necessary state of physical/biochemical, mental/emotional/psychological, body/mind/spirit/Soul equilibrium … **69, 77, 180**

BANDAID APPROACH: Patching up/relieving the symptoms instead of the real cause/problem … **61**

BATTLE OF THE SELVES: The internal wars created between the different parts of ourselves, which are separated and living in conflict, causing us dis-ease, crises, and traumas … **117**

BIBLIOTHERAPY: The systematic and focused process of learning through reading other's creative written works … **41**

BIOCHEMISTRY: The composition, structure, properties, and reactions of biological/living, and in this context, human substances and processes ... **61, 62**

BLESSING: To invoke Divine attention to, to surround with Divine Grace … **115, 160**

BLOCK BUSTING: Releasing, removing or transforming constricted energy (BLOCK) … **19, 20, 63, 100, 110**

BODY/MIND/SPIRIT COMPLEX: A Soul's sojourn on Earth has to include using mind to form a spirit or etheric body which then is part of an earthly physical body when human … MINDSPIRIT a Soul's intelligence and energy being… BODYMINDSPIRIT a Soul's intelligence and consciousness (mind), energy or etheric being (spirit), and physical human body… **throughout book**

BRAIN LEFT/LOGICAL AND RIGHT/INTUITIVE: The portion of the central nervous system in the vertebrate cranium that is responsible for the interpretation of sensory impulses, the coordination and control of bodily activities, and the exercises of thought and emotion. The Left Brain or mode of thinking relates to the logical and analytical. The Right Brain or mode of thinking relates to the intuitive and spiritual … **105, 140**

BRAINSTORMING: A thinking tool that enables our mind to explore any area uncensored ... **12, 16, 20, 131**

BRAIN WAVES: There are four different types of waves or electrical impulses coming from different states of consciousness that the human brain makes and needs - Alpha, Beta, Delta, and Theta ... **140**

CHAKRAS: Swirling energy vortexes that extend out from our bodies through our aura ... **19, 49, 59, 73, 80,101**

CHAKRA DIAGNOSIS: Using the chakras to understand what is imbalanced in our physical, mental, and spiritual bodies ... **49-59**

CHAKRA MASSAGE: Using various massage techniques and systems to help rebalance the energy that flows through our chakras ... **84, 85**

CLAIRAUDIENCE: The ability of hearing at higher vibrational levels and to hear words or thoughts from nonphysical entities/beings... **24, 152**

CLAIRSENTIENCE: The ability to feel or sense energy that cannot be physically touched/seen... **24, 152**

CLAIRVOYANCE: The ability to see higher, subtle energy patterns and to perceive things that are beyond the ability to see with only normal human vision... **24, 152**

COCREATOR/COCREATING/CAUSATION: To cause to exist, bring into being, originate in physical form an effect, result, or consequence through connecting with one's Higher Self and being a Cocreator by using one's higher abilities and guidance... **36, 37, 41, 142, 157**

CODEPENDENCY: A dynamic of relationship addiction where we need someone else in order to feel and be OK. An intertwined interdependency among two or more beings that requires at least one "giving their life away" in order to meet the other's needs... **125**

CONSCIOUS BIRTHING: Being aware of Soul's intention regarding birthing choice and honoring the Soul-to-Soul commitment consciously... **176**

CONSCIOUSNESS: The state or condition of being aware... **22**

CONTEMPLATION: Whole, thoughtful, and thorough observation, meditation, consideration... **161, 164**

CREATIVITY: The power and ability to make something new, to originate, and cause to exist... **142, 143**

DARK NIGHT OF THE SOUL: An intense psychospiritual process that comes as a result of learning and being involved in SOUL EXAMINATION, where one is purposefully tapping into one's SOUL MEMORIES bringing into consciousness one's thoughts, feelings, and behaviors from other lifetime's as well as from this current lifetime... **35, 117**

DEFENSE MECHANISMS: Psychological patterns of thinking, feeling and behaving oriented to taking care of oneself when perceived threatened, such as denial and projection... **126**

DEVA: A spiritual being of Earth nature who is concerned/involved with a particular area or group species in the plant and animal worlds... **168**

DISCERNMENT: The act or process of perceiving distinctions and differences without judgment of right/wrong or good/bad... **23, 73**

DIS-EASE: Illness or sickness that is the result of being at ill-ease with some aspect or aspects of one's life... **59-73**

DIVINE LIGHT AND LOVE: God or Infinite Intelligence's energetic manifestation... **57, 162**

DIVINE ORDER: The natural or Divine timing and structure of all things based on intelligent holism. Divine Order moves beyond personality and works on a Soul level... **167**

DIVINE SAFETY: The natural Divine right to have what one needs as a Soul to move forward on one's Soul Journey. Divine Safety moves beyond personality, working on a Soul level... **167**

DIVINE WHITE LIGHT: The most powerful protective energy available... **57, 73, 155, 160, 167**

DOWSING: Use of an object, such as a pendulum or even one's hands, through which to pick up on certain energies... **152**

DREAMS: Series of mental images, ideas, conversations, and emotions occurring in certain stages of sleep... **101**

ECCENTRIC: A person who acts different from others, departing from the established norm in belief and behavior... **26, 130**

ECSTATIC DANCE: Movement where the mind gets out of the way and lets our spirit/Soul express itself through rhythmic motion... **93**

EGO/EGOCENTRIC: The personality component that most immediately controls behavior and is in touch with external reality. Thinking and acting with the view that one's self is the center, object, and norm of all experience... **16, 32**

EGO TRAPS: The destructive games/patterns one's lower or false self has learned to play in order to keep from changing... **155, 180**

ELEMENTALS/ELVES: Earth's etheric nature spirits of various forms... **168**

EMOTIONS: Currents of energy with different frequencies that form through one's feelings/thoughts/beliefs... **97-105**

ENDOCRINE SYSTEM: The ductless or endocrine glands of the human body, such as the thyroid and adrenals, whose chemical secretions pass directly into the blood stream as directed by our brain and the chemical reactions produced by our thoughts and emotions... **61**

ENERGETIC PATTERNING: The things we do, the thoughts we think, the beliefs we operate from, the intentions we run, the emotions we feel that through time and repetition form interwoven patterns of habit... **96**

ENERGETIC SIGNATURES: Each spirit's way or mark of energy and how they feel to you... **167**

ENERGY MANAGEMENT: The process of consciously choosing, balancing, and working with the various energies we as Souls in spirit and physical bodies attract and interact with... **19, 81, 87, 96**

ESP/HIGHER SENSE PERCEPTIONS/METAPHYSICAL ABILITIES: Perception by reading the vibrational rates of energetic manifestations. Attunement to things, beings, and situations beyond the physical through the development and stimulation of "beyond normal" senses, although they are actually very natural ways of sensing that have been closed down for various reasons... **15, 18, 21, 24-26**

ESSENCE: The energy, spirit, principle of life, and most important or effectual crucial element of something, someone, a situation, circumstance, and system beyond its outer attributes... **30**

ETHERIC/CHI/ORGON/PRANA/SUBTLE: The energy of the life force vibrating at a frequency just beyond the physical and at speeds beyond light velocity with magnetic character (what our spirit bodies are made of)... **49**

FASTING: Abstaining from eating certain or all foods for cleansing and spiritual discipline... **92**

FAULTY LIVING PATTERNS: Daily ways and habits we live our lives, based on misbeliefs and disbeliefs about what life really is, that are destructive and unhealthy... **61, 64**

FLOW STATE: A state of mind or consciousness which occurs in the act of creation where one is so completely engrossed in an activity that they loose track of time... **142**

FOCUSING: The mental skill of calling attention to, being aware of, honing in on, deeply concentrating, and exploring in a whole-encompassing mode a particular thing, concept, idea, principle, or situation making a felt sense that indicates the real essence behind a particular action and emotion... **44, 72**

FOOT ROLLER: A devise usually made of wood or hard rubber with ridges in it that rolls underneath feet stimulating reflexology points... **86**

FORGIVENESS: The act or process of letting go, working through, and transforming angers, resentments, and negativities... **34, 43, 66, 113-115**

FREE ASSOCIATION: A mental technique that aids one in becoming aware of what is in their thinking and feeling processes, opening them up to less restrictive/more creative directions... **16, 20**

GETTING IT: Wholly understanding a concept making complete connections within one's thinking programs, enabling one to integrate behaviorally and emotionally that truth/reality in daily life and living... **13**

GOD/GODDESS/THE ALL OF LIFE: A fundamental, creative power/energy and Higher Intelligence in the Holoverse which is the source and substance of all existence... **14-16, 22, 89, 93, 94, 157, 158**

GODCIDENCES: Syncronicities which create validating experiences of God in Earthly life... **167**

GRACE: The state of living in connected awareness of Divine Love, Order, and Protection... **161**

GROUNDING CORD: An energetic or mental removal apparatus that extends down from our pelvic areas helping us to drain out unwanted energies from our etheric & physical bodies... **51**

HANDS ON HEALING: Using Divine Life Force energies emitting from one's hands to influence the health of ones self and others... **152**

HARA: The area between the human rib cage and pelvis in oriental energy medicine that is very important for energy flow and therefore relaxation and health... **86**

HERO: The part of us that can explore the unknown to uncover mystery, discovering new information and skills, gaining new assets or allies, and then bringing all these things back for the benefit of the whole... **130**

HIGHER SELF: Being attuned to one's Soul and developing personality characteristics that enable Soul to be expressed... **18, 22, 24, 173 & throughout**

HIGHER SELF INTEGRATION: The process of becoming and applying one's *Higher Self* in everyday life ... **8-10, 18, 23, 36, 40, 87, 136, 173, 179, 183 & throughout**

HOKU POINT: A tsubo/Nadis used in acupressure/acupuncture that is located in the webbing of both one's thumbs and first fingers... **86**

HOLISTIC: An approach emphasizing the importance of the whole and the interdependence of its parts, including physical, mental, emotional, spiritual, and Soul aspects of human health… **33, 59, 182**

HOLOVERSE: Every physical universe as well as every spiritual dimension at every level… **14, 49, 100, 157**

HUMANITY ACHE: The Soul Pattern that occurs when we are advanced enough to read and feel the energies of all of humanity throughout history, yet are still judging from a lower-self personality view point… **35, 103**

HUMANITY RAGE: The Soul Pattern of anger that we feel when we begin taping into our Soul memories reliving our involvement with human pain and suffering that we haven't let go of… **35, 103**

INDIVIDUATION: The process of becoming a differentiated Soul Being… **16**

INNER CHILD: Our child persona, which often becomes repressed, containing natural wonder and joy of life. Unsocialized, unfiltered SoulSpark we're born with… **34**

INSPIRITING: Inspiring, envisioning, affirming, motivating in order to think, feel and behave in happy, joyful, hopeful, and Soulful ways… **76**

INTEGRAL PRACTICE: Studies, activities, techniques, tools, skills, and experiences that involve and connect the physical, mental, emotional, spiritual, and Soulful elements and aspects of being… **40**

INTENTIONS: One's aim, purpose, and state-of-mind that influences all action and reaction. The real reason, purpose, and aim behind an action/plan/goal, sometimes covered up or hidden behind "should's and have to's"… **36, 75, 94, 180-182**

INTERDIMENSIONAL COMMUNICATION: Contact and exchange with spirit beings in different dimensions at different vibrational spheres… **153**

INTUITION: The act or faculty of knowing without the use of rational processes… **18, 24, 149**

KARMA: The sum and consequence of a Soul'sactions during the successive phases of their existence. An energetic system of checks and balances that allows the Soul to experience the full range of perspectives on life… **28, 66**

KARMIC INFLUENCES: Those things that have guided or penetrated a Soul's individual energy… **28, 66, 68**

KIRLIAN PHOTOGRAPHY: An electrographic process, pioneered by electrical engineer Semyon Kirlian, which uses the corona discharge phenomenon to capture the bioenergetic processes of living systems on film, actually capturing aura's or energy fields… **49**

KUNDALINI: The creative, evolutionary spiritual energy stored as potential energy within the root chakra… **160, 161**

LEVITATION: Lifting one's body or other physical objects up in the air only through the power of mind… **148**

LIFE'S PURPOSE/PLAN, LESSONS/TASKS, GOALS/MISSIONS: The Soul's reasons and intentions in choosing to sojourn as a human on Earth at a particular time in history. The Purpose is the overall commitment made. The Lessons are the learning the Soul has set out to accomplish. The Goals are the ways The Soul helps or serves (self, others, Earth, and spirit)… **177-179**

LONG DISTANCE VIEWING: Mentally picking up on something that is happening physically many miles away… **148**

LOVE: In its pure form, love is The Divine or highest emotional and spiritual energy/power that's more powerful than any other form of energy… **94**

LUCID DREAMING: Controlling one's dreams while in the sleep state for a prestated purpose… **146**

MAGNETIZATION: A part of the Manifestation Process or Power that involves drawing to one what's needed… **170, 171**

MANIFESTATION/DEMONSTRATION: To show, demonstrate, prove, reveal, teach, describe, or illustrate by experiment or practical application, to make real… **170, 171**

MASSAGE: A healing art that is the practice of rubbing and pressing specific areas of the physical body to relieve pain, prevent illness, ease muscular tension, open up energy blocks, dispel tiredness, and reinforce depleted or unbalanced energy… **81, 82, 86**

MASS CONSCIOUSNESS: The prevailing human view of life usually based on misbeliefs and disbeliefs programmed from people to people through centuries of restricted human programming… **13, 30**

MASTER TEACHER: Being expertly skilled in helping others learn/master The Art Of Living, Soul Attunement or *Higher Self Integration*… **39, 139, 180**

MATERIALIZATION: The art/skill of causing something to become real or actual… **24**

MEDITATION: The disciplined observation of thoughts, feelings, impulses, and sensations along with the turning towards a presence beyond the ordinary self… **33, 44, 68, 144, 158**

MEDIUMSHIP/ SPIRIT CHANNELING: Communicating with the spirit world… **147, 153**

MEMORY SCANNING: Consciously reviewing one's own memory banks through accessing mental thought forms and pictures... **17, 20**

MERIDIAN LINES: Fourteen major energy currents or lines of the physical body as distinguished by oriental medicine... **84**

MIND/BRAIN COMPLEX: Our interwoven abilities to be human by operating our mind, spirit (Soul) through our brain and body... **135-156**

MINDFULNESS: Paying attention in a particular way that involves purpose, being present in the moment without judgment... **138**

MIND WAVES: Flows of interrelated thoughts... **12, 146**

MISBELIEFS/DISBELIEFS: Misbeliefs are wrong or faulty mental acceptances or connections in the truth or actuality of something. Disbeliefs are the refusals or reluctances to mentally accepting that something is true and real... **16,64,65,100,110**

MODERN MADNESS MEMENTOS: Present day patterns of feeling, thinking and behaving based on our addictive society and its modern problems... **121, 126**

MULTISENSORY AND MULTIDIMENSIONAL BEING: Human's ability through the development of their Higher Sense Perceptions to live in this physical world and at the same time communicate with other dimensions or levels of life/lifeforms... **14, 39, 148**

MULTI-TRACKING: A brainmind development and expansion technique and ability where we can think, do, feel, and see two to five different things or functions all at once... **148**

NEUROPEPTIDES: Biochemical messengers or chemicals that are directly triggered by emotions and hook up to receptors in our cells located throughout our bodies... **61, 62**

NONJUDGMENTALNESS: Not criticizing or condemning, neutrality...

OUT-OF-BODY TRAVEL: Lifting one's spirit out of one's body while in a sleep or trance state... **152**

PAST LIFE WORK/EXPLORATION/THERAPY: The techniques and processes involved in remembering, releasing, and integrating knowledge of the different issues/personalities/ relationships/situations from our other lives as Souls for the benefit and karmic transformation of this life's personality and Soul Stage/Level... **152**

PERCEPTION/READING ENERGY: Becoming aware of, achieving understanding in one's mind by detecting/observing, through metaphysical senses, the state of energetic and vibrational condition something is in, which in turn gets interpreted into language we can relate to... **138**

PERSONALITY: Patterns of thinking, feeling, and behaving influenced by our past lives, genetic and biological programming, earthly environment, planetary influences, and the modeling we receive from those who surround and teach us their ways of adapting to Earth living... **16, 17 ,121**

PERSONAL PROCESS WORK: Peeling back the layers of our personalities and the emotions we run excavating, releasing, and reworking negative, separating and life destructive beliefs, thinking patterns, emotions, habits, and ways of behaving and communicating... **40, 63, 97, 108, 122, 126**

POWER/EMPOWERMENT: The ability to make things happen in all aspects of living, becoming able to live fully integrated as one's Higher Self... **67**

PRAYER: Act of communion with The Divine/God/Goddess... **33, 68, 128, 144, 158, 159, 162, 176**

PRECOGNITION: The knowledge of something in advance of its occurring... **152**

PROPHESY: To reveal or predict by Divine Inspiration... **152**

PROSPERITY/ PROSPERITY CONSCIOUSNESS: The study/practice of The Spiritual Laws of Wholeness, developing all the energies and skills necessary to attaining *Higher Self Integration* with the results being that one has all the material, human, nature, and spiritual resources one needs to be balanced and whole... **24, 25, 60, 169, 170**

PYSCHIC SABOTAGE: When conditions, people, and your own mental misconceptions work against you achieving your Soul Goals... **180, 181**

PSYCHIC SELF-DEFENSE: The ability to take care of and protect oneself on a psychic, metaphysical , and spiritual level... **155**

PSYCHOLOGY OF THE SOUL: The science and study of the emotional, behavioral, spiritual characteristics of our Soul/*Higher Self*... **8**

PSYCHOKINESIS: The production of motion, especially in inanimate and remote objects, by the exercise of psychic or metaphysical powers... **24**

PSYCHOMETRY: The energetic reading of an object, being able to know information about a person through picking up on that person's energy which has collected on their personal object, such as a ring... **24**

PSYCHONEUROIMMUNOLOGY: The study of the interaction between the mind, body, and the immune system in health and in illness… **61**

QUANTUM LEAPING: A part of the Manifesting Process that increases one's energy in order to attract, demonstrate, or manifest more than one has been able to do previously… **170, 171**

REFLEXOLOGY: Zone Therapy is the study and massage of the reflexes in the feet and hands corresponding to specific parts of the physical body through the nervous system… **80-85**

RESPONSE-ABILITY: Our ability to respond based on whole Soul knowledge… **throughout book**

RITUALS: Detailed method and procedure faithfully followed which has spiritual significance… **174**

ROLFING: A specific type of massage-healing system working with deep connective tissues of the body… **81**

SACRED SPACE: Inspiriting a certain area or space for the purposes of communion with spirit… **174**

SELF-TALKING: A Personal Processing Technique that involves talking silently and out loud to one's personality self as if they were a wiser counselor type. It helps in starting to allow our Soul to be heard… **17**

SEPARATION SADNESS: The intense emotional Soul pattern of loss, separation, and disconnection we feel when we have enough awareness of God/Goddess and the realization that we have consciously disconnected from God or Goddess… **35, 103**

SHADOW OR DARK SELF/SIDE: The negative, destructive parts of ourselves hidden in our subconscious, yet influencing our feelings, thoughts, and reactions in our daily lives… **117**

SHAMAN: One who journeys in altered states of consciousness while remembering and integrating throughout everyday life what has been experienced and learned in those states… **159, 160**

SHAMANIC JOURNEYING: Exploring nonordinary realities while maintaining control of one's own consciousness… **159, 160**

SHAPESHIFTING/TIMESHIFTING: The ability to control and utilize one's energy to the fullest to meet whatever the particular life situation of-the-moment requires… **138**

SOUL: The animating & vital principle in humans credited with the faculties of thought, action, & emotion. Conceived as forming an immaterial entity distinguished from but temporally coexistent with his/her body. The spiritual immortal nature of humans considered in relation to God, separable from the body at death… **14, 15, 20, 28, 62, 69, 74, 182, 185 & throughout**

SOUL BAGGAGE: Leftover situations, lessons, and unresolved karmic situations from one's Soul History… **117**

SOUL CONSCIOUSNESS: Being aware of and integrating as one's own Soul… **8, 15, 20, 22, 28, 62, 69, 74, 182, 185 & throughout**

SOUL CORE ISSUES: Our particular, individual lessons concerning the understandings and knowledge of life we are working on learning as Souls in Soul Evolutionary Stages… **99, 119**

SOUL EMOTIONAL PATTERNS: Particular ways we run our energy based on the beliefs and experiences we have collected as Souls taking on various personalities… **99**

SOUL ETHICS: Principles of truth in action, appropriate to the whole of life coming from Soul… **117**

SOUL EVOLUTION: The process of consciously communing with The Divine through Soul Consciousness… **165**

SOUL EXPRESSION: Bringing forth, manifesting, and communicating from and as Soul… **142**

SOUL FRUSTRATION: A Soul Pattern in which we have reconnected enough to have higher visions of the potential of life here on earth as a human, but still lack the knowledge of how to create such a life…**103**

SOUL MASTERY: Being expertly skilled with integrating one's Soul/Divine into the human and spirit worlds… **22, 116**

SOUL MATE/COMPANION/GROUP: Persons (or Souls) who one is committed to traveling through time together in order to foster one another's growth and to complete their karmic entanglements or lessons… **167**

SOUL PATTERNS: Energetic emotional complexes that tie in directly on the Soul level, all coming from Soul Separation such as: Separation Sadness, Humanity Rage, and Humanity Ache… **40, 103**

SOUL SEPARATION: When we inhibit our conscious awareness of being Soul… **117**

SOUL SHIFT: An evolutionary move from Soul Separation to Divine Reconnection which happens when one has accepted, forgiven, and reworked what one has been and done in one's various incarnations… **117**

SOUL VOICE/TRUE VOICE/TRUTH VOICE: Divine knowledge that comes through Soul… **100, 182**

SOUL WORK/RETRIEVAL: The effort, techniques, processes, skills, and abilities it takes to consciously reconnect with Soul and integrate Soul here on Earth… **18, 24, 108, 109, 120, 179**

SPIRIT/ SPIRIT BODY/ ETHERIC BODY/ SOULSPIRIT: A Soul's etheric or energetic body… **14, 138, 157, 167**

SPIRIT FRIEND/GUIDE/TEACHER: An advanced Soul in spirit form, who tries to work with a Soul in human form towards the advancement of the human's growth and Soul Consciousness... **15, 166**

SPIRITUAL PARTNERSHIP: A psychospiritually intimate human-to-human commitment with another to help each other in development of one's *Higher Self*/Soul/Divine Attunement... **175**

SQUELCH OF SOUL: Keeping one's Soul covered up with lower-self personality... **117**

STAGES OF RELEASE: Stage One In The Moment Release/ Stage Two Connected To Your Life Release/ Stage Three Connected To Soul Release... **106, 107**

STINKIN' THINKIN': Destructive/negative patterns of thinking based on Addictive behaviors... **126**

SUBCONSCIOUS: Part of the personality which dwells below the surface of working consciousness and which controls automatic human functions... **22, 65, 140**

SUBPERSONALITIES: Different patterns of characteristics, behaviors, temperaments, emotions, and mental thoughts and traits that form sub or less intact personalities within one's larger or more pervasive personality configuration... **121, 127-129**

SUMMONS: A "Call to Attention" to do something specific that has Soul purpose and mission...**119, 172**

SUPERCONSCIOUS: Part of the higher Soul structure containing Higher Wisdom and Connection that is accessible when consciously freed... **22, 140**

SYMPATHY/EMPATHY/COMPASSION: Helper styles relating feeling or in relationship with another based on:
SYMPATHY - Pulling another's energy or problem into one's being, becoming stuck with their negative energy,
EMPATHY - Pulling another's energy or problem into one's being, projecting it back,
COMPASSION- One is clear and unattached to another's energy/problem understanding their problem as a whole and thereby supporting them in their ability to solve their own problems... **112, 113**

SYNCHRONICITIES: Events and circumstances that occur through energetic attraction, often appearing as "coincidences" to the unaware... **23**

TELEPATHY: Communicating mind-to-mind without spoken words and gestures... **184**

THE JOURNEY HOME: Consciously working on one's Higher skills and characteristics which help one to evolve out of earthly karmic cycles bringing back one's consciousness and Soul to The Divine... **16, 28, 178**

TONING/SOUNDWORK: Using tones, musical notes and rhythms, verbal/instrumental/natural noises and sounds in ways that work with and heal our physical and etheric bodies/spirit... **56**

TOXIC ATTITUDES: Negative mindsets that sabotage, harm, or defeat our beings... **92**

TOXINS: Chemical reactions which produce chemical substances within our human bodies that are poisonous or harmful to us... **92, 174**

TRANCE/TRANCE STATE: A state of detachment from one's physical surroundings enabling one to journey inward to the recesses of one's mind, spirit, Soul, and in other dimensions... **21, 109**

TRANSFORMATION/HEALING: To change the nature, function or condition into balance and wholeness... **59, 62**

TRANSITION TIME: The passage of changing from one form, state, activity, or place to another... **170**

TRANSMUTATION: The act of changing from one form, nature, substance, or state into another... **117**

TWISTED THOUGHTS: Negative destructive thoughts that feed off one another warping our attitudes and behaviors... **136, 137**

UNIVERSAL LAWS/PRINCIPLES/TRUTHS: Unbreakable, unchangeable Principles Of Life that operate inevitably, in all phases of our life and existence, for all humans and all things, everywhere, all the time... **20, 21, 35, 43, 163, 164, 167**

VISUALIZATION: Mental images/visions consciously solicited through mental process... **17, 20, 22, 144, 146, 150**

WHOLE HEALTH: Fully healthy, prosperous, and joyfilled living in balance with our bodies, minds, spirits, and Souls... **59-73**

WHOLE-THINKING: The ability and skill to know things in their completeness, to be able to use all the senses, intuitions, and information about something, including its past, present, and future, to assess the best-for-all-concerned... **44, 67, 138, 148, 149**

WITNESS CONSCIOUSNESS: Objectively, with nonattachment, and void of unreal expectations, being able to see the truth of our own body, thoughts, emotions, spirit as Soul (SELF-WITNESSING)... **69, 159**

WOUNDOLOGY: A way of relating to others and our lives through and with our pain/traumas... **66**

YIN AND YANG: The feminine (YIN and Anima) and masculine (Yang and Animus) elements or energies of The Dualistic Energetic Pattern that appear to be of opposite nature, yet which are always in complement... **121, 123, 124**

YOGA: A mind/body/spirit discipline with a system of body movements aligned with breath... **90, 91**

ISBN 155212599-8